CERYS, *CATATONIA* AND THE RISE OF WELSH POP

CERYS, *CATATONIA* AND THE RISE OF WELSH POP

David Owens

EBURY
PRESS

First published in UK in 2000

1 3 5 7 9 10 8 6 4 2

Ebury Press
Random House, 20 Vauxhall Bridge Road, London SW1V 2SA

Random House Australia Pty Limited
20 Alfred Street, Milsons Point, Sydney, New South Wales 2061, Australia

Random House New Zealand Limited
18 Poland Road, Glenfield, Auckland 10, New Zealand

Random House (Pty) Limited
Endulini, 5A Jubilee Road, Parktown 2193, South Africa

Random House UK Limited Reg. No. 954009

A CIP catalogue record for this book is available from the British Library

ISBN 0 09 1874122

Cover design by Glen Reynolds
Plate design by Dan Newman
Front cover photograph © Mark Guthrie, Camera Press
Back cover photograph courtesy of WEA Records

Typeset by SX Composing DTP, Rayleigh, Essex
Printed and bound in Great Britain by Biddles of Guildford

Papers used by Ebury Press are natural, recyclable products made from wood grown in sustainable forests.

For my parents

Acknowledgements

I would like to thank: for their help and encouragement, Rhys Mwyn, Huw and Tash, Iestyn George, Mark Radcliffe, Adam Shutes, Gruff Jones, Alun Llwyd, Tony Schiavone, Conal Dodds, Paul Buck, Geraint Jarman, Lisa Jarman, Charlie Pinder, Jayne Houghton, Geoff Travis, Richard Parfitt, Andy Barding, Steve Johnson, Greg Haver, John Robb, Lloyd Powell, Emyr Richards, Paul Sampson, Mike Peters, Ginny Luckhurst, Rolant Dafis, Darren Jones, Andy Rudenko, Aidan Byrne, Sioned Davies, Miriam, Cristine, John Cornfield, Paul Jeff, Romina, Donna 'Catfic' Balsdon, Stephen Middler, Laura D, Gaspode, Chantal Patton, Beth C, Hugo Schwyzer, Debs Prowse, Debbie Manley, Sawmill Studios, The Western Mail & Echo Ltd, all the Welsh bands that have soundtracked my life; Natalie Jerome at Ebury Press; for their unstinting support Nicky and Stuart Rich, Stephen and Mary Owens, Christopher, Peter and Matthew, Jordan and Joshua, David Atkinson, Andy and Dania, Mr and Mrs H, JJ and Georgia; and, for everything and more, Claire Farrell.

Introduction

> As any astronomer will tell you, a star is not born, but made and fashioned from random bits of space dust just awaiting their galactic moment. And so, each pop supernova has their own rubble, the sediment from a pre-brilliant past that lies, undisturbed, until they take their place in the firmament.
>
> (Kitty Empire)

Catatonia were not some dazzling supernova that was created overnight. They are the sum of many different parts, not least a colourful history that stretches back and forth from the mid-80s political minefield of the Welsh-language movement, riding the first wave of Welsh pop in the 1960s and back to its logical inception with the caricatured excesses of Bassey and Jones.

Theirs is also the story of how three words, 'Welsh', 'music', 'scene', took on an altogether different resonance from what it meant before Catatonia, to a tidal wave of bands that crashed out of Wales and firmly embedded themselves into the UK's collective consciousness. These were vital and dynamic bands who were reacting to their country's past and rewriting its future; and Catatonia with their innate pop sensibilities, bittersweet lyricism and superstar singer, were leading the charge.

Once the butt of jokes, Welsh pop music had broken free from its confines as a nation trapped in a time-warped history of harp players and male voice choirs, and spun on its axis with a revitalised music scene at its beating heart.

I was writing about the Welsh music scene for newspapers and magazines in South Wales when the fuse was lit that ignited the Welsh pop revolution. Its defining moment came when Welsh-language bands made the hugely controversial decision to sing in English. Despite the ensuing furore from Welsh-language radicals, for the first time a dynamic union was formed between both Welsh and English-speaking musicians. Catatonia were pioneers of a new bilingual, musical ideology and I was immediately smitten by their first release on the Welsh Crai label. The *For Tinkerbell* EP was a shimmering parade of other-worldly pop music, topped off to dazzling effect by a singer with a unique and captivating vocal style.

By landing killer blows with a flurry of intensely evocative pop tunes, Cerys Matthews and Catatonia were storming the barricades of what had gone before and were revelling in rewriting the present. With her extravagantly emotive voice, off-kilter glamour – she's like the barmaid as supermodel – sparkling surreal sense of humour and ineffably warm charisma, Cerys has become a pop enigma. But it's obvious she would be nothing without the spectacular songwriting of Mark Roberts.

Beloved of the serious music press, worshipped by the teen crowd and adoring parents alike, Catatonia have risen from dole-queue drinkers achieving very little large-scale recognition in a lengthy space of time, to A-list champagne glitz. This is the story of a nation's striving for respectability and one band's captivating struggle at its core.

It tells of how Catatonia had to exorcise the ghosts of their pasts to forge a new beginning. How a bewitching voice dared to be Welsh, well before the principality became the heartland of UK pop. Of how their hedonistic excesses and the disintegration of Mark and Cerys's relationship nearly ruined their career. How uncertainties about their future dogged their early days at Warner Brothers. And how they crash-landed into the nation's psyche by virtue of writing glorious songs masquerading as tabloid headlines.

With an angel on one shoulder and a devil on the other, the angelic voice and the bar-room queen, the sweetest disposition and the fiery proposition, this is also the story of one woman's elevation to the regal heights of the unofficial Princess of Wales.

From the luminescent, starry-eyed glistens of their early Crai releases, and the crystalline kisses and waterfall dynamics of *Way Beyond Blue*, to *International Velvet*'s joyous million seller anthems, through to the evocative evolution of *Equally Cursed And Blessed*, Catatonia have got a lot to answer for, but baby we love them!

David Owens
Cardiff, May 2000

1
Wales 1968–91 BC . . . before Catatonia!

> Every day when I wake up I thank the Lord I'm Welsh
> (Catatonia, 'International Velvet')

No really.

Cerys Matthews smiled a broad smile as she surveyed the ecstatic scene before her. With a wine bottle in one hand and a microphone in the other, she tilted her head back, opened her mouth and breathed in a deep gulp of air. This was the pinnacle of dreams, the fulfilment of life-long ambitions.

Now perched on the edge of the stage, shrouded in the stage lights and the glow of late-evening sunshine, she placed the mic close to her lips and, roared on by 30,000 adoring fans, let loose one of the most amazing voices in British pop history.

Accompanied by the breathtaking rumble of an 80-strong male-voice choir, a musical Wales past and present collided in blissful union as Cerys was drowned out by her own words, 'Everyday when I wake up I thank the Lord I'm Welsh,' being sang back at her with a fierce and fervent pride by a rapturous crowd. The band's 'unofficial' Welsh national anthem not only trumpeted Catatonia's arrival to claim the success and rewards they had struggled so long for, but Welsh music had pulled itself up from the depths of ridicule to the unthinkable heights of worldwide respect and renown.

Tell any Welsh musician at the turn of the Eighties/Nineties that this seemingly unbelievable story would unfold over the ensuing decade and they would have laughed in your face. Now, as the last year of the decade burnt itself out towards a new millennium, 1999 typified the stellar success of Welsh bands. The Stereophonics, The Manic Street Preachers, Gorky's Zygotic Mynci and The Super Furry Animals were all squeezing plaudits out of even the most hard-nosed cynics.

And Catatonia sat proudly at the vanguard of this Welsh musical revolution.

But to trace the DNA steps of the cultural uprising that spawned Catatonia and their brave new dawn of musical brethren, you have to tread fearlessly backwards to the dim and distant past, and immerse yourself in the murky embarrassment of Wales' dark ages. To get a blueprint of the future unfortunately you have to fingerprint the past.

IT *IS* UNUSUAL . . .

Bonnie Tyler, Shakin' Stevens, Shirley Bassey, Harry Secombe, Tom Jones, Michael Ball, Aled Jones, you took one hell of a beating, a hell of a beating. And, well, let's face it some of it was warranted.

'Wales was just viewed as a joke by the rest of Britain,' Cerys Matthews explains just what the cultural landscape was like before she and her fellow pop renegades stormed the music scene. 'To them it was all coal mines and mountains. We were second class and as far as music went we were bedevilled by the clichés of choirs and dodgy rock 'n' rollers. Musically, we weren't renowned for pushing back the frontiers, but that was fine, as it just hid the talent that was bubbling below the surface.'

To be a Welsh music icon pre-Nineties was to vault the twin pommel horses marked 'laughing' and 'stock'. Being Welsh then was none too dissimilar to committing some sort of heinous cultural crime.

Personally, I always dress in a shawl and a stove hat. I am never without my harp and a lunch box full of leek and lava bread. And when not over affectionately 'troubling' my pet sheep, I can be found in the hills insanely muttering 'whose coat this jacket' while looking for coal. Goes without saying. To be Welsh was like being bludgeoned with a history you didn't have and a cultural heritage that didn't exist the other side of the Severn Bridge. Stove hats, leeks, daffodils, druids, dragons, harps, lava bread, choir practice, women in shawls, male-voice choirs, decaying coal mines, three houses for a pound, widespread sheep abuse and a phlegm-inducing native tongue are the populist currency of a Wales that only exists in the minds of people who don't live there.

Save the works of Dylan Thomas, the acting of Richard Burton, the voice of Shirley Bassey, and the golden era of Welsh rugby in the 1970s, the Welsh were the butt of more jokes than the Irish and Scottish put together.

There's almost too much realism in the Welsh culture. Failure's got a lot to do with it – just look at history. The stark decline in the country's once proud industry runs as deep as its once rich mines, stretches as far as the golden beaches that line its coastal length and loops as wide as the Bristol Channel – the watery divide between Wales and England. Until the 1980s, Wales was one of the epicentres of the Industrial Revolution. Coal, steel and slate were the engines that drove Welsh industry – it gave jobs and security to hundreds of thousands and provided the country with a sure financial footing and a proud strength of identity.

The damaging politics of recession and closure that underpinned the Thatcher vision of the UK ripped the heart out of the heartland and dismantled every nut and bolt of Welsh industry. It left the country reeling like a punch-drunk boxer, quickly having to bring itself to its senses while unemployment spiralled and men over forty faced up to the future on the unemployment scrapheap.

Wales was wracked with uncertainty, a depressive state that fed down to its populace who were fighting for self-belief. 'When I was growing up there was nothing to do,' explains Cerys Matthews. 'And you look around now and there's this whole feeling of "You can do this, be whatever you want to be." But before it was, "Oooh, you don't wanna do that. You can't do that—you're Welsh."'

A nation has to stake its identity from an indomitable source and Wales was left as nothing more than a living industrial museum, haunted by its broken past and having to live with the heartache.

Ironically, and rather tragically, Wales's biggest industry is now tourism. Many of the mines and steelworks that heaved under the strain of heavy industry now heave under the weight of curious tourists wanting to fill their gills with echoes of Wales past.

But if Wales has anything to thank Thatcher for it's that although she bludgeoned a nation into submission, Wales is fighting back twice as strong and twice as determined to exorcise the insecure demons of the past. Success both economically and culturally has been quietly assembled and a nation on its knees now walks tall with a long-desired confidence and pride.

And this rebirth, the pure heartfelt emotion that comes from a sense of pride in identity, has much to do with music.

'CAST ADRIFT ON MEMORY BLISS'

Until the Nineties, when Wales conjured up an explosive cultural renaissance with the emergence of a music scene that revelled in its own glorious diversity, the Principality's English-language music scene was burdened by the weight of its own under-achievements.

Read this roll call and hear the wind whistle across the barren rock 'n' roll conquering plain. The Sixties and Seventies served up Amen Corner, Badfinger, Mary Hopkin, Dave Edmunds, Man and Budgie, while the 1980s saw The Alarm, The Pooh Sticks and The Darling Buds gamely attempting to inject some credibility into a country's music scene that was all but comatose.

Although not exactly a line-up to strike fear into the hearts of chart compilers for their string of multi-million selling number ones or causing epochal cultural earthquakes, many of these assortment of Sixties popsters, prog rockers, punky rabble rousers and indie kids laid the foundations for the triumphs that lay ahead. If nothing else, they – each in their own small way – formed a sketchy blueprint of the melting pot of musical styles that would contribute to the Nineties' renaissance of bands that were unified by their Welshness but divided by their own individual musical styles.

Since the Sixties Wales had spat out a phlegmatic fist of bands that had hardly hazarded to make any impression on the charts, let alone leave its sketchy imprint on the pages of musical history.

Thirty years and just a handful of notable success stories. Understated profligacy, that's the Welsh scene! Three decades between a succession of successful bands is some wait, but the turn of the Sixties into the Seventies was the only other time when Welsh music was equally as lucrative as it is now. The long-haired gathering of Cardiff's first genuine pop stars Amen Corner, Merthyr's rock psychedelists Man, heavy rockers Budgie, Swansea's Beatles-sounding Badfinger, rock 'n' roller Dave Edmunds and West Walian singer-songwriter Mary Hopkin all garnered major success with varied musical approaches, and equally consistent and successful careers.

That was the point when Welsh rock music began and harp-playing and joining fifty of your mates for choir practice down the chapel stopped being the musical recreation of a nation's youth.

Much of what went before is gently represented in the present. As a collective unit Catatonia show very slight traces of their Welsh forebears. There are shadowy glimpses of the pure pop simplicity of Amen Corner, the pastoral folkiness of Mary Hopkin and psychedelic innovativeness of Man. The legacy has been felt in many Welsh bands, although in very small doses and in varying measures. Cwmanan's Stereophonics are much more influenced by the gritty heavy rock vibe that pervades in the Valleys, while The Super Furry Animals are turned on by Badfinger's downbeat harmonies and Man's epic psychedelic soundscapes.

MARCHING ON

The first signs of any new life in the Welsh music scene came courtesy of The Alarm – the fiery, cerebral and passionate outfit that blazed a trail out of Rhyl, North Wales in the early Eighties. Although they didn't know it at the time, The Alarm were to become Wales's most loved rock band, revered by their fanatical followers and the huge home support they could count on. They would also pave the way for the uniting of both Welsh and English languages, a bilingual stance that would bear fruit as a common thread among the successful bands of the Nineties. The Rhyl rabble rousers came together in 1981 after a stint as dodgy mod-punk outfit Seventeen and they were as important a band to Wales in the Eighties as The Manic Street Preachers would become in the Nineties.

Both bands not only shared a penchant for spiky hair and a garish blouse early on in their career but also a common purpose of attaining a greater political good through their blistering music. However, whereas The Manics' agenda was built solely on nihilistic intent and underpinned by sneering arrogance, Mike Peters and Co. were devoutly peaceful soapbox revolutionaries – a much more imperturbable but nevertheless intense proposition.

The band's first two albums, 1983's *Declaration* and 1984's *Strength*, had album titles carved straight out of Orwell's Ministry Of Propaganda. However, the music was not contrived – just brimming over with unstoppable enthusiasm. Nevertheless, the cowboy outfits and clothes, exhibited on the cover of their debut 'The Stand' single were too much for the cynical British press. The Alarm were lambasted as 'a storm in a teacup'. It was a time in the UK when the critics were realising that the promise of punk had turned into plastic-sounding, commercial new wave. The press wanted to find their own darlings, and The Alarm just did not fit the mould. To them, a band espousing the DIY aspects of punk, while trying to inspire their fans to 'join hands make plans and take a chance' was just too idealistic and naive for the Eighties. The Alarm brought back memories of a promise gone sour, something critics would just rather forget than acknowledge.

'The press never liked us and we never worried about it,' mused Mike Peters, who despite receiving the sniping barbs of the music press, remains philosophical about The Alarm's relationship with the press. 'They had their line and stuck to it,' he said. 'Being Welsh didn't help us much. Remember when we started out there we were the Welsh music scene's flag bearers. There really wasn't anybody else but us. It was tough at first, but the special bond we had with the fans always saw us through.'

Although The Alarm were worshipped in Wales as folk heroes and their gigs were always unforgettable rallies – stirring gatherings of some of the most fanatical and dedicated fans you could ever wish to meet, the music press dubbed them 'the Welsh Clash' and 'sub-U2 clones'. Early singles '68 Guns' and 'Where Were You Hiding When the Storm Broke' only reinforced the rabble-rousing social conscience the band wore earnestly on their sleeves. They sang fervent songs that urged social change and spoke of the industrial prostitution of Wales; and their devout following clung on to Peters's every word like he was some sort of ecclesiastical preacher. The music press hated that. They couldn't fathom Peters out at all, believing he and his band were some sort of act, suckering people in with their false manifesto. But falling short of carving 4 Real into his arm, he meant it man!

If British journalists were suspicious of Peter's emotional outpourings, then America lapped up the band's confessional songs. Whenever The Alarm toured there, they would play to sell-out crowds. I was lucky enough to interview Mike Peters several times, first as a fanzine writer and then working for a Welsh evening newspaper. On every occasion that we met, and however highly his fans lauded him and the press derided him, he was always one of the most charitable and humane of people, seemingly unflustered by stinging criticism and single-minded in his pursuit of the common touch – music with a message that moved both him and his indomitable fanbase. Like most Welsh musicians at the time he had a thick skin and had learnt to take the predictable knocks about his country's lack of musical success.

While writing songs for the 1987 *Eye Of The Hurricane* album, Peters embarked on his Welsh odyssey – a round Wales journey, it was a pilgrimage that had a profound effect on him and his music.

> I can never forget some of the places I visited while I was travelling through Wales writing songs [says Mike, casting his mind back to his eventful Welsh trek]. I remember going to Blaenau Ffestiniog, sitting above the town looking down at the slate mines. It was raining. I had my video and guitar and just started singing into the mike. Some of these slate grey images would end up on tape and I'd write them down in my book. Another inspired moment I had on that little journey was when I was sitting up on a bench above the Rhondda Valley writing – just where the Rhondda Fawr dips into the Rhondda Fach, and this old guy came up to me and started telling 'em about 'how it wasn't the same here anymore' and you listen to things like that and they can't help but influence you.

Peters was documenting bleak times for his fellow countrymen, but the singer was struck by his people's propensity for overcoming adversity. 'Welsh people have this tremendous "never say die" spirit that typifies us all as a nation,' he says. 'In the Rhondda especially they really didn't have too much to smile about, but however bad things were they had this great admirable spirit that kept them going through the bad times.'

After years of touring the world, he fell back in love with his birthplace and set about learning to speak Welsh. The single song that made the case for the album was 'A New South Wales'; a huge orchestrated homage to Wales that Mike Peters had been working on for the better part of three years. It featured the thunderous and spine-tingling accompaniment of the massed voices of The Morriston Orpheus Choir and quickly became not only a classic, but a national anthem.

Peters was the first Welshman to bridge the gap between the English and Welsh language, by simultaneously releasing an album in English and Welsh, The Alarm's 1989 *Change*.

To lend support to their cause, The Alarm recorded an alternative version of *Change* named *Newid*, with all the lyrics sung in Welsh. Instead of mere posturing, the band had started creating change by themselves. *Newid* was The Alarm's effort to help bridge the gap between the people of Wales trying to hold on to their own heritage, and those who had fully assimilated into the English culture. The Alarm's album went some way to healing the wounds. It was a reparation of sorts and a huge success story; one which opened up the language to many English-speaking Welsh Alarm fans and introduced them to the burgeoning Welsh-language rock scene that was reaching its zenith in the late Eighties. So, when they split in 1991, due to time-honoured musical differences and an inability to get on with each other, they left an impressive legacy – six albums and many successful singles. The Alarm also established a blueprint for the many Welsh bands that emerged later in the way that they were able to inspire a passionate following of fanatical fans.

At the same time as The Alarm were conquering America, a starstruck Swansea band were hatching equally ambitious plans.

POOH, WHAT A SCORCHER . . .

The Pooh Sticks were rock's most inside joke, Wales' greatest 'lost' band – a monumental yet affectionate prank on the very mythology of pop music itself. The Pooh Sticks were led by frontman Hue Williams, (the son of former Man and Dire Straits drummer Terry Williams). He had an encyclopaedic knowledge of pop cool, and his first-hand experiences of his dad's successful rock 'n' roll career made him hungry to sample the same giddy success. Although admitting he couldn't sing and 'he liked to hear guitar but he couldn't play one' (as one of their songs went) Hue brought a stately ironic presence and devilish guile to his band. These single-minded, almost arrogant but wholly cool attributes would be admired and adapted by four Manic Blackwood revolutionaries who would soon burst onto the Welsh music scene. Hue himself would put his skill at scamming to good use in later years as a lynchpin of the Nineties Welsh music uprising.

However, in October 1987 Hue was just teaming up with Swansea-area schoolmates Paul (guitar), Alison (bass), Trudi Tangerine (keyboards) and Stephanie (drums) – the band were too cool for last names – and debuted with the single 'On Tape,' a humorous jab at the po-faced, C86 indie mentality that had been sweeping the country with bands such as Primal Scream, Tallulah Gosh and The Shop Assistants. In 1991, The Pooh Sticks added Tallulah Gosh and Heavenly vocalist Amelia Fletcher to their ranks and a glimmer of pop success broke through. The album, *Great White Wonder*, was their masterpiece, a collection of sunkissed, bubblegum pop songs built entirely around other people's ideas! From the Neil Young - pilfering on 'The Rhythm of Love' and the fourteen-minute 'I'm in You' right down to the album's title, borrowed from a legendary Bob Dylan bootleg, this was a band in thrall to the Seventies-styled AOR of Todd Rundgren and the colourful bubblegum excess of The Partridge Family and The Banana Splits.

'Other bands lifted things from obvious reference points like The Byrds and The Velvet Underground,' explained Hue. 'We were more likely to filch from Neil Young, Meatloaf, Tom Petty and Peter Frampton. We didn't sit down for hours thinking it would be cool to nick this or that like a lot of the bands at that time, we were totally the opposite.'

Legendary animators Hanna-Barbera, even agreed to immortalise the band as cartoon caricatures, and they would play live with their cardboard cut-outs on stage. At this time I spent a day with Hue in Swansea. He turned up wearing a 'Welsh And Proud' sweatshirt, that he would wear at gigs, years before the Welsh bands that are household names would proclaim their Welshness.

'Nobody wanted to know then, but I like to think I had a hand in all this Welsh tub-thumping,' he laughs ironically. 'Although at the time we had to go to America and Holland to work because Wales was dead musically, no one was interested.'

Hue arrived at the interview with his cardboard cut-outs which we lugged down to the seafront for a photo session in front of perplexed pensioners outside the city's Patti Pavilion. *Great White Wonder* was an amazing album but, like everything The Pooh Sticks released, it stiffed as rigidly as those cardboard cut-outs.

The UK was still suffering a hangover after the baggy excess of Madchester and The Pooh Sticks' American flavours were just not to the taste of the general public. 1993's sublime *Million Seller* took much the same path. Released on the Zoo imprint, a worldwide subsidiary of BMG Records, despite its cheeky title it was anything but a unit shifter. It was, though, yet another wondrously iridescent album brim full of giddy bubblegum pop and sunny psychedelia. It included the 1 minute 48 second histrionic sugar rush of 'The World Is Turning On' which, released as a single, propelled the band to the hitherto untold heights of daytime Radio 1 play. Its eventual chart placing typified much of The Pooh Sticks story – it stalled at 41!

Another album, *Optimistic Fool* followed in 1995 on the cult US label Seed, but only heightened the band's seeming ability to be in the wrong place at the wrong time. With Britpop evolving into a distinctly English proposition, a band enthralled by American music found it hard to strike a chord. And that was about it for The Pooh Sticks – a band that will undoubtedly be exhumed as an 'overlooked gem' some time in the next century. However, as Wales's answer to Malcolm McLaren, Hue Williams was to resurface as a pop svengali responsible for much of the great music that was still to come out of the country. He managed The 60ft Dolls, recommended The Stereophonics to the A&R who signed the band to V2 and, more importantly for this book, advised Catatonia in the early stages of their career.

BUDDING TALENTS

A band that that did take its chance and was patently in the right place at the right time was Newport's spiky guitar popsters The Darling Buds.

The Buds, fronted by the delectable and diminutive Andrea Lewis (vocals), with Harley Farr (guitar – his real name was Geraint but he reckoned that the English public wouldn't be able to pronounce Geraint!), Bloss (drums) and Chris McDonough (bass), formed in Gwent in 1986. They were part of the brief 'Blonde' movement, a spurious music press scene, which traded on the trend for a band to have an alluring blonde female singer backed by blokes wearing black trying to look moody. Along with Voice of the Beehive, Transvision Vamp and The Heart Throbs, the Buds looked to the past – chiefly Blondie and The Buzzcocks – and forged a derivative yet hugely likeable sound that traded on fizzing melodies, barbed guitars and Andrea's luscious vocals.

The band were signed up by Epic in 1988 and had moderate chart success with a string of singles – 'Shame On You', 'Burst' and 'Hit The Ground' and an album, *Pop Said*, which was full of their trademark relentlessly chirpy tunes.

As well as the singles, the gorgeous 'Let's Go Round There' and the exuberant 'Things We Do for Love' were the standouts. At this time they played a number of storming gigs in Wales. A gig that forever sticks in my memory was one of the finest shows they ever played, upstairs at Cardiff's Welsh club, Clwb Ifor Bach. It was a packed claustrophobic affair that saw the walls dripping – there was no air-conditioning and any breeze that did waft over the audience came from people clambering to open any window they could find. Adrenaline rushed like conducted lightning through an excitable, ebullient crowd that bounced up and down so hard the floor below was in danger of falling through.

At an altogether different-sized end of the live spectrum, The Buds played the biggest gig of their lives supporting Scottish rockers Simple Minds at Cardiff's Arms Park in 1989. The home crowd loved it, but the band's indie pop sound just wasn't made for stadiums, and the sound drifted into the ether from about 40 rows back, such was the sheer size of the stage and the 50,000 strong crowd. Yet it was amazing not only to see them perform to such a huge crowd but seeing a Welsh band playing to such a huge audience. Ironically, it would be ten years later that a Welsh band would return to the scene of The Buds' mini-triumph, although this time on an altogether grandiose and ambitious scale.

AND ONCE MORE UNTO THE WILDERNESS!

So, apart from The Pooh Sticks and The Darling Buds, as the Eighties spun into the Nineties, Wales was still firmly considered a musical backwater, as likely to spawn the 'next big thing' as Labour was to form the next government. But the Welsh scene at this time was thriving, full of bedazzling talents that remained hidden through the blind ignorance and utter contempt of London's record companies.

Gwent was showing itself as a breeding ground for guitar bands such as The March Hares, Crazy Jane and the breeze block punk-rock of The Abs. Cardiff was no less prolific, with a clutch of bands that were just as talented. Prunus Tenella were a young band that spun out beautifully decadent and wilfully strange psychedelia: Peppermint Parlour, The Third Uncles, Papa's New Faith, Velvets fronted by the intense Jensen brothers; Hollyweird and the fabulously named Proud Marys. All fantastic, all overlooked. The valleys too were resonating with the sound of amps being plugged in and guitars being picked up. Treorchy's Watermelons fronted by gravedigger Paul Rosser peddled some of the most passionate heartfelt vignettes of the daily struggle of life in a valleys town. Their tough but delicious noise held a clenched fist in its velvet glove, showcasing an agenda of hope over under-achievement. If you view The Stereophonics' Kelly Jones as an über-commentator of small-town life, Paul Rosser's contemplative storytelling was equally as enriching.

Picking up on the new breed of emergent Welsh bands were Darren Jones's excellent Porth-based Welsh music fanzine *White Lemonade* and my own tongue-in-cheek *Taffbeat* fanzine – both peddling enthusiasm in excelsis for ultimately little or no reward. The South Wales public were willing, but the record company executives weren't able.

'Nobody was mentioning Wales ten years ago, but that didn't mean that there weren't any good bands around,' explains Darren Jones. 'The major problem was getting exposure and to get noticed Welsh bands had to work extra hard, as all the record companies were based in London.

'It got to the stage, and this is true, where Welsh bands travelled to England to post their demos. This will sound a horribly contrived apocryphal tale, but it was rumoured that anything that arrived with a Welsh post mark on it went straight into the record company's bin.'

Judging by the amount of success that Welsh bands had at the time, you tend to believe it.

But those who kept the faith knew there were so many good bands around and we were shouting 'Come over here and take a look', but unfortunately no one was listening. Trying to get a record company to send an A&R man to Wales at the end of the Eighties was tantamount to shopping at a greengrocers after a robbery. Fruitless.

I'm sure many of them feared they would never be seen again, ending their days sharing a dank cell on a decaying council estate with some Welsh militiamen and a couple of Terry Waite-lookalikes. They would rather stop off at the edge of their civilisation, or Bristol, as it's also known.

But the talent was there because many Welsh musicians who are now forging successful careers since moving to London have long-forgotten pasts spent in Welsh bands. None more so than electro dance pioneers Underworld, whose Welsh dance revisionaries Rick Smith and Karl Hyde first licked the sugar coating of pop success as Freur in the early Eighties. The arty synth-pop band from Cardiff were notable for initially using an unpronounceable symbol as their name over a decade before the concept occurred to Prince and also for scoring a minor hit in 1983 with the single 'Doot Doot.'

Feeder, one of Britain's brightest new rock bands, features singer Grant Nicholas and drummer Jon Lee, both of whom were in Newport bands Temper Temper and Raindancer in the late Eighties, while the similarly coruscating, but ever-so-slightly more glam, thrash posers – Rachel Stamp – features green-haired firebrand David Ryder-Prangley. The boy-rocker from Dinas Powys in Cardiff was frontman of Cardiff's bubblegum rocketeers Hollyweird before heading for the bright lights and big city.

Then there was David Gray. The inspirational Welsh singer-songwriter, hailed as the 'British Bob Dylan', started his career in Wales.

And if we're being overly indulgent over this exile-picking nonsense – gin-soaked literary types Jack, signed to Stereolab's Too Pure label, features the talents of frazzled wordsmith Anthony Jones, once formerly of this parish as singer with the equally highbrow Cardiff band Misery.

But little did we, our over-achieving exiles or those short-sighted A&Rs know that the blue touchpaper of the Welsh revolution had just been lit and was about to blow up in our faces.

GENERATION TERRORISTS

'Er, Dave, four aliens have just landed in reception for you.' The voice on the other end of the phone line sounded puzzled and not a little perturbed.

This wasn't the sort of call I was expecting from the *South Wales Echo* security desk. And, when I headed downstairs from the first floor newsroom to investigate, I could see why. Terry, our affable 60-year old front-office commissioner and unofficial look-out post was eyeing my guests suspiciously.

There, dressed in homemade, tie-dyed shirts were four mascara-clad, dagger-edged spiky-haired youths named Nicky Wire, James Dean Bradfield, Richey Edwards and Sean Moore. All four wore skin-tight white jeans and looked a dazzling collision of mod, punk and casual chic.

The effect was unforgettable – just as if a spaceship had spilled its contents into the newspaper's offices. The place had ground to a halt and was staring wildly at these four soon-to-be riders of the rock 'n' roll apocalypse. Of course, I didn't know that at the time. All I was expecting was some punk band called The Manic Street Preachers that I was to interview for the newspaper. Once I'd reassured Terry that he could in fact take his finger off the 999 button, and that the four weren't going to trash the place, he calmed down. The last time the old fella had seen men dressed like that was evidently in his worst nightmares.

But his horror was compounded when the hardest-looking of the four, James – whose hair was shockingly bleached with streaks of yellowy-blonde – introduced himself to me and then the rest of the band, before asking if he could borrow a black felt-tip marker pen.

Terry duly handed over the marker and then watched in overstated astonishment as the band began to write slogans on their chests and arms. When the paper's photographer arrived, he gave me and the band a swift nervous double-take before starting to rummage furiously through his bag for film. I think this was more out of fear of having to talk to them than anything else.

Seemingly oblivious to the fuss they had caused, the band wheeled on their Dunlop White Flash heels straight out of the reception with stoic looks etched on their faces, and firmly informed the photographer they had seen a great place to take the pictures.

As first meetings go it was the most impressive I'd ever experienced. I'd been alerted to The Manics in 1989 by Philip and Martin Hall, the enthusiastic brothers that ran hip London music PR company Hall or Nothing.

I'd met Philip at a gig by North Wales' rabble rousers The Alarm the year before. Philip was handling the press for the Welsh firebrands and I was immediately impressed by his passion and knowledge of music, and the fact that he was one of only a few of the London media who was not flippant or dismissive of the Welsh music scene.

So when he raved about this exciting young band that the company had taken under their wing and 'was wondering if I would interview them' – I agreed immediately.

I already knew that the band had released a single 'Suicide Alley' on the Gwent-based SBS label but unfortunately, not possessing one of the 500 copies in existence, I had not heard anything by them. Because The Manics came from Blackwood near Newport, a town renowned for feisty guitar bands and its burgeoning hardcore scene, I was expecting just another bunch of three-chord punks but the band were everything I hadn't expected. They were confident, articulate, passionate and their knowledge of politics, history and literature was astonishing.

After the photo shoot we decamped to Burger King – no food was ordered they were far too skinny for fast food. We sat upstairs where rhythm guitarist Richey Edwards held me with an unerring and intense gaze and held forth on all things MSP-like.

They hadn't even released their 'New Art Riot EP' on Damaged Goods – the follow-up to 'Suicide Alley', and yet they were talking as if they were the greatest and most vital band that ever walked the planet.

Although I was immediately suspicious of their grandiose claims and arrogant impudence, you couldn't help but be drawn to their idealistic manifesto. For remember this was a Welsh band who had only played a handful of gigs, yet had released their debut single, signed a management deal, had a single of the week in *NME* (*New Musical Express*) and had a live review of their very first appearance in *Melody Maker*. You'd be a fool not to think that you weren't in the presence of something vital.

As I listened uneasily to Richey holding forth and informing me without a trace of irony that 'we're the only band in Britain who has anything to say' and 'if we ever write a love song we'd kill ourselves', I was thinking: this guy is either the greatest actor in the world or the greatest orator since Aneurin Bevan. They were just wildly alluring and immediately beguiling.

They were also pent-up and pissed-off, alienated by the boredom of small-town life in Blackwood and fired-up with nihilistic anger at anything and everything.

Being Welsh of course they were met with wholesale suspicion, but their blistering attack and defensive gang mentality – they all looked out for each other – meant the barbs and the criticisms of their Welshness and everything else just bounced off them like a tennis ball off a wall.

Although fiercely patriotic The Manics still told truisms about Welsh culture and the divides brought about by language. I remember Nicky Wire famously saying: 'You have to be wary of romanticism. Wales is a much more complex and divided place than some people think. It isn't this glowing ember of close-knit communities. There's animosity there too. Some North and West Walians resent us talking about Welshness because we can't speak Welsh.'

Richey was even more forthright: 'People should be prepared to accept reality. The Welsh language is basically dead, it doesn't matter to the majority of people in Wales, so just let it die a natural death. You can't reinvent a language or culture. It gets to a scary level when people are so obsessed with nationalism, it just borders on fascism.'

At the time of The Manic Street Preachers' emergence, the question of language was being fiercely fought out between two staunchly partisan groups – the pro-language Cymdeithas yr Iaith (the Welsh Language Society) which was campaigning for the equal use of the Welsh language and those non-Welsh-speaking members of the Welsh community who viewed the Welsh language as dead. These protagonists thought the language as culturally redundant as the coal mines that lay dormant throughout the country.

It was a fascinating time, underpinned by a Welsh-language rock scene that was about to reach its zenith and act as the catalyst for Catatonia and a host of brilliant Welsh bands.

2
Way Before Blue

EVOLUTION, REVOLUTION AND THE STATE OF A NATION

Music and Video Exchange is London's biggest established retailer of second-hand records, CDs, minidiscs, tapes, 8-track cartridges and music memorabilia.

Now numbering eight shops, its first shop opened in Notting Hill, West London in the early Seventies. The trendy area made famous by the film starring Hugh Grant was then a vibrant mix of ethnic tribes, much more earthy and bohemian than the ultra-chic, *de rigueur* image it wears like a garish Versace suit nowadays.

In 1975, 23-year-old graduate teacher Tony Schiavone was making ends meet by working part-time at the Notting Hill shop, a cavernous resting place for London's unwanted second-hand music.

This stuffed shrine to the waifs and strays from high-street record shops was a treasure trove for the diligent bargain-hunters who flocked there on a weekly pilgrimage in the hope of sighting a rare 7 inch or priceless white label.

As a music obsessive it was a job that indulged Tony's passion while providing money to supplement his career teaching deprived kids at a tough comprehensive school in East Acton – a roughhouse area of West London.

The native North Walian had enjoyed his time studying in London. Who wouldn't? If you were music-mad like Tony there was no better place to indulge your passion. Like most students in the capital he had spent most of his time at the city's multitude of live venues, checking new bands and the emergent scenes that London served up. Coming from an area where a show by a big name band was as rare as a sighting of Halley's Comet, London's burgeoning live circuit, with its regular A-list gigs, was like manna from heaven for the music obsessive.

Although London was still to meet the full force of punk head on, reggae was taking a foothold in the capital and captivating Schiavone, who lapped up the sun-splashed sounds of Dennis Brown, Bob Marley and the emergent Caribbean music. Their earthly captivating roots music was a sweet antidote to progressive prog rock dinosaurs like Genesis and Yes who bestrode the charts in the mid-Seventies.

He wasn't the only young white guy turned on by the colourful reggae sounds resonating around West London. Joe Strummer was a permanent fixture on the London pub rock circuit with his band The 101'ers, when reggae and punk rock shook him to the core. Ditching his former incarnation as a pub rock singer, he teamed up with fellow guitarist Mick Jones, bassist Paul Simonon and drummer Nicky 'Topper' Headon to form The Clash.

Based in West London, The Clash may not have been the first British punk rock band, that honour going to The Sex Pistols, but they were the definitive British punk rockers. Where The Pistols were nihilistic, The Clash were fiery and idealistic, charged with righteousness and a leftist political ideology. From the outset, the band was more musically adventurous, expanding their hard rock 'n' roll with reggae, dub and rap among the other roots musics that London's cultural melting pot was serving up.

It was definitely a case of being in the right place at the right time, as Notting Hill's vibrant Afro-Caribbean community was the first to inject London with the sunshine sounds of the Caribbean's leading reggae exponents, notably Bob Marley.

So taken by the magic of Marley was Tony Schiavone that he took a class of kids to see the reggae superstar in concert at London's renowned rock 'n' roll venue The Lyceum.

Although, a veritable reggae giant back home in Jamaica, Marley had yet to find the same measure of success in the UK. The gig at The Lyceum would change all that. It was the beginning of his swift elevation to reggae-godlike status. This impromptu outing was a resounding success, with a class of reggae converted kids thanking their teacher for taking them to such an amazing show by a man who was just about to be anointed as a musical legend.

As a geography teacher, by rights the only rock formations Tony should have been espousing were those jutting skywards from the towering mass of his native Snowdon. However, that night, his educational unorthodoxy had borne radical fruits. He vowed to himself that whenever possible he would try everything in his power to coerce kids in his charge to listen to cool music and encourage them to experiment and discover the power of musical eclecticism.

Tony left London in 1976 to return to North Wales, where his manifesto for music and education to mix was soon to realise the rock 'n' roll dreams of one of his most talented pupils.

TEENAGE KICKS

Mark Roberts was a fanatical 15-year-old music fan, crazy about The Clash and wanting to form a band when he sat down in his form four geography class and first met his equally music-obsessed teacher Tony Schiavone.

Mark was born on 3 November 1968 in the market town of Llanrwst in North Wales – a rich agricultural area that stands on the edge of thick forest, mountains and the river Conwy situated in the Conwy Valley to the north of beautiful Bettws-y-Coed. The town is steeped in Welsh folklore – Llanrwst's St Crwst's Church is famous as housing the burial case of the last king of Wales, Llewelyn Fawr. The location of the final resting place of the remains of this Welsh legend still remain a mystery today.

Mark attended the town's comprehensive school Ysgol Duffryn Conwy and was a diligent pupil who, although academically advanced, only ever had designs on a music career. As soon as he started secondary school, those thoughts started to pick up pace.

'It was when I was about 11 that I first thought about getting a band together,' he remembers. 'I think it was just seeing bands, but not one particular moment. People used to bring records into school, new wave-type singles at the time, that's how I got into music.

'I think we had a notional band when I was 11, but it involved having loads of girls in it, they were the singers. But we didn't have a rehearsal or anything. Then I had another notional band when I went to the big school, but nothing came of that either. None of us could play anything, we just kept saying that we'd learn to play all these instruments, and we designated people to play different instruments.'

Although, with Catatonia, Mark is now one of the UK's most imaginative guitarists, strangely it was as a drummer that the aspirant musician first excelled. 'I took up guitar, but wasn't very good at it,' he explains. 'So I had drum lessons in school because it got me out of French. I learnt to play the drums before guitar.'

But it was in between lessons about oxbow lakes and cirrus cloud formations, that the dreams started to become reality, and in no small way this was thanks to Joe Strummer.

'Mark and I used to swap notes about The Clash after geography lessons,' says Tony Schiavone. The reggae music that had so inspired Tony as a teacher in London had had the same effect on a nascent Joe Strummer, who infused a zestful reggae edge to much of The Clash's inspirational music.

Tony remembers that there was general enthusiasm for music especially of the indie variety with The Smiths being especial favourites among the pupils he taught. However the flame of musical passion burnt brightest in Mark Roberts. 'I could see that Mark was serious about a career in music and had the dedication that was needed. So when he formed the band Y Cyrff in school I was determined to help him and his bandmates in any way I could.'

Y Cyrff (The Bodies) were formed around the fifth form with classmates

Dylan Hughes on drums, Emyr Hughes on rhythm guitar and Barry Colley on bass.

Like so many new bands, Y Cyrff went through a transitional phase, learning their craft and experimenting with songs and songwriting. Those early songwriting efforts left a lot to be desired.

'I used to write so much, and thankfully some of it will never see the light of day,' Mark admits. 'There'll be some embarrassing stuff in there as well. I got these notebooks full of horrible lyrics. It was like rockets, bombs and gangsters – all that sort of terrible stuff.'

Evidently the punkoid influence of Strummer and The Clash loomed large over the young Roberts's early songs!

Playing a first nervous gig in front of their mates at Ysgol Duffryn Conwy, Y Cyrff soon got into their stride and quickly became local legends, not least for a series of storming gigs they played at the Llanrwst Community Centre. Tony Schiavone, who was booking the band gigs and generally acting as their unofficial manager, was particularly proud of the name he gave to these ambitious early Cyrff performances.

'We were naively ambitious in those days,' he laughs. 'We couldn't help showing our influences. We wanted to do a residency just like all the punk bands like The Jam had done at The Red Cow in 1977. We called them "Llanrwst Yn Llosgi", which translated means "Llanrwst Is Burning"!' A tribute to The Clash's seminal *London's Burning* album and yet another indicator of just how much an influence The Clash were on the band.

Although those punk influences were there, Y Cyrff were steadfastly post-punk. They weren't about three chords, two-minute songs and one idea. They were luxuriously crafted, producing an ambitiously lush sound that twisted and contorted around Mark's dark and brooding guitar structures. It echoed early REM, Echo and The Bunnymen and The Smiths, not only musically, but Mark's songwriting was ambitious and the words powerful. Not as political as some Welsh bands, but loaded with imagery of the starkness of everyday life. With songs like Yr Haint (The Plague), The Housemartins they certainly weren't.

Tony was instrumental in getting the band gigs at local schools and persuaded the headteacher of Ysgol Dufrryn Conwy to put on gigs there – not only to promote Y Cyrff, but also the indie-styled Welsh-language bands that were beginning to emerge as quickly as the English music scene was breeding new indie labels and extolling a DIY ethic.

'The school's caretaker and I made a pact to not tell the headmaster or anyone else about the damage that was invariably made to the school hall after each gig,' says Tony. 'We always managed to cover it up, otherwise the school's heads would have stopped us. As it was they saw the pupils flocking to the shows and having a good time, so that was good enough for them!'

The early incarnation of Y Cyrff didn't last long past those early school gigs. Drummer Dylan Hughes's brother Emyr wasn't up to scratch on guitar and Barry Colley moved to rhythm guitar, while a new bass player was sought. Paul Jones, a long-time older friend of Mark's, used to hang around town with the teenage musicians, waxing lyrical about the respective merits of Welsh favourites The Alarm, Echo and The Bunnymen and the mid-Eighties music scene. More importantly he could play bass and was quickly invited to join Y Cyrff.

From working as a National Trust instructor in dry-stone walling techniques to bass player in a fiery, idealistic punk band isn't the natural progression for most tentatively stepping up the career ladder, yet that was the state of play when the band who were just finishing their GCSEs (Tony: 'I'm proud to say Mark got a B in Geography!') tempted Paul to jump on the ever-growing Y Cyrff bandwagon.

Like Mark, Paul also grew up in Llanrwst. Born in 1960 and being older than the rest of the band, he was already taking his place as the older, wiser sage figure in the set-up. Paul was the most unorthodox music fan in the band, professing a love of anything from The Beatles and The Stones to Ice-T and NWA. He also had his exotic element, being a big fan of Jacques Brel.

By this time, the band had left school and Mark had started a joylessly inauspicious job at Pero – a local dog-food factory. Although soulless, it allowed him to make money to plough into the group and to spend his days dreaming up songs. Thanks to Tony and the band's hard-working approach, Y Cyrff had started to take their reputation further afield. They had also acquired a quiet determination and self-belief. 'This was markedly different from most other bands at that time,' Tony points out. 'They weren't like a lot of other bands in the Welsh-language music scene before then which was dominated by middle-of-the-road, middle-class university types.'

'SAY, YOU WANNA REVOLUTION . . .'

1986 was an important year for music in Britain. The Eighties had been clogged full of manufactured, disposal pop music spewed out by bland bands like Spandau Ballet, Aha and Duran Duran. But the underground was about to go overground and reclaim some lost ground. The *New Musical Express* had coined the term C86 after a free cassette they had given away with one of their issues. It reflected an exciting time with independent labels and fanzines starting up at a rate of knots. Bands like The Pastels, The Weather Prophets, The Soup Dragons, Biff Bang Pow, The Jasmine Minks, The Television Personalities, The Razorcuts, The Shop Assistants and labels such as Rough Trade, Postcard and Creation were reflecting a flourishing Do-It-Yourself scene that was gaining a head of steam.

And in much the same way the Welsh-language scene was about to undergo a radical explosion with a similar multi-styled, experimental approach. To raise Y Cyrff's profile Tony Schiavone not only promoted their gigs with other Welsh-language bands, but published *Llmych*, a liberal fanzine that featured Mark and his band, as well as anything related not just to the Welsh-language scene but to any music that he was interested in.

'*Llmych* doesn't mean anything, it's just a sound,' explained Tony. 'The idea was to create a buzz for Y Cyrff and also feature music that we liked. I remember we wrote articles on renowned African musician Thomas Mapfuno, country legend Hank Williams and all our favourite punk bands, so you can see our eclectic approach!'

Through the fanzine and the gigs Tony and Y Cyrff quickly came into contact with many who shared their enthusiastic approach. Key among these was Rhys Mwyn. A fired-up iconoclast whose profligacy in organising gigs and publicity for his band resulted in much of the Welsh-language scene's early profile being bulldozed by Rhys and his band, Bangor punkers Yr Anhrefn (The Angry). Their non-stop talking up of the scene made them the first point of contact for English music media interested in the cause.

The band were something of an enigma, by virtue of their pioneering Welsh-language punk tirades and position as one of the hardest gigging bands ever. A normal year of touring would see them playing over 150 gigs, not only in the UK but also abroad. In countries like Germany, France and Czechoslovakia, where there was not so much of a stigma attached to singing in Welsh as there was in the rest of the UK, they would regularly play in front of crowds of 500 plus. Anhrefn's adrenaline-driven punk sound was as vociferous and persuasive as their championing of the Welsh music scene.

'As a teenager I was very cynical and hated everything Welsh,' Rhys explains. 'I saw the Welsh thing as being the Eisteddfod (an annual and historic event which features competitions for poetry, literature and music) and shit folk music.'

But that all changed in 1977 when punk and two seminal Welsh-language bands turned his world upside down.

'There was a Swansea-based punk band called Llygr Fynych that released a self-financed single and a new wave band called Trwynau Coch who set up their own indie label Recordiau Coch and released a single "Methu Dawnsio". These were both played on John Peel's Radio 1 show. I was 16 or 17 and was influenced by The Sex Pistols, but also these Welsh-language bands. Hearing these Welsh-language bands who had released their own records on Peel's show turned me on to the Welsh-language thing. I thought, cool – I can do that.'

With his brother Sion Sebon, and two of Rhys's friends Gwyn Jones on drums and Sion Jones on guitar, Anhrefn's vibrant punk manifesto and dynamic cottage industry were about to come alive.

'The key turning point was when we decided to put out our own records on Anhrefn Records,' remembers Rhys. 'The first record was in 1984. Everything we were doing was influenced by fanzines, Rough Trade, indie labels all that culture. Our punk rock was very DIY. In Wales it was almost a necessity because we had no music industry.'

The second stage to this awakening of the Welsh-language scene was the meeting of Anhrefn and Y Cyrff. Rhys: 'I'd heard of what Tony and Y Cyrff were doing – putting on gigs and their fanzine – and realised that we shared so many ideals, so I got in touch and we hit it off straight away.'

Inspired by Y Cyrff and Anhrefn, as well as the new productive DIY underground that had gripped the British music scene, a rash of bands were forming within thirty miles of each other in North Wales. There was the leftfield, off-kilter lunacy of Datblygu, the mercurial Gorwel Owen's Kraftwerk-ish electro outfit Plant Bach Ofnus and the weird twisted pop of Y Fflaps.

'The common thread was we all realised that this was a new scene, and we were all mates, all at each others' gigs, all gave each other support slots,' says Rhys. 'So if Y Cyrff got a gig Anhrefn would get a support slot and vice versa. We had a fanbase and the gigs were selling out. It's funny because the audience was full of people who have gone on to better things. There was Rhys Ifans (the actor) in the crowd at one gig and Gruff and Dafydd Ieaun (from The Super Furry Animals) in another. Then we thought, let's put out our own compilations featuring all these Welsh-language bands because it was much more cost-effective than say putting out 10 singles.'

Rhys remembers the day he first went to London to spread the gospel of Y Cyrff, Anhrefn and the Welsh scene to journalists and DJs, who were half-intimidated, half-impressed by his evangelical zeal.

'I went armed with copies of the first two compilations *Cam O'r Tywyllwch* and *Gadael Yr Ugeinfed Ganrif*,' Rhys recalls. 'I went everywhere – *The Face*, Capital Radio, all the music press editors, I knocked on doors and demanded to be seen. I think they liked my cheek and started to write about us. Mick Mercer at *Melody Maker* who thought we were mad, David Quantick from the *NME* thought we were thugs. But we didn't care, we were doing what we wanted. It was a home-grown thing, achieved naturally and done on our own terms.'

John Peel was one of the first to meet the maelstrom that was Rhys Mwyn and a man who would become the main outlet for Welsh-language bands to be heard nationally.

Brought up in Shrewsbury, Peel had close links with nearby Wales from an early age. He went to a boarding school for boys in Deganwy in Conwy, and spent most of his military service on Anglesey.

But it wasn't until Rhys Mwyn sent him some demo tapes of his bands, that the perceptive Peel began to realise that Wales had a rock scene all of its own which was very much alive and well.

'Rhys had put together and sent me two worthwhile compilations on his own Anhrefn Records,' he remembers. They were quite primitively produced in their way, because of the financial constraints the bands faced. However, when I eventually met Rhys, he was such a persuasive and dedicated person – the sort who just couldn't be ignored – that he started me off on Welsh music. Before that I had zero interest.'

To Peel's surprise, once he began playing Welsh records, requests started flooding in for Welsh songs from the most unexpected listeners.

Letters asking for more of the same arrived from people from Germany, Australia and Czechoslovakia, who all regularly picked up the show and enjoyed the music – even if they didn't understand the lyrics.

'There is more of a language barrier facing Welsh music in the UK than there is abroad,' Peel explained. 'In other countries, people are more used to listening to music in languages which are not their own, and they don't see anything strange in it.'

But still the English media, in the main, remained strictly ambivalent. Save Peel and a double-page-spread article in the now defunct music newspaper *Sounds* in 1988, the Welsh-language scene remained as underground to the rest of the UK as it was beginning to clamber overground in Wales.

A whole host of bands were excelling at singing in their mother tongue backed by an eclectic array of sounds and styles. Journalist John Robb who wrote the article for *Sounds*, and who himself was a musician at that time with legendary Manchester noiseniks The Membranes, remembers the scene for its rapid diversity. 'It was a rumbling collection of countless outfits creating a multi-styled assault of Welsh music,' admits John. 'There were the Fall-esque landscapes of Datblygu, the electronic weirdness of Plant Bach Ofnus, the twisted hip hop of Llwybr Llaethog, the techno indie pop of Ffa Coffi Pawb, the noise manipulators Traddodiad Ofnus, the indie weirdness of Y Fflaps and seemingly a thousand others.'

Apart from the seminal influences of Trywnnau Coch and Llygr Fynych in the late Seventies, up until this point the Welsh-language scene had been littered with middle-of-the-road rock bands and folk singers, but this rapid expansion reflected both a love of the music and the language.

'It was the first time the people who were directly involved were motivated as much by promoting the music as the language,' Tony Schiavone reckons. 'It was a very political time. We were promoting gigs through the Welsh Language Society (Cymdeithas Yr Iaith – a radical pressure group campaigning for the Welsh language) so for the first time a real support network existed with a number of venues for bands to play. There was a core of people who were very active like myself and Rhys and it was a very exciting and dynamic time.'

Despite Paul Jones's description of the early Y Cyrff as 'these scruffy punks without much idea of what we were doing', the band took advantage of this new creativity and released their first single 'Yr Haint' (The Plague) on Rhys's Anhrefn Records in 1985. 'Their brooding melancholia was indicative of the times, wasn't it,' opines Rhys. 'You could hear The Bunnymen and The Smiths in their sound, but it was also wordy, powerful and intelligent.'

Tony Schiavone's dedication to the band gloriously showed itself in his unorthodox sales technique, so as well as gaining an audience with Welsh speakers, the single also broke into the unlikeliest of places – school tuck shops and Russia included!

'I was so into the band and wanted everyone to hear them, so at breaktime I would set up in the school tuck shop and sell the single to my pupils!' He even smuggled some out of the country on a school trip. 'I took a class of kids to the Soviet Union in 1985 and took about a dozen copies of the single with me! So there are 12 really cool Russian kids with copies of Mark's early work.'

As Y Cyrff played more gigs and evolved a real sense of community and affinity with other Welsh-language bands, so their confidence grew, especially Mark's songwriting, key to Catatonia's later success.

He was an acute observer of everyday life even then,' reckons Tony. 'A sensitive and intelligent guy, but very grounded, who just wanted to play music and wasn't starstruck by the fact that his band were rapidly becoming one of the biggest in Wales.'

Anhrefn Records was then the main record label for bands wanting to release singles, having put out the first releases from Y Fflaps, Datblygu and the promising Heb Gariad. However, Rhys thought it time that more bands did it themselves.

'We had started to gig a lot in the UK and Europe, so the second part of the strategy was to say to these other bands you should put these records out on your own labels, let's have more labels. I remember having this conversation with Gorwel Owen, who went on to produce many of Super Furry Animals records. He set up Ofn Records and Ofn Studios, which became a home for Gorwel's Plant Bach Ofnus and the bands Nid Madagascyr and Eiryn Peryglus, who both shared a similar experimental, maverick electro feel to Plant Bach.'

Y Cyrff too started up their own label and released 'Pum Munud' (5 Minutes) in 1986.

With the Welsh-language music scene becoming both rock 'n' roll and sexy, it invariably attracted the attentions of Welsh-language media and new Welsh-language channel S4C in particular. But at the time this attention wasn't embraced comfortably by the bands who, with their strict underground agendas, were very suspicious.

Rhys remembers being in Paul Jones's house when Y Cyrff were the first Welsh-language band to get offered a TV gig.

'Paul, Mark and I had a meeting to decide whether it was politically correct to do S4C,' says Rhys. 'I said I think you should do it because it's good exposure. We all had that underground thing maybe we shouldn't be doing telly, which showed how DIY we were. I mean it was a little bit Clash doing *Top of The Pops*. But if it brought the music to a wider audience all the better.'

There was not only a lot of hard thinking done during these radical times for both Welsh music and the language, but a lot of tough talking too. In the Eighties there was much abrasion between Welsh speakers and non-Welsh speakers on how the language was promoted. Both Y Cyrff and Anhrefn felt the sharp end of these factional politics.

'In the Eighties in Wales there was a division between English-speaking student unions and Welsh-speaking student unions,' explains Rhys Mwyn. 'My thinking was that anyone coming to a Welsh university should hear some Welsh culture. So when Y Cyrff and Anhrefn started playing so-called English student union gigs in Wales, the Welsh nationalists went up in arms, as in "you're playing in front of English people you can't do that". We said we would play in front of anyone. So there was a rift with the harder line narrow-minded nationalists who were upset, which was ridiculous. And they're still there today, the people who have never been further than Dogellau [in North Wales] and have an "ap" in the middle of their name!'

My opinion was that it's all music whatever the language. Everyone should be invited to the party. But it was a puzzling time.

The extreme politics of Meibion Glyndwr and their terror group tactics – burning down cottages owned by English residents – caused unease among the English-speaking Welsh who distanced themselves from their Welsh-speaking compatriots. Cymdeithas Yr Iaith, the Welsh Language Society – although a moderate organisation trading on an agenda of non-violent protest – were also guilty of what I saw as separatist snobbery.

In the early days of Cardiff's Welsh club, Clwb Ifor Bach, there was a strict Welsh-speakers-only policy of admission. This, in essence, meant that although I too was a patriotic Welshman, whenever I wanted to see a band play at Clwb, I was excluded, even though I was an enthusiastic supporter of Welsh-language bands. I'd bought the records and naturally wanted to see the gigs.

I remember one night Y Cyrff were playing in town and naturally having picked up on the band's reputation I was eager to experience the tumultuous live performances I had heard of. But the only way I could see them was to play my trump card and say I was a journalist reviewing the gig for a fanzine I was writing. It worked but even then I was begrudgingly allowed in only if

I was signed in by a Welsh speaker.

I remember going up to the bar and debating whether I should attempt to order a pint of lager in my pidgin Welsh (un paint o'r lager – I think!) or just ask for it in English. Feeling sure I would make a fool of myself either way, I stumped for the English option and was shot such a look of abhorrent horror by the barman that I had spoken English, that I made that pint last all night. Talk about feeling like a stranger in your own land. The one simple answer is that everyone in Wales should be equal, regardless of whether you speak the language or not. (The large Somali population that lives in Cardiff are as Welsh as anywhere else in Wales and that's where it should start and end.)

Still, the gig more than made up for it. Y Cyrff were powerful and dynamic, but also elegant and wistful. There was something intense and resonant about the chiming guitars and their artful agenda was perfect for Mark's haunting vocals. I was hooked.

After releasing two singles, appearing regularly on S4C, and selling out shows in Wales wherever they played, Y Cyrff were looking to be more ambitious. An alliance was formed with a Welsh record label that was renowned for its more traditional Welsh music acts, but not for anything as remotely alternative as Y Cyrff.

Sain (which is the Welsh word for 'sound', and pronounced like the English word 'sign') is one of Wales' leading record companies. It was founded in 1969 in Cardiff by protest singer Dafydd Iwan, as well as Huw Jones and Brian Morgan Edwards. Sain retained a close affinity with the political resurgence in Wales. Many of its releases arose out of the language campaigns, and the theme of Welsh freedom ran through the songs of several singers and groups.

Heading into the Sain Studios in August 1987 with in-house engineer Eryl B. Davies Y Cyrff reaffirmed their grand ambitions by recording a mini-album, the biblically titled *Y Testament Newydd* (The New Testament). The album comprised seven songs of ornate grandeur and stark lyricism. The religious title worked on several levels – the Welsh-language music scene was writing a new chapter in Welsh history: it was a new beginning and those Welsh-speaking kids who were following the bands had a new radical agenda to cling to.

Y Cyrff's musical aftershocks were being felt all over Wales, but particularly in West Wales where two university students loved this strange and alluring Welsh band. Alun Llywd and Gruff Jones were two students at Aberystwyth University, located on the West Wales coast. They were promoting gigs at the student union and were huge fans of Y Cyrff.

'I met Mark Roberts at a gig in Menai Bridge in 1986, but had already heard of his band before that,' recalls Gruff Jones. 'Myself and Alun were very much into them from the very start. They were the most musically proficient of all the bands around then. They had a more evolved style and image, and were very professional. A lot of bands were in it for fun, to earn enough money for a few drinks at the end of the night, but Y Cyrff had their own bank account and any money earned from gigs would be ploughed into the band's funds.'

Much like Tony Schiavone, these West Wales lads promoted gigs and published their own photocopied fanzine, *Ish*. But they also had grander plans.

'In 1988, Welsh pop music releases, with a few notable exceptions like Anhrefn and Ofn Records, were for the most part limited to recordings of choirs, old men and harps, and re-releases of wartime Welsh tenors,' says Gruff.

Not to be perturbed, the two students formed a shaky partnership and one of Wales's most important record labels, Ankst Records, was born. Leaving Aberystwyth, they relocated to Cardiff and with a close friend Emyr Lewis, they set up the label in a damp one-room office, taking advantage of the limited funds the Enterprise Allowance Scheme had to offer.

For its formative years survival was on a shoestring budget . 'We used to wait for releases to sell out before being able to plough the small profits back into the next,' explains Gruff. 'The early days saw cassette-only releases, progressing to 7" EPs and eventually a host of 12" singles. Although sales of Welsh pop releases continued to be low, there was great grassroots interest and plenty of potential.'

Y Cyrff, meantime, were still in the ascendancy, but still skint. Mark was trying every way he could to make ends meet – chiefly holding down jobs as a butcher, an electrician's mate and a potato picker. They had also lost a drummer, Dylan Harris, who had left to join Anhrefn. The loss of a drummer was quickly overcome by Mark acting quickly to keep Y Cyrff's all-Llanrwst connections alive by recruiting another friend that he had hung around town with. Mark Kensal – who had ironically been taught to play drums by Mark himself at Ysgol Duffryn Conwy – quickly slotted onto the drummer's stool and the classic Y Cyrff line-up was complete.

The band's fortunes quickly swung in their favour when Ankst's Alun and Gruff, who were understandably keen to work with the band after following them as fans, signed them to Ankst on a combined management and recording deal.

Although a very informal arrangement, it would allow Y Cyrff to record what would become some of the most classic music ever recorded in Welsh.

But it was in Cardiff at the television centre of Sianel Pedwar Wales (S4C) that one music show was at the eye of this revolution in Welsh-language music. *Fideo 9* – so named because it allowed bands to make videos and have them shown on Welsh national television at 9pm on

Thursday evenings – ran from 1988 to 1992. It gave Y Cyrff a regular platform for their majestic performances and fostered the careers of nascent versions of many of the bands that now sit serenely as Welsh pop royalty.

Fideo 9 saw the first sighting of a 15-year-old genius called Euros Childs and his strangely offbeat, neo-medieval Gorky's Zygotic Mynci. And then, Ffa Coffi Pawb, a psychedelic thrill pop machine featuring future Super Furry Animals Gruff Rhys and Dafydd Ieaun. The formula was simple but the results were startling. S4C in conjunction with the show's makers, production company Criw Byw, allowed four bands every week to make a video.

Nothing earth-shattering in that, you might think, but which other UK music show was allowing bands access to state-of-the-art recording equipment, TV studios and a sizable payment at the end of it? Exactly. None.

Strangely there was no shortage of takers. 'You could tell how healthy the scene was by the numbers of bands that were forming,' says Geraint Jarman, the show's executive producer. 'When you had bands like Y Cyrff and Ffa Coffi Pawb appearing, they were influencing the kids who were their fans to form bands and not be afraid to sing in their mother tongue. It was a tremendously exciting time with a real sense of community between all the musicians.'

Musicians were not only afforded the sorts of gratis recording opportunities that most bands would have to save diligently for, but they were often taken on foreign trips to record videos and play gigs in Europe.

'We'd made connections with promoters in Europe who were sympathetic to Welsh-language music,' Jarman remembers. 'We took Y Cyrff to play Warsaw in Poland and they were awesome. I remember them supporting me and my band at a benefit gig in North Wales in '86 and they were very frenetic, very fired-up, just like The Clash. But now they had quickly developed into writing amazing songs full of depth and feeling.'

Another band that were a product of *Fideo 9* was Cardiff's Y Crumblowers. If Y Cyrff were the artful Welsh existentialists, literate deep thinkers shrouded in a cloak of navel contemplation, then Y Crumblowers were 24-hour party people – a rumbling, tumbling, carousing confection of The Stone Roses and The Happy Mondays. Their gigs were parties and their parties were usually gigs!

In Cardiff they accrued legendary status. Gigs at Clwb Ifor Bach were always riotous assemblies of drink, drugs and Bez-like dancing. They were also the only Welsh language band that attracted hordes of groupies. I still find it hard to see why, as they were a band with staggeringly big hair – each of their rank attempting to outdo each other by sporting a pudding-basin bowl cut or something resembling a poorly advised white boy afro.

The band consisted of brothers Lloyd and Owen Powell (voice and guitar; Owen later becoming the guitarist with Catatonia); Lloyd Mahoney (guitar); and Owen Stickler (drums). They formed in Christmas 1986 when they discovered drummer Dave Rizzo as they waited at Llandaff train station in Cardiff on their way to see The Damned at the city's Ritzys venue. Dave was going to go on his own but that night the English-speaking drummer was corralled by four drunken Welsh speakers to join their band.

'He still doesn't speak Welsh, but then he is a drummer and they're not supposed to say anything,' reasons Lloyd Powell. It got interesting at Welsh-speaking-only gigs, as the rest of the band would communicate with him in hand signals. 'Of the two-fingered variety usually,' laughs Lloyd.

Playing their first gig as support to Edrych Am Jiwlia – a short-lived but semi-legendary band that featured The Super Furry Animals' Huw 'Bunf' Bundord – at the Urdd Centre in Conwy, Y Crumblowers quickly gathered a following, much to the incredulity of Lloyd Powell who confessed: 'I was really shy to start with, not much good for a frontman, but Owen was really into guitars and needed a singer. At the first gigs, we just made it up as we went along initially. Sometimes I didn't know what I was going to sing. I just improvised!'

And they weren't exactly angling to set the world alight. 'We just wanted to have some fun and if we got anything else out of it that was a bonus,' Lloyd admits. 'We weren't really sure what we were doing. We thought we would put out some singles and see what happened.'

Through the network of gigs set up by the Welsh Language Society they ended up supporting Y Cyrff, who were the biggest band in Wales at the time, but Lloyd remembers he and his brother weren't overly impressed.

'Yeah, we hated them at first, we thought they were arrogant,' says Lloyd. 'But it probably had more to do with the fact that they were so much better than us!'

Despite this, their 1990 EP *Colossus*, with its waterfall guitars and euphoric melodies, transformed them into the Welsh Stone Roses. More importantly the national music press put their head above the parapet and Steve Lamacq, then just a lowly scribe on the *NME*, nominated it Single Of The Week.

After years of being ignored by the music press the Welsh scene was finally gaining the attention of usually cynical London journalists – although to be honest it was a Welshman who set the *NME*'s ball rolling.

Swansea-born Iestyn George was news editor of the *NME* when *Colossus* landed on his desk. The son of famous S4C TV presenter Betty George, he was a graduate of the Polytechnic of Central London, where he had edited his own fanzine, the imaginatively titled *Zine*, with the former editor of

Loaded, Tim Southwell, and the woman who would end up marrying Steve Lamacq, Juliet Sensicle. After a stint working for the now-defunct pop weekly *Record Mirror*, he became *NME* news editor in 1990.

As a Welsh speaker, attending a Welsh-speaking school, he had always been aware of the Welsh-language music scene and its associated bands. He'd grown up listening to Geraint Jarman, folk hero Meic Stevens and Y Brodyr (The Brothers). However, the scene of Iestyn's youth had never been cool enough or vibrant enough to harbour the sort of dynamic movement that would see bands like Y Cyrff, Y Crumblowers and Datblygu vying for column inches in the rock inkies.

Iestyn was sharing a flat in Brixton with Steve Lamacq and spent his time gently brainwashing the future Radio 1 Evening Session host into the wonderful ways of Welsh bands.

'I received a copy of Y Crumblowers' *Colossus* and this was about the time when indie dance and baggy was taking off,' recalls Iestyn. 'I was a sucker for a funky drummer backbeat and loved the record. So I gave it to Lamacq who was reviewing the singles for *NME* that week and to my amazement, as Steve was always a three-chord, punk sort of bloke, he made it single of the week.'

Luckily, 1990 was a rare vintage for Welsh bands, and there was more to come. After prolonged exposure by John Peel to the charms of Anhrefn, Y Flaps, Datblygu and Llwbyr Llaethog, Peel disciple and *NME* writer, Stephen Dalton, wrote a Welsh-language music scene article that shed light on the scene, its bands and its labels. Now this was progress.

'It was an exciting time,' says Iestyn. 'But Y Cyrff were the band that really intrigued me. They seemed so serious. They were like The Bunnymen, The Jam and The Smiths rolled into one. They meant it man. I wanted to interview them because I was really impressed. They were quite surly, intense and serious, you knew they weren't tapdancing, but they did have that faultless passion and commitment to their music.'

Iestyn had heard 'Hwyl Fawr Heulwen' – Y Cyrff's tumultuous 1990 debut single on Ankst and was intrigued. Understandable, as it was a serrated, spiky pop anthem reverberating with echo and Mark's urgent vocals. But it was the band's debut album *Llawenydd Heb Ddiwedd* that fired the journalist's imagination.

'I was working for the BBC at the 1991 National Eisteddfod in Mold, North Wales,' Iestyn recalls. 'And all I remember was playing that album over and over in my car. I thought it was as good as anything I'd ever heard.'

Again, he sneaked a goal for the Welsh past Steve Lamacq. 'It was quite handy,' laughs Iestyn. 'He was editing the "On" section of *NME* which features new bands, so it wasn't too difficult for me to get Y Cyrff in there, although I think he said yes because I kept going on about them!'

Ironically, just as Y Cyrff were beginning to be buried beneath a mountain of critically exclamatory press cuttings, they were obviously doubting how much further they could go with this. It had taken them to 1991 to release their debut album – seven years – and there really wasn't anywhere else for them to go. Despite the *NME* coverage and a few favourable shows with Y Crumblowers, Fflaps and Anhrefn on St David's Day at London's Powerhaus venue, Y Cyrff twigged that bands singing solely in the Welsh language were only ever realistically going to make a limited living from sales in Wales.

By August 1991 you could see the cracks appearing.

I interviewed Paul for a local magazine and although he paid tribute to the role that Ankst had paid in getting their debut album out, you could sense that if it wasn't for the label's enthusiasm Y Cyrff would have already ground to a halt.

'The guys behind Ankst started out as fans, then they signed us,' explained Paul. 'They believe totally in what we're doing and are so enthusiastic about our music. They've been doing a lot of the groundwork for us, making sure the albums are in all the record shops, getting us interviews, publicity and handling management duties as well as promotion.'

And it was just as well that Alun, Gruff and Emyr were there to push the band as Paul freely admitted to them not being the most upfront of bands. 'I suppose we're all quite shy,' he confessed. 'We're definitely an insular band, we don't push ourselves as individuals. We do tend to let the music do the talking.'

1991 was the year when the band achieved their greatest successes so far, yet it was their last year together and maybe a glimpse of their future intentions could be seen in Paul's comments: 'What's been most pleasing though is the fact we're now getting more English-speaking people coming to our gigs. We're trying not to get stuck on the endless circle of playing Welsh clubs, because you can get trapped in that situation. But we make an effort to try and not play strictly Welsh-speaking places. And recently we've had some great nights with a mixed crowd of both Welsh and English speakers.'

Geraint Jarman, who had been banned by the Welsh Language Society for singing in Welsh outside of Wales to English audiences, could understand why Y Cyrff had decided to make their move across to singing in English.

'There's a feeling when you know the time is right. You could tell at that time something was going to happen. Not only with Y Cyrff. Musicians were collectively talking about it, but keeping their plans very quiet for fear of reprisals.'

Y Cyrff, Ffa Coffi Pawb and Y Crumblowers had worked tirelessly for years supporting the language but for little or no financial reward. Finally, as musicians they wanted to attempt to make long-lasting careers out of their talents, something that just could not be achieved within the medium of the Welsh language.

Anhrefn's Rhys Mwyn summed it up perfectly: 'They learnt their craft, but they all grew up and realised that they had gone as far as they could. I think people eventually realised that you could be big in Wales, but it doesn't keep the wolf from the door. You know, respect don't pay the bills.'

If any date could be sited as the day that the Welsh-language music scene called time on five glorious years of awakening and regeneration then Saturday, 7 December would be it.

The Pavilion, Pontrhyfendigaid, in West Wales, was the venue for one of the biggest fundraising gigs ever staged for the Welsh Language Society.

It featured Y Cyrff, Y Crumblowers, Fflaps, Ffa Coffi Pawb and over thirty of the Welsh-language scene's leading bands. It ran from midday to midnight and not only did it serve as a fitting curtain closer for a scene that had outgrown itself, it marked a meeting of minds. It was the place where Mark Roberts and Cerys Matthews's stars collided and the good ship Catatonia was to set sail on a hazardous journey to pop glory.

3
The Squeak Shall Inherit the Earth!

> To be born Welsh is to be born privileged, not with a silver spoon in your mouth but with music in your blood and poetry in your soul.
>
> *Anon.*

Rock 'n' roll tales are the fabulous fables used by press officers to make their bands seem more sexy and appealing. In most cases you'd be hard-pressed to squeeze an ounce of truth out of any of these character-building myths.

Catatonia were no different, having experienced their own piece of rock 'n' roll press impropriety early on in their career.

Despite the widely held belief that Mark Roberts spotted Cerys Matthews busking outside Debenhams in Cardiff, this is just a media myth – a romantic and apocryphal notion to give Catatonia an intriguing press biography. True, they did go busking, but this was invariably together, when they had to make ends meet on the dole, while they were holed up in their new home writing songs for their yet-to-be-named musical project.

Bursting with ideas and brimming with the sort of confidence and romantic notions that only two people who are in the first full flush of love can muster, the pair were fired with enthusiasm and ready to take flight into the English-speaking music world as a new breakaway alliance. More importantly they wanted to break free from the confines of a Welsh-language scene that was stifling them.

1992 was a year when Welsh music had turned full circle and started to implode on itself. It signified the death of Wales's most influential pop music programme, *Fideo 9*, and the outbreak of a civil war within Welsh-language factions. There were those who were split between the groups who supported those cool Welsh-language bands' decisions to reform under new guises with a set full of English-speaking songs, and those who accused these new bands of being traitors to the language.

After the epochal Welsh-language society benefit at Pontrhyfendigaid, new plans were being hatched and new directions laid. The leading bands had collectively decided that times were a changing. Ffa Coffi Pawb's Gruff Rhys was scheming under the new monicker of The Super Furry Animals, brothers Owen and Lloyd Powell had mutated from Y Crumblowers into the gloriously poppy Colour 45, and Mark Roberts had moved to Cardiff with his new girlfriend Cerys Matthews. The Welsh-language scene itself at that time was a tightknit community with everyone knowing everyone else. If you regularly went to gigs at Cardiff's Welsh club, Clwb Ifor Bach, then you would invariably see the same faces, and it didn't take long to get to know them.

This close-knit community was made up largely of Welsh-language bands and their friends – many of whom were artists or who worked in the arts, as well as those employed at S4C or who were involved in the local media. HTV and the BBC in Wales are notoriously populated by the Taffia – an exclusive clique of Welsh speakers whose backgrounds at Welsh-speaking schools and Welsh universities, coupled with their ability to speak the language, has led to the sorts of nepotism notorious among Oxford and Cambridge graduates in London media circles.

Cerys Matthews was a regular at Welsh-language gigs throughout the late Eighties and was a very big fan of Y Cyrff. She had already accrued a reputation as one of the more colourful supporters of Welsh bands and been out with one or two Welsh-language musicians. Soon-to-be-Catatonia guitarist Owen Powell remembers one night when his band Y Crumblowers had played a gig in West Wales, and he was crashing on the floor at Cerys's house. He was about to be truly introduced to that voice and that animated personality. 'I remember trying to sleep in one of the rooms, because at four in the morning she was hammering out Spanish folk songs on this guitar. For the first hour I was thinking, "Oh this is really good, she's got a really nice voice", but as it got later and later, I grabbed a sleeping bag and sneaked off into the kitchen lying on the floor thinking, "No, no, please stop."'

Cerys had a fearless and peerless reputation that evidently preceded her ascension to pop queen, if not quite the glorious voice that marks it out as memorable as any other singer of the twentieth century (and twenty-first hopefully!). She just didn't know that her full-tilt hedonism, ribald lust for life and a voice that was to be memorably described in *The Times* as 'the sound of Kirsty MacColl, Courtney Love and Liz Fraser from the Cocteau Twins bonding so well one drunken night, they'd decided to morph into one lullabying superbird!' would leave her and her band equally cursed and blessed by their fearless notoriety and outspoken reputation.

WHEN THE SAINT CAME MARCHING IN

> Well, if you want to draw lines everywhere, my mother came from a very working-class background and the other half is middle-class, so it's an amalgamation, and they're both as relevant and influential as each other. But I'm not queen of any bloody council estate.
>
> (Cerys Matthews)

The character of Cerys Matthews has been formed from a host of contradictions and mixed emotions. While she loved to make trouble, she was also a rebel who did well. She was an academic with an edge, a girl who excelled in school but who caused her teachers and her parents endless consternation. She was brought up both in the city and the country by parents from mixed-class families. A strong personality, brimming with confidence, and a passion for life, are the cornerstones of Cerys's character.

It may have taken her years to attain star status, but in her own head she was convinced that she would be a success. The young Cerys was set on doing something that was unorthodox and exciting.

'I didn't aspire to be famous exactly,' mused Cerys to Select magazine. 'I think "famous" is the wrong word. I think "special" is better. I wanted to do something special. I had a friend who was a girl, and she used to try and kip in my bed all the time. We weren't lesbians or anything, she just used to share my bed with me and talk all night long, going, "You're special and I'm special." And I never believed her, I thought it was bollocks. But I'd like to meet up with her now. The point is, I wanted to do something unpredictable. Out of the ordinary.'

Cerys Elizabeth Phillip Matthews was born at St David's Hospital in the Canton area of Cardiff on 11 April 1969. Growing up with two brothers and a sister, Cerys was born into a stable, comfortable family – her father Phillip became a surgeon after abandoning his parents' farming background, while her mum Pamela is a hospital administrator.

The family's medical background seemed to have had a profound effect on the curious young Cerys and much to her bemused schoolmates' amazement she once took a human index finger to school and tried to grow a chicken's foot tendon in a teapot! At primary school Cerys was christened with the nickname The Dentist – on account of her habit of yanking out classmates' loose milk teeth. Already noted for her impulsiveness and grand idealism, the young Cerys Matthews was also dubbed 'Squeaky' by her fellow pupils because of her high-pitched voice. But Cerys paid little attention, sustaining a dayglo imagination in her head that was already working overtime.

Little did Cerys know that those early days travelling to primary school were spent in the company of her future guitarist Owen Powell: 'Yeah, we'd actually been to school together. We used to get on the same bus,' says Owen, 'but I didn't know until much later that this was the same person.'

Cerys was certainly different from most of her fellow youngsters and had quickly established her own set of rules by which she was going to live her life. Perhaps it was her unorthodox upbringing in a house that had a fridge stocked with bones, as a result of her dad's work and a mother who refused to mollycoddle her offspring, allowing them independence from an early age, that gave Cerys a single-minded approach. It was this alternative agenda and lack of regard for authority that would become some of her most endearing assets, but was to prove difficult for a man who would play a key part in her later life.

The *NME*'s Iestyn George was brought up in Swansea and became great friends with a girl called Rhiannon Matthews whom he met when she and her family came to live in the middle-class Mayals area of Swansea. Iestyn was a prefect at Bryn-Y-Mor Junior School. His remit was to keep the younger children under check, making sure they didn't run riot. But Rhiannon's younger sister Cerys was one kid he just couldn't control, running the future music journalist ragged:

'Rhiannon was a really normal, bright, friendly, easy-going girl,' explains Iestyn. 'But Cerys was like a Tasmanian devil. She seemed genuinely angry with life. She was also very non-conformist, she just didn't want to behave and reacted really badly with me!'

Because Iestyn and the Matthews children attended a Welsh-speaking junior school, they had to travel to school by bus every day:

'Because this bus journey would take about 20 minutes and you had a bunch of kids in the one place, the older kids tried to get the younger ones to sit down and be quiet,' says Iestyn. 'With success in the most part, apart from Cerys of course. She saw no problem in racing up and down the aisle of the bus shouting and screaming. The kid had no fear. And she had no real reason to rebel because she came from such a comfortable background.'

It was perhaps because of her secure background that Cerys threw herself full tilt into being a nuisance. Being one of the youngest members of the family she was used to being spoilt and getting her own way. 'I guess she was born with punk rock in her veins,' laughs Iestyn. 'Somewhere there's a part of her that is forever at The Roxy on stage with The Clash!'

Cerys didn't attend the same high school as her sister and Iestyn – Ystalyfera High School in the Swansea Valley. 'I think the family tried to put her on the straight and narrow by sending her to St Michael's, a private school in Llanelli. I remember whenever I asked Rhiannon about her younger sister, she would just arch her eyebrows. She was a handful and I would hear stories of her drinking exploits when she was 15. I despaired for her because I just thought she was a self-obsessed attention seeker!'

One of Cerys's old classmates at St Michael's was Kirsty Williams, Liberal Democrat member for Brecon and Radnorshire. Kirsty remembers Cerys living up to the tough, ballsy image she would become renowned for as a one-woman school peacekeeping force. 'She stood no nonsense but she was also very fair,' explains Kirsty. 'I remember how she always stuck up for the underdog. If someone was being bullied she would sort it out.

'I was being picked on once and Cerys came along and stopped it. She was a good person to have around, especially when you're the youngest in your class. She was very popular in the school and when she told someone to stop picking on another pupil they certainly listened.'

As Cerys was evolving her feisty character, she was also experimenting with another of the traits that would later define the cult of Cerys Matthews – her infamous fashion sense.

'The school uniform wasn't very popular and all the girls were always looking for ways to introduce their own clothes,' recalls Kirsty. 'Cerys used to get into trouble for wearing outrageous things.'

The headmaster at St Michael's, Daniel Sheehan, remembers well Cerys's love of flouting the school dress code. 'We have a very rigid policy of uniform here and myself or my deputy stands at the school gates every morning to inspect the pupils. The girls have to wear grey skirts to just above the knee. Cerys used to wear shorter skirts and clothes which were the wrong colour. But we never sent her home.'

One of the reasons Cerys got away with flouting the dress code was because she helped push up the grades at St Michael's. Despite her gently rebellious ways and penchant for the unpredictable, Cerys excelled in exams and sport, although, ironically, not music.

Mr Sheehan says that Cerys was academically strong and in her third year came top out of 40 pupils. 'She gained top grades at maths, physics and Latin and came over as a very intelligent girl. She was a model pupil and was particularly good at sport – she thrived at hockey and netball.'

Although with the benefit of hindsight it's safe for the headmaster to say that Cerys was destined to be a star, he says most teachers at St Michael's reckoned she was going to do well when she left school. 'Cerys was quite charismatic then, with a strong personality and definitely knew where she was going,' explains Mr Sheehan. 'She was a very confident young lady and her teachers said she was always going to be a big success at something.'

Her teachers were also very aware of another of the now-famous Cerys traits – her outspoken behaviour. Cerys's former art teacher John Roberts remembers her 'rebellious streak'.

'She was an incredibly bright girl,' he says. 'She was very artistic and definitely had a mind of her own, but she was a bit of a rebel in the sense she was always questioning the status quo. But she was never disruptive even though she was very popular with her peers. She could have undoubtedly followed an academic career if she had chosen to. She was an all-rounder, good at everything.'

Well almost. Despite playing the violin at school her teachers said she was 'not exceptionally musical'.

These were the two sides to the Cerys Matthews that would map out her intriguing character. The work ethic that her parents had instilled in her allowed her to grind out good qualifications, despite her rebellious streak, but with her propensity for daydreaming and indulging in flights of escapist fantasy, she was seeking a world far beyond that of her fellow pupils. With an imagination that would run wild, and a teenage temperament that would boil over with all the confusion and angst that those years bring, Cerys Matthews always believed she would be going places. She just didn't know where yet.

One person who was happy to see Cerys leave behind her school days and her teenage rebellion was her long-suffering mum. Describing the end of those teen years, Cerys commented 'I think my Mum felt it was like sitting at the edge of a motorway breathing a sigh of relief and thinking, "Thank fuck that's over!"'

Cerys's flights of fancy had taken her to many places in her head, such as enlisting in the foreign legion, but now she had hit upon a plan of action that centred around her escaping what she considered a humdrum existence in West Wales for the bright lights and big city of London.

She decided she wanted to spread her wings and discover the world. As a result she not only ended up in London where she studied psychiatric nursing but also worked as a nanny in Spain. Abandoning the nursing when she discovered she was ill prepared for the emotional rigours of the job, she realised that her quest for foreign situations weren't exactly what you would describe as 'life-enhancing'. She recalls: 'You'd wake up in Tooting with two strangers trying to cop off with you – which wasn't too healthy, really!' The nannying stemmed from an advert she saw in posho British servant-finding mag *The Lady*. Having had an aptitude for languages, it was during her spell in Barcelona that she learnt to speak Spanish, adding to her fluency in Welsh and splintered French and Catalan.

While there she came over all Mary Poppins and played her little charges folk songs on her guitar, while they mischievously water-bombed her in return. This voyage of self-discovery also marked the beginnings of Cerys Matthews's much-vaunted dress sense. She recalls how she once dressed up as a mountain for a Spanish fancy-dress do.

'It was awful though – nobody knew what I was!' she says. 'I had my face painted green, and I had green hair, and I had sheep stuck all around my thighs! Mountains don't come without sheep, do they? I liked my hair green, though.'

Spain taught Cerys many things. She discovered that childcare and mountain imitation was not for her, but that singing was. A prophetical meeting with an old guy on a bus journey in Spain, persuaded her that she should really make good in following her dreams. Cerys got talking to the friendly, elderly gent who asked her what she wanted to do. She replied that she was a nanny but really wanted to sing. He said, 'Go on then, sing for me.' She did, and he was amazed, and spent the rest of the journey complimenting her and saying what a wonderful voice she had.

Back to Wales she went with a head full of dreams, but these were to be momentarily dashed on the rocks of West Wales's beaches where she worked on her return.

Cerys, in typically conflicting fashion, had said that her major influences on leaving school were The Sex Pistols, Pippi Longstocking and The Wombles, and now she had found a job that allowed her to combine The Wombles' recycling ideology with Ursula Andress-like glamour – picking up dead seagulls for the local council!

The nascent pop star was someone who evidently relished in the surreal. Her influences were a jumble of some of the most diametrically opposed cultural icons, yet in the Cerys Matthews mindset they all made perfect sense.

She told *Select* magazine: 'I used to drive around in a van all day with the radio on. Then I'd get to the beach and do a bit of cleaning up in my bikini and these massive council work gloves. I was Madame Cholet in The Wombles' swimsuit issue – removing dead seals was my speciality. I've always admired The Wombles and their philosophy of finding a use for everything!' Spending her days trawling the beach allowed her time to dream up songs and lyrics in her head and practise them back home on her acoustic guitar.

Unbeknown to the rest of her family she'd picked up the acoustic guitar in her early teens and began learning a combination of Beatles songs and folk and blues tunes. 'I never told anybody I had long wanted to be a singer because I thought they'd laugh, she recounted in an interview with the *Western Mail*, the national morning newspaper of Wales. 'My brother used to come into my bedroom when I was playing and recording my songs on my tape recorder. I've still got the tapes and you can hear me in the background shouting at him to get out.

'I blame my neurotic auntie for my voice. She used to come round to our house all the time when I was young and sing. I think I've got her genes. I love losing myself in music and there's no better way than by singing.'

Cerys confessed she mainly started off playing old folk stuff and owned a book called *How To Play The Blues*. Now just imagine it. This little white Welsh girl from Swansea playing the blues, Mississippi delta blues. 'I'd play anything really, I just wanted to learn.'

She also admitted to teaching herself some lusty Irish folk songs with 'one song in particular by this 16-year-old serving lass. It's pretty rude stuff – all cuckolds and birds' nests which really meant male and female genitalia. It shows the likes of Snoop Doggy Dog where to get off!'

Cerys admitted that although there wasn't a shortage of music in her household, much of it failed to interest her: 'The stereo system in our house was so bad I didn't know what treble sounded like until I was at least 21, and when we went on holiday we'd have to listen to these dreadful tapes my dad made up – "pops" he called them. We ended up hearing them about a million times because he would only bring three away in case he lost any [getting more animated as she remembers], and they used to put foil inside the car windows to keep us cool. It was like a volcano in there!'

It was while making her first tentative steps into live performances that Cerys and her honeyed voice was first spotted. She was working in a bar in Pembrokeshire singing folk songs with a gang of appreciative old fellas, when a guy over from America told her that she sounded like Melanie (cult American singer of the Sixties beloved of Morrissey) and that she should do some recording.

With her love of the Welsh language and music, it was only natural for Cerys to be a regular at the subsided Welsh-language gigs organised by Cymdeithias Yr Iaith (the Welsh Language Society). Steadily she immersed herself in a scene that was about to reach its zenith and became a regular at the annual August Eisteddfods that would act as a showcase for the best bands in Wales.

She had been writing diligently for about a year – while also attending Fishguard High school to do two more A-levels, in French and Welsh (just in case her dreams weren't fulfilled) before she attended the huge Welsh Language Society Benefit at The Pavilion, Pontrhydfendigaid on Saturday, 7 December. The Christmas spirit was just kicking in and Cerys Matthews didn't need an excuse to indulge one of her favourite pastimes. So, armed with a bottle and an 'optimistic winning way with the guys', there was one band and one man in particular that she wanted to see that prophetical day. Her favourite band Y Cyrff, and her favourite Welsh songwriter Mark Roberts.

Cerys was a long time fan of Y Cyrff and had bought all their records. As the charismatic frontman of the group Mark Roberts was used to the attention of the band's female followers. However, Cerys had got to know Mark over a number of months when she would go the band's gigs or when she would offer musicians from various Welsh bands accommodation at her parents' large West Wales home. She didn't want to be associated with the groupies that would follow some Welsh bands, but she was smitten by Mark's good looks and his consummate songwriting. He in turn, was turned on by her larger than life personality and impressed by her love of music.

It was a long day of drinking and music, with thirty bands performing. It didn't finish until the early hours of Sunday morning, but by that time the last post was sounding for the Welsh-language rock scene, a new dawn was about to crest over the horizon for two people in particular. Cerys and Mark were to become an item. Sharing a mutual admiration for a disparate collection of cultural and musical icons – John Lennon, Billie Holliday, Eric Cantona and Rolf Harris – 'the rest', as the cliché invariably tells it, 'is history'.

SWEET CATATONIA, I SHOULD HAVE TOLD YA!

At the turn of the Nineties Cardiff was buzzing. The city and its former thriving docks were playing the Regeneration Game. The once-famous Tiger Bay had long since lapsed on hard times and was undergoing a facelift of multi-million pound proportions. Renamed Cardiff Bay, the area was reawakened with modern flats and houses and a thriving bay area was peppered with bars, pubs, restaurants and cinemas. Leisure had become the new industry and Cardiff knew how to play as well as work hard. The city centre was similarly at the centre of the modern regenesis. New shopping centres and pedestrianised walkways had given the city a distinctly European flavour.

All this meant Cardiff was home to over a quarter of a million people, while the city's numbers were thronged by shoppers who would flood there on weekends. It rapidly acquired a reputation as one of the best places to go shopping because of its low prices and its many shopping centres. And the city itself was voted for four years as the cheapest in the world. This meant rich pickings for everyone, shoppers and shopkeepers alike. And Cerys Matthews and Mark Roberts didn't do too badly out of this retail rebirth either, these two dedicated buskers needed the shoppers' spare change to make ends meet. The two would busk songs by their favourite artists – 'Superman' by REM and The Jam's 'That's Entertainment' being among them – outside a lucrative pitch near The Hayes entrance of St David's Shopping centre.

But this was a new start in every sense of the word. A new beginning, a new relationship, a new musical direction and even a new language to write songs in. So, if Mark Roberts was to start again it would be at the bottom.

After embarking on a relationship only weeks before the end of 1991, the pair had moved into a house on Gold Street in Cardiff's bohemian Adamsdown area. The house was owned by S4C television presenter Eleri Sion, who had got to know Mark through his numerous Welsh language television appearances with Y Cyrff. The street was bordered by other similarly metallic addresses – Copper Street, Metal Street, Pearl Street, Zinc Street and Iron Street – all named after the metalworks that stood near to where the houses were first built. But this house on Gold Street, would gain notoriety of its own in Cardiff music folklore. It was a three-bedroomed party house and safe haven for the Welsh-language scene's movers and shakers. It also became synonymous with Mark and Cerys's appetite for hedonism – hosting some of the wildest parties seen outside of Keith Moon's mansion!

As they signed on and busked to supplement their giro they began writing songs together.

These songs took self-empowerment and personal liberation as their central creed. They were also implanted with a soft heart and a steely shell. The medium would be guitar-rock, but their ambitions stretched way beyond the indie toilet circuit: they wanted to be unashamedly pop but with a venomous almost menacing heart. These skewed melodic visions and lust for grand ambition, were aptly represented in the name they chose for their band.

Although admittedly they misinterpreted it's meaning initially – the name fitted perfectly with the light and dark of their songwriting. They took the name Catatonia based on Cerys's experiences of working in a mental health institution in London and the Aldous Huxley book *Doors of Perception*. They chose the monicker because they thought it meant 'being in an extreme state of happiness'. They were mistaken, but when they discovered its true meaning they had already used it.

Mark Roberts explained the initial confusion: 'In the dictionary in which we looked came the optimistic meaning of the word, only later we found out that it was a kind of schizophrenia. Anyway, it sounded good on the posters.'

Originally calling themselves Sweet Catatonia only added credence to the bittersweet songs they were penning. They were sweet schizophrenic visions, songs that kissed you on the lips and then stabbed you in the back.

'The name of the band came out of the song,' remembers Cerys. 'It was the first song Mark and I wrote. It's sort of about lying there in the middle of the night, when you're with someone new, semi-conscious, in the midnight hour or whatever and you want to ask questions, and then you don't because you're in this sort of lovely trance.'

The couple's relationship was in the first full flush of love and the twosome were inspiring each with their dreams of pop fame and fortune. Money raised from busking and any left from the weekly giro was spent recording demos at Cardiff's City Centre Youth Project, otherwise more widely known as 'Grassroots'. Located on Charles Street, a side street just off the main pedestrianised city centre Queen Street shopping area, Grassroots has long been a stopping off point for new bands wanting cheap rehearsal and recording studios.

Grassroots first blinked into life during the days of punk and mutated into a squat cum co-operative favoured by anarcho punk bands like Crass who played riotous gigs there at the onset of the Eighties. The place was a salvation for the destitute musician, offering special deals for the unemployed on recording, rehearsing and music tuition. Mark and Cerys, who easily fitted into the penniless category, were quick to take advantage of the recording studio.

'We did our first demos at the Grassroots project which had a 16-track studio that was only £50 a day,' explained Mark. 'It's still going, only now it's 24-track, it's got a programming room as well.'

Mark and Cerys were in estimable company at their new second home. They regularly bumped into fellow Welsh-language star turned English-language sampling musician Owen Powell. His new band Colour 45 were recording a clutch of English-language songs and getting used to life as 'the band formerly known as Y Crumblowers'.

Owen's brother Lloyd remembers that initially Colour 45 had made more ground than the embryonic Catatonia, having recently triumphed in a local band competition. 'The competition was run by Cardiff recording studio Soundspace for the best ten bands who entered to record a song at the studio which would be put on a compilation tape,' he explains. 'The ten would also win a place on the bill at the Cardiff Bay Music Fiesta, a new event set up to promote music in the bay.'

The gig would feature both national and local bands playing over two days on a big stage erected at the Cardiff dockside.

'I remember Mark and Cerys being gutted because they only came something like 45th, while we sneaked in as the tenth band,' adds Lloyd.

Ironically, Mark and Cerys's housemate at that time Gareth Potter and his innovative dance fusionists Ty Gwydr took the fourth slot, while just to rub salt into their collective wounds, The Hepburns, featuring future Catatonia drummer Aled Richards, came in eighth!

The fallout of all these new bands and their new directions was still settling. The decision by many of the musicians to metamorphosise from Welsh to English-language bands had upset people in certain quarters of the Welsh-language movement, but after years and years of hard labour it was inspired by wanting to sell rather than sell-out.

The nascent Catatonia utilised that Welsh-language music community by recruiting notorious drummer Frog, a madcap loon from the equally mental Welsh punkers U-Thant, a band famed for their infamy. Cerys memorably described him (Frog) as 'completely mental, he used to wear a pink lurex catsuit and a silver hat and he'd play so hard he'd collapse at the end of a show!' More sedate, however, was bass player Guto Pryce – the future bass player with the newly formed Super Furry Animals. Recruited from the same camp as Frog – well, sort of – he was the younger brother of U-That guitarist Iwan Pryce.

The scratch band went into the studio and recorded a clutch of mesmerising bilingual songs – 'whatever language felt right fitted', said Cerys by way of explanation of their bilingual approach, which would mark their early years as a band. 'l was bilingual, but I never came across contemporary Welsh-language music until I was 18, so initially it sounded really odd. And we'd always said we'd sing in English as well because I wanted to be as successful as Shirley Bassey. That was the condition by which we all got involved.'

Listening to Catatonia's early demos you are struck by one startling fact

– the songs sound as fully formed and bewitching as any of the songs that were to come. Live was a different matter, however, but in the studio Mark and Cerys's songs were brimming over with confidence and quality. Those years Mark Roberts had spent in 24-track studios learning his craft while recording songs for a myriad Welsh-language pop programmes were evidently paying off. Catatonia's songs were good from day one: with this band there were no embarrassing pasts or dodgy incarnations.

1992 was the year that grunge went supernova and REM conquered the airwaves with the unit bulldozing *Automatic For The People* – an album which was like grunge-lite, but pandered to America's screwed-up, Prozac chic kids. It also signified the death of the 'baggy' scene that had regenerated British pop through the psychedelic grooves of The Stone Roses and The Charlatans.

And despite the release of Flowered Up's classic hedonist's anthem 'Weekender' and the establishment-scaring drug jingle 'Ebeneezer Goode' from The Shamen, the sunsplashed days of Madchester were just a distant memory.

But whatever the musical climate outside, Catatonia were holed up in a hothouse of their own, blissfully ignorant of changes in temperature and tastes. Mark and Cerys were two people who had a cool contempt for whatever was 'in', and an instinctive sense of what they were going to put out.

Many songs were recorded in both languages, evidently to see if the songs fitted. So for 'Snail Ambition' you had 'Difrychwelyd'; for 'New Mercurial Heights' see 'Gyda Gwen'; and for 'Confucius Stare' read 'Dimbran'. Whatever the language these were songs justifying superlatives. Moody, sensuous and unearthly tunes that were deliciously dipped in Mark's luscious melodies and gently wrapped around Cerys's otherworldly voice, completely belying the menacing content that stuck the songs together with their own strange glue.

As songs they were truly uncategorisable, forcing critics to scratch their heads in bemusement. Demos went out and those lucky enough to receive them struggled with comparisons.

As a unit they garnered descriptions as varied as The Velvet Underground, Buffalo Springfield, Penetration, The Pixies, The Throwing Muses, The Cocteau Twins and The Stone Roses. Meanwhile Cerys's voice was causing an equal measure of unpindownable consternation – Tanya Donnelly, Björk, Liz Frazer, Debbie Harry and Nico were all mentioned in general befuddlement.

Those first two demos recorded at Grassroots included versions of future singles 'Sweet Catatonia' and 'Whale', as well as the never-to-be-released 'Sugar Loaf Mountain'. This intriguing song features both Mark and Cerys singing, while Mark conjures up some magically sweeping, chiming guitars.

It's notable for not only the quality but that it features the line 'I know that I could never fall from grace, I'm far too clever'. A line that would crop up some six years later on a song called 'Game On', from a certain triple platinum-selling album. With this band, obviously, nothing went to waste! And many people were going to be hooked before they had even released their debut single.

NEW FACES AND OLD PLACES

September 1992 saw Cerys and Mark again back busking outside their favoured pitch. As well as the usual appreciative Beatles lovers who will always throw in a £1 coin for a well-played version of 'We Can Work It Out', a more statuesque figure was studiously casting her eye over the two buskers.

Natasha Hale, had recently moved to Cardiff from Swansea with her partner Huw Williams, Welsh pop icon and erstwhile scamster frontman of Wales's great white wonder The Pooh Sticks.

'I was just out shopping and saw these two great-looking people playing guitars,' explains Natasha. 'I went over to them and told them I think you look really cool. I said I knew The Pooh Sticks and we just started talking. Huw was thinking about getting a female singer for The Pooh Sticks and I thought Cerys would fit the bill perfectly.'

She just looked really cool and was going for it,' adds Natasha. 'She seemingly had no fear and appeared very cool. They were both singing and both seemed to be having fun.'

Cerys told Natasha that she and Mark were about to play their first-ever gig at Cardiff's Meltdown – a Sunday night Cardiff institution that gave musicians – both established and otherwise – a stage for the evening. That was the simple and alluring idea behind Meltdown – an organisation run by music lovers for music lovers, that ran for over ten years at the city's Welsh club – Clwb Ifor Bach and before that at The Four Bars Inn, Cardiff's late and legendary jazz venue.

Of course, realistically anybody who had expected the same crystal clear and lucidly lush versions that had adorned their technically precise demos on their first live appearance would have been greatly disappointed. As the expectant Huw Williams discovered.

Huw and Natasha, as well as Pooh Sticks' manager Steve Gregory were keen to see the nascent Catatonia perform. Sadly, they weren't overly astounded. 'Huw and Steve didn't like them,' recalls Natasha. 'It was shambolic but I still thought they were very cool, even for a first gig.'

In the studio you have room to breathe, there's time available and certainly not nearly as much pressure as the one-take immediacy of a live performance. Never mind a first gig where nerves are crackling like electricity.

Huw explains the reason for his indifference. 'At that time we still had our arrogant pop star heads on and I wasn't really impressed by them. Steve and I didn't want her in the band. Tash was more of a fan initially.'

What did impress Huw though was finding like-minded people in South Wales and that night at Clwb Ifor Bach he had unearthed some musical soulmates.

'Like I say I didn't particularly like the gig, but it was good that there were people who were in it for the same ends as us,' he says. 'Sussed, honest people who weren't trying to reinvent themselves or hide dodgy pasts.'

Despite it being her first official gig, Cerys was mortified at Huw's reaction, as he remembers.

'Funnily enough after that gig Cerys sent me a tape with demos on it with a letter saying please come and see us again, I can sing! They'll admit it was shambolic themselves. I remember Mark joking that he knew we were coming so they all decided to take acid! I think he was joking!'

Cerys says of that first gig: 'We were awful. I'd regularly been to this place and seen other bands, and now I was up on stage behind the microphone for the very first time. I was really scared so I drank loads of brandy, which I don't think helped my voice any!'

Despite the nervous catharsis of a first gig, Mark and Cerys were unstoppable – their relationship was in the throes of a blissful honeymoon period and their lifestyle was equally eventful.

Their Gold Street house was being shared by artist Elfyn Lewis – an old friend of Mark's – whose work would feature heavily on the covers of Catatonia's future CDs. Also in the 'house of fun' was musician and actor Gareth Potter, frontman of Welsh-language dance terrorists Ty Gwydr and the guy credited with bringing rave to Wales.

As well as the pursuit of rock 'n' roll fame and fortune, the endless parties and general bohemian nirvana, many money-making schemes were hatched in an attempt to alleviate their skint predicament.

'We did want to open a pie shop, but there's a place down the road called Maggie's Pies that sells great pies for only 28p so that was no good,' said Cerys. 'Then we wanted to get an ice-cream van, but that didn't work out, because we would have to had bought one!' They were barely scratching a living but they were having the sort of life-affirming fun that only the brash confidence of youth can muster.

That total belief in what they were doing would have been perceived as arrogant in some quarters but it was equally as infectious and completely justified. *Fideo 9* mainman and Welsh music TV exec Geraint Jarman was one of the next to be swept away by the Mark and Cerys tide.

'The two of them came over to my house,' recalls Geraint. 'They had just come from Grassroots and had a tape with three songs on it, "Gyda Gwen", "Dimbran" and "Difrychwelyd". I thought it was great. The songs had that sort of psychedelic late Sixties feel to them. Very Syd Barrett with the flowery guitars, and I thought Cerys's voice sounded very much like Sixties singer Melanie.' (Not the first time she had gained favourable comparisons to the enigmatic singer.)

Unsurprisingly after his visit to Geraint Jarman with Cerys, Mark Roberts didn't take long to unveil Sweet Catatonia to a Welsh public that was eager to know what the Y Cyrff frontman had been plotting. Appearing again as Sweet Catatonia, Mark and Cerys, once more backed by Frog and Guto Pryce, recorded a single at the 24-track state-of-the-art Music Factory Studios in Cardiff and made a video for *Fideo 9*. The video was memorable for having the look of a classic Andy Warhol production – all art-school monochrome. It not only encapsulated the times – this was the last series of the seminal pop programme that had led the vanguard of Welsh-language bands – but introduced the first lineage of the new Welsh rock order.

The song chosen as their first step to national exposure was 'Gyda Gwen' ('New Mercurial Heights'). It allowed Cerys to stretch her starry-eyed twinkling vocals over a gently swirling psychedelic melody and Mark's mesmeric backwards guitars. It was a bewitching, beautiful song as immediate as it was beguiling. In one deftly crafted evocative moment of celestial bliss Catatonia had introduced a nation into their ethereal netherworld, and put the ghosts of their past where they should stay, in the past.

Those who had canonised Mark Roberts as the patron saint of Welsh-language rock would now have to bow to a new religion. One of the first to be indoctrinated was Rhys Mwyn.

'I thought it was phenomenal, the best thing I have ever heard,' says Rhys Mwyn of 'Gyda Gwen'. Rhys, the punk stalwart of the Welsh-language scene with his band Anrehfn was working for Crai Records, set up in 1990 as a cool indie label offshoot of the resolutely MOR Sain label. Crai means raw materials in Welsh and that's exactly what Rhys had started to deal with – raw young bands. He saw much potential in Sweet Catatonia.

'Obviously having worked with Mark in Y Cyrff I knew him, so, after seeing the "Gyda Gwen" video I rang Mark up and said what you are doing is brilliant. And Mark being Mark, replied "What exactly are you saying Rhys?" And I just said we should do something you know very informal.'

So Rhys headed down to the house at Gold Street. Ironically, their first meeting with him took place on 1 March – no bigger date in the Welsh calendar, being St David's Day.

'It wasn't intentional, but it sticks in my mind because of the date,' explains Rhys. 'I think I bought them spaghetti on toast in a local cafe that they frequented. It's the usual story with bands – they're always skint.'

Although Rhys had known Mark for years he had never met Cerys before, but she made an immediate impression on him. 'I remember walking down the street with Cerys and Mark to the cafe, and thinking to myself, "These two are fucking cool." I'd never met Cerys before but she was striking. I thought she was a bit of a star straight away. She just had great presence! Mark is an exceptionally gifted songwriter, always has been, always will be, so I thought these two together could really be something. So we had this meeting and I think we agreed that I'd help them out. We agreed to give it six months to send some demos out and get a vibe going and just see what happened.

He adds: 'It was very informal, but a managerial position in inverted commas! The first six months is always a trial period with bands, and obviously they needed live experience. They didn't have a band so the next step was to get a band together.'

4
Where Were You When We Were Getting Crai?

FOR TINKERBELL WEAVES ITS MAGIC

Finding a band wasn't exactly difficult in early Nineties Cardiff. Frog and Guto Pryce, Catatonia's initial band members, had just been stopgaps. Both had their own things going on musically with U-Thant and other assorted musical projects.

But those were the times. All these Welsh-speaking musicians knew each other, so they would all invariably collaborate on each others' projects. If anyone was ever mad enough to attempt to draw up a Welsh rock family tree, they would quickly discover it has more branches than Woolworths and WH Smiths put together! There were plenty of musicians around, it was just a case of which ones.

Dafydd Ieaun had drummed with Rhys in the final line-up of Anrehfn and he was kicking his heels messing about with music and looking for a band. As the drummer with Welsh baggy popsters Ffa Coffi Pawb he had shared the same bill many times with Y Cyrff and knew Mark very well. Although, originally from North Wales, Daf was sharing a house in Cardiff with former Edyrch Am Jiwlia guitarist, Huw 'Bunf' Bunford who was working as a teacher at the time. A third member of this house-share was actor Rhys Ifans. Rhys was a childhood friend of Daf's and a regular Welsh-language gig-goer with his mate during the late Eighties. He, Daf and Ffa Coffi's singer Gruff Rhys were in the front row at Anrehfn's memorable 1990 gig on top of Mount Snowdon to celebrate the first release on the newly formed Crai label.

Rhys, whose star was set to go supernova as one of the drug-addled brothers in 1997's Welsh cult classic *Twin Town* and then as the scene-stealing comedy Welshman Spike in *Notting Hill* alongside Julia Roberts and Hugh Grant, was roped in by Daf and Bunf as a guinea pig for their 'house music' experiments.

'Daf had a little four-track and my bedroom was where they kept everything, I was their guard dog,' Rhys explained later to *Select* magazine. 'Daf and Bunf started dabbling with tunes, and they thought, "Let's get the skinny one to sing a bit." So I sang and played the goat. I've always enjoyed me rock 'n' roll.' Of course, little did Rhys know that he had written his place in Welsh rock history as the first singer with an embryonic Super Furry Animals.

Daf was only messing around musically with Bunf, so when Rhys Mwyn offered him the chance to drum with Mark and Cerys's band, he bit his arm off. Almost!

Next was a bass player. This was easy. Mark had been in touch with Paul Jones since they were in Y Cyrff together. 'They knew each other so well as they're from the same place, so it was natural,' explains Rhys Mwyn. 'Paul joined on bass. It was very informal, I may have suggested Daf, and Paul was a mate of Mark's, we all knew each other, so it was simple.'

Completing the line-up was Clancy Pegg. Originally from London, Clancy had arrived in Cardiff looking for work and had befriended a group of Welsh speakers that had included Daf, Mark and Cerys. Because all the people she knew were Welsh speakers Clancy quickly learnt the language. She also proved to be a talented musician. She played keyboards and was also an actress, most noticeably as a member of Brif Goth, the acclaimed Welsh theatre company.

Believing the addition of a keyboard player would add weight and fullness to their sound Clancy completed the line-up.

Finally there was a settled line-up, one that included Cerys both singing and playing guitar. The newly formed group had also decided to lop off the 'Sweet' for the more user-friendly Catatonia.

Combining his job at Crai Records with furthering the ambitions of this new band, Rhys Mwyn and his contacts book went into overdrive. First to be called in were all his Welsh-language contacts.

'Because Catatonia were good from day one we got them a lot of Welsh-language TV,' says Rhys. 'I remember I got them on an S4C kids TV programme. I think they doubted it initially. Some of the programmes were ropey, but my argument was that if the band is cool, you can't not do programmes because the programme is shit. You don't do the National Lottery show because the programme is quality TV, you do it because of the exposure and experience.'

And given Cerys's much avowed goal of distancing her band from the trainspotterish indie ghetto and aiming for the grand mainstream, kids TV would have seemed the ideal platform for their unashamed pop ambitions.

Catatonia played a few of their early gigs at the Yellow Kangaroo in Roath – one of the band's regular daytime haunts where they would sit and excitedly plan their futures. However, these local gigs were a bit of a false economy.

Because they were playing in front of their mates every time they appeared there, Rhys believed that gigs away from Cardiff's media-centric crowd were the best lesson for the band.

He took them on a mini-tour of Germany with his own gang of merry punksters Anrehfn and subjected them to two eye-opening gigs in Germany. Eye-opening because of the large crowds they played in front of. The first gig in Losheim near the French border was in an 800-seater venue with a big stage.

'The band loved that,' says Rhys. 'They took one look at the stage and said "cool"!'

The following day the band played at an open-air festival at a city-centre park in Bonn with about 20 other bands from all over Europe. 'I remember it was a beautifully sunny day,' says Rhys. 'Perfect for an open-air gig. There was a big crowd, must have been over 10,000 and the band were excited about playing such a good gig. I think Cerys was a bit terrified at first but she and the band played really well.'

Able to get these gigs because of the extensive touring he did with Anrhefn, Rhys decided that a few dates in Europe were just what was needed to gel this new outfit as a unit.

'We had a good time in Germany. I felt the pressure was off them because Mark and Paul had been in Y Cyrff and the spotlight was on them in Wales,' he explained. 'So I thought let's get away from everybody and just do some shows and get a band vibe going. It's good in all ways, it boosts morale and the band has a laugh.'

Rhys also remembers a conversation he and a wide-eyed Cerys had on the ferry going over to their debut European gigs. 'Cerys and I had a meal and we were just talking about what was in store. I always remembered that there was just the two of us and it felt good because I was able to give advice and she was more than willing to listen. She wanted to learn, you know. That was a pleasurable little moment because you realised that, right, you are working together toward something.'

SINGLED OUT FOR SUCCESS

The first summer of Catatonia was proving to be an eventful one and it was quickly going to get better. The Strand Hall in Builth Wells in August 1993 was the only place for Wales's music-loving kids to be. It was the site for that year's annual music Eisteddfod and Catatonia were booked to play a Welsh-only set as headliners above a bill that included Gorky's Zygotic Mynci and U-Thant.

Rhys had signed a contract with the promoter Plaid Cymru (the political party of Wales) agreeing that it was a Welsh-language set, but 'of course it wasn't', says Rhys. 'They were a bilingual band, simple as that.'

On the night the band were skint, as new bands always are, and Rhys managed to blag £50 off the promoter for them on top of their fee. 'Which of course went on drinks,' he laughs. 'It was an amazing gig, it was early days for them but it was very exciting.'

Catatonia were playing in front of 500 people and it was packed. 'You knew it was the first time a lot of people would have seen this band and you knew that this was the most exciting band in Wales for a long time,' enthused Rhys. 'They were still developing as a band and as I sat at the back of the hall at the mixing desk I felt proud because it was coming together.

'Mind you I was expecting us not to be paid because they played an English set. But no one said a word, mainly because they went down a storm. The crowd loved them.'

Things were rolling along nicely then. But there was still no sign of a record label for the band to release their clutch of brilliant songs on. Catatonia were signing on and availing themselves of the department of social security's full benefits scheme, including housing benefit for their rock 'n' roll pad in Gold Street.

Any stage gear was bought from Cardiff's multitude of cool secondhand clothes shops. The band's image, then, wasn't really an image, just a collection of the clothes they liked best thrown together in whatever haphazard manner they could manage, although, as figurehead of the group, Cerys was living up to trainee rock star status by sporting all manner of wierd and wonderful designs.

Of course, there was also the odd handout from long-suffering parents who backed their kids all the way – but, like all parents, just wished that they would gain some success. Cerys's parents in particular were really supportive. After having had Cerys and her single-minded ways to deal with when she was a troublesome teenager, they were just happy for her to be happy.

A remedy for their destitute ways was soon to be found. Despite his work with Crai, Rhys was tentative about suggesting that the band record for his label. 'The ideology at the beginning was to sing bilingually and get a record deal, as simple as that,' he explained. 'When they didn't get a deal it was Mark specifically who suggested that they do a couple of EPs for Crai. It was their suggestion, I didn't push it.'

Nevertheless, Rhys wanted to make sure that there were no internal arguments between the Welsh music factions and made a phone call to the Cardiff-based Ankst Records who had signed Y Cyrff. 'I rang the Ankst guys because I didn't want to poach anybody, because you know Y Cyrff were on Ankst and Mark was good friends with Alun and Gruff. So I was surprised when they didn't want to know Catatonia. I guess there was still this hangover from the storm over Welsh bands singing in English.'

If that was Ankst's initial standpoint it was one they would soon relax, releasing bilingual CDs from The Super Furry Animals and Gorky's Zygotic Mynci.

However, at that time Rhys and Catatonia just got on with it. 'I was excited, yeah, but I would have worked with the band in any capacity because I had loved what I had seen and heard already,' says Rhys. 'So it was easier putting out records on Crai than trying to get a deal.'

The Crai main man was wary that the band's bilingual stance might prove tricky with the hierarchy of Sain, who owned the Crai subsidiary, as it would be the first English-language release by any band on the label in its history.

'Ironically Dafydd Iwan who owns Sain was extremely cool about it,' Rhys admits. 'He liked the band from day one. He never ever questioned it, so he was behind it from the first time they entered the studio. And Dafydd Iwan's background is in protest songs about promoting the Welsh language, so that augured well for the future!'

Ironically the most resistance came from Rhys himself. 'I was surprised that the lead track "For Tinkerbell" wasn't going to be sung in Welsh, but to be fair it hadn't been discussed,' says Rhys. 'I just thought it would be easier to market a Welsh-language song to a Welsh scene who were aware of Mark's previous incarnation in Y Cyrff, than trying to sell an English record further afield than Wales.'

Catatonia's debut CD, the *For Tinkerbell* EP, was released in September 1993.

It featured five songs – the title track and 'New Mercurial Heights', 'Dimbran', 'Sweet Catatonia' and 'Gyda Gwen' – the Welsh version of 'New Mercurial Heights' – all self-produced by the band.

'Bassist Paul was very hands on, being the technical wizard among them,' recalls Rhys. 'I was strict on the studio time because we were working to a budget.'

'For Tinkerbell' is a song about holding TV responsible for the loss of innocence, for clogging up your dreams with useless images: 'Tinkerbell should've waited before turning on the TV show.'

'TV, it's always there, innit? It's just the teasing quality of it. I think it's a major thing in a way, showing you things that might not be real, but making you try to attain them anyway,' explained Cerys at the time. 'When I was younger, I used to watch the telly and the news, and it was too much information. I suppose you can't have too much information, but you're losing the wonder as well, aren't you?'

The cover art for the single was produced by photographer Rolant Dafis who was a friend of Mark and Cerys. He had taken photos of Y Cyrff for Welsh language music magazine *Sothach* and had also snapped the very first photos of Mark and Cerys at their Gold Street house. The cover of *For Tinkerbell* featured one of Rolant's ornaments, a cherub snatched from his sideboard.

'A cherub from Poundstretcher to be exact,' reveals Rolant. 'At that time I was in to collecting kitsch items and that caught my eye. The band really liked it and it looked great as the cover artwork.'

'For Tinkerbell' could not have had such a profound and massive effect as it did, although it took a little time for the music media to catch on! It was a full two months after its release that their debut was not only made *NME* Single of The Week with a thrillingly colourful review by Steven Wells, but was also played on Radio 1 by the station's king of night time radio Mark Radcliffe.

'Radio 1 phoned me up late afternoon and said your record is being played on Radio 1 tonight,' recalls Rhys. 'I rang the band and told them that at 10.45pm tonight the record was going to be played on the Mark Radcliffe Show. We were all thrilled, as you can imagine.'

Respect has to go to Mark Radcliffe because he played the song without pluggers (people employed to promote records to radio stations to try and get them played on air). The record was sent directly from Crai to him.

'It was great that he could just play what he liked,' says Rhys. 'You don't need some fucking producer putting a list on a computer to tell you what to play.'

Mark Radcliffe has his own recollections of the Catatonia single coming into his office. 'I remember it for a few reasons,' he explains. 'Firstly the remarkable voice. Secondly the fact that in 1993 we were getting sent endless records by identikit grunge bands. However "For Tinkerbell" was a breath of fresh air because thankfully it was nothing like any of those Nirvana-u-likes. Thirdly it was such a good record for a debut single. They weren't trying to be anything except themselves. And finally I remember being impressed by this small Welsh indie label sending the record direct to me.

'I'm all for independence, so it was good hearing that Wales was making such good music, music that was detached from London.'

Then there was the *NME* Single of the week only a few weeks later. Rhys remembers ringing the band the day they got single of the week in NME. 'We were all buzzing I was just as excited as they were, because when you get involved with a band you become a team and get as excited as if it was your own record!'

The buzz was also reverberating about the ears of Iestyn George, who had acted as the catalyst for the *NME* single of the week. Just as the journalist had attempted to spread the Y Cyrff manifesto to the masses, he was again hopelessly smitten by Mark Roberts' songwriting. Although he freely admits that the first time he heard of the nascent Catatonia he wasn't overly impressed. 'Well, knowing Cerys as I did from her past I couldn't take her seriously. So when she rang up to tell me she had formed a band with Mark I didn't think anything of it. Bluntly I thought "Cerys is hanging out with musicians and she just wants a piece of the action. She's jumping on the bandwagon."' Although Iestyn's immediate slanted view evaporated instantly when Rhys sent him a copy of 'For Tinkerbell'.

'I remember thinking "This is absolutely wonderful." It blew my head away,' he confesses. 'It was the first time in my professional life that I had lost all sense of objectivity!'

The *NME* has always regarded itself as the coolest music newspaper in the world. With its offices situated at the elevated heights of the 25th floor of IPC magazines' Kings Reach Tower near Waterloo Bridge, that same sense of lofty detachment and resolute casualness has to be deployed by its writers. The hallowed floors of 'the world's biggest selling weekly rock newspaper' is not a place where a writer runs in berating his fellow hacks for not picking up on a band, or slapping them around the head, gurning like a fool, shouting, 'You have to listen to this it's incredible.' No, London's serious music press deploys an arch, knowing persona, where bands are introduced and broken with a restrained nonchalance.

So it was with that same aloofness that Iestyn George casually slipped the *For Tinkerbell* CD into the *NME* office CD player, pressed play and hoped for the best.

'I was gnawing my hands off trying to be so cool about it, but I really wanted to shout that I wanted everyone on the earth to listen to this record,' he recalls wryly. Iestyn needn't have had any worries, as a voice piped up.

John Mulvey (now *NME*'s deputy editor) was the first to mumble something along the lines of 'what was this record and who was it by', and for him to ask, I knew it was really something!'

One notoriously difficult *NME* obstacle had been won over, but Iestyn was yet to face his most difficult task. Steven Wells would be the *enfant terrible* of *NME* if he was young enough to be an *enfant*. A shorn-haired, firebrand skinhead, he writes with the sort of iridescent, speed-freaked prose that suggests every word is exorcised like demons from the tormented souls of *Smash Hits* writers on crack cocaine. Or something. He is fiercely political and particularly fierce. And this was the man who would write that week's *NME* single reviews – a pile of records that included 'For Tinkerbell'. Oh lord help 'em!

'I gave it to Steven Wells, who is a miserable reactionary bastard at the best of times,' laughs Iestyn. 'He was reviewing the singles and I just feared the worst. I just feared he wouldn't understand it at all.'

Well, like the parting of the Red Sea and Tom Jones still having hits at his age, miracles do happen. So to Mr Wells's dayglo review, repeated here in all its exhaustive and exhausting glory, for the simple reason that you may never ever again read a review written with more zip than a trouser factory and more fizz than a Coca Cola warehouse. Under the ever-so-slightly understated heading of ROMPY STOMPY WELSHO PUNKPOP SEX RECORD OF THE WEEK, it reads:

> Starts off all soppy and luvverly and suddenly turns into an X-Ray Spex-ish heavy metal orgy with a Sugarcubes-style blitzkrieg of total funpop. If I could I would hum it for you. It goes soppy SNARLY soppy SHOUTY soppy SEXY – a rollicking rollercoaster that will leave you shagged and gasping and screaming for more. The woman singer has a voice capable of deathly whisper and full throttle RAWK rebel yell and she leaves no buttons unpressed, giving full attention to the ones marked YES! UH! UH! UH! and sounds a bit like Aerosmith's 'Dude Looked like a Lady' done by Shampoo if they could sing. What's it about? It's about lurve and sex and it is very, very clever. You know how every now and then you hear a pop record that makes you feel as if someone is stroking your spine with an ice cube? Or that you're being dangled upside down from a jet helicopter and dragged through an ocean of ice cold champagne? It's one of those!

NME's main rival, the *Melody Maker*, was also getting the message. Former *Maker* writer John Robb remembers a phone call from Rhys Mwyn alerted him to the band in 1993. 'The cassettes he sent over sounded good. They were more pop than the usual stuff that came out of Wales and right from the start Cerys's powerful vocals cut through giving them a definite edge.'

John did their first national press interview with Catatonia for the *Melody Maker*. The article was only about 300 words but it gave the band much needed exposure and some much welcome lauding from one of the UK's coolest rock writers. Robb aptly described 'For Tinkerbell' as 'reeking with atmosphere and melody', while the band themselves were a 'multicultural pop experience', a band who were crafting 'moody pop making its own unhyped space'.

CAUGHT BY THE BUZZ!

It took off for Catatonia. According to Rhys there was massive interest in the band almost immediately the day after the single was played. 'I must have spent six months if not more from that day just handling Catatonia calls, there was huge interest from media, promoters, music publishers and the occasional record company sniffing around,' he says.

While the rest of the country was stoking itself over the fires lit by grunge and a scene dubbed by the music press as New Wave Of New Wave – featuring bands like S*M*A*S*H and These Animal Men who were flailing their stick-insect bodies and sunken cheekbones to their amphetamine punk sound – Catatonia were spinning out classically cut but defiantly leftfield pop exotica, that was as inspired as it was different from the signs that were mapping out the musical times.

Still, *vive la différence* and all that. This was a band who had paid their dues and were going to do it on their terms. No sell-outs, no cop-outs but plenty of take-outs. This was tender music woven from a rough-hewn heart, not an imitation nor a reproduction of slavish homages to bands past. It was something new, something good and something appetising for those London music journalists to chew over. Remember this was a band from a country that had never been in fashion, so Catatonia were simply never going to work at being in fashion. They had their own minds and how.

With a healthy disregard for the English capital's myriad music industry excesses, Catatonia were unbowed, unbroken and totally true to themselves. And of course, they were making music that shimmered and shone, illuminating them as one of the music scene's most intriguing new prospects.

Back in Cardiff it was almost a year since Huw Williams had encountered the embryonic Catatonia at their debut gig at Meltdown in the Clwb Ifor Bach.

However, the next time he heard them his reaction to them was going to be vastly different from his initial indifference. Once in his possession Mark Radcliffe had played 'For Tinkerbell' quite a few times on his Radio 1 show. If it was being played to attract new fans it had worked.

'It came on the radio and I remember thinking this is fucking great. Then Radcliffe came on and said that this was Catatonia from Cardiff and I thought "Fuck, that's Sweet Catatonia who I'd seen at Meltdown,"' explains Huw Williams. 'They'd certainly come on a bit since their first gig!'

Huw got in touch with his old friend Iestyn George (Iestyn had interviewed Huw for his fanzine years previously) to find out more about the label that had put the record out, 'and he put me in touch with Rhys. And that's how the alliance was formed. I just became a fan basically and the three of us tried to help Catatonia as best we could.'

With Rhys in North Wales and Iestyn in London, the band would often turn to Huw and Natasha for advice because they lived in Cardiff.

'We used to go and meet them in Marcellos, a lovely Italian restaurant in Cardiff's city centre,' Huw explains. 'They'd asked our advice, they were very keen to take in as much as they could about promoters, managers, recording, everything really.'

'I think myself, Iestyn George and Huw Williams – who were very hands on with them in the early days – knew what we had straight away,' says Rhys. 'We were absolutely certain of that. Catatonia were good from day one, we didn't need national press or music press to tell us they were.'

The band themselves were focused, serious and ambitious, knowing that London gigs would help them capitalise on the fantastic publicity they had accrued from 'For Tinkerbell'.

'I was telling them that the London shows sometimes take three months to book up in advance, so they did give me a hard time about getting them to London,' Rhys remembers. 'They wanted it all and they wanted it now. And I guess there is nothing wrong with that drive and determination. They always had a vision, there was never a lack of commitment.'

Rhys did manage to book the band their first London gig at the Samuel Beckett pub on Stoke Newington High Street in North London on Saturday, 13 November 1993, playing with Anrehfn and Margi Clarke. The punky actress was mates with Rhys and was then pursuing a musical career.

Until that gig came around the band were busy playing gigs anywhere and everywhere. Rhys had even managed to book them a mini-tour for November with dates either side of the London gig. Catatonia were booked at Aberystwyth Students Union on Wednesday, 10 November; Bangor University on Thursday, 11 November; Birmingham's Toreador Club on Friday, 12 November; the London show on Saturday, 13 November; back to Bangor for a gig at the Curved Lounge club on the 24th; a long overnight journey down the A470 – the main road that runs from North to South Wales – for a gig at Cardiff's Stage Door on Thursday, 25 November; and at Atlantic College, Rhoose, near Cardiff Wales airport on Friday, 26 November.

As London gigs went Catatonia's first appearance in the big smoke was a success. Stoke Newington in North East London is much like Brixton with its multicultural population. It also has quite an anarcho crusty population so gigs at the Samuel Beckett were always populated by punky kids.

'Anrefhn had played there a few times,' explains Rhys. 'They were great gigs because of the crowd, who were very earthy, passionate and honest, far removed from the posey excesses of Camden. So for a first gig it was a good one for Catatonia.'

Despite not being as punk as Anrehfn, Catatonia were still very raw when they were playing live. And that probably helped at the Samuel Beckett gig.

'It did definitely. The crowd wanted to see a band with an edge,' says Rhys. 'Because of the following Anrehfn had at that time, it was a Saturday night gig and the place was heaving. So early on in their career Catatonia were still learning live, but they were being tested by having to play to crowds like this. Some bands might have found the punk crowd intimidating, but remember that Mark, Paul and Dafydd had seen it all before, so they were a real steadying influence.'

And Cerys? 'She loved it, loved a challenge. She had a few drinks and was well into it!'

Gigs like the Samuel Beckett in front of big crowds were exceptions to the rule in the early life of Catatonia. Just like any new band starting out they had to do it the hard way. They were playing gigs that were earning them £150-£200, but when you cover all your costs there's very little left at the end of the night. There's also the uncomfortable journey in the back of the transit van, the hernia-inducing lugging of your own equipment and –

until you soared to rock 'n' roll supernova status – the invariable playing in front of crowds, which especially as a support band would amount to a full bar and an empty venue. Student gigs weren't much better fare. These would invariably amount to a load of pissed up students ignoring you while either trying to vomit on each other or cop off with the person next to them.

Is it any wonder then that bands resort to imbibing vast quantities of alcohol and the compulsory inhalation of as much dope as is humanely possibly without having to secure a pilot's licence as you're getting so high?

Being Welsh and from a country where drinking would be an Olympic sport if ever the International Olympic Committee were drunk enough to offer it to us, Catatonia excelled at supreme drinking skills. They were black-belt drinkers, gold-medal imbibers. They could drink you under the table and to the centre of the earth if need be.

Which all meant that in those early days they were doing exactly what new bands faced with the horrors of arduous hours in the back of a van and then a gig that had all the appeal of a night in Stalag 31 would do – getting blasted. Except in their case they would do it at least ten times more voraciously than most of their contemporaries.

Thursday, 11 November is a case in point. Booked to play at Bangor University's students union, the night's events brought a new meaning to the words 'hitting the bottle'.

Aidan Byrne was a first-year student at Bangor, and also a massive music fan. He'd heard 'For Tinkerbell' and came along to see what the band that had produced such a startling debut release were like live.

'This was their first gig in the union and they played in the tiny bar at the bottom of the building, called Jocks,' Aidan explains. 'There was a noise abatement order on the union at the time. The council came to tell us to turn it down, so the security gorilla approached Cerys, who was wasted. She smacked him round the chops with a bottle of wine and carried on!'

Luckily the gig didn't turn into a riot, but it uncovered the first signs of the feisty Cerys Matthew's temperament that would garner her plenty of notoriety in the gossip columns in the years to come.

Despite the drunken altercation, the end of 1993 was packed. Thanks to Rhys's hard work the band were booked in for radio sessions on Radio 5, Radio Wales, Radio Bristol and Cardiff's Red Dragon radio; there were TV appearances on a host of Welsh-language shows and there was a memorable appearance miming to 'For Tinkerbell' and 'Gyda Gwen' on *Heno*, Welsh-language TV's version of *This Morning*.

The year finished with Iestyn George coming to Cardiff to interview the band at Cardiff's Chapter Arts Centre for the *NME*'s 'On' section, which featured hotly tipped new bands.

The afternoon was memorable for a couple of reasons – the conversation Iestyn had with the band and the photos that were taken of them by *NME* snapper Roger Sargent.

'I was just imparting my knowledge about what I thought they needed to do,' Iestyn remembers. 'I said they should stay on Crai until they felt that they could take it no further because I'd seen plenty of Welsh bands that had gone chasing what they thought were "big" deals, taken the first thing that came along because it was "a deal" and ended up regretting it when they disappeared without trace. They sat there and listened intently. It was just plain, simple, obvious advice. I almost felt a little bit embarrassed because I think they thought of me as some sort of oracle because I worked for the *NME*.'

What a difference the years make. Cerys was sitting quietly, listening intently to Iestyn, when all those years back in Swansea an eight-year-old Cerys Matthews would cause nothing but trouble for the 11-year-old prefect, Iestyn George!

Iestyn was accompanied to Wales for his assignment by photographer Roger Sargent. It was a welcome return for 'Sarge' who, as a student photographer at Newport College of Art, had worked for me on *Venue* Magazine – a Cardiff-based listings magazine. We'd send him out to gigs with a photo pass and he would duly return with some of the best rock 'n' roll gig pics we'd ever seen. He was a special talent and no surprise he ended up taking pictures for the *NME*.

He always had the photographer's instinct of seizing the unusual. And on his return to the city, a Cardiff roundabout and a pop band gave him ample scope for some unique pictures.

As the city of Cardiff was being redeveloped, so artists were being given opportunities to figure in the reconstruction of the city. On one of the roads that act as a linkway to Cardiff Bay, there's a roundabout populated by road signs. Nothing unusual in that you would think, except these are road signs of every different shape, size and colour, all stuck together into giant cubes and spheres. It looks amazing and is nothing if not a pop art masterstoke. If you are ever in Cardiff seek it out, you won't regret it. So Sarge took Catatonia to the roundabout and snapped some great pictures of them on this fantasy traffic island.

After the band's photo sessions the band relaxed at a nearby pub. And it was here that Iestyn was asked something he wasn't expecting. 'At one point in the conversation Cerys asked me if I would manage the band,' he says. 'I was shocked because I just wasn't qualified. I remember from years previously, when I had tried to put a gig itinerary together for a band. It was so hard.

'Besides I was working full-time at the *NME* and it would have been too much work, even if I had wanted to. See, me, Rhys and Huw were just glorified fans helping them out, realistically we weren't what they needed. What they did need were full-time managers who could take them forward.'

And that, although they didn't know it, was just around the corner.

5
London Calling

> 'It's a faraway world come out of your gutters you boys and girls'
> (The Clash, 'London Calling')

As 1994 swung into full view, Catatonia were acclimatising themselves to increased exposure of their own – outside the confines of the Welsh-language world they had previously orbited.

While word was just beginning to spread nationally, with both *NME* and *Melody Maker* newly resolute fans of the group, locally the English media was as usual slowly coming to terms with a talented new band. Despite the Welsh-speaking media's predilection for showcasing the best new young Welsh musical hopes, the English-speaking media in Wales had always been painfully slow in recognising the talent on its doorstep. So while S4C, Radio Cymru and Welsh-language newspaper *Y Cymro* and Welsh-language magazines *Sothach* and *Golwg*, all gladly offered an open house to a bilingual Catatonia – with extensive coverage from the outset – the English-speaking media were riddled with lethargy and disinterest.

Their view was obviously that local bands didn't sell newspapers nor attract listeners or viewers. Subsequently, their coverage was minimal, confined to once-weekly pop columns, token late-night radio shows and uncomfortable slots on embarrassing middle-of-the-road TV shows presented by retired rugby players. If Wales was on the brink of a cool new dawn, the English-speaking media were still forever in the dark.

However, luckily for the band, they had sympathetic supporters in the local English media. These were willing subversives who were ready to infiltrate their newspaper's pages and radio station's airwaves with news of this cutting-edge new Welsh band.

Rhys Mwyn had carried out a PR coup of targeting those journalists and radio broadcasters who had a fine track record of supporting local bands. Having had a single of the week in the *NME*, the band stood out from the opposition. No other Welsh band singing in English had had that honour bestowed on them since The Darling Buds a few years previously, so it wasn't particularly difficult to get those local music supporters involved. Still, infiltrating the hallowed hallways of these media institutions and convincing the powers to be to give Welsh pop music a chance was a different matter.

The biggest newspaper group in Wales at the time was the Cardiff-based,

Thomson Regional Newspapers. It's now been taken over by Trinity Mirror, but at that time (1994) the company responsible for the majority of British package holidays was at the helm. The newspaper group's building is situated a drop-kick away from the home of Welsh rugby – dwarfed under the towering presence of the massive Millennium stadium. It houses the South Wales evening daily, the *South Wales Echo*; the national morning newspaper of Wales, the *Western Mail*; and the national Welsh Sunday newspaper, the *Wales on Sunday*.

The bustling newsrooms of these papers were invariably populated by two types of journalist. There were those in it for the long haul for whom their chair and desk were for life and those eager young university graduates who were using their days in Cardiff as a foot up to Fleet Street.

It made for an interesting community of wizened old hacks and ambitious whizz kids. Sat uneasily somewhere in between was Andy Barding. 'The Bard', as he's known to his cooler colleagues, was something of an enigma in the corridors of the *Western Mail*, where he was a reporter.

For many years Andy had been the newspaper's Gwent correspondent, working from a small office in Newport. By day he might have been the mild-mannered reporter filing humdrum council stories, but by night he was a key figure on the burgeoning Newport music scene. The more mainstream hacks thought him a bit strange for his alternative pursuits, but he could talk you into tomorrow about obscure Mudhoney B-sides and the complete works of Sub Pop. Let's face it though, filing stories about the Welsh local council community required a strong heart and a sturdy constitution, and no end of night-time escapism to shake off any untoward after effects the daytime job might have brought.

The main man behind Frug – his own resolutely DIY indie record label and fanzine – he was a tireless supporter of Welsh music, promoting local gigs at Newport's legendary TJs venue. Combining his obsession with a job on a daily newspaper was not easy, especially when attempting to infiltrate the pages with cool Welsh bands, while putting on a sober face at council meetings.

Trouble was that the Principality's national morning newspaper is a resolutely conservative and middle-class paper with a readership formed exclusively of farmers, politicians and the Welsh business community. The last subject on its editorial agenda was the promotion of rock and pop music.

Still, Andy's unstinting perseverance and wholesale haranguing of his fellow editorial staff allowed him brief scope to feature his favourite bands. A CD copy of *For Tinkerbell* and a letter from Rhys, who had met Andy when his band Anrehfn played TJs some years previously, alerted the journalist to the band's talents.

Despite Andy's fondness for coruscating thrash guitars and the sort of punk noise that was the staple of the soon-to-hit-the-headlines Newport sound, Catatonia's bewitching vocalist and blissed-out music hooked him whole.

Andy featured them heavily in his fanzine and was one of the first journalists to interview them. His first encounter with the band came in his weekly rock column in the *Western Mail*.

'Wales is pretty much theirs for the taking it would seem, and national acclaim is just around the corner,' he prophetically forecast. And writing about 'For Tinkerbell', he recognised that this was a band that weren't stuck in a stylistic rut:

'The debut CD whizzes through a variety of styles and influences on its five tracks from the Sgt Pepper swing of "For Tinkerbell" to the moody "New Mercurial Heights" and the repressed emotion of "Sweet Catatonia", giving ample indication that this band can turn their hands to anything.'

If the English-based print media was being turned on to the Catatonia sound, so was local radio. Cardiff's commercial radio station Red Dragon Radio was like any other commercial station. It pumped out a saccharine mix of pop chart hits and classic oldies for South Wales's less discerning musical listeners. And, like most UK commercial stations, it didn't care about cutting-edge music, much less music being made on its own doorstep. It just obsessed over the quickest way to make money. The place was Fab FM in excelsis, populated by sub-Smashey & Nicey clones with the sorts of cloying voices that made Tony Blackburn or Dr Fox sound like John Peel and Steve Lamacq. The place was as false as the DJs' phoney smiles.

It wasn't the first place you would immediately think of finding one of Catatonia's most vociferous early supporters. But then Steve Johnson wasn't a normal sort of radio DJ. The former musician had been the frontman of elegantly crafted Cardiff band The Miracle Brothers. Imagine Travis fronted by David Byrne. They were an outfit ahead of their time.

A chance meeting with the DJ who was fronting Red Dragon's graveyard Monday night 'Biz' local music programme gave Steve the chance of a career-change. The DJ confessed that he was, unsurprisingly, not at all interested in the show and would Steve like to put in all the hard work and research the programme for him.

Steve was kicking his heels after The Miracle Brothers had split and jumped at it. Soon he was presenting the Biz, and thankfully offering South Wales' more astute radio listeners a glimpse of light in a place of darkness.

One night, after recording the show Steve had left the building in Cardiff's West Canal Wharf, and made a short walk across the wharf to Soundspace Recording and Rehearsal Studios, which was situated about 50 feet from Red Dragon.

Steve regularly visited the studios to check on what bands the owners Andrew Thomas and Pete Williams had had in that week. As he was chatting with the pair that night, he was distracted from his conversation by the sound of a girl singing. It was coming from one of the rehearsal rooms and he quickly sped off to investigate. He pushed open the door into the cramped room and was met by the sight of Cerys Matthews belting out the words, 'Don't you fall asleep there's lots of things I need to say that just won't keep. Sweet, Sweet Sweet Sweet, Catatonia, I should have told ya.' The lyrics rode beautifully along on the back of Mark Roberts' slowly shimmering guitar and another media player was hooked.

'I thought they sounded amazing and looked even better,' says Steve. 'Cerys had a presence, something about her that was star quality even then. You could see they were serious about making it and they had the songs to make that wish come true.'

Steve immediately fell in love with Cerys's voice and 'Sweet Catatonia' in particular. 'Her voice had a real lushness to it and I used to play that song on the show all the time after I got to know them,' he says. After meeting the band for the first time he invited them on to the show. 'Cerys and Clancy did the interview,' he remembers. 'They loved it. It was all new to them so they were lapping up all this appearing on radio malarkey.'

Steve was a key supporter of Catatonia in those early days, as he was of all the new Welsh bands that were set to stir a once lifeless scene into life. Unfortunately, he found that his excited protestations to his colleagues that Welsh music was about to enter a bright new age fell on deaf ears.

Steve was like a square peg in a round hole at Red Dragon and it wasn't long before working under a management who 'just didn't have an idea or get what was going on' forced him to leave for a job on Radio Wales.

'The biggest irony is that now, Red Dragon Radio proclaims itself as a champion of Welsh music,' he explains. 'But when bands like Catatonia, Super Furries and Stereophonics couldn't get arrested, the station just didn't want to know. It had as much interest in Welsh music as I have in giving up alcohol! Now the Welsh music scene is making money, Red Dragon is oiling the wheels of the bandwagon as much as anyone.'

Away from the English media, Catatonia were becoming cult icons on S4C. The band had made umpteen appearances on Welsh-language TV already – encompassing children's, pop and daytime TV programmes. They were about to update their CV with an appearance alongside Dafydd Ieaun's housemate Rhys Ifans. A considerable way away from *Twin Town* (well 70 odd miles from Cardiff to Swansea anyway) and a million miles away from *Notting Hill*, *Ffranks* was an educational programme about two characters called, strangely enough, Frank, who were learning to speak Welsh. Indicative of the way the close-knit Welsh-speaking media works – everyone knows each other, so everyone helps each other out – Rhys persuaded the S4C producers to get Catatonia on the show. A demonstration of charitable nepotism maybe, but probably more to do with Rhys's housemate pocketing an appearance fee, so allowing Rhys to be treated to a few beers down at their favourite Cardiff pub The Yellow Kangaroo.

Being in a pop band puts you in some bizarre situations. However Catatonia were about to chalk up one of their strangest appearances past, present or future. Wednesday, 12 January 1994 saw them setting up their equipment on location at Sully Hospital, a private hospital situated in the countryside between Barry and Cardiff, in readiness for a slightly leftfield TV experience. The production company's synopsis of the band's part in the show makes for interesting reading. It reads: 'Catatonia to appear in an episode of the "Ffranks" where one of the Ffranks is semi-conscious in hospital (i.e. a Catatonic state). The choice of music would be up to them, although the more upbeat the better.' As a tenuous link to get a band onto a show, it's class without a doubt. And as TV appearances go, performing to playback and attempting not to inflict interminable damage to Rhys Ifans's health, as he pretends to be teetering on the edge of lapsing into a coma, has to be marked down as one of the more colourfully surreal moments in televisual history!

STAGE STRUCK AND NOT SOBER

Whether it was mucking about on a TV programme with their mates or sitting in their favourite pub plotting their destiny Catatonia were a carefree proposition. Powered on by the confidence of two people very much in love, the band had everything to look forward to and nothing to fear. Cardiff was beginning to buzz, all their friends were either involved in local bands or in the arts, so it was a dynamic time to be in Wales. No one could quite grasp it then, but the Welsh music revolution was taking shape. Not least thanks to a network of people helping each other out and a real spirit of co-operation existing between band members and musicians. So, while Catatonia were revelling in their new-found media star status, the band's unofficial support group – Rhys Mwyn, Huw Williams and Iestyn George – were calling in favours and spreading the Catatonia gospel like a bunch of messianical preachers.

These were key moments in the band's career. The people they would link-up with in the next six months would be with them for the rest of their career. Rhys was ringing around all the people he had sent copies of *For Tinkerbell* to and was attempting to get them on support tours; Huw was talking to all the music biz contacts he had made with The Pooh Sticks, and Iestyn was wielding his big NME contacts book like an offensive weapon!

The three would phone each other up – from London to Cardiff to North Wales – around 7pm each day for a progress update report. All three of them had their own success stories. Rhys befriended Dave Harper, the manager of emerging indie band Salad. The leafy-sounding quartet were fronted by leggy MTV presenter Marijne. They were receiving good reviews in the music press. However, the acclaim afforded Salad seemingly had more to do with what their sexy singer was wearing than the presence of any discernible tunes. Nevertheless, these were the times when female-fronted bands like Echobelly and Sleeper were cropping up and the male-dominated music press sensed some scene-shaping bandwagoneering. The lack of any noticeable talent hadn't stopped them from creating scenes before (anyone remember 'the Camden Lurch' or 'Shoegazing'?), so why stop them now? Anyhow, Dave Harper was impressed with what he had heard and offered Catatonia a support tour with Salad for June and July.

Huw meanwhile had contacted the former Pooh Sticks booking agent Paul Buck. He was working for the London-based Asgard agency and held much clout when it came to booking bands gigs and more importantly the London gigs that Catatonia needed to play if they were to showcase their talents in front of the greatest number of A&Rs, publishing scouts and journalists. Paul was turned on to the band after hearing a tape that Huw had sent him and was bewitched by one track in particular. With its dark, brooding and mysterious orchestral-like feel and oddly angular guitars, 'Dimbran' swept the agent off his feet.

'Although I liked the other tracks, I loved "Dimbran",' admits Paul. 'I'm a big fan of ethereal music like The Cocteau Twins and The Young Marble Giants (cult 80s band who featured Cardiff singer Alison Statton), so Catatonia's sound struck a chord with me.'

Rhys sent Paul a clutch of tapes and CDs to use as promotional aids to get the band gigs and within days of becoming official Catatonia support group member number four, Paul had booked them their second and third London gigs, at the Camden Falcon and the Splash Club, both in February.

Iestyn had been beavering away diligently as well himself. He had used his contacts to arrange for some of the leading record industry types to see the band play at the Falcon on 2 February and the Splash Club on 25 February.

But before those two important London gigs there was the little matter of a support slot at a gig in Newport. There they would make their first encounter with the man who would become their promoter. This was the guy who would, some years later, arrange for them to play the biggest gig of their lives in front of 50,000 rabid fans in a country park near Port Talbot. But until then there was the prospect of playing at the bottom of the bill at one of the most famous venues not only in Wales, but the world.

The Legendary TJs first started life 28 years ago, half its size and christened Cedars Rest, a restaurant specialising in steak and seafood, before it was turned into a burger bar called the Pittsburg Diner. It was around this time that John Siccolo bought the property next door, joined them together and renamed it El Sieco's, before he eventually decided on TJs Disco which has survived albeit in abbreviated form for the last 12 years.

TJs stands for Trilby and John. Trilby was John's late wife; a remarkable, feisty, character who once kicked Iron Maiden out of the venue when they happened upon the club and tried to have an impromptu jam on stage. It acquired the 'Legendary' tag because it was becoming so famous, that DJs like John Peel and Steve Lamacq were calling it 'The Legendary TJs'.

John Sicolo is half Welsh, half Seychellian and a big bear of a man. He has owned the venue for the last 28 years since leaving the merchant navy where he served as a cook. TJs is remarkable for many things not least the hospitality the bands playing there received courtesy of John's culinary skills.

I remember interviewing Bobby Gillespie from Primal Scream in 1990, in the flat above TJs. This was pre-*Screamadelica* era Primals, when they were still clad in leather and wanted to sound like The MC5 and The Stooges. I'll never forget it. One, for the relief I felt and two for the food. We both sat there enthusiastically tucking into some delicious chicken stew that John and Trilby had served up for the band, while Bobby who had attacked a journalist only weeks previously sat there a vision of politeness and manners. Thankfully!

Unlike many venues this was a place with a homely welcome and a warm heart at its core. Here were people opening their house, feeding the musicians out of their own pockets and giving them space to sleep on their floor. That's why bands returned time and time again, because they simply loved playing there. TJs was one of Nirvana's favourite venues, and it is alleged, although this may just be a wilfully apocryphal story, that Kurt Cobain asked Courtney Love to marry him after a particularly riotous Nirvana gig there.

TJs has hosted gigs by some illustrious names: The Cranberries, Elastica, The Lemonheads, Mercury Rev, The Offspring, Oasis, Supergrass and The Manic Street Preachers – who used to hang out there on weekends – have all kick-started their careers at TJs. And Catatonia were about to join those illustrious ranks.

The gig on Monday, 24 January saw the band booked on a bill put together by Elephant Music – a local gig promoter run under the auspices of Hereford-based Conal Dodds.

Catatonia were booked as support act to two rising stars of '94's resolutely indie-generated scenes. Headlining were Cornershop, who were then a shambling agit pop punk band who had yet to realise that they were really Asian pop dance exponents 'Born On The Seventh Sign' and soon to be blessed with 'A Brimful Of Asha'. Below them were the New Wave of New Wave punkers S*M*A*S*H.

They were memorably described on the poster for the gig (a cut and paste DIY photocopy by Conal) as 'a quite preposterous punk-whipped whirlwind founded stoutly on the basis that the Tories are bastards, apathy is, er, boring and "Never Mind The Bollocks" was the best record ever'. For a Monday night in Newport and £3.50 on the door this was, thanks to Elephant Music, something of a bargain night out.

Conal Dodds was a young promoter and Elephant Music was still in its infancy when he first promoted Catatonia. He had started out putting on gigs in Hereford. His first promotion was, amazingly, a charity gig featuring Led Zeppelin's Robert Plant at Monmouth Leisure Centre. Promoting a rock superstar for your very first gig—that's no mean feat!

Newport was the nearest main town to Hereford so Conal approached John Sicolo to put gigs on at TJs. From there Elephant Music moved into Bristol promoting at The Fleece & Firkin and The Tropic Club, before Conal started becoming the main promoter for Wales and the West Country. He moved on to working with one of the UK's biggest promoters MCP before joining the equally renowned Metropolis Music where he works today. All throughout his career he has promoted Catatonia, from pub gigs to festivals, but the first night he encountered them he wasn't exactly overwhelmed.

'They were just a local band, bottom of the bill and they didn't get paid,' Conal remembers. 'I was looking for a local band for a support act for this double header and I think it was Huw (Williams) who recommended them to me. I remember they were quite shambolic. It was a very drunken evening, quite a punky night. Both Cornershop and S*M*A*S*H were very punk, and Catatonia were very raw as well. Ironically on the poster I had a line saying "This is the future", so I must have known then they were going to make it!'

They might have sounded very clean and polished on record, but live Catatonia were just finding their feet and learning. Remember, Cerys was still playing guitar and her voice was still to reach its perfect pitch. And if there was a crate of beer lying around, it was they who were going to educate everyone in how quickly they could demolish it! Catatonia's drinking would soon be getting as much publicity as their music but at that time Rhys Mwyn, who was in the crowd at the TJs gig didn't think anything of it. 'I tell you one thing: people drink and girls drink from pint glasses,' he laughs. 'There's a real drink culture in Wales, London wimps should get used to that!'

Rhys said he didn't worry about Catatonia's early live performances. 'Mark, Paul and Dafydd were experienced, they'd all been in bands before, so they were strengths in that sense,' he says. They knew the ropes and weren't going to fall apart if the monitors weren't working. They had wise heads on stage. You had a band who could hack it.' Rhys watched Catatonia play as he stood next to one of the S*M*A*S*H guitarists who was more than interested in Cerys. 'He thought she was Debbie Harry,' he says. 'Not that Catatonia sounded like Blondie but she had a real attitude and strength.'

The Debbie Harry comparison wasn't remiss. In the years to come Cerys would bedazzle not only for her ballsy attitude but her ability to combine that strength of character with both an offbeat allure and a smouldering sexuality.

Of course, there was also the little matter of the singer having a relationship with the lead guitarist, just like Debbie Harry and Blondie's guitarist Chris Stein.

Although their first TJs gig was something of a success, their second a few months down the line would officially go on record as being the worst gig they ever played. Still, these were exciting times for the band – there were London gigs to play and a new single to record. 'Hooked' was the follow up to the *For Tinkerbell* EP. Again recorded at Crai studios in Llandwrog, Caernarfon, it was put together over the weekend of 19-20 February with Ken Nelson – a producer the band had met when recording a session for Radio Wales in Wrexham at the tail end of 1993. The band recorded two tracks, 'Hooked' and 'Fall Beside Her', at Crai; the third track 'Difrychwelyd' was one of those that was laid down at Grassroots studios. 'Hooked' was scheduled for release at the end of May to coincide with the band's tour in June and July with Salad.

Rhys sent out pre-release copies of 'Hooked' to Iestyn and Huw to give out to their contacts and act as a clarion call to all those record company A&Rs who had begun to swarm around the band.

'They were becoming hot property,' recalls Rhys Mwyn. 'I was dealing with calls from record companies who were feeling their way and finding out about the band. They knew it was a band at the early stages, so initially they were content to bide their time and keep an eye on them.'

Meanwhile in London, Iestyn George was lining up a host of industry figures to check out Catatonia for the very first time at their gigs at the Falcon the Splash Club.

'I got a load of people to commit to going to the Falcon,' says Iestyn. 'There were people like Paul Buck who Huw had alerted to the band, as well as Ben Wardle from Indolent Records (who would give a home to The 60ft Dolls), Simon Williams (music journalist and mainman at Fierce Panda Records), Mike Smith from EMI Publishing and more importantly for Catatonia's future career, Charlie Pinder, A&R scout at Sony Music Publishing.

LONDON DAZE

The Falcon gig would be as support to Speedway – a sort of baggy punk band who couldn't make up their minds whether they wanted to be The Happy Mondays or These Animal Men. Sadly, for them, they were neither, as their disappearance into oblivion proved.

The Falcon is one of the key London venues for any of the bands wanting to showcase their talents to the music industry. Tucked midway between Kentish Town and Camden, the Falcon is basically a pub with a large bar and a backroom where the bands play. Like similar venues – the Monarch and the Dublin Castle in Camden, the Bull & Gate in Kentish Town and the Splash Club at the Water Rats pub in Kings Cross – these are places populated by packs of A&Rs all hoping to spot the next big thing and all paranoid that their colleagues will snatch them first.

For bands being thrust into the London spotlight it can come as something of a culture shock. As Catatonia were about to find out.

The band had travelled up to London in a hired transit van. They had arrived early and spent all afternoon in the pubs around Camden and Kentish Town, exploring the watering holes that would become a second home to them over the next two years. All this was new to the band, and although Mark, Paul and Daf had played at the Powerhaus venue in London on consecutive St David's days as part of a bill made up of leading Welsh-language bands, this was finally the real thing.

They wanted to make it and now they were going to mix it with The Man (or the music industry as its otherwise known!).

It was no wonder they were filled with a mixture of nerves and excitement. However, if you've got all afternoon and then some before you have to play a gig, there's not much else to do than sit in a pub and drink. And if the talent of a band was measured in pints, then Catatonia would be world beaters, platinum-selling superstars. It wasn't that they could just drink – they were more than adept at trashing themselves into such a stupor you would have mistaken them being born of the same gene pool as Oliver Reed and Peter O'Toole. London's pubs and venues opened up a new world of wonder to them and they evidently wanted to embrace the rock 'n' roll lifestyle and swallow it whole.

'They were a shambles basically,' says Iestyn of the Falcon gig. 'The worst thing of all they made themselves look like a youth club band. They were falling apart. They had a keyboard player playing a synth, it was like a poor man's EMF, it just didn't look right. That night they just didn't look the part.'

As an attempt to impress the assembled industry hordes, the gig was nothing short of a disaster. 'We played the Falcon in London, a while back,' Paul recalled to the *Melody Maker* some years later, 'and there were loads of record companies there to see us. We'd been on the piss all day and it was a long day as well. Then you have a couple of lines and you're bundled onstage, and it's like, "What the fuck am I gonna do with this guitar?" It was a very fast gig, I remember that much. After a couple of lines, you don't really give a fuck anyway. But I remember seeing a lot of bemused faces in the audience.'

Ironically, not everyone was underwhelmed by their trashy showing.

There were those in the audience smitten by the band's rough-edged approach and Cerys's "girl-don't-give-a-fuck" stage presence. 'She had attitude by the truckload and wasn't really bothered by who had turned up,' admits Paul Buck. 'I quite like punky gigs anyway. That's the sort of music I like, but yes, some people didn't think they were very good, that's for sure. I think a lot of people were expecting them to sound as angelic as they did on record.'

But that was Catatonia all over. They displayed a hugely schizophrenic talent for conjuring up lush and eerie bittersweet symphonies, but live they were as raw as a force 10 gale. The band stayed in London that night, as Paul Buck had also booked them a gig at Kingston University in Surrey, again with Speedway. The band had already played gigs at Bangor and Aberystwyth universities, so were used to running through their set in front of a pissed-up student crowd. This suited them better, because they could be just as drunk as the crowd and no one would notice.

At this time Cerys was still the naive feature in the group – someone who wasn't so bothered about the politics of indie music and who knew nothing about the business of putting records out. She had room in her own personal iconography for the likes of Shirley Bassey, Judy Garland, and, erm, Whigfield, so you can imagine how much contempt she held for playing the indie toilet circuit. The diva had still to escape from the devil-may-care madam, but her voice was still stretching out for the stars, even if she had always expressed a desire to be cooped up in a transit van heading up and down the M4!

Cerys admitted: 'The best thing about touring is, like, when I was fourteen, I used to see bands and all the lads would get into a transit with all the gear, and I used to just die to be sat in the front of the van and to be driving off – just driving places. That used to be my one ambition.'

That was the young Cerys Matthews and her escapist fantasies coming to the fore. The dreams to fly away that propelled Cerys to uproot herself and leave for London and Barcelona a few years previously.

However, the drive home after the Kingston gig was more of a sobering experience than her dreams might have first suggested. The band didn't get paid the night before. As a support band your cut of the door take is minimal, and anything they did make had been spent on transit hire, petrol and alcohol. Their fee at Kingston was a flat fee of just £50 – between five! They even had to borrow money from a fan to pay the toll on the Severn Bridge to get home.

The band had always wanted to play London, but if they had dreamt of these gigs as anything other than tough then they would have been wrong. Bands on the first rung of the ladder certainly don't make any money. Venues realise that bands have to play these London gigs to get themselves known, so the venues can pay the artistes they book a pittance.

Catatonia would find that out again soon, when they made another pilgrimage up the M4 to try and redeem themselves after the Falcon gig with a Friday night slot at the Splash Club in the Water Rats pub. Situated on Grays Inn Road, a stone's throw away from Kings Cross railway station, the Water Rats is a pub even smaller in size than the Falcon, but with a back room that has the appearance of a plush little theatre. It doesn't have any seats but it has long, sweeping, crushed-velvet curtains and a chandelier hanging from the ceiling that give it an air of theatrical respectability.

Sandwiched in the middle of a bill that included the never-to-be-heard-of-again Pretty Blue Gun and headliners, the decidedly leftfield noise merchants Fin, Catatonia would have to bring their own crowd with them if they were to make any money. Some venues paid bands by operating a strict system whereby however many paying punters handed over tickets with the band's name on them, the band would get a cut of those tickets. The Splash Club contract read thus: 'The management agrees to pay the artist/es £1 per Catatonia payer after the first 20 Catatonia payers. And then £2 per Catatonia payer after the first 50 Catatonia payers. The artist/es will receive no payment from the audience who have come to see no artist/es in particular.'

This meant that for the band to make any money from the gig they had to invite as many friends and fans to the gig as they could to have a chance of making any money and also make sure they all paid with their Catatonia tickets. The venue gave Rhys the tickets. These were photocopies that were run off on the venue's xerox. He duly doled them out to as many people as he and the band could find. Luckily, there is quite a large contingent of Welsh speakers in London, and many of them had been corralled by the ubiquitous Rhys Ifans who was acting in a play in London at the time.

Another interesting line in the contract, gives an insight into just how difficult it is for bands first starting out to keep their London profile high – 'The artist/es agree not to appear at any other London venue two weeks before and one week after their appearance at the Splash Club. Any artist/es doing so are subject to breach of contract.' Although primarily done to allow the venue the benefit of the maximum number of fans of the bands booked to turn up, it seems unfair to limit bands who are promoting singles and albums to the number of London gigs they can play in a three-week period.

But that's London gigs for you. Not as glamorous as you might expect – just ask Catatonia. They didn't even have anywhere to get changed that night, as the one Water Rats dressing room was exclusively reserved for the headline band only.

There might have been two other bands on the bill, but the assembled throng was full of industry figures. Huw had invited an old friend of his, Charlie Pinder from Sony Publishing, to check out the band. 'I heard the

Crai EPs, and I loved them,' explains Charlie. 'Cerys' voice reminded me so much of The Sundays' Harriet Wheeler and Liz Frazer of The Cocteau Twins. When I went to see them I thought they were good if not a little rough-edged. It took Catatonia a while to develop, while Cerys' voice sounded amazing on record, in those early days it never tended to hit the mark. They were really pissed but had a lot of promise. Ironically, I think I fancied the keyboard player Clancy! The band were pretty shambolic, but I vowed to keep an eye on them. That's how I would operate. There were bands who I thought were good but it was obvious they just weren't ready to be signed at that time.'

Charlie reckons that it was not only the Catatonia sound they needed to work, the image could do with a makeover as well. 'The other problem then was her image. Now she is an amazingly sexy and confident frontwoman, but then she wore football tops and tracksuit bottoms. It was as if she was almost trying to be one of the blokes. She also hid behind her guitar which is a common trait of someone not fully confident at being out front.' Other esteemed figures in attendance were Alan James (one of London's coolest PRs) and Dave Ambrose (who signed The Sex Pistols) as well as A&Rs from Island Records, EMI, Epic and Steve Lamacq's label Deceptive.

DAZED, BEAUTIFUL AND BRUISED

The Catatonia set then was made up of earlier penned tunes. 'Sweet Catatonia', 'Hooked', 'Fall Beside Her', 'Difrychwelyd', 'Cariadon Ffol' and 'Message' (later renamed as 'You Can') as well as the more recently written 'Bleed', 'This Boy Can't Swim', 'Painful', 'Dream On' and 'Whale'. There were even appearances for two early songs 'Mr Stops' and 'I Can Hear You' that would soon disappear, never to be resurrected.

Mark and Cerys were quite prolific as their set of earlier-penned songs and recently written gems proved. However, many of these songs that were written in 1993 and 1994 would have a patient wait, until 1996, before they saw the light of day on an album. It was unsurprising that the unfettered beauty and lyrical depth of these songs rang out, despite their early frenetic live performances. They were simply a band that was not the sum of their influences.

While 1994 saw an uprising of uninspired, insipid female-fronted guitar bands that relied heavily on image over substance and a wholesale pilfering of punk pop indie styles, Catatonia were only ever indebted to themselves for their sound. That's why reviewers had such a hard time trying to pin them down. Many of their songs like 'Bleed' and 'This Boy Can't Swim' were electrifying buzzsaw gems that reviewers were quick to pocket in compartments marked 'the sound of the new Blondie' or 'melodic Buzzcocks-like pop punk'.

But trip-topped tender epics like the somnambulant, sleepwalking 'Dream On', the lushly serene 'Cariadion Ffol' ('Foolish Sweetheart') and the mesmeric, starry-eyed 'Gyda Gwen' ('With A Smile') weren't as easily dismissed as anything other than two songwriters diving headlong into the depths of human emotion and resurfacing with something both beautiful and unsettling, delicious and disturbing. Although Catatonia would, for music press convenience sake, find an unfortunate home through lazy pigeonholing alongside other female-fronted outfits like Sleeper, Elastica and Spacemaid, those in the know were well aware that Catatonia were anything *but* one-trick pop kids.

Scratch beneath the surface of the other generically indie female-fronted bands vying with the Cats for music press headlines at that time and you found nothing but a big-mouth singer with opinions that struggled to cover the creative holes where their songs should have been – Echobelly's Sonya Madan and Sleeper's Louise Wener being the worst 'rent-a-quote' culprits. However, scratch beneath the Catatonia surface and you found an ambitious range of lyrics laced with complex emotions about the fragility of the human psyche. Just as the band sailed close to the edge with their fondness of full-scale hedonism, so did the songs – all bittersweet and warped, walking a fine line between love and hate – a soft coating concealing a hard-hearted centre.

The assembled music industry brigade present at the Splash Club gig knew they had something special. Backstage after the gig Cerys spent an hour fending off the over-keen advances of the easily excitable A&R brigade, because it wasn't just the songs that were intriguing those present – Cerys was unlike anything many of them had ever encountered. Here was someone with a remarkable voice that fluidly switched between gut-wrenching rasp and mellifluous croon, yet still managed more torque and intrigue than Björk. She had a voice that was pure helium filled Welsh cartoon character and a look that was the epitome of cool. A look that relied solely on Cerys's own vivid anti-fashion agenda that gleefully rubbed the fashion brigade up the wrong way. Cerys's fashion sense was based around the dictum that when it comes to what you wear, you don't rule anything in nor rule anything out.

Although this was early days, no music press reviews just yet, the London-based *Sun Zoom Spark* fanzine summed up Cerys's iconic stage presence nicely. 'She's got the shades on and she swigs her beer and chews her gum exuding movie-star cool,' they bubbled enthusiastically. 'This woman deserves to be idolised.' How prophetically correct they were.

Despite the grungy, divey venues that Cerys found herself in, she invariably attempted to lighten the gloom and inject a little bit of glamour into proceedings. She must have got that from her mum, who gave her a satin-lined vanity case to take on tour! Mind you, Mrs Matthews would have feared the worst for her offspring if she'd seen some of the places her daughter ended up in.

Early gigs in London, especially the Water Rats gig, saw the band having to run the gauntlets of record company A&Rs who would flock to their gigs in packs hunting for the next big things. At this time the Welsh music scene was slowly showing signs of life. Its heartbeat was centred around Newport. The industrial town, 20 miles from Cardiff, was spinning out a clutch of thrilling guitar bands – The 60ft Dolls, Dub War, Flyscreen and Novocaine – who were as fiery as the Welsh dragon, and twice as pissed-off. The Manic Street Preachers may have initially blazed a trail out of Wales, but the punky frontiersmen for the Welsh scene were being followed by a population of bands that were as diverse as they were different.

The more sussed of the A&R community were wising up to Wales for the first time and, God forbid, some were even planning trips to uncharted territory – the other side of the Severn Bridge! A&Rs by dint are strange creatures. As most of them work nights they very rarely have that many friends, so the A&R community is tight knit. Although there is a rivalry to sign bands, most of them are very good friends, spending hours each night propping up various venues' bars.

Their sense of community also invariably comes from the fact that they are viewed as the pariahs of the music world, parasitic creatures out to out do each other, living on their nerves and keeping their jobs on the success or otherwise of their signings.

Rhys Mwyn had met many A&Rs in his time and held them in nothing but contempt.

'I remember the Water Rats gig when Cerys told me she had had one of these A&R dickheads telling her the band should be this and that, trying to tell them that if they wanted to be signed they should be like this or like that,' he spits. 'It upsets people, it's fucking out of order, it's a pain in the arse and it's boring. Bands should evolve for themselves, not design themselves to the dictates of what A&Rs want.'

'And these people are minions anyway, people giving business cards out,' adds Rhys. 'They go back to report on how many bands they've seen in a week. Bands don't need that kind of bullshit, they should leave that to the managers. Although A&Rs would rather bypass the manager and get straight to the band.'

But this was the problem. Catatonia didn't have a manager. They had three or four well-intentioned, supremely enthusiastic people fighting their cause, but no one that was their ultimate guiding hand.

After Iestyn had received his surprise proposal from the band to manage them two months previously, he had put the feelers out to London's many management agencies. It was a case of throwing out as many tapes and CDs as he could and seeing what stuck. But the exercise was not without its successes.

'Anyone who was enthusiastic could join the party,' explains Iestyn. 'What we did was target as many people as possible and wait to see what came back. Lots of people were interested, it's just that Catatonia were still finding their feet live, and many industry people we approached thought they either didn't have enough potential or just weren't good enough because of their live frailties.'

As Iestyn points out, these were cautious times in the music industry anyway. The UK scene was undergoing another reticent regeneration after the diametrically opposed excesses of Madchester and grunge, while record companies were still holding up a wetted finger to gauge which way the musical wind was blowing. Britpop had yet to be brought into the world and was still being incubated in a pub in Camden along with the careers of both Pulp and Blur.

'Record companies weren't signing bands,' says Iestyn. 'Times were tough for young bands and I think Catatonia needed managers to tighten them up and improve their live shows, before they could realistically dream of a record deal.'

Despite the uncertain environment they were operating in, there were people willing to take a chance and invest in the band. As well as a booking agent who loved their raw pop sensibilities and an enthusiastic young promoter pushing them forward, Catatonia were about to gain some much needed management.

6
Hooked on Classics!

> 'I'd rather not go where the people I know have no hooks to hang from'
> (Catatonia, 'Hooked')

Richard Lowe has Iestyn George to thank for a phone call the Welsh journalist made to him. Iestyn implored the one half of the London-based management team MRM to come along to the Water Rats to see for himself the band that had garnered *NME*'s Single Of The Week. So it was that Richard was in the throng at the Water Rats. Fortunately, he was suitably impressed with this exciting band and their beguiling singer.

At the time Richard and his management partner Martin Patton were looking after two bands, Thieves and Ultramarine. Described as 'a heavenly meeting of Al Green and the lush instrumentation of the Cocteau Twins', Thieves featured the exquisite voice of David McAlmont, who would later go on to record a memorable album with former Suede guitarist Bernard Butler. Ultramarine had similarly experimental elements. Never slaves to fashion they revelled in ambient electro sounds like a Nineties Soft Machine. Their avant-garde experimentalism brought cult appeal but little financial or commercial rewards.

It was Catatonia's unpindownable, compelling sound and Cerys's shimmering, otherworldly voice that had struck Richard. Like the two bands in the MRM stable, Catatonia had ethereal leftfield leanings that appealed to his keen musical sense.

'They (MRM) were interested from the start,' admits Huw Williams, who fielded many calls from the management in those weeks after the Water Rats gig. 'Paul Buck had told them that we were involved so they rang up quite a lot to suss us and the band out!'

Richard was convinced that he could work with the band, but wanted to let his management partner Martin Patton see Catatonia play in London again, before MRM made a collective decision on whether they would become the band's managers.

The band were both flattered and impressed by MRM's interest. Catatonia knew they needed London-based management to carry on their dream, and they were impressed that Richard and Martin were both very sussed about the machinations of the music business, but also had a roster of bands that were distinctly different from the mainstream.

Catatonia were next due in the smoke on Thursday, 14 April, supporting

Salad at the Borderline. Sadly, a mix-up with Salad's management meant their support slot had to be pulled. However they still had the summer tour with Salad to look forward to so it wasn't too much of a disappointment.

Their next gig after that had been booked for Monday, 25 April at the Dome – not, sadly, a forerunner of the monstrous eyesore adorning Greenwich, but a former ballroom in North London's leafy Tufnell Park. Ultramarine were playing Brunel University the following night and it had been agreed that Catatonia would play a support slot to these prospective label mates, so that both Richard and Martin could run the rule over them before making any decisions.

Until then the band were busy. The three Catateers Rhys, Huw and Iestyn and the new fourth member Paul Buck were doing an admirable job of booking them gigs anywhere and everywhere.

After the Splash Club show there were two gigs days later at Bangor University and the Coal Exchange in Cardiff with former Alarm frontman Mike Peters and his band The Poets of Justice, who were made up of members of Welsh-language group Jess. The Cardiff gig was especially memorable. The Coal Exchange is a grandly ornate building at the heart of Cardiff's dockland and was once the administrative centre of Tiger Bay when the docks heaved with ships transporting coal around the world. For many years it lay in a ruinous state, but at the start of the Nineties the Coal Exchange had been transformed into a hugely appealing venue; one of the more salubrious places to host gigs in Wales.

Mike Peters has a devout following in his homeland. The Alarm were nothing short of folk heroes, so any gigs by the former rabble-rouser were going to be met with rapturous crowds. Peters had recently recorded his first solo material since The Alarm had split at Crai's studios in Landwrog. Rhys had met Mike and recommended Catatonia to him as a support band.

Mike's new work had been hugely anticipated and both the North and South Wales gigs were mobbed, with kids hanging off the balcony in Cardiff.

For Catatonia it was a chance to introduce themselves to an audience full of the English-speaking Welsh kids who so loved The Alarm but weren't overly familiar with their Welsh-language pasts.

That night they revelled in playing in front of their hometown crowd and, by the end of the night, an army of new fans had joined the Cat crusade. Ironically, it was a night that neatly bridged the gap between the Welsh rock hero of the Eighties and unveiled the new Welsh rock cool of the Nineties.

BEST LEFT FORGOTTEN

The band's second single 'Hooked' was in the can and awaiting its May release and those important London gigs were looming large. Back in Wales, Catatonia were making the most of their growing stature with appearances on BBC Wales television. At that time BBC Wales and its commercial brethren HTV Wales were like the televisual land that time forgot. Most of the programmes they produced had as much imagination as a coma victim. They were invariably presented by second-rate comedians who made Max Boyce appear to be a comedy genius or ex-international rugby players, whose monosyllabic drawls were a walking advertisement to the dangers of extensive scrummaging.

There may have been a bright new dawn of Welsh culture rising, but Welsh television worked with its blinds down and minds shut. They were still locked in the past, in a land of harps, daffodils and male-voice choirs. Youth culture was as alien to them as an English-sounding name in their Taffia ridden hierarchy.

Still there was always Roy Noble. Catatonia appeared on the imaginative *Roy Noble Show*, a televisual winner that featured the saintly Welsh housewives favourite, a sub-Terry Wogan clone with a Captain Birdseye's beard but his own hair, droning on about 20 uses for disused coal mines. Imagine Marilyn Manson appearing in the cookery slot on *This Morning with Richard and Judy*, and that's how uncomfortable Catatonia's appearance on the show was. Still, they were on TV and reaching the masses. I doubt a nation of Welsh housewives ran out to place their orders for 'Hooked', but it was a subversion of sorts, however bizarre.

And then, at the other end of Catatonia's promotional schedule, there was S4C. The golden age of Welsh-language bands may have passed, but the Welsh-language station was still making space for pop programmes in its schedules. It may have copped flak from young Welsh speakers who believed it to be deeply uncool, but compared to BBC and HTV Wales, S4C was the coolest station on earth. A few days after undergoing the Roy Noble treatment they appeared on *Syth 94*, a replacement for the late, lamented and wholly seminal *Fideo 9*. The band wowed the Welsh-speaking masses with a haunting rendition of 'Difrychwelyd' from the new single.

The future then was looking brighter than a skip full of dayglo dancing flowers. But with Catatonia in those early days, it was wise never to rule out the band's thrilling unpredictability. Thrilling in that Catatonia gigs were difficult to call. Consistency was not a word they recognised easily. Gigs could swing from glorious shows where Mark's guitars would sparkle and Cerys's voice would shimmer with luxuriant ease to shows that were just shambling, rambling, beer-swathed drunken romps.

Although they had come this far with a mixture of help, luck and talent, discipline was a word they just didn't comprehend. Just like the title of Guns 'N' Roses most famous album, they had an 'appetite for destruction'. And they were about to display just how healthy their appetites were on their return visit to Newport. Thursday, 7 April will go down in the history of Catatonia as the day when the music almost died.

It was by some considerable stretch the worst gig they would ever play. As well as his reporting job at the *Western Mail*, Andy Barding was putting records out on his Frug label, writing a fanzine of the same name and also promoting gigs at the Legendary TJs. As part of a Frug Nite Out, Andy had booked Catatonia with Gorky's Zygotic Mynci as support. The industrious Newport scenester had just put Catatonia on the cover of the latest issue of his fanzine and was a hoping for a good night.

However, the signs of how the evening might progress were there for all to see when the band arrived at TJs. Andy recalls how the gig may have been at the Legendary TJs but it was remarkable for the band's equally legendary drinking. 'As far as I can remember they didn't get paid,' says Andy. 'They played for a crate of lager. And they drank that within an hour of getting to the venue. Then they went out and bought another crate and a few bottles of wine. I think the local off-licence had one of their best night's ever!'

He can joke about it now, but Andy wasn't happy on the night. Huw Williams, who had just taken on the responsibility of managing Newport's most-likely-to's, The 60ft Dolls, was DJ-ing on the night and remembers how the proceedings unfolded.

'Newport was buzzing, the gig was right at the start of when the Newport scene and Wales was beginning to really take-off, so there was a big buzz surrounding the gig,' explains Huw. 'It was also a late-night show, Gorkys didn't go on until gone 11pm and Catatonia didn't get on until 1.15am.'

The band's late slot was obviously their downfall. They'd spent hours and hours since soundchecking in the afternoon drinking vast amounts of alcohol. 'Catatonia came on, just after I'd pulled a drunken 60ft Dolls guitarist Richard Parfitt, out of the DJ booth because he was playing Bruce Springsteen,' laughs Huw. 'I mean everybody was in varying shades of drunkenness, but Catatonia were more pissed than anyone there. The crowd started to walk out because the band were so pissed. Cerys didn't see her guitar let alone play it. They were awful.'

Huw remembers Andy Barding being hacked off when everyone started walking out. Andy said at the end of the gig that the band were, ironically enough, really fucked off that everyone had gone. But he was fuming himself and rang Rhys Mwyn the next day to tell him as much. Andy had arranged the gig through Rhys, so the North Walian who had missed the gig, copped the flak.

'Yes, I had a call from a distraught Andy Barding saying 'Oi, what happened with them?' He wasn't happy.'

Rhys had said that 'Mark, Paul and Dafydd were experienced gig-wise, they were strengths in that sense. They knew the ropes and weren't going to fall apart if the monitors weren't working. They had wise heads on stage. You had a band who could hack it.'

But that night at TJs, even if Carlos Santana and Eric Clapton had drunk as much as Catatonia they too would have sounded like a dirgey pub rock band.

The peripheral byproducts of being a rock 'n' roll band were important to them. Like the proverbial kids holding shop assistants hostage in a sweet shop, they were being offered the world and they were gonna eat it whole. As much as Keith Moon was a demon destroyer, the hedonists' hedonist, he still went on stage and played like the best drummer in the world. Catatonia's excessive zest for excess was causing them to miss the point. You're in a band for the music first and everything else is secondary. Or it should be.

The morning after the night before, there was no rest for the wicked. Cerys had a phone interview to carry out with Steve Duffy, the *South Wales Echo* pop writer. Steve is the brother of Primal Scream's keyboard player Martin Duffy, so he's more than familiar with bands who party like their lives depend on it. Steve's interview with Cerys makes for colourful reading, especially Cerys's confession about their performance the night before.

> Enough has been said about Cerys Anazapela's [Cerys was still using the name that appeared on the *For Tinkerbell* sleeve] wispy voice. As we speak this April morning it's particularly fragile. But nothing apparently that a foaming glass of resolve can't cure. 'I've got a terrible hangover. We got really wrecked at TJs in Newport,' she laughs painfully. 'We were playing really late and we'd all had a bit too much to drink, and we were crap, it was a bit of a disaster. We're supposed to be playing a session on the Mal Pope show on Radio Wales tonight, and that's live!'

Luckily, they did play the session and despite their monster hangovers it went so well that Mal Pope (an old Welsh musician who plays in Max Boyce's band and managed to somehow wrangle a radio show) wrote about how much he liked the band in his column in the Swansea-based *Evening Post*.

MRM PEOPLE

Catatonia had two weeks until their crucial London gigs, ample time for them to rehearse, play a few more gigs, do a bit more promotional work and regain what momentum may have been lost in the alcoholic haze of TJs.

They played a gig at the Feathers pub in Aberaeron, West Wales on Saturday, 9 April, were interviewed on the BBC Radio Wales *Revolution* programme on Friday, 15th, played Sam's Bar in Cardiff on Tuesday, 19th, and were interviewed on *Hwyrach* on BBC Radio Cymru on Sunday, 24th. The next night they travelled up to London for two of the most important gigs of their career.

The music industry was out in force again at the band's gig at the Tufnell Park Dome. There were some newer faces in the crowd, noticeably Rough Trade's legendary head honcho Geoff Travis. Rough Trade was a renowned indie label that had made its name in the Eighties by signing The Smiths. Geoff knew Richard and Martin well and had released an album on Rough Trade by the MRM managed Ultramarine, 1992's *Every Man And Woman Is A Star*. He was more importantly a fan of the emerging Welsh bands and had also shown interest in The 60ft Dolls.

The band played a great set, which was sweet relief after the disastrous TJs gig. This set them up nicely for the second-leg of this London play-off supporting Ultramarine at Brunel University in North London.

Catatonia knew this was to be a big weekend in their career, but if they were nervous, apprehensive or just plain scared, they didn't show it. This was a band who, when they got it together on the night, were peerless. They wanted success – to ensure they escaped the dole queue that was Mark and Cerys's reality until they started to build up their bulk of UK gigs and start to earn a litle money. And that night they played like the world was theirs for the taking.

Both Richard Lowe and Martin Patton were entranced by the band's cool pop exotica and skewed melodic visions. Immediately after the gig they told the band they wanted to manage them. The band duly agreed. The Catatonia machine had moved up a gear.

To celebrate their management deal the band travelled to Bristol the following day to play a Conal Dodds promoted show at the Bristol Fleece and Firkin. During the day they had recorded a euphoric live session for *Loaded*, BBC Radio Bristol's youth culture programme.

And it was with the youngsters that the band stuck the following day, when they literally went back to school. Ysgol Dyffryn Teifi is situated in West Wales, in the town of Llandysul. It sits on the River Teifi and is a place of outstanding natural beauty. When the Welsh-language music scene was at its strongest, many of the bands used to play at Welsh-speaking schools as a way of promoting the language in a cool, accessible medium. Catatonia's gig at the school was set up by Rhys through contacts he had made when touring with Anrehfn. Catatonia headlined a bill that included two local bands, Bronwen and Ensyniadau. The poster for the show is pure DIY fanzine. Written in felt tip and badly photocopied, it illustrates a band revisiting a scene that they were about to leave behind forever.

It wasn't just these off-the-cuff gigs they would no longer be playing. Now they had proper management, the roles of their support group, Iestyn George, Huw Williams and Rhys Mwyn would no longer be needed in such an involved way. While both Iestyn and Huw were more than happy about this – Huw was managing The 60ft Dolls and Iestyn was full-time on the

NME – Rhys was about to feel the full force of the new management's involvement. And he wasn't going to like it.

'At the time MRM came in we were planning the promotion and release of "Hooked",' explains Rhys. 'However, we had extreme difficulty co-ordinating it because MRM had just started working with the band and had their own ideas about their developement. We were left with a second single and a band not available to promote it. MRM wouldn't supply a release date, so in the end we just put it out.'

Rhys admits that he could almost understand the management wanting a clean slate and not having to deal with himself and Crai.

He adds, 'I was absolutely aware that the band were going to get a deal and that we wouldn't be working together forever and I was absolutely supportive of it. When it started to take off I wished them all the best and I meant it genuinely. I said get a million in the bank, tour the world and love it. I knew I wasn't going to be part of that deal so fine. I didn't have any hidden agenda. We were just the label that developed the band initially.

'Every record company, every management company tries to make money out of these things. All labels like Sub-Pop, and Wiiija, survive on selling records, and Crai is just the same. We sold "For Tinkerbell" and "Hooked" because they are great records. These are not some shitty demos that we were aiming to make a quick buck out of, so MRM's legal letters seemed a bit excessive to us. All they had to do was call!'

PLAYING HOOKY

'It was a very luxuriant, great record but it was never fully accepted,' says Rhys of 'Hooked'.

'It was a bit more quirky, a bit more leftfield than "For Tinkerbell". However, despite not garnering another Single Of The Week, *NME* were dazzled yet again by Catatonia. This time the paper drew comparisons between the band and absent kings of Manchester The Stone Roses. Young *NME* staffer John Harris was reviewing the singles and he wrote of the three tracks:

> Taffoid oddbods Catatonia start whispering a song that's as fragile and delightful (and slightly more redolent of Belly), before tumbling into a chorus that betrays their love of garish beat-pop, as minted by The Stone Roses; so large segments of 'Hooked' come over like 'Standing Here' or 'Mersey Paradise' rendered by rural innocents. It is incidentally, nigh-on marvellous. Furthering the point, 'Fall Beside Her' is the ghost of Spike Island resurrected and dressed in white robes: all spooky keyboard effects, angelic vocals and overwhelming urge to dance like a heroin-addicted retard with a loosely-packed cigarette and triangular trousers. 'Difrychwelyd', we can safely assume is Welsh for 'rather

> inadvisable and indulgent third track that world can comfortably live without'. But stuff it. There is currently a Ready Brek-like aura of ecstasy around the review room because 1) we have a new genre (etherio-baggy, or something); and 2) only the faintest memory of the Wee Papas remains. Huzzah.

Despite their attempt at pigeonholing and their amazing dismissal of the stupendously beautiful 'Difrychwelyd' – with its gorgeous, spine-tingling backwards guitar and spooky French vocals – the *NME* weren't far wrong. 'Hooked' was a record that flooded the senses with its ethereal atmospherics and was blissfully euphoric with its waves of crystal guitarlines. 'Fall Beside Her' was littered with eerie and unusual sounds and 'Difrychwelyd', a murmuring heartbeat of ghostly loveliness.

John Harris obviously had unearthed the fact that here was a band that transcended pigeonholes, but who were more than adept at such an early juncture in their career at producing songs of such ornate splendour. And he wasn't the only one who thought so. The kids were getting Catatonia as well! The band had built up a massive following in Wales, especially among Welsh-speaking teenagers who had made sure that the *For Tinkerbell* EP had sold out of its first pressing, 1000 copies, before it was even released!

A review of 'Hooked' by teenage critic Owen Hughes in the *North Wales Weekly News* nails 'Hooked' perfectly. The review reads:

> This whole record creates an eerily soft musical atmosphere. The brainchild of Catatonia, a Cardiff five-piece formed from the remains of the Llanrwst-based Cyrff boys, the slow indie style of this three-track CD is moody but mellow. The backing mixture of strings, drums and keyboards is tuned into a complete package with the biting vocals of female singer Cerys, whose soft Celtic accent cuts to great impact. It favours comparisons with Bjork or The Cranberries singer Dolores O'Riordan. The first two songs, 'Hooked' and 'Fall Beside Her', are played out in English and scream a distinctive excellence. The third track is a ballad sung in Welsh and titled 'Difrychwelyd'. But bilingual soon becomes trilingual when a splash of French is added – a strange concept. This release is more evidence of current talent in Wales and you shouldn't need any persuasion to go out and pick this one up – I'll spare you a corny pun on the title!

The reviews were again billowing with praise. So, two euphoric singles then, and some equally joyous press cuttings to match. Whatever the respective arguments that MRM had with Crai, there was no doubt that Rhys Mwyn and his label had given the band a remarkable launching pad to fulfil their ambitions. But if the band thought they would have a smooth passage into the exclusive realms of pop's hinterland, they were to be mistaken.

SPLIT DECISION?

Photographer Rolant Dafis, who had taken the first pictures of Mark and Cerys when they were still Sweet Catatonia, accompanied the band on their next dates after the Llandysul school gig. These shows at Southampton Joiners Arms on Wednesday, 4 May and London Garage on Thursday, 5 May were some of the first gigs after the management had come on board. But the atmosphere was anything but celebratory. Rolant admits that incredibly the band were very close to splitting up.

'I was sitting in a pub in Kentish Town in the afternoon of the Garage gig with Daf, Paul and Clancy,' he explains. 'Basically the general feeling was that MRM were concentrating too much on Mark and Cerys. The others felt as if they were being pushed out. Meetings were held with just Mark and Cerys, without the others involved. I think Paul, Daf and Clancy thought that the management saw them as expendable, and that they were going to be replaced.'

With Mark and Cerys the main songwriters, the management stood guilty of mollycoddling their star charges without paying too much attention to the rest of the band. When new people come into any situation, they like to stamp their authority and MRM were obviously making their presence felt.

The situation was finally resolved after the others made their feelings known to Mark and Cerys; however the trio's suspicions were closer to the facts than they had realised.

This was a testing time for everybody. The two Englishmen who had taken on the task of managing this über Welsh band were about to be uncomfortably indoctrinated into their wild Welsh drinking ways.

Backstage after the Garage gig, a swarm of party-loving Welsh friends had descended on the band's dressing room, led by chief hedonist Rhys Ifans.

'MRM looked a little lost,' laughs Rolant. 'Rhys Ifans was conducting the riotous assembly backstage and everyone was babbling away in Welsh. I don't think they quite understood the Welsh psyche and our ability to drink. They were a little shocked by it all.'

What was needed was a break away from London's excesses, an escape to somewhere that would re-energise the band. So what better than a French mini-tour. From 11 May until 17 May, Catatonia played small bars and clubs in Brittany and Nantes. The dates had been set up by Rhys Mwyn, through contacts he already had there and new ones he had picked up through a great review of *For Tinkerbell* that had appeared in France's leading music magazine *Les Inkoruptibles*. The band played five dates, including an open-affair festival in Brest, and recorded a radio session for Radio Nantes.

'I know they had a great time in France,' explains Rhys. 'It was all valuable experience for them. You know things like this are exciting when you're just starting out. They're what makes it all worthwhile.'

Suitably refreshed and raring to go, the band returned to the UK for their first major support tour with Salad. The dates, at Reading After Dark (29 June), St Helens Citadel (30 June), Middlesbrough Arena (1 July), Birmingham Edwards (3 July), Bournemouth Hothouse (5 July), Cardiff Clwb Ifor Bach (8 July) and Northampton Roadmenders (9 July), were all promoted by MCP and promoter Conal Dodds accompanied them throughout, buying the riders and generally looking after the band.

'They were rough diamonds basically,' he says. 'They definitely had something – Cerys was a very charismatic front person. They were still big drinkers, I never saw them without a drink in their hand. I'd give them 12 cans, and they probably asked for another 12 quite quickly. But they were young and exciting, charged with energy and enthusiasm!'

Catatonia also played at the Cnapan Festival in Wales on 2 July. It was memorable because Rhys had to get Cerys into the gig as the security didn't know who she was. Added to this Catatonia made a welcome return to the Splash Club as support to Sleeper at the Water Rats, where they blew loud-mouthed Louise Wener and her band of faceless Sleeper blokes off stage. After the Cnapan gig, that was the last time Rhys would see Catatonia for a few years. All the gigs he had arranged had now come to an end and so had his working relationship with the band.

'It was sad, but you work with bands, then you don't work with bands,' he says philosophically.

In later years Rhys would receive a platinum disc from the band as a thank you for all the hard work that he had done to launch their career. Years had passed but they evidently never forgot his industrious efforts for them.

So as one chapter was closing another was just beginning. Catatonia were not yet the finished article and MRM had their own ideas about how the band should be. This though would cause friction within the Cat's ranks and cause the inevitable departure of band members.

7
Having a Whale of a Time!

'YOU SHOULD HAVE LEARNT BY NOW . . .'

Oxford Street in London is one of the world's busiest streets. Millions of curious tourists and eager shoppers walk along its famous pavements each year. The few pubs dotted along this world-renowned address are some of the most lucrative hostelries in the UK. These watering holes are more than used to serving up hundreds of pints by the hour.

But in the summer of 1994 sales records for pubs saw a marked upturn in fortune. Not really surprising. Catatonia were in town and there was drinking to be done! Of course, there was also the little matter of recording demos for EMI publishing and working with their first bona fide producer. But with all things Catatonia, work and pleasure went very much hand in hand.

Now that MRM management, Martin Patton and Richard Lowe, were on board, the good ship Catatonia was being resolutely steered towards music business success. Their first port of call was EMI Publishing's demo studios, just off Oxford Street. The band had been invited to record some demos after EMI Publishing's Tony Smith had seen them play at a recent London gig. He liked what he heard and wanted to hear more.

It's common practice for publishing companies to invite bands who they have an interest in to lay down tracks as a way of developing their interest and to monitor how the band they have seen live translate to the studio. The recording studios usually demo bands to a 16-track and eight-track. Catatonia had just finished a successful tour with Salad, where the headline band's woeful musical deficiencies were swept away by Catatonia's elegiac agenda. They were on a high and rightly so.

MRM had moved quickly to bring their own producer in to work with the band at EMI's demo studios. Paul Sampson was the man entrusted by MRM to get the most out of the band. From Coventry Paul was himself a musician and producer. He had played on and produced many of the great songs penned by The Primitives, the colourful late Eighties indie pop band. The Prims were leading lights of the spurious, music press generated 'Blonde' movement by dint of the colour of their singer Tracy Tracy's hair.

That scene also included Newport's equally blonde singer Andrea and her band The Darling Buds. Both bands' energetic buzzsaw tunes and rampant bubblegum melodies weren't a million miles removed from what Catatonia were doing, although there was more depth and vulnerability to Catatonia's repertoire.

Paul Sampson had also produced many projects and releases commissioned by MRM – a resolutely ethereal, inspirational and experimental set of musicians including Ultramarine, Kevin Ayers (the former member of Seventies cult avant-gardeists Soft Machine), David McAlmont, The Playthings and the wonderful, but wholly underrated Band of Holy Joy. TBOHJ were pioneers of a swaggering English urban folk sound, free of guitars, which brought frequent comparisons to their Irish counterparts The Pogues. Their songs were uplifting and optimistic, a call-to-arms against the oppressions of Thatcherism.

'If you hunt out any of these obscure releases, you will discover them to be works of art, poetry and music rather than pure works of pop,' says Paul Sampson. 'Catatonia's music opened wide doors in my commercial music inspiration and, looking back, MRM hooking them up with me fired up a soulful chemistry.'

Paul and the band connected on many levels. 'A major link was my arrangement and production work with guitars and blonde girl band The Primitives, and engineering and performing on Indian Classical and Bhangra albums. I liked Catatonia's Welsh lyric songs the most at first, even though I had no idea what they were singing about. Like with Indian music, I'm into rhythm and melody no matter what the language. True musical soul can't be hidden.'

Paul remembers the EMI sessions well and that first meeting sticks in his mind. 'MRM arranged for myself and the band to have our first meeting on neutral territory,' he explains. 'This being EMI demo recording studios, we were thrown in together to just come out with whatever happened. I got on with them really well straight away, they seemed similar to me in culture and attitudes.'

Unlike many recording studios where sessions invariably don't start until late morning and carry on until the middle of the night, EMI's premises had more orthodox opening times.

'Considering the studios are just off Oxford Street, the studio hours open and close like a village shop,' laughs Paul, 'Something like 10am till 7pm, quite restrictive for musical creativity – yet we still managed to record a number of songs and spent the evenings in the pub.'

The demos recorded included the lilting gentle strum of 'Tourist', the jagged 'Part Of The Furniture', the rip roaring 'Beautiful Sailor', the icy drama of 'Infantile', 'Some Half Baked Idea Called Wonderful' (also known as 'Mickey') a bittersweet vignette about a former housemate of Mark and Cerys, a rugged, reworked 'For Tinkerbell' and the spiky 'Cut You Inside'.

Catatonia were never a band to let anything go to waste. So the tracks recorded at EMI's studio's were all demos of songs that would later appear on early singles and their debut album, and in the case of 'Part Of The Furniture', a song that would appear on the album after that.

'Some pieces evolved into later titles and were reworked for future releases,' explains Paul. Although they were being lumped in with the Sleepers and Echobellys, they always had more substance than those bands. Mark and Cerys wrote great songs and she had a unique voice.

'They also had a refreshing honesty and unimpressedness with the whole music business, which I liked,' he adds. 'They had a great sense of humour and, of course, they worked and created with total efficiency!'

Although these sessions reaffirmed the band's undoubted ability, EMI didn't take the option to sign the band. But these were cautious times and cheque books weren't being wielded haphazardly by either record companies or publishers. In any case, Catatonia now had a set of stunning demos which, alongside their equally amazing releases for Crai, formed a powerful portfolio which they could use to hook themselves a recording contract.

DEPARTURE LOUNGE

Before any thoughts of that recording contract could enter their heads there was a stark task for Catatonia to undertake. MRM wanted Clancy out of the band, and Cerys was the one who had to break the news. There was the possibility of the management informing Clancy, but the band didn't think this would be right, after all she was their close friend.

It was becoming all too apparent from live performances that Clancy just didn't fit the bill. The band didn't gel with her on stage, and her musical skills, or the lack thereof, weren't adding anything to their sound.

The warning signs had been seen at the earlier Garage gig in London when Cerys and Mark had their own meeting with MRM, without their bass player, drummer and keyboardist. MRM didn't feel the band could go on in their present form. It needed to be reshaped because a keyboard player didn't fit the image.

Iestyn George recalls a conversation he had with Cerys and Mark much to the effect of telling them that in his opinion Clancy just didn't fit in. 'They didn't look right, there was no reason musically for Clancy to be there,' he says. 'I actively said that Clancy was a bad idea. While they had someone plonking away in a haphazard manner they weren't going to get signed.'

After the frayed episode of the 'nearly split' before the Garage gig in London a couple of months previously, relations in the band were slightly ragged. It was as if they knew something would give, and unfortunately it was Clancy who was to take the brunt of the management's tough decision.

Although Crai's Rhys Mwyn parted company with the band a few weeks before, he had to deal with strained phone calls from two upset women within hours of each other. Cerys called him first to seek advice because she was distraught at what she had to do, then this was followed hours later by an equally upset Clancy wanting to pour her heart out to Rhys after being informed. Rhys admits it was difficult for him because although he was flattered that they sought to confide in him, he wasn't working with them any more.

'Cerys phoned and it was really out of the blue,' remembers Rhys. 'And she told me she had to tell Clancy she was no longer in the band. Cerys wanted advice, you know it's not an easy job having to do something like that, because Clancy didn't expect to be out. She had been in the band for over a year and although she might have had an inkling, you don't expect it to happen.

'I felt sorry for Cerys – it put her in a difficult position,' he adds. 'I just told her that this is what you get with London-based managers, they're more ruthless. This was slightly tongue-in-cheek, but I knew that they [MRM] wanted to iron out any rough edges and they saw Clancy as a rough edge. I just said that these things happen in the music industry. I mean what else could I say?'

Paul Sampson saw for himself first hand how hard it was for Cerys and the rest to break the news. 'To be honest I think it was difficult for them to stop working with her because she was a friend,' he says. 'I remember Paul saying that he sat with her and comforted her. He was like her best mate. What was hard was that she was a friend and they were all nice people. Okay, she wasn't really that competent a keyboard player, because Mark and Cerys could probably play keyboards better than her in the studios. So I think it was one of those cases where she was close to them and it's hard to have to tell a friend something that difficult.'

Rhys answered a harrowing phonecall from a suitably broken Clancy. 'She phoned me about 20 minutes after Cerys's call,' he explains. 'She was really upset, she was saying that she didn't have a choice, she had to leave. Obviously I really felt for her. I offered my sympathy but it was difficult. I could only try and gee her up. I said that she shouldn't take it personally and that that was London management companies for you, they aren't worth bothering with, they're all cut throat bastards! You know the sort of thing. I was trying to think of how to help her get through it. It wasn't easy for her to handle. One minute you're in the band and looking forward, the next your history is cut short.'

She didn't take it well and retreated to Cardiff in a state of distress. It must have been doubly hard for her given that her friends were Catatonia's friends and they all hung out at the same places. For a few years there was a strained relationship between the two parties. According to those involved in the Cardiff-based Welsh-language scene Clancy's departure from Catatonia was something you just didn't talk to her about. When she formed her new band, a punky Welsh-language outfit called Crac (meaning 'angry' in Welsh), the subject was taboo among journalists who interviewed them. She refused to talk about it.

You could understand Clancy's anguish. Think of The Beatles' ousted drummer Pete Best or the girl that left The Spice Girls before they became famous and you think, 'Well, it must have been doubly difficult for them watching them travelling the world, living the rock 'n' roll dream and gaining so much success.' It's just human nature to feel slightly bitter about it, and let's face it, who wouldn't?

Clancy's new band Crac, co-incidentally, featured the frenetic talents of Frog, the drummer from legendary Welsh punkers U-Thant who had featured on Mark and Cerys's very first recordings as Sweet Catatonia at Grassroots in Cardiff. It was an interview with Crac by Rebecca Burns for the Virtual Cardiff website in February 1999 that maybe hinted at Clancy becoming used to her past, with a dismissiveness of what had happened to her. 'It's really weird because I don't aspire to being a pop star,' she told Rebecca. 'I used to. If you'd asked me three or four years ago I'd have said "I want to be number one and be a pop star" but I've seen it actually happening to people I know, and then you know how little it means. It's not me, either.'

One member down they might have been, yet it was seemingly business as usual as August saw the Cats and Paul Sampson laying down tracks in another studio.

Another selection of songs was recorded at Fishco studios in North London. The band were firmly in the manor of the Nutty Boys, as the studio was used by Eighties ska heroes Madness.

'We were looking to release something at the time. Although there was nothing firm planned there were a few things in the offing,' explains Paul. 'We got a free day at Fishco through MRM setting it up through a contact they had.' So in one day the band recorded demo versions of 'Lost Cat', 'This Boy Can't Swim', 'Painful', 'Dream On' and 'Bleed' – again another batch of demo songs that would end up as singles or on the band's debut album. And it was a clutch of songs that aptly illustrated the band's freehanded versatility. On the one extreme there was the crunching, pop punk of 'Bleed', a vicious scything stormer, and on the other there was the luxuriant netherworld of 'Dream On' – a bilingual song that twinkled as brightly as a stellar constellation.

'From this and the EMI sessions we selected the tracks to arrange and record for public consumption,' explains Paul.

And if they were waiting for some kind of deal to facilitate a release they didn't have to wait long. In fact just a matter of days. Rough Trade's legendary music industry svengali Geoff Travis had seen the Cats play at Tufnell Park Dome earlier in the year and desperately wanted them to record a single for his Rough Trade Singles Club – a limited edition 7″ vinyl-only release.

Popular among collectors and indie aficionados, the release would allow the band increased exposure in the music press and give them the opportunity to reinforce their ever burgeoning reputation.

Plus they were to release a record on the famous Rough Trade label. Not a bad bit of business, all in all.

MAKING A SPLASH

Rough Trade is one of those legendary record labels that will forever be charted in the annals of rock history as the label that signed and nurtured The Smiths. The label actually started as the Rough Trade shop which first opened in 1976 in Kensington Park Road in Notting Hill, London. Originally intended to reflect the owners' interests in the US and Jamaican music scene of the time, the shop quickly became one of the many focus points for the rapidly expanding UK punk movement.

In the next couple of years Rough Trade expanded into a distributor and a record company, distributing early Factory releases and releasing records by new wave pioneers The Swell Maps, Raincoats and Stiff Little Fingers, among others.

By 1982 the rapid expansion combined with what can best be described as 'business problems' led to the shop and the record-label side of the business splitting in two, independent of each other.

Rough Trade Distribution and the label continued to expand during the Eighties, especially with the arrival of The Smiths and the dynamic song-writing coalition of Morrissey and Johnny Marr. The band's subsequent huge success, evidenced by their chart hits and slavishly devoted fans, made Geoff Travis's name in the UK music industry.

But in the early Nineties it all went badly wrong. Rough Trade Distribution collapsed, taking the label and publishing companies with it. However, to keep the name alive Geoff had set up the Rough Trade singles club to promote new young bands and stay true to the ideals that the label was originally born with.

Catatonia were well used to the indie way of life, having released limited edition releases on Crai. They were establishing a fine reputation for their fiery live performances and astute pop sensibilities and Geoff Travis loved that:

'They are quite unique,' said Travis at the time. 'What stands out is the quality songwriting and Cerys's voice, which has real soul. I first saw them at a gig in Tufnell Park when they had a keyboard player. They were less coherent then, and I think their new work demonstrates the virtues of playing a lot.'

After recording 12 demo songs in two studios in the space of a couple of weeks, there was no time to spare as they found themselves heading for the East Midlands and a third studio to record their Rough Trade single. Paul is from Coventry and when he recorded with The Primitives he had worked out of a local recording studio called the Cabin that he knew like the back of his hand, but with more buttons and faders! It was the ideal studio for Catatonia to record their 'rushed' opus.

'We didn't have much time,' remembers Paul. 'Geoff Travis's Rough Trade singles club really wanted to release something quickly by the band. As it was recorded in August and released in September 1994 no time could really be taken over the recording.'

The single chosen was the lustrous pop rush that was 'Whale' and the B-side was the equally thrilling if slightly more heavyweight 'You Can', also commonly known as 'Message' during live performances. Don't ask me why, Catatonia just loved to have two or three different titles for a song.

'We never had time to properly mix and tweeze the song,' says Paul. 'Hence the final release of those songs are the monitor mixes we quickly did for reference at the end of that week's session. Trainspotters of the band will have already noticed Cerys giggling on the end chorus, when she sings "I blew it."'

Before 'Whale' was released, the band didn't have time to catch their breath, as their recording stints were interspersed with live gigs. As training for rigorous schedules they were going to have to endure later on in their career, this was solid experience.

The most famous of the gigs at this time was a show on 27 August at the Manchester Roadhouse. The gig at the smoky 250 capacity venue was a landmark for the band, their first live review in the *NME*.

The music paper's north-west stringer Emma Morgan was part of the packed crowd that night. The band's reputation had started to build after the critical rave reviews of 'For Tinkerbell' and 'Hooked'. As reviews go, it's a masterstroke of invention and humorous praise.

> So Phil Spector's strolling down Rodco Drive, right? And he's thinking 'I'm right cheesed off with bloomin' California', so he pops down to Hogg Robinson and books a flight to somewhere totally different. Having thus arrived in Wales, he's listening to some Beatles tracks and ponders whether he could pull off the old 'wall-of-sound-meets-fab-four-riffola' scam again. And he decides that, yes, perhaps he could, but seeing as how John, Paul, Luke and Ken aren't hanging around together anymore, he'll have to find some new angle.
>
> Perusing the racks of the local alternative vinyl emporium for inspiration, Old Phil espies a crinkly-edged copy of 'Star' by Belly, which he plays to death,

until he hits upon the idea of having a velvet-throated yet hard-rockin' female singer for his new beat combo. 'Zowie!', he cries, 'The future of rock is in my hands!' So he puts a card in the newsagent's window and waits . . .

. . . Or something like that, anyway, because there can't be a simpler reason why a band like Catatonia can suddenly appear, with their effortlessly cool-yet-tight rhythm section (cue insistent wobbly basslines and Grohl-indebted drumming), the most rounded hooklines this side of Elastica's record collection, and all the 'La la la' singalongs that were too giddy to make it on to 'Parklife'.

It would seem that the future of Welsh Rock is not in such dire straits as the Manics rumours would have us believe. So ring out the bells and tell Shirley Bassey the news.

With an ecstatic review and a newly recorded single under their belt, any friction caused by the departure of Clancy had long since been forgotten as the band could seemingly do no wrong. Yet, there was unbelievably even better news to come. When that third single, 'Whale' hit the record shops in the first week of September 1994, it was a sell-out. It also had the music press again slavering over their over-worked thesauruses for apt analogies to ably pin down the Catatonia sound.

It all seemed so easy. Whatever the reason – it could easily have just been Iestyn George ruling his fellow journalists at the *NME* with a rod of iron, or maybe just that the staff were in love with this feisty Welsh woman and her band's white knuckle ride social habits – 'Whale' garnered them yet another *NME* Single Of The Week. The *NME* review enthused:

Among the pick of the crop of this week's guitar bands, Catatonia stand head and shoulders above the rest – by virtue of their effortless grace alone. 'Whale' is a breathy pop classic, loose-limbed and groovy even in this rather perfunctory form, displaying a similar reverential regard to the basic delights of melody that you'd find in the work of the brothers Gallagher. Ok, so maybe it's a bit early in the day to be bandying around the Oasis comparisons, but there's at least one great album buzzing around the brains of songwriting partners Cerys and Mark. And their track record thus far ('Tinkerbell' and 'Hooked' having been received with similar enthusiasm within these pages) is promising enough to provoke more than a mild frothing at the mouth, which is always a good sign. Unless you've got rabies.

In customary Catatonia fashion they celebrated with a few drinks or so. 'Well the only reason we come to London is the train ticket costs as much as a night on the piss in Cardiff,' Cerys famously remarked at the time. 'But once we arrive we get all our drinks free, so it works out just as cheap!'

The lyrics of 'Whale' are about blowing a relationship, but they could almost aptly allude to how close to the wind the band sailed and the chances they took with their resolute drinking, excessive hedonism and hardcore rock 'n' roll lifestyle. 'You should know by now . . . disappointment I'd take but there's no point to it I blew it . . . things go wrong and we deny it together . . . you should have learnt by now, that the common thread is taut but it's hard to reflect when your world is sighing . . . I blew it.'

There were some poor live performances that were purely down to their shattered frames being reduced to wrecks by alcohol, but they still managed to pull through. But it was only a matter of time before their irresponsible love of hardcore hedonism would force them to finally make a change. The music press may have been endeared to their celebratory way with an evening out, but record companies were still wary. They knew that the band's reputation could do as much harm as good, so they kept a cautious distance. Yes, they were impressed, but not quite enough to lavish them with a lucrative financially rewarding, house-in-the-country-securing record contract. This, despite the slew of exclamatory reviews that 'Whale' gathered from a variety of published sources, *Time Out* being the pick of the bunch:

> Swirling adrenalin guitars duel with warped world-weary harmonies to knicker-wetting effect. Catatonia are a) from Cardiff b) unfeasibly ace c) about to become bigger than Godzilla's piles.. I've strapped myself to the Clairol footspa for the entire weekend with only this humble seven-inch for thrills. Furthermore, Catatonia's singer is called Cerys. You don't know how happy this makes me!'

Even *Melody Maker* had finally caught up with the fuss. Once the *Maker* had started their adulatory approach to the band they apparently couldn't stop. Almost two weeks after *NME*'s live review, *Melody Maker* were about to reward the Cats with their first live review in their hallowed pages. Freelance writer Victoria Segal had her pen and pad primed and ready at Catatonia's next show after Manchester – a third visit in a year to the Water Rats for another show with Fin, the band they had played with on their first outing at the pub on Grays Inn Road.

The review was great but the paper's sub-editors were probably shot that week. First, the heading has Catatonia playing with 'Fly', and Cerys is referred to throughout the review as Carys. But who cares when the review reads as positively as this.

> Are you 'bored, curious and unsure'? Then watch out, because Catatonia have designs on you. They want to get you dolled-up, drunk and into big trouble. There's loads going on for them, most of it beginning and ending with singer Carys [sic!] who, with her silver boots and sunglasses and the sort of confidence

> that could be activated as an intergalactic defence shield, shines brightest. And her voice! You could lure small children into cars with it. It's a voice that grabs the dizzy, staggering punk pop swirl and forces it on before it pales and faints away. 'You Can' is gorgeous on every count though, Carys sounding like she's pleading for her life through gritted teeth while the music hurtles around with increasing desperation. More songs like this and they're away. Expect quite good things soon, here's hoping.

Although at this stage Catatonia's press and PR was still being handled by MRM, the band was harvesting column inches as if they were going out of fashion. The music press gossip columns were the first port of call for aspirant pop superstars. The *NME*'s PublicNME and *Melody Maker*'s Rumour Mill were the main source of rumour-mongering, spinning out spurious stories that invariably involved tales of hedonistic high-jinks in excelsis. However it is worth noting that these tales were renowned for their flexibility – bending the truth as efficiently as a government spin doctor.

However, Catatonia humorously bypassed the conventional route for their first two music press stories, which were two tales of confrontational wonder. By now the band were making regular trips to London by train. On one such occasion, the band was slumped in the buffet car, when they started an argument with the train's conductor about the validity of youth revolution. The conductor was an old punk who was evidently still coming to terms with selling-out his nihilistic 1977 principles by taking a job with (the then) British Rail. He was so disgusted by the band's stance against his hackneyed punk views that he threw them off at Swindon! That was famously gossip story number one.

Their second entry in the hallowed halls of gossip centred around Catatonia's next gig after the Water Rats show. This time the band was supporting Banglesey Oz pop exponents, the subtly melodic Clouds, on 16 September at Camden Underworld. Alongside the Dublin Castle, the Monarch and the Falcon, the Underworld is another of the Camden triangles essential indie gigs. Essentially a pub-cum-venue, located directly opposite Camden Town tube station, it's slightly larger than the other venues and has two levels. As with most London gigs the band had all afternoon to ponder the night's performance over a beer or 17. Subsequently, they were suitably well-oiled when they arrived at the venue. They played the gig, but as they were clearing away one of the bouncers seemed to take exception to the band speaking Welsh and a row ensued. Cerys was at the forefront of haranguing the bouncer who obviously didn't know what he was letting himself in for. As a result of the rumpus, Catatonia were banned from the Camden Underworld for swearing at the bouncers in Welsh!

'They should have sworn at them in English, then they wouldn't have understood,' quipped the *NME* at the time.

TALKIN' THE TALK, WALKIN' THE WALK

Mark and Cerys had always had a love of The Stone Roses, the magical Manchester group that revolutionised the music scene at the start of the Nineties with their eponymous debut album. The Roses pulled no punches and were an unstoppable force as the Nineties swung into full view. A hybrid mix of supercharged arrogance, spat out by simian like singer Ian Brown and magical psychedelic pop conjured up by guitarist John Squire; their music spun on a funky axis courtesy of their watertight rhythm unit, bass player Mani and drummer Reni.

There were many early comparisons between the two groups. Journalists sketched a portrait of Catatonia as 'an otherworldly Stone Roses' and of 'transporting the Roses' Madchester sound into altogether eerier territory'.

But it didn't stop there, the band were warming to their role as chief hedonistic flag bearers for the Welsh music scene, a scene that had been criminally ignored for as long as the words 'criminally' and 'ignored' had been resident in the Oxford English Dictionary. Along with the equally party-loving 60ft Dolls, who were firing up their own press outrage with tales of histrionic rock 'n' roll behaviour, they blazed a trail for Wales, and in no uncertain terms announced their arrival on the British music scene. The dragon had reawakened. Confidence, or the lack of, has always been a factor for the Welsh race, but now here was a scene and groups that were charged with energy and who really didn't give a flying fuck what anyone thought of them. As far as they were concerned it was payback time.

That confidence was oozing out of Catatonia like molten lava when they were interviewed for *NME* by John Harris for their first major music press interview.

Like boxers trapped in a corner they came out fighting, jabbing furiously and landing their verbal punches with furious ease. They were relishing the fight.

'Echobelly, These Animal Men, Sleeper, all those groups . . . they've got the gift of the gab, they know what to say, they live in the right places. But you put their records on and you're fucking disappointed. Every time. You're not going to go back and listen to them in ten months, let alone ten years. People are wasting their money. It's all full of shit.'

Cerys was in the backroom of a London pub when she shouted these words into Harris's tape recorder. He might have seen similar cocky confidence before, but he was easily impressed by their raging Welsh singer. Here's his vivid description of Cerys:

> Cerys, apparently the product of a freakish experiment in which cells scraped from Tanya Donnelly (Throwing Muses, Belly) were mixed with a toxic residue taken from Lou Reed circa 1972. She's prone to sound like a washed-up fairy –

replete with deliciously cracked voice – and she manages to carry herself with all the broken glamour of a messed-up East Village barfly. This, for a twenty-something dole-ite from Cardiff, is no mean achievement.

The key to these interviews was securing the backing of music press journalists who got it, who understood completely how the band operated and what they were about. And Harris got it straight away. He knew they were leagues ahead of the female-fronted bands with whom his lazy colleagues had lumped Catatonia. There was so much more to Catatonia than the empty style over substance of their rivals. Harris observed:

> Catatonia have tunes that steal the trick of simultaneously sounding both sweet and sneakingly evil from the Velvet Underground. Others (like brilliant new single 'Whale') that bravely pioneer a new genre – 'etherio-baggy' (Wah-hay! Yes! Flaregazing! – Ed), at the last guess – based on launching the ghost of The Stone Roses into territory that's eerie other-worldy; and a handsome clutch that escape any stereotyping at all, simply leaving you befuddled . . . enchanted.

As an exact assessment of their talent and songwriting ability, John Harris was right on the money. Of course, Mark and Cerys didn't have to be told. They were swaggering with the confidence of two people certain of their beliefs in their ability. 'We've got great songs basically,' said Cerys in the *NME* interview.

'When our debut album comes out,' added Mark. 'It'll have every sort of sound on it. And I'm not talking about orchestras, that's the usual thing. I'm talking about a record that'll be better than The Stone Roses. I think we can do that.'

On recorded evidence Mark Roberts wasn't wrong. Their songs rang true with unbridled variety and musical innovation. They had lyrics that plunged into the murky waters of relationships and everyday heartbreak, while consuming the listener with bewitching melodies and a singer whose beautiful voice was simply not of this world.

'Deep breaths, then, the world will soon be theirs. Probably.' John Harris's hopeful conclusion summed up Catatonia perfectly. As much as they oozed confidence and held supreme belief, their inconsistent flashes of brilliance live still counted against them. The band believed they would break through, MRM believed their group were good enough and the critics hoped it would happen. Now it was up to the fickle music industry to decide.

CITY LIFE

Every year the industry's movers and shakers decamp to the hotels and bars of Manchester for the 'In the City' music seminar. It's a five-day, five-night music industry beano where

> three thousand CEOs, musicians, vice-presidents, MDs, lawyers, producers, TV execs, accountants, promoters, A&Rs, pluggers, managers, radio programmers, publishers, DJs, distributors, agents, journalists and the brightest gonabees in Europe talk music and do real business.

That's according to the official poster blurb anyway.

As a shop window for a new band it's an invaluable way to put your name in the frame for a record deal. You do though have to be invited. Thousands of tapes flood into the 'In the City' offices months before the event, and out of these, bands are invited to perform at the 'In the City' unsigned bands event. At its basic level it's a glorified battle of the bands with a cash prize at the end for the band to be adjudged as the most promising. At its best, it allows you to perform in front of the most 'important' people in the music industry.

Catatonia, and a contingent of new Welsh bands, Gorky's Zygotic Mynci, Novocaine and The 60ft Dolls, ensured that 'In the City '94' was the year of the Welsh band. Journalists had had a field day inventing the New Wave Of New Wave scene, but at 'In the City '94' it was the Welsh bands that held their gaze.

While NWONW had faded under the weight of its own hyped expectations, the Welsh bands stamped their arrival with a series of blistering gigs. There were those astute A&Rs that were wising up to Wales, but 'In the City '94' set off an alarm call across the industry. From then on the Welsh music scene just wouldn't be the same again.

Catatonia were in their element. While they took the piss out of the assembled hordes, showing their disdain for the whole music circus with a performance of searing indifference to the A&R heavy crowd, NME neatly informed the music industry's masses that they 'would begin to understand Catatonia if you imagined dream pop as performed by Brix Smith and Sterling Morrison'.

The Cats played with Gorky's and the unsigned event's eventual winners, the ironically soon-to-be forgotten Flinch. Iestyn was in the crowd at Catatonia's gig at Al's Music Cafe in Manchester city centre on 21 September.

'I remember Mary Anne Hobbs [former music journalist and now Radio 1 DJ] saying to me that she thought Cerys was a broken beauty. Mary Anne described her as like Marianne Faithfull, beautiful and tough but looks as if she has lived a little!'

Iestyn remembers that the whole band looked arresting. 'They were dressed quite odd really,' he says. 'It was three or four years after baggy and they were still wearing flares. They seemed to be on a different planet. But they did exude a sort of cool, they weren't over eager to please, like some bands can be. I think the more astute A&Rs who had just started to wake up to Wales liked that.'

After 'In the City' had ended it was a running joke in Newport and Cardiff that you couldn't move at a gig in South Wales before being accosted by a record company representative or an over zealous A&R waving a chequebook. Everybody was about to get lucky. And Newport was the goldmine for those record company prospectors.

Newport is a steel town that's been on the wane for years with high unemployment and low morale. Few tourists come to Newport, only working men from the nearby valleys, looking for a pint, a bird and fight on a weekend night. The locals think that their town is the worst in the world, but conversely it's the perfect breeding ground for a rock scene.

Newport's population in 1994 stood at 137,000, but the town and it surrounding valleys boasted what may have been the world's highest concentration of young, quality rock bands. There were more than 60 of them, led by The 60ft Dolls, Flyscreen, Dub War and Novocaine.

Famously dubbed 'the new Seattle' by American music journalist Neil Strauss, for its dynamic proliferation of powerful guitar bands, Newport and the Welsh scene had exploded into a colourful regenesis.

'I think it was the new Seattle,' says Huw Williams. 'It was exciting because of the bands in Newport and then there was Gorkys, Super Furries and of course Catatonia. I'd never found like-minded people to work with before – there was never any inter-band activity. Things were now germinating and people were working together for the first time.'

Just like Seattle, as Neil Strauss put it, 'before the music industry prised open the cellar flaps of a burgeoning rock underground', people didn't give a shit and there were all these brilliant, uncompromising bands getting signed.

And there were also fanzines, record labels and bands – lots of them. Before this, it was too much like hard work to do anything in Wales, you had to go to London to try and make it. Now the difference was simply astounding. However, if journalists were looking for a common thread between all these musicians there wasn't one. They were all wilfully different, revelling in their own individuality. Despite all the band members coming from the same country there were marked differences between bands from the North and South.

Newport – a predominant bastion of English-speaking Welsh – was spinning on the axis of angry white-boy rock 'n' roll – sounds culled from the council estates that had spawned the Manic Street Preachers. It was the sound of alienation and boredom, a pissed-off vibe that told stories of crime and unemployment. At the other end of the spectrum, bands like the emerging Super Furry Animals and Gorkys Zygotic Mynci – from the Welsh-speaking North – were more artistically obtuse, peddling a more gentle indefinable brand of wilfully different psychedelic pop. Where The 60ft Dolls snarled nihilistically, Gorky's Zygotic Mynci sang about love in sweet falsettos.

Being based in Cardiff, Catatonia embraced both camps. They were both tough and tender, punk and psychedelic. They could rock as hard as a stormy day and radiate the warmth of a hazy summer afternoon. I would have called it schizo-pop, but luckily there were no takers for that particular tag.

After their 'In the City' appearance, the following day brought an invitation to play a set on the show of one of their biggest fans – Mark Radcliffe.

This was the first time the band had actually met Radcliffe after he had set the wheels of their career in motion by playing 'For Tinkerbell' on national radio. They were delighted to meet him and he to meet them. 'I just remember them being dead friendly,' remembers Mark Radcliffe. 'They liked a drink, I could see that because they were all swigging from cans when I met them, but that's all bands for you really. They were funny, relaxed and cracking jokes. Cerys seemed particularly pleased that they were on national radio, in fact they all did. They were just nice down-to-earth people.'

Among the songs they played that night was an acoustic version of 'Whale', that would later appear on *Tourist*, a Japan-only release collecting together early B-sides and demos.

TIME TO SPILL SOME BLOOD

By now London had truly become Catatonia's second home. As an unsigned band it was important for them to play as much as possible. Although it must be said that with the Welsh music scene attracting A&Rs like moths to a flame, just the very fact of their nationality was enough to have record companies sending over half their staff to a Catatonia gig. By now the band were being tracked as closely as fugitives.

A gig with Creation Record's hopefuls Adorable and the long-forgotten but memorably named Chainsaw Kittens at the Marquee in London on 29 September, was previewed by *Time Out* who raved, 'Catatonia jangle and purr in all the right places with Cerys's rather lilting delivery topping off a rather gorgeous pop mixture.' While humorously *The Independent* dubbed the band 'bristle kids from Wales!'

Catatonia were grateful for all the press adulation, but Cerys, who had always wanted Catatonia to be a fully fledged pop band, was especially wary that they didn't get ghettoised with an indie tag. 'If good reviews in the *NME* and the like get people who are not sad indie bastards, in other words, anybody normal(!) to come to our gigs then that's brilliant,' she told *Sun Zoom Spark* fanzine, after the Adorable gig. 'That's why we bother coming all the way to London.'

The constant journeys to London were telling on the band who were wearying of their trips to the English capital. 'Audiences [in London] are just so afraid of themselves,' Cerys explained to the fanzine, before memorably adding. 'Being on stage is like wanking in front of people, if they don't want to join in, you don't want to do it by yourself!'

Luckily respite from London was just at hand as their booking agent Paul Buck had secured them a support slot with The Senseless Things in October.

Included in the tour itinerary was a welcome hometown gig at Cardiff University, as well as first-time trips to Brighton's Pavilion Theatre and Nottingham University. It was a sobering tour for the band (not that they drank any less alcohol). They were seeing at first hand how a band can quickly scale the heights and just as quickly fall down again.

The Senseless Things had been Britain's poppier take on grunge. Their melodious thrash pop sound marked them out as a sort of junior Nirvana. But as grunge had dissipated and a new musical climate was forming, The Senseless Things were becoming irrelevant.

'It was a bit sad really,' said Cerys. 'They were on a downward curve. They were playing these quite big venues and they weren't filling them.' Catatonia were determined that that wasn't going to be them. And that tour would forever stay in their minds as they too made a careful ascent up the music industry ladder.

Despite the hordes of record companies that were regularly in touch with MRM, the band were becoming unsettled at the fact that no concrete offers had yet been made. It was decided that to give them that last push to securing a contract, they should record another single.

So in November, Catatonia reconvened with Paul Sampson at Cabin Studios in Coventry to record their fourth single. 'Bleed' was chosen as the A-side with 'This Boy Can't Swim' and 'Painful' as the B-sides.

'There were actually three studios used for the record,' explains Paul Sampson. 'Bleed' and 'This Boy' were recorded at Cabin Studios and mixed at Berwick Street Studios in London, while 'Painful' is from the Fishco sessions and left unchanged from that recording.

At the same time as the 'Bleed' recording, a new conceptual music magazine called *Volume* approached the band. *Volume* was a publication that also included a cover-mounted CD featuring the bands interviewed in each issue. Now since gone to the conceptual music magazine rack in the sky, it was a great idea at the time. Catatonia readily agreed to be interviewed, and Paul salvaged a demo version of 'Dream On' and quickly remixed it for *Volume*.

'It was an incomplete track recorded at Fishco,' he explains. 'I took the master tape up to Coventry and I finished it off at Cabin. I had to post the mix back the next day and I remember I worked all night because it was a really tight deadline.'

While 'Bleed' was scheduled for release in February 1995, *Volume* hit the newsagents' shelves in December. Catatonia shared the pages of the magazine and its compilation CD with fellow Welsh colleagues Novocaine, as well as the then relatively unknown Spiritualized, Moby, Garbage and Massive Attack.

The interview with *Volume* is revealing for the insights it gives into Mark and Cerys's songwriting partnership.

Like the rest of the music press *Volume* was wholesome in its praise of the band, raving that 'what they do is to craft effortless pop songs that artlessly encourage personal empowerment. Songs like 'You Can' are about balancing fantasy with reality, less about wanting to be adored than learning to respect yourself. It's also the first pop song I've heard that effortlessly incorporates the word "recumbent".'

'We both write the words,' Mark told the *Volume* writer. 'I might come up with a verse, then Cerys'll get hold of it, and she'll change the bits she doesn't like, and, ahem, it'll lose all meaning from what I intended!'

Cerys ignores her boyfriend's sly quip. 'They like it to mean something to them – I do, anyway. I listen to something and think, yeah, I know what you're going on about even if the whole song doesn't make sense. I like to think there's a meaning, even if you have to dig deep.'

1994 was drawing to a close and save another gig in Camden at the Dublin Castle with American pioneer of the lo-fi revolution, Bill Callahan – alias Smog – and a December date at Aberystwyth University, Catatonia's year was winding down nicely. It was a good job they had a few weeks to relax and recharge after a hectic year, because 1995 was shaping up to be momentous in so many extraordinary ways.

Dreams would be fulfilled, working relationships would reach breaking point and they would court controversy at every turn.

8
Beer Here Now

'FASTRISINGBEERSOAKEDRIPROARINGPOPTART!'

Remember when Nicky Wire proclaimed that he wished Michael Stipe would die a miserable death from AIDS and when Noel Gallagher wished much the same on Blur's Damon Albarn? Their respective press officers must have been making world record length phone calls to the Samaritans after their charges let their mouths run ahead of them and spewed out those unfortunate soundbites.

Behind every great band there is invariably a press officer attempting to stop them from destroying their careers in a flurry of libellous vitriol, outrageous slander and a media circus-attracting court case. Of course if you are Noel Gallagher or Nicky Wire then that sort of big mouthed mischief-making is usually positively encouraged. That's their well-honed, controversy-courting image and they resolutely stick to it like Spiderman to the side of a skyscraper.

However, for a young Welsh band just honing their interviewing technique, press officers were as foreign to them as the Albanian tax system. Then, as now, music press people operated on schizophrenic agendas. They could easily morph from protectors of the truth to speed-freaked exponents of gossip-fuelled spin, dependent on whether they needed to keep their clients away from or in the headlines, of course.

London-based, independent press company Excess has a name that aptly portrays its image. Owned by former music press photographer and writer, Jayne Houghton, the company was conceived at the onset of the Nineties with major clients who weren't too impartial to the odd bout of über-hedonism and a liking for a lively quote. First there was New Order, quickly followed by fellow Mancs, The Happy Mondays, who ensured that Excess quickly became one of the grooviest, hip-slinging PRs in the music business. Jayne Houghton had a way with the wayward. Unsurprisingly, then, they and Catatonia were undoubtedly made for each other!

'Richard and Martin came in and played me some of their stuff and asked me if I wanted to get involved,' explains Jayne Houghton of MRM's first approach. 'I already knew them both because they had a pokey little office a few doors down from my pokey little office in Farringdon.'

Richard Lowe and Martin Patton rightly figured that feisty bleached-blonde Northerner Jayne Houghton would hit it off with the equally feisty bleached-blonde Welshwoman Cerys Matthews. That or they would end up in the biggest music biz ruck this side of a Blur versus Oasis rematch. Luckily for everybody concerned it was the former.

'I think it was probably the me and Cerys thing, knowing that I would get on really well with her,' explains Jayne. 'I think that's why they chose us. We get on really well with all the band. I had a capacity to drink as well. They were really sweet and every single day would be exciting for them.'

Jayne says they were quite in awe of it all. 'They were meeting legendary people who worked with us and who they wouldn't have dreamed of being as famous as, like Shaun Ryder and New Order. I think they were both intrigued and impressed.'

But she adds: 'It was never nerve-wracking for them, we'd go for a few drinks to plot, plan and scheme. We were nurturing them, putting it all together. We would spend a lot of time telling them how they could do this and do that. They were getting their first mentions in the music press and it was an exciting time. To be honest, it was lovely to see that wide-eyed amazement that they had about everything. But of course you feel really protective as well.'

Jayne's initial plan was to introduce them to the music press. 'They enjoyed meeting all the journalists and photographers we would introduce them to socially. We'd try and find people who we knew were really going to champion them and get them like we got them. We started to build relationships with writers. Everett True and Taylor Parkes at the *Melody Maker* were big fans and Babara Ellen and Iestyn, of course, at the *NME* also loved them.'

As it transpired it wouldn't be a problem for Jayne to harness the band a few choice column inches, judging by the publicity that had gone before anyway. January 1995 had already seen Cerys securing *NME*'s 1994 Newcomer of the Year for and I quote: 'being the most inspired female piss-artist since Janis Joplin!'

Jayne and Excess had a few initial successes straight away. Monthly music magazines *Vox* and *Select*, picking up on the buzz created by the weekly music press and Jayne's seal of cool PR approval, both mentioned the band in flurries of promising prose. *Vox* described Catatonia as 'more Sonic Youth than Suede . . . a South Wales quartet that bring spunk and attitude to indie guitar pop without sacrificing cool melodies'. The mag also described Cerys as a 'bleach-blonde firebrand . . . with a stroppy mastery of the two minute pop blast'.

Select were equally complimentary but neatly captured a snapshot of the 1995 Catatonia with these words: 'Have been patchy live, but are improving all the time. Currently being eyed by various record companies while plotting their debut album.'

The band's live unpredictability may have been charming to those more indie-inclined journalists that loved the band's punkish air of just-thrown-it-all-togetherness, but it was their inconsistent performance that was holding them back. These rough diamonds needed shining. Although with MRM and Excess at the helm the hope was high that Catatonia would snare a deal, a realistic assessment was that they needed to sort themselves out quickly. As it stood the band just weren't good enough for a record deal. If they wanted to escape the ramshackle indie ghetto they were hemmed into, they had better get down to polishing the performance, learn some discipline and play like success was a meaningful right, not an afterthought.

The next single 'Bleed' was due to be released in February. As far as the band's reputation went, the machinery had been put in place and now it was time for everyone to pull together and drive the band forward to the next level: to spread the word outside the confines of Cardiff and London's sheltered acclaim, as well as securing the Cats a record contract, of course. Excess had the skill and knowledge to transform this reasonably successful indie band on the London margins to a highly successful band courting publicity on a national scale. Although it's enjoyable, (for a time) you can't make a living out of being the doyennes of the *NME* and spend your life propping up the bar at the Camden Falcon, unless you have some reasonable success to back it up.

So it was that 'Bleed' was the song Catatonia hoped would plant itself in a nation's subconsciousness. The single itself, was released on Nursery, a label set up by MRM's Martin Patton to promote bands managed by him.

'Bleed' gave critics great reign with critical analogies about the band. The wonderfully monickered Britpop fanzine *Fantasy Y-Fronts* memorably over-enthused:

> You know the scene in Boys From The Blackstuff where Yosser Hughes's daughter smiles sweetly then headbutts the social worker? Cross this with Omen 1 and Omen 2 and you're some way towards capturing the Catatonia experience – a childlike, high-pitched, cutesy pie voice which deceives the listener into a false sense of security, then suddenly snarls and pounces leaving a hideous bloody mess.

You could understand these comparisons. Witness the songs on 'Bleed' for evidence. There's Bleed itself, where feisty vocals spit out the lines: 'He claims that he knows you/Says its written in the stars/Do you believe this bullshit?', 'This Boy Can't Swim' with its vicious lyric, 'I hope he sinks', and 'Painful', a song that speaks of youthful desolation: 'Swallow anything that suits, dress it up as truth', while the guitars build up from a whisper to a rumble. They may have been two-thirds sugar and spice but also one third pure psychosis – just as their name suggested.

Rather disappointingly given their past record – two out of three Singles Of The Week, *NME* didn't award the band their highest accolade but were still impressed.

> Having crafted a succession of quiet marvels, Welsh misfits Catatonia step into a fierce splenetic lake that while looking a little predictable in a punk-pop/girl singer style, delivers sackloads of pleasure. 'Bleed', though it cynically lifts the central riff from Pulp's 'Do You Remember The First Time', is something of a delight, peaking at the moment when singer Cerys looks into the eyes of a smitten friend and sings, 'He claims that he knows you, says it's written in the stars . . . Do you believe this bullshit?' 'This Boy Can't Swim' and Painful', meanwhile, exude Catatonia's consuming interest in the darker side of smalltown intrigue: hurt, death and scattershot despondency. The mixture, as expected, works wonders.

The trouble with 'Bleed' was that, as the *NME* said, it looked predictable in a punk-pop/girl singer style. It was shamelessly commercial in an indie chart-headed way. It may have been cynically chosen to heighten the band's chances of success, but did nothing to set the band apart from their competition. While many of their songs were wilfully different from the admittedly excellent fizzing punk/pop of 'Bleed', there was nothing there to distinguish them from the similar angular guitar pop of Elastica or Sleeper.

Melody Maker meanwhile saw hope for the future in 'Bleed's grooves.

> Quelle surprise! We actually thought Catatonia was a place in Spain, with 24-hour siestas. As it turns out, it's actually a zombifying form of schizophrenia. The group Catatonia are a Welsh pop combo and, were it not for the ridiculous slickness of the guitars, they would actually be pretty good. The singer sounds like a malicious Clare Grogan, and they write tunes you can actually hum along to – always a sign that a little trouble has been taken. A hope for the future.

Even out in the provinces, magazines and newspapers were talking about Catatonia, and in some places a scrap was ensuing between believers and non-believers. Whereas Birmingham's *Buzz Factory* declared that 'Bleed' 'was Sleeper with more urgency, vitriol and vibrance' and that Catatonia 'are destined for greater things', the pop reviewer at the *District and Driffield Post* (Yorkshire's last staging post for searing rock criticism) reckoned that the problem with 'Bleed' was the vocalist. 'The lack of vocal power does these three otherwise decent tracks no favours at all, and I will be shocked if Catatonia make the grade.'

Although Driffield's expert pop analyst would be ultimately wrong in his assessment, he was one of the first to touch on the problem that many singers with distinct vocals face – some people just don't like their voices! While you wouldn't exactly say that Cerys's breathy rasp was an acquired taste, you could see that some people would be put off by her distinct Welsh brogue, just as there are discerning record buyers who detest Liam Gallagher of Oasis and Brett Anderson of Suede for what they reckon are annoying nasal whines.

Elastica, a band fronted by knuckle-hard Justine Frischmann, former girlfriend of Suede's singer Brett Anderson and the then current beau of Blur's Damon Albarn, were kicking up a fuss on the indie scene with the release of their energetic punk pop song 'Connection'. Although Catatonia's inspirational music wasn't as widely acknowledged as Elastica's new wave retreads, 'Bleed' was released at the same time as Elastica's single and outsold it in record shops all over the country.

The single was chosen for just this purpose – to propel the band further into the limelight, even if Mark Roberts described it 'as not out best work.' But he knew that the record would knock down a few walls for the band. 'It was just so easy to do,' he explained. 'It's like our Trojan Horse, so that we can do what we want eventually. We aren't saying that we don't like it, but it was a case of "Right, let's release something that will make us more popular than we are."'

Welsh music magazine *Sothach* echoed what most Catatonia fans were asking themselves on 'Bleed's release: 'This is better than anything else around at the moment – including Oasis. Isn't it about time Catatonia got the attention they deserved?'

Little did *Sothach* know that the major leap forward they had been dreaming of since those busking days outside Debenhams was just at hand.

DRAWING A BLANC

February was buzzing as furiously as a hive of pissed-off bees. As well as the release of 'Bleed' and a number of important gigs lined-up around the country, they were also holed away in Cardiff rehearsing songs for the recording of a debut album. Record companies had been sniffing around for what seemed like an age, but MRM were negotiating furiously, attempting to secure the band a good deal. So confident was everyone that a contract was imminent, the recording of an album was being talked and thought of as a certainty rather than a maybe.

And how true they were. At last there was the breakthrough. After a couple of years of frustration and constant wondering; gigs that could fly between fantasy and farce; and a reputation that had been built on all the wrong reasons, a record contract was finally offered to the band – by a man who was willing to take a chance on them. Geoff Travis, who had been a huge supporter of the band and who put 'Whale' out on his Rough Trade singles club, offered the band a deal they couldn't resist. He signed them to Blanco y Negro, a subsidiary of the giant Warners Music Corporation for the not-too-inconsiderable sum of £350,000.

Blanco was formed in 1982 when Geoff Travis took a proposal to Warners for a new label to be housed within the Warners system but to act effectively as an offshoot that would attract, A&R and nuture bands the major could not. The idea was for Blanco Y Negro to possess an indie mentality but with the resources of a major. The upshot was that the label could offer bands considered 'commercially challenged' the resources and financial security to develop as fully fledged chart contenders while not compromising their artistic integrity.

Blanco had an enviable track record for unearthing leftfield talent. Blanco's open-house policy to all genres of quality music attracted the kind of varied and reputable roster that actually gave major labels a good name. For a change.

Blanco had already nurtured the diametrically opposed careers of exotic dance exponents Everything But The Girl and those Scottish Stooges, notorious chainsaw punkers The Jesus and Mary Chain. Now Catatonia's shining brilliance was about to luxuriate in the glow of a major label spotlight.

Geoff Travis, who was then Blanco's head of A&R, ironically admitted to being puzzled as to why he hadn't offered the band a contract sooner.

'I should have signed them a year ago, because I love them and it would have been a lot cheaper,' he joked at the time. Not only were they newly made stablemates with Madonna, Prince, REM and Elvis Costello, but they were also the first bilingual group on a national record label.

Cerys could hardly contain her joy, and neither could the Welsh press. 'This is brilliant for us and we are really enjoying it,' Cerys enthused to the *Wales on Sunday*. 'We had to get our acts together a bit, cause we didn't think we were good enough before. Now we are going to a new city all the time, it is the ultimate fantasy. We are really enjoying it now, touring and partying. I suppose it is part of the Welsh legacy.' That Welsh legacy evidently revolving around getting so drunk you can speak Welsh even if you are not a Welsh speaker.

As the band were putting pen to paper, one music journalist wrote: 'Everyone knows that Cerys is one of the few pop stars still waving the rock and roll flag, a bird who stays up all night and probably drinks beer for breakfast; in short, one of a dying breed: the proper pop star.' And that was, in essence, why Catatonia had to be signed. Cerys was a star in the making and the rest of the band were the perfect foil to Warner's lofty ambitions for them.

At that early stage of their career the rest of the band knew that Cerys would become ever increasingly seen as the figurehead of the group. Of course, at this euphoric moment in their career no one was thinking of future problems that the elevation of Cerys into the limelight and the boys dissolving into relative anonymity might have on the group. They were all happy with Cerys taking the lion's share of the promotion and publicity work that was put their way. Anyway they always maintained they were in it for the music, not to be stars, so why worry? All fine and well obviously, until egos and the democracy of opinions come into play. Still, this was not the time for future worries, but a time for celebration.

Newly installed as a bona fide signed act, the band threw themselves into rehearsal for their live dates and for the recording of that much anticipated debut album. The band's producer Paul Sampson had been spending much of this time in Cardiff with the band. He would crash at Mark and Cerys's Gold Street house and spend a large amount of time with them outside the recording studio rehearsing and routining them in local rehearsal rooms.

'This is how we prepared the arrangements for the album that was to become *Way Beyond Blue*,' explains Paul. 'That's what we did by day. By night we drank at local pubs. I remember one night drinking with a bunch of Dafydd Ieaun's friends, who turned out to be an early line-up of The Super Furry Animals. I remember he also introduced me to a mate of his, a drummer called Aled Richards!'

Paul must have met half of what was soon to be the most important musicians ever to come out of Wales. Of course, in those days they were all still on the dole. Then thoughts of record contracts, world tours and hefty royalties were just pipe dreams to be enthused over after a few pints of Brains Dark (pronounced D-a-a-a-a-r-k – Cardiff's favourite tipple) in their two favoured pubs the Yellow Kangaroo in Roath (staggering distance from Gold Street) and the legendary City Arms.

The City Arms is a pub stuffed with Cardiff folklore. The last time it had a new lick of paint Queen Victoria still ruled but its frayed decor hides a hostelry filled to the gills with Cardiff characters. There's names like Welsh rugby legends Barry John and Mervyn Davies mixing it with the winos and journos, doleites and barflies, and Taffia schemers and rugby first-teamers – all of them gabbing away in broad Kairdiff accents about the respective merits of their city. To give it even more kudos, the pub is situated mere feet away from the entrance to the Millennium Stadium. On international rugby match days you had about as much chance of getting a drink in there as the Welsh rugby team had of repeating their Seventies golden era heyday. None. Whenever Catatonia were in Cardiff town centre, this is where you would find them. Slumped at the back of the pub with a pint or two on the go, surrounded by their Welsh-speaking mates from the local music scene.

Paul Sampson soon became familiar with the drinking places, the faces and the accents, and quickly became the unofficial fifth member of the band. His place in the Catatonia picture was exemplified by an out-of-the-blue invite from France's answer to John Peel, Bernard Black.

The renowned French DJ invited the band over to France to record a Black Session for him at Studio 105 in Paris. Catatonia had scored rave reviews after the mini-tour of Brittany, arranged by Rhys Mwyn in 1994. They had also built up a reputation from an exclamatory review of 'For Tinkerbell' in France's leading music magazine, *Les Inkoruptibles*.

Paul takes up the story: 'In those days Catatonia weren't as well known as they are now obviously,' he explains. 'So, if someone gave you a spot on their radio show you upped and went and did it. At the time that the Bernard Black show rang us up, Paul Jones was on holiday with his wife. He wasn't able to get back, so I filled in and played bass for them at that show.'

Catatonia left within hours of the phone call. Admittedly, they were filling in for a band who had cancelled, but it was a prestigious invite nevertheless, and would do their European profile the world of good. It also gave Catatonia's singer the chance to put her multilingual skills to good practice.

'Cerys, in particular, enamoured herself to Bernard Black and his people,' remembers Paul. 'She won them over straight away because she spoke fluent French. The band had a bit of an affinity with France, because of the language. I think French speakers like the Welsh language, so the band were very welcome when we arrived in Paris.'

The session, recorded on 12 February 1995, has now become a highly collectable bootleg, much sought after by Catatonia fans. They played a full set of fantastic quality at Studio 105 Maison de la Radio in Paris. The songs performed were 'For Tinkerbell', 'Beautiful Sailor', 'Whale', 'Painful', 'Mickey', 'Message' (also known as 'You Can'), 'Way Beyond Blue', 'This Boy Can't Swim', 'Sweet Catatonia', 'Acapulco Gold', and 'Bleed'.

Everything was seemingly picking up for the band. Bolstered by their new-found Gallic cred, they sped back across the English channel, bobbing along on a wave of optimism and readying themselves for another round of vital live appearances.

THE QUEEN OF TARTS

Despite their propensity for shaky live performances, Catatonia had already made a great leap forward by playing their first headline appearance at what was quickly becoming their second home, The Splash Club at the Water Rats. The band had played a storming gig in January with a scuzzily exotic support bill that included the brooding, narcotic splendour of New Zealand's The Starlings and New York's low-slung punkoids NY Loose.

Catatonia's booking agent Paul Buck was again working miracles for the band. He was calling in favours and hawking the band for support slots wherever he could. As a result, Catatonia did find themselves slotting in some pretty strange supports. They had already played those mismatched dates with grunge-lite popsters The Senseless Things and now found themselves pencilled in for three February dates with widescreen US rockers Live.

Dates at the Garage, London, the brilliantly named King Tuts Wah Wah Hut in Glasgow and Birmingham Edwards No. 8 saw the Cats playing in front of hordes of pierced, earnest rock fans who worshipped Live's intense performances and had that annoying habit of forming devil's horns with their fingers. I doubt they picked up hundreds of new fans, but as an abject lesson in turning in great live shows against the odds, this was the band that relished a fight.

Still, they had their own headline gigs to play in front of packed crowds and there were plenty of those. Two in particular would go down in the annals of Catatonia folklore for the creation of review quotes that would be lovingly reproduced in every rock interview with the band for the next two years.

The first came from the pen of the *Melody Maker*'s Taylor Parkes, a promising writer who had built up a cult reputation with the *Melody Maker*'s young readership for his florid writing and flourishing female following. He also loved Catatonia's strange and exotic music, so much so that he made a pilgrimage to North Wales to review the band at that renowned fortress of legendary rock 'n' roll performance, the Glastyn Hotel, Penrheg.

Situated on the isolated, windswept fringes of Snowdonia National Park, mere miles away from Llanrwst where Mark Roberts and Paul Jones grew up, the Catatonia gig was the highlight of the locals' social calendar. Every minicab firm in the surrounding towns was completely booked up and for many of the enthusiastically drunken crowd this was the only gig they were going to get to for months. Given that fact, the hybrid mix of bowlcut-haired indie kids and rambunctious rugby players were going to make a bizarre-looking but riotous assembly.

Taylor's memorable review perfectly mirrored the gig, the choice of venue and this strange rural happening:

> Catatonia's pop is sharpened, bristling, melody-heavy, but glazed with a psychotic strangeness that captivate some in ways I can't define, but tonight they must Entertain Or Die. So their mercury-drip is plugged, and the whole thing is stripped down to WITCH MUSIC, which is fine with me! Cerys sounds drunk, unafraid, rough as a robber's dog. In more civilised years, she'd be a pile of ashes at the base of a stake by now, anyhow – 20 minutes before Catatonia went onstage, I caught her slamming down a pint glass, hitching up her skirt, pouting and screaming, 'Swansea tart! Who's a Swansea tart?' as bulky,

> moustachioed faces frowned all around – but, framed by feedback and a sound mix that sounds like dying, she loses it completely, throws back her head and simply screams (like you would were you taking on 10 people at once armed with a chairleg!). 'You Can' was recorded as a glazed, triumphant rush; tonight it becomes a long, agonised rip. 'Painful', top track from their new 'Bleed' single loses the tumbling, xylophonic counterpoint that lends it a feel akin to the sensation of passing out, emerging as a simple torn-throated gust of disgust. Someone starts moshing in between Cerys and Paul and almost knocks the drums over. No one really seems to care. Maybe all bands should have to take on crowds like this now and again. The lambs would shiver, cop out, wither. The rams, meanwhile, seize the moment and squeeze.

Despite inevitably descending into League Of Gentlemen style occasions these frenzied gigs in wildest, darkest North Wales would become an annual staple of Catatonia's gig calendar. The band would use them as secret warm-up shows and also as a way of paying lip service to their roots.

More presciently, these gigs far from London' ever-polarised, schmooze-oriented environs, were manna from heaven for Catatonia. Their growing disgust with the English capital was manifesting itself in nearly all the interviews they gave. Mark and Cerys would neatly wind up the London-centric media with vicious anti-London tirades. Their diatribes were partially aimed at the holier-than-thou London music business that was predisposed to stuff its own bloated ego with its own sense of self-importance, and also as a payback for the years Catatonia's country had been dismissed as a musical and cultural backwater.

In a motel room after the Penrheg gig, Cerys vented her anti-London spleen to Taylor Parkes. 'In London everyone is hung up on dress and attitudes, which is fine in itself, but it means you get people getting really big when they just sound like stuff that's gone before,' she railed. 'You go to the Outer Hebrides, the Outer Hebrides! And I bet you'd hear more fuckin' innovation in music there than you'd ever hear in London. Ever! Nobody'll ever hear it, but it's there, I'm telling you.'

It's noticeably ironic, with hindsight, that Cerys expresses a grand distaste for anything London oriented given that later on in her career she would make herself at home in the star-struck climes of London's egocentric party scene. Until then though, she was still playing the brash upstart, brandishing a quote-friendly regional ire for anything English capital-like.

Equally ironically, it was back in the capital at the Water Rats, that Cerys would be bestowed with a nickname that would neatly summarise her status as Queen Hedonist. Just as Ian Brown is otherwise known as 'Monkey King', Mick Jagger and Keith Richards are joined at the hip (replacement) as 'The Glimmer Twins' and David Bowie spent his Seventies heyday spreading foppish grandeur as 'The Thin White Duke', Miss Matthews was about to be decreed a glorious tag of her own.

Heaven Up Here was just one of a growing number of fanzines sprouting up around 1995. After the scuzzy onslaught of grunge, the British music scene was still dazed and confused, lacking any focus or direction. However, its grassroots were still as prosperous and edgy as ever. Fanzines are vital to new bands. Not only do they offer a less-cynical, weary hack view of those musicians hoping to break big, but they write about them in a style that may be decreed amateurish but which fizzes with boundless enthusiasm.

Heaven Up Here, which gets its title from a song by Gene (foppish Brit guitar band oft compared to The Smiths) was a fanzine that had both boundless energy and, what was a rarity among many other photocopied fanzines, a clutch of extremely cool writers.

The fanzine was edited by journalism student David Atkinson, a music fanatic and maverick writer who possessed a wizardly way with words. He, like many other British music writers, had a penchant for girl-fronted bands. Much as he loved Sleeper's Louise Wener, Elastica's Justine Frischmann and Echobelly's Sonya Madan, it was Cerys Matthews that caught his eye.

'Jayne Houghton's assistant at Excess Press, Martine, rang me and also sent me a CD single of 'Bleed',' explains David. 'I stuck it on, thought it was great (still got it and still do, in fact) and so I called up Martine and asked to go along to the next London gig.'

David decided that he would rather enjoy the gig than have to review it, so he took along one of his writers, Australian Liz Cattermole, to review the gig.

'Liz had written a few reviews and had enthused to me about this cool new Welsh band with a gutsy female singer, known for her penchant for the odd quiet beverage. Or ten,' says David. 'So I thought she was better qualified to write the review, and I was happy just to take in the full splendour of Cerys Matthews live!'

Cut to the King's Cross Splash Club at the Water Rats on 25 February. Catatonia were headlining, with supports from The Voodoo Queens – a punky riot girl outfit, and Eva Luna – who are memorable for the fact that I know nothing about them!

David recognised that the band in the live arena still had to smooth out their rough edges, until they were the real deal, but he could see that Cerys was becoming something of an icon even then. 'Liz and I were both near the front and we were both blown away,' he remembers. 'They sang quite a few songs in Welsh, they were pretty raw and didn't look like they gigged that much but there was definitely a spark of something there.'

David was also struck by how Cerys was turned out. 'It's funny now looking back at how Cerys was that night,' he says. 'She was really dressed down – just jeans and T-shirt I think. Weird as she's turned into such a vampy glamourpuss subsequently, but then again, even then I think we both could see a star quality in her performance and in her voice – the way it went from fragile falsetto to gravely rock chick growl in the course of a song. Liz thought she made a perfect frontwoman, she had so much more presence than some of the early Britpop bands around at that time like Sleeper and Echobelly.'

Liz Catermole's review was filled with all sorts of exclamatory adjectives about Catatonia's live prowess, but also a line that would sum up the 1995 Cerys Matthews perfectly. It was also a monicker that would find its way on to T-shirts and become a legend for the frontwoman to bear. Here's a snippet of this momentous review:

> Cerys only sports half a can of lager so we know it'll be a short set, but in the seven twinkling little numbers you could see the silver lining in everyone, from 'For Tinkerbell', to the single 'Bleed', via few Welsh-language numbers in between. Cerys's voice is an angelic choir girl one moment and fast-rising, beer soaked, rip-roaring pop tart the next!

That cool bastardisation of Pepsi's famous 'Lipsmackingthirstquenching' advertising slogan would be quickly picked up and made equally notorious by a piece of sharp thinking by Jayne Houghton.

PICTURE THIS

At this stage Catatonia hadn't yet had any press photos taken for their new label. Excess Press had been given money by Warners to spend on pictures, so decided to make a splash by choosing a name photographer to take the band's first proper press pictures. Excess figured it would be great to have pictures taken by a legendary rock photographer printed in the music press.

'We wanted it to be like Jill Furmanovsky's legendary pictures of Oasis,' explained Jayne Houghton. 'So we chose Gered Mankowitz, a renowned rock photographer who had made his name by taking amazing photos of the Rolling Stones in the Sixties.'

Unfortunately, circumstances didn't work out quite as planned. As Jayne recalls. 'Martin Patton brought the pics in for me to look at and Cerys looked terrible. They weren't what we were after at all. The rest of the band looked great but Cerys didn't look like herself.'

The result was that everyone hated them even though they had spent a sizeable wedge of the record company's money on the photo sessions. Meantime, Cerys had her confidence knocked by these awful pictures. 'She was thinking "Oh God, that doesn't even look like me, how could they possibly go out?"' explains Jayne. 'She was quite apprehensive, she realised things were starting to pick up momentum and then there were these pictures that she didn't want to be sent out.'

Luckily the duel forces of Excess, MRM and Cerys managed to persuade the record company it was a bad idea and blocked them from sending the pictures out. 'The record company wanted us to use them because they didn't want the money to be wasted,' says Jayne. ' It was the first time I had to lock horns with them, as did Richard and Martin and so did Cerys. Luckily they listened to us.'

There was only one solution to this pictureless situation. Jayne got her camera out.

'I said, "Why don't I bang off a few rolls of black and white pictures and see what we get?"' she recalls. 'Cerys was really nervous so I said, "Come to my office, let's get a few bottles of cheap wine in and we'll take some pics".'

Martin and Jayne had struck gold on the idea of using Liz Catermole's famous 'Fastrisingbeersoakedriproaringpoptart' quote on the front of a mocked up T-shirt that brilliantly lampooned the 'thirstquenching-lipsmacking' Pepsi slogan.

'We thought the quote was perfect and we also thought let's get a skinny little T-shirt with that on it,' says Jayne. 'We didn't want it to be too sexy, like a "Louise Wener from Sleeper tries-too-hard to get her cleavage out" sort of picture.'

A few drinks and Jayne was ready to roll. 'Cerys was just sitting on the floor messing with her hair. There were some close-up shots I took where she looks like a baby Courtney Love before the drugs and Kurt and before she got so fucked and addled!'

Jayne took tons of pictures and was thrilled to bits with the results. 'I didn't get my camera out too much then, so they were far better than we could even have hoped for. They were perfect, it captured the moment of someone on the brink of stardom who possessed an innate innocence and coolness.'

For those who saw the pictures it was hard to disagree. It was so obvious that Cerys wasn't trying hard to look cool like other female singers at that time, she just was. 'We used those pictures and they started to be used everywhere,' explains Jayne. 'Then Warners bought some of me to use and it became a really important early shot.' And the rest as they say is history.

As for Liz Catermole's famed quote, David Atkinson says: 'She's returned to Australia and I've lost touch with her, but I'm sure she would be delighted to discover that her bons mots found their way to be emblazoned across Cerys's chest. Just goes to show, nobody might actually buy fanzines but someone somewhere is taking notice. And you never know who!'

CORNISH POSTINGS

Despite not being the band's big crossover hit, 'Bleed' had served Catatonia well. A big indie hit, it peaked at No. 4 in the British independent charts (those charts made up of sales of records released on independent labels as opposed to the major labels that make up the mainstream charts). It was an encouraging step forward for the band in terms of recognition and broadening their fan base.

However, in terms of mainstream, chart sales success, it hardly troubled the scorers. 'Bleed' did have broad shoulders – it held the rest of the UK chart up – peaking at No. 104.

Although they would have hardly been pleased with the single's progress, the releasing of records on their new major label with the marketing and publicity muscle that it brought couldn't come soon enough for them.

Cerys, who had always distanced herself from comparisons by lazy hacks with so-called 'indie queens' Louise Wener of Sleeper and Echobelly's Sonya Madan, wanted to reach the greatest number of people she could with her music. This was a woman who was unashamedly pop and whose influences were far grander than the residents of the indie ghetto. She aspired to the grandly classic heights of 'famed belters' like Aretha Franklin, Janis Joplin and Shirley Bassey.

Geoff Travis and Warners viewed Cerys more like Chrissie Hynde, Debbie Harry or even Courtney Love, strong, sassy women who easily transcended the indie niche into a wider mainstream appeal without ever selling out their musical principles.

'Most of the time none of our friends or family can even buy the records we put out,' Cerys said of life spent ploughing through the indie malaise. 'It's sad, like. This elitist ideology about independent music, I can't understand it, it's bollocks! Get out to Joe Public, let them decide. If it's shit, it's shit. If it's good, it's good. Fuck the rest of it. It's like art, innit? Art's not just for a minority. Let everybody have it.'

Of course, Catatonia were not only about to leave the dole queues behind for good, but there was to be no more slumming it in the indie ghetto. They were about to move upmarket. The band were set to leave Cardiff behind for two weeks, and have their first experience of recording in a large residential recording studio – one of the best in the UK. Before they departed their hometown they left behind a track on the wonderfully titled *S4C Makes Me Want to Smoke Crack* compilation. The four-track 7" single, released on Ankst records, was limited to 500 copies and featured three other Welsh bands – Paladr, Rheinhalt H Rowlands and Ectogram. Catatonia's contribution to this spiky Welsh-language package was the gorgeous 'Caradion Ffol'. With its mellow strings, beautiful harmonies and Cerys's luscious voice gently whispering 'Pwy wnaeth ti fel y diafol?' (Who made you like the devil?) the track just reinforced the view of those that interpreted Catatonia as a delicious clash of schizophrenic proportions – one minute brash and bold the next lush and serene.

A SAW POINT

Set in its own unspoilt tidal creek on the banks of the River Fowey in Cornwall, South West England, Sawmills Studios certainly qualifies for the description lush and serene.

Catatonia's Cornish destination was established in 1975 as one of the first residential recording facilities in the UK and can probably claim to be the most unique, picturesque and atmospheric locations for a recording studio anywhere in the world. The main building is an old water mill, whose documented history stretches back to the eleventh century. Situated a mile from the sea on the south coast of Cornwall, Sawmills sits on the western bank of the River Fowey in its private tidal creek. It is surrounded by acres of natural woodland and one of the main features of the studio's location is the access by boat along the River Fowey; a refreshing way to go to the local pub!

With their producer Paul Sampson, this would be where Catatonia would finally start to record their first tracks for Blanco Y Negro. Robert Plant, Oasis, The Verve, Supergrass and the Cat's personal favourites The Stone Roses, had all recorded at Sawmills. That legacy had quickly rubbed off on the band, as they geared up for their first sessions at the studios. It was an exciting time for them. Rehearsals in Cardiff had gone well and Cerys had already enthusiastically spent a chunk of her first advance on the biggest 12-string acoustic guitar she could find in anticipation of the recording sessions.

'Catatonia had been used to operating on an all too familiar shoestring budget of equipment, studio time and crusty guitar strings,' explained Paul Sampson. 'I remember the band having to sleep on the floor each night in Cabin Studios in Coventry, but Sawmills was a different world.'

The accommodation was certainly luxurious. There was the living area with a patio, sun room and a spacious lounge, all bedrooms had superb views looking out across the water to the woodland beyond. Then there's the satellite TV, playstation, pool table, large video library and it's a wonder any work gets done.

Sawmills undoubtedly conjured up a special creative vibe – one that weaved its magic on the band. 'Both myself and Catatonia live in grey industrial towns, yet even hard cynical, real city kids can't help but space out into the world of ambient art in this location,' explained Paul. 'It became a running joke with the Sawmills guys while they watched the studio's magical, mystical surroundings change a band from the assignment of delivering a pop single to the: "Oh! they must have been really off their heads that day" concept album!'

The intention originally was to go and record 'Sweet Catatonia' as the first single and 'Acapulco Gold' as one of the extra tracks. 'That's right,' confirms Paul. 'Although we also ended up recording a few tracks for the album of which we ended up doing quite a lot. We probably did half the album. It was very productive.'

Although Paul Sampson admitted the session at Sawmills was 'one of the most enjoyable times I have ever experienced in a recording studio to date', he also confessed that 'by now my relationship with the band was a lot closer, as much as I try to assert my role as producer. But it's plainly obvious that I've fallen towards arranger and band member as I had also done nearly 10 years previous with Coventry band The Primitives.'

Little did he know at the time but this was to be his ultimate downfall. After the Sawmills session, Paul would be replaced as the album's producer by renowned Blur producer Stephen Street. John Cornfield was the in-house engineer at Sawmills at the time of Catatonia's arrival. He remembers the sessions in much less glowing terms.

'The band were committed and passionate about what they were doing and Cerys had a voice that was outstanding,' says John. 'But there was friction on both sides. Paul Sampson was more of a guitarist-producer, than a straight producer. He wanted to play on a lot of the tracks and I don't think the band wanted him to.'

It was Paul's closeness to the band that John reckons was his undoing. 'I think because he had almost become a member of the band, he was too near to it. I think they needed a producer who would just concentrate on producing and have a bit of distance between himself and the band.'

Paul Sampson though concurs with the view that the band were uncomfortable with his input.

'Being involved in arranging and playing a few things was never a problem,' he says. 'I mean I would admit I'd become close to them but that was inevitable.'

It was quite a unique position for a producer to be in. Paul readily admits as much. 'I'd probably spent near enough a year of my time working totally with Catatonia and that meant going to Wales and staying there quite a lot with them at Cerys and Mark's place,' he says. 'I think because I buddied up with them quite a lot, I started to feel like I was a member of the band rather than the producer. When we turned up at Sawmills they thought I was the guitarist and Paul Jones was the producer, because we are about the same age.'

Ironically, Paul reckons his only failing was enforcing the management and record company's bidding.

'They [the management] wanted me to insert a 'stop drop back' bit [a break in the continuity of the arrangement], in the middle of "Sweet Catatonia". I personally thought it was a bad idea.'

This decision led to a disagreement with the band, one that Paul regrets. 'I've subesequently learnt to do my own thing artistically in the studio and to go with my gut instincts.'

This was the last time that Paul would work with the band, he would be dropped in favour of a new producer.

The band's time at Sawmills also saw friction between Mark and Cerys. John Cornfield remembers their bust-ups well. 'I knew they were an item, but it seemed to be very on-off,' says John. 'They seemed to have a very tempestuous relationship, splitting up all the time after blazing rows.'

Spending so much time together was evidently taking its toll. Ask any couple who not only live together and work together and they'll tell about the stresses and strains that brings. Add to this working together in a high pressurised environment and sparks are bound to fly. Inter-band relationships are not renowned for having a high percentage of success stories, so Mark and Cerys's partnership had the odds stacked against it.

Paul Sampson plays it down, attributing it to the fact that passions are bound to rear when two people who are a team in life and in songwriting are thrown together. 'Because they were partners in both music and in love, I would imagine that anything is likely to cause friction,' reckons Paul. 'I didn't see it as strange at all. That's what relationships are like anyway, especially when you care a lot about your partner and you care a lot about your music. When they're both the same thing it's like there's nowhere to hide.'

FINDING HER VOICE?

Although there had been problems at Sawmills that would result in a new producer being brought in to finish off the recording of the album, the Sawmills sessions had still been fruitful. The Paul Sampson produced tracks 'Sweet Catatonia', 'Dream On', 'This Boy Can't Swim', 'Whale', and 'Way Beyond Blue' would find their way on to their debut album.

While they waited for a new producer to be found, the band did what all rising talents did in order to spread their own personal gospel of troubled relationships and excessive alcohol abuse. They gigged. Relentlessly. Catatonia's agent Paul Buck had again been working his magic. He had secured them a UK tour with other hotly tipped hopefuls Marion and Puressence. Meanwhile, Paul had also got the band on the bills of two of that summer's largest festivals, the Phoenix Festival in Stratford-upon-Avon and the Heineken Festival in Leeds.

First, though, there was a welcome return to Cardiff for a gig at the

University on 11 March, as well as dates at Sheffield Leadmill on 18 March and London's Camden Sausage Machine Club on 24 March.

The tour with artful widescreen indie rockers Puressence and anthemic Joy Division obsessives Marion, would be eventful for the searing live shows they played and the gigs they had to cancel due to Cerys's losing her voice. The tour stretched over a month between the end of April and start of May and stopped off at small venues with capacities between 400 and 800. The triple-header stopped at Leicester Princess Charlotte, Brighton Concorde, Liverpool Krazy House, Newcastle Riverside, Glasgow King Tut's Wah Wah Hut, Leeds Duchess of York, Derby Wherehouse, Birmingham Edwards No. 8, Bristol Fleece and Firkin, Portsmouth Wedgewood Rooms, London LA2 and Manchester University.

When Catatonia played critics were rapt by their spellbinding performances. Although some reviews stretched the boundaries of artistic licence more than others! At the more obtuse but nevertheless entertaining end of live reviewing was this from Leeds magazine *Insomnia*:

> Catatonia definitely keep their pop under the bed and pay regular night time visits to it. Singer Cerys has an amalgam of treacle, grit and lemon juice for a voice. The treacle oozes seductively into your ear, the grit sandblasts you into submission and the lemon juice drips into the cuts that are left behind. 'Bleed' takes you skipping into Hansel & Gretel territory picking bluebells and before you know it granny's bunged you in the oven and you're simmering nicely on gasmark 5! On 'This Boy Can't Swim', Cerys's wispy little Red Riding Hood voice transforms into the big bad wolf and gobbles you all up (ooh er pardon!).

The tour saw the gigs at Bristol and Manchester being cancelled because of Cerys losing her voice. Conal Dodds was promoting many of the gigs for MCP on the tour and he remembers the difficulties Cerys had.

'She did have a lot of problems with her voice,' he says. 'She had to learn to look after it a lot more and cut back on the boozing because it couldn't have been doing her voice much good. I don't know whether she had had singing lessons but it took a couple of years for her to learn how to project her voice properly.'

A review by the *NME*'s Andy Richardson at Birmingham Edwards No 8 noted with surprise the band's lack of imbibement and also encouragingly, given Cerys's desire to graduate from the indie tenements to the palace of pop, an indicator by the reviewer that they were doing just that.

> Your typical Catatonia gig consists of the following. Rip-snorting pop songs edged with razors, heavenly vocals that dart and veer and crafted guitar-led tunes that breathe new life into the ageing indie variant. Oh, and there's usually lots of beer.

So it's no surprise that Cerys from Catatonia has a new t-shirt that proudly shouts, 'Fast-Rising, Beer-Soaked, Rip-Roaring Pop Tart'. Except the moniker is strangely out of place tonight, because, perhaps for the first time, Catatonia are playing and they aren't pissed.

Without their customary Pils-fuelled arrogance they transform from nonchalant seven-out-of-ten indie slackers to diamond-encrusted pop stars with a cherub-like frontwoman. Alcohol is replaced with cocksure confidence and mistakes are supplanted with casual elegance.

The rest of the t-shirt slogan – which is the important bit – sticks, Catatonia are reaching the point where 'indie' and 'pop' collide and tonight they spiral ever higher with the blistering pop shock of 'Painful', the electric burst of 'This Boy Can't Swim' and the 24 carat melody of 'Bleed'.

Critics were beginning to 'get' Catatonia in ever-increasing numbers. Ian Watson, reviewing the band at their first ever festival appearance alongside such rock legends as Bob Dylan, Paul Weller and Van Morrison at the Phoenix Festival recognised their pop potential, despite Cerys's snotty voice! He wrote:

Catatonia appear sandwiched between Skunk Anansie and neo-Eighties group Marion, which presumably explains why vocalist Cerys has come down with such a heavy cold. As a result her normal oblique, helium-filled tones are rendered more accessible. At least half the set is sparkling and invigorated in an abstract Sugarcubes/Throwing Muses style. This, presumably, is why critics call Catatonia 'weird'. Weird. Right. And next to Throbbing Gristle (seriously leftfield bonkers noiseniks) they'd sound like Whigfield! Not that I'm put off by this, of course. No. Catatonia do have fringe avant-garde tendencies but they work so much better as a pop group.

Catatonia were definitely headed in the right direction, even if they were encountering obstacles on their way. Most noticeably those problems with Cerys's voice and the search for a new producer delaying the release of their debut single.

'Sweet Catatonia' had been mooted for an autumn release date, but had now been postponed to the New Year. It was frustrating but also introduced them to just what life is like on a major label. Release dates have to be optimised to tie in with marketing campaigns, press interviews and tour dates. Not altogether an easy schedule to juggle, but when handled properly can result in the full weight of major label muscle flexing in your direction.

All they needed now was a producer who was right up their street. Now funnily enough . . .

9
Streets Ahead

SOME MIGHT MARSEILLE . . .

Stephen Street is one of the most famed producers in the UK music industry. As the award-winning production guru behind the desk of acclaimed albums by The Smiths, The Cranberries, Morrissey and Blur, he's got the sort of enviable, 24-carat gold CV most producers would kill for.

Street became known as 'the fifth Smith' in the Eighties after producing the Manchester band's seminal albums *The Queen Is Dead* and *Strangeways Here We Come* as well as co-writing and producing Morrissey's debut solo album *Viva Hate*. In the Nineties he performed much the same task as Blur's longtime producer.

In 1995 he was fast becoming the hottest music producer in the business. Rising stars don't come cheap, but so determined were Warners to fix Catatonia up with Street's studio skills that money wasn't really an issue. Employing a star producer who they believed could help the band achieve their ambitions of delivering the album that Mark and Cerys had widely touted as being as good as The Stone Roses' debut was the issue.

It was a tall order to scale the lofty heights conquered by the Madchester megalith, especially as the recording had suffered such a fragmented construction. It didn't help the ebb and flow of the album to use more than one producer, nor to record it in different studios.

But that was the situation that Catatonia found themselves in. Searching for a producer had set release schedules back, but at least now they could ensconce themselves in the studio and once again embrace recording like a long-lost friend.

Whereas Cerys had sampled country life, canoeing in the creek outside Sawmills picturesque studios listening to mixes of their tracks, now four sound-proofed walls and the urban jungle of London were their surroundings as they holed up at Maison Rouge studios.

Catatonia were more than happy with the choice of Stephen Street as producer. Not only for his track record but for his flexible approach, as Cerys explained to the *South Wales Echo* evening newspaper. 'It went much more smoothly with him [Stephen Street] I mean, we had all the ideas anyway which Stephen took into account whereas the old producer wasn't allowing us to put them into practice.'

Street is renowned as quite a strict disciplinarian, insisting on drink and drug-free recording; however, Catatonia were about to enter the annals of pop history as the first band allowed by Street to knock back the booze in the studio – although, to be fair, this wasn't because the band threatened Stephen Street with physical violence if he didn't allow them to continue their renowned indulgence for imbibing. Strangely he relaxed his drinks ban to aid Cerys's voice. Unsurprisingly, given this information, *Way Beyond Blue* started life with the working title of 'Out of the Blue' (from the Bottom of a Bottle of Wine).'

'The first time we met Stephen I had vocals to record and walked into the studio stone-cold-sober,' said Cerys. 'I started to sing and my voice was all over the shop. I don't know why, but I didn't normally get that nervous in the studio. So he sent out for a couple of lagers.' And the rest, as they say, is history, albeit a blurred one at that.

Catatonia's stay at Maison Rouge was productive. As well as knocking back the booze, they knocked out six songs for the album. There was the recently penned 'Lost Cat', stuffed full of bitter melodic melancholy as the lyrics weave a story of failed romance; 'Some Half Baked Idea Called Wonderful', the kitchen-sink drama pop song formerly known as 'Mickey' that was written about a former housemate of Mark and Cerys who was hopeless with women; the grandly fragile but archly bittersweet 'Infantile'; the slow-burning 'Painful', spiked with jagged guitars; the debut single 'For Tinkerbell', transformed from its former guise as a crunching maelstrom into a swirling orchestral monster; and Cerys's entrancing voice wrapping itself around the bewitching psychedelia of 'Gyda Gwen' – the song that first appeared on the *For Tinkerbell* EP that would hide itself as the hidden track on the forthcoming album.

What's striking about these recordings is not only the staggering variety of styles – euphoric guitar blasts one minute, blissed out trip hop grooves the next – but the wealth of ideas that underpin the songs. Any journalist who misguidedly lumped the band in with the Echobellys, Sleepers and Salads of the indie pop world, would only need to listen to their debut album to be convinced that they were far more versatile than those other bands' poorly disguised, two-dimensional punk pop fakery.

There were good reasons why Catatonia weren't A&R-ed. The band knew exactly what they wanted and exactly how to achieve it and no one could tell them differently. Remember these were supreme musicians who had spent their years in Welsh-language bands wisely, utilising the best studios in Wales to hone their craft.

'We try out songs in a load of different ways until we find the best sound for that song, we don't want to pigeon hole a song before we have had a play with different styles,' said Mark Roberts, explaining how Catatonia approach the recording of each song. 'We don't want to stick with just the usual guitar set-up or just use strings like loads of other bands have in the past. When we are in the studio we don't want to limit ourselves. If you're in the studio you might as well not sound like a crap live band, you might as well try and get a song sounding like it does when you have it in your head. All our ideas are quite well formed so everyone might just call us 'clever fuckers'!

Having a producer come in and handle those ideas can cause friction though. In an interview with style bible *ID* magazine Cerys explained – with a typically blunt Cerys analogy – how Stephen Street's presence took some getting used to.

'When you're used to shitting in your own bathroom, it's odd to have someone tell you what your best shit is! Stephen pulled us through just by keeping a clear head in the studio.' And evidently also by listening to Catatonia's own highly formed ideas. 'We've actually been told that he had the least input of ideas to an album anyone's ever known!' she recounted to *ID*.

As a precursor to their first material released on their new label, Catatonia again made an appearance on a Welsh-language compilation. This time they popped up on *Triskedekaphilia*, a collection of session tracks recorded for Welsh DJ Nia Melville's essential Radio Cymru show Heno *Bydd yr Adar yn Canu* (Tonight the Birds will Sing). The compilation was released on Ankst Records and features Catatonia performing two of the songs recorded as demo tracks at the onset of their career, pre-Crai. They play 'Gwe' (a Welsh-language version of 'Whale') and 'Iago M' (an alternative version of 'New Mercurial Heights'). The collection also includes tracks by Gorky's Zygotic Mynci, The Super Furry Animals and Ectogram. Copies of *Triskedekaphilia* are still available by mail order from Ankst Records, and it's well worth purchasing not only to hear a nascent version of Catatonia in all their evocative glory, but also to listen to the embryonic beginnings of a dynamic Welsh-language scene.

GOING DAF FOR A LIVING

With the *Way Beyond Blue* album finally in the can, although it still hadn't been given a definite release date, Catatonia could throw themselves back into gigging. With the weight of Warners behind them and a booking agent working overtime on their behalf, gigs were being pencilled in at a rate of knots, although their agent Paul Buck admitted that it wasn't altogether the easiest thing booking the band dates at that time.

'Although they had had singles of the week in the NME, it was still quite difficult getting them good support tours and bigger gigs,' he says. 'Bands who get singles of the week either get signed straight away and make that graduation to bigger gigs or as in Catatonia's case it just doesn't happen straight away. In London and Wales, there was the buzz, but most of the provinces were still getting used to them, so you really had to sell Catatonia.'

Catatonia's progress wasn't as glorious as it might have been for two main reasons. First, they were still fighting against comparisons with other female-fronted bands at the time and, secondly, they were also attempting to live down their reputation as supreme hedonists, which was clouding the issue of how good their music actually was. In interviews journalists only wanted to talk about their drinking exploits and not about the music. Of course they only had themselves to blame for making a rod for their own back. If they had shown some serious commitment, hard graft and discipline earlier on in their career they would definitely have got signed sooner.

Catatonia hadn't yet released anything on Warners, so the level of gigs they were playing wasn't exactly a surprise, although the amount of gigs they would play throughout the coming year would see them building up a loyal following through sheer hard work and a resilient approach.

Most surprising though was the fact that not all the band's members would be coming along for the ride. Dafydd Ieaun had decided to leave Catatonia to join The Super Furry Animals. In the cold light of day it wasn't the most surprising news. The Furries were about to be signed to Creation Records and although Daf was great mates with the rest of Catatonia, his best mates were The Furries. Daf had shared a house in Cardiff with Furries guitarist Huw 'Bunf' Bunford and The Furries' first singer, actor Rhys Ifans. Daf also grew up with Furries' singer, Gruff Rhys, and was Gruff's partner-in-crime in Welsh-language legends Ffa Coffi Pawb. When the Furries begged him to fill the drummer's stool there was only going to be one answer.

Oddly enough, Catatonia bypassed the crisis that usually inevitably ensues when most members leave a band, having already ridden the storm when Clancy had left. Luckily, a replacement was found almost immediately – the band having a combination of Mr Urdd and the close-knit Welsh-language music scene to thank for delivering them a drummer.

Mr Urdd (or Mistir Urdd to be precise Welsh language-wise) is the figurehead of Urdd Gobaith Cymru, the Welsh-language youth movement in Wales. A grinning red, green and white triangle (with arms and legs), Mr Urdd helps to promote the Welsh language to the youth of Wales. Urdd Gobaith Cymru was founded in 1922 by a man with the Welshest of Welsh names, Sir Ifan ab Owen Edwards. The organisation has the aim of keeping the Welsh language alive among young people in Wales. One of the ways it achieves this is by organising holidays for Welsh schoolkids to its residential centres situated in two of the most stunning locations in Wales. I can say that, because as a teenager I attended both camps and experienced some of the best weeks of my life struggling with the Welsh language while I lapped up the amazing scenery.

Glan-Llyn is situated on the shores of Llyn Tegid – a huge lake that stretches for miles, near Bala in Gwynedd. Meanwhile the other centre at Llangrannog is situated on a site which overlooks Cardigan Bay on the golden coastline of West Wales. You'd be hard pressed to find a coastline with such golden sands and beautiful deep blue sea than the one that stretches along Cardigan Bay. It's simply stunning.

It was at these holiday camps cum Welsh-language education centres that a 13-year-old Dafydd Ieaun met the similarly aged Aled Richards. Although Dafydd was from North Wales he got on famously with Llanelli-born Aled Richards and kept in touch over the years, until they both found themselves drumming in different bands playing gigs in South Wales, albeit in markedly different camps. While Dafydd occupied the stool for unorthodox arch psychedelists Ffa Coffi Pawb, Aled was drumming for the resolutely doomy English-language indie band The Hepburns – a jangly trio made in the image of C86 outfits like The Pastels and The Weather Prophets.

Aled wasn't going anywhere in The Hepburns: although they gained a cult following in South Wales, they were strictly old school indie. Success to them would have been selling out, so it was lucky that Aled was recommended for the Catatonia job by Daf. At least he wouldn't have to admit to the rest of The Hepburns that he harboured a secret desire to be in a band whose aspirations lay beyond navel contemplation and limited edition DIY coloured vinyl singles.

Although Aled successfully auditioned and got the job, an advert had already been placed on the musicians notice board in Spillers record shop in Cardiff. There was more than one reason for the ad. Firstly, there was the vacant drummer's position, but Catatonia had also made the decision that they needed a second guitarist to allow Cerys to concentrate on singing. The amount of guitar work Paul Sampson played in the studio at Sawmills proved that although her voice was a strength, Cerys's guitar playing was a weak link. Still, with a voice that powerful it was best that Cerys freed herself of the guitar to allow her to do her singing justice. Problems with her voice had resulted in cancelled gigs so it wasn't helping that she couldn't concentrate on making full use of her amazing vocals.

Spillers Records, in the Hayes in Cardiff, is just around the corner from Mark and Cerys's old busking haunts. It is one of the oldest shops in the country – over 100 years old and counting. It's also famously the place that Richey Edwards and Nicky Wire would flock to in the late Eighties to pick up all the latest indie releases from their favourite bands like The Bodines and My Bloody Valentine. They were also attracted to the legendary record shop to pick up the famous Spillers bags, with the shop's logo emblazoned on the front. The ad placed on the shop's notice board memorably read: 'Gullible tossers required to make up dodgy beat combo. Laundry skills a must. DO you like Mud?'

This wasn't some coded, prophetical message that the band would in the years to come find themselves playing in the rain-splattered quagmire of the Glastonbury Festival, but a love of the soiled-sounding Seventies glam stompers famed for their hit 'Tiger Feet'. 'I thought it was really mud!' Aled famously quipped at the time.

POWELL TO THE PEOPLE

Although Aled had joined the band by now, Catatonia fielded their appeal for new members by fending off advances from flare-wearing members of dodgy Seventies-style tribute groups and crusty road protesters.

Luckily they found their new guitarist right under their very noses. Owen Powell was an old friend of Mark Roberts and Paul Jones from his days when he played lead guitar for Welsh-language groovers Y Crumblowers. Both Y Cyrff and Y Crumblowers shared the same bill at gigs around Wales. When Mark and Paul moved to Cardiff, Owen was one of the faces on the Welsh-language scene. He was always to be found propping up the bar with his brother Lloyd, at Cardiff's Welsh club, Clwb Ifor Bach.

Owen was working as an engineer at the Music Factory in Cardiff, the studio where many of the Welsh-language music scene's leading lights had recorded tracks for Welsh television during the late Eighties and early Nineties.

Y Crumblowers had long since given way to Colour 45, who were ostensibly Y Crumblowers with the same line-up but singing songs in English. They only lasted a year, until their agreeable, if a little lightweight, jangle pop sound was usurped by the discernibly far heavier whacked-out rock bluster of The Family. Owen and Lloyd were evidently ahead of their time, as The Family out-Verved The Verve before Richard Ashcroft was even a 'Bittersweet Symphony' away from greatness.

'The Family were myself, Owen, Owen Stickler [the original drummer from Y Crumblowers and Colour 45] and a mate of mine called Dennis on bass,' explains Lloyd Powell. 'We did some demos and I thought we were ace. Ironically, and this is a true story, we met a bloke from Wigan at one of the gigs we played and he said, "You were brilliant, have you heard of this new band from Wigan called The Verve, you sound alike!"'

Owen was also working as a guitar tech for The Super Furry Animals at the time, and The Family supported The Furries on a few of their first-ever gigs in Wales. However, once Owen had heard of Catatonia's desire to draft in a second guitarist he was frankly over-qualified for the job. Catatonia knew all about Owen and he all about them.

Owen was preordained to be a pop star from the days he would play a tennis racket in front of the mirror, or as he recounted the tale to the *NME*: 'Yeah I used to do that. But one day my dad caught me singing with a tennis racket.' What did he say? 'Well, he'd caught me having a wank the day before, and he said – 'Look son, I don't mind wanking . . . but this rock star business has got to stop!'

Owen's warped anecdotes aside, he was the only man in the race to be fair. All you had to do was look at the dreams Cerys was having at the time to realise Owen was the man for the job.

She was telling Welsh magazine *Golwg* about a dream where 'I had adopted a little boy, and everyone said "Don't do it!" He grew really tall and was like a freak and I couldn't calm him down, and everyone was saying "We told you so."'

Owen is one of the tallest guitarists in the UK. He's well over 6ft 3 inches and must have been excited to be joining Catatonia. I'm not sure about the freak part although he has confessed to having had dodgy heavy metal tendencies in the past.

Cerys admitted to *Vox* Magazine that the band started to sound better as soon as Owen arrived. 'He can play guitar and, er, that's a big help,' said Cerys. 'Playing the guitar is the only thing I've ever been particularly bad at learning how to do. This is the big change in the band. We started to gain a successful reputation when I threw my guitar away. It's no good trying to make beautiful music when I'm there sounding like a dog and cat playing guitar. Or a cat and a cat.'

'Actually, it's only now that we're beginning to take it in at all. Before, I was just in a blind nowhere land. We were terrible. I could never hear the rest of the band, so I'd just shout into the microphone. One time, Mark managed to play the whole gig just playing one note, because he thought it was so good. I was shouting "Mark, play your guitar PLEASE." We're good now though. We want to be big – go to Japan, and see the hotels and eat the sushi.'

Those Far Eastern ambitions wouldn't be too far off, nor would the development of Cerys's new found guitarless stage presence and her 'unique' dancing. Vox pointed out that a guitar would get in the way of the distinctive shapes she throws on stage. 'What do I do on stage?' she challenged *Vox*. 'Now, be careful what you say. Don't say farmer, or barmaid, or Tina Turner, or knock-kneed lad in stilettos. I've heard them all. I can't change the way I dance.

I had this really good friend who said, "Look, Ceh, here's some advice for you on stage: just shut your legs a bit." But I can't do it. I can't sing with my legs closed. It's impossible. Shirley Bassey's voice coach says you've got to open your airways. I got it wrong! I took it the wrong way!'

With her new found bow-legged stage style and two new members in tow, the new look Catatonia, by my reckoning Catatonia Mark 4, headed for another eventful, fun-packed, riotous jaunt around the UK's less salubrious highways and byways.

December is traditionally the month to be merry. And Catatonia certainly knew all about making merry. They were pastmasters at over-zealous hedonism. The ensuing weeks and months would see them storming the music press gossip columns and claiming them for their own, with enthusiastic hacks gleefully documenting their colourful on-road high jinks. Of course, Jayne Houghton and her Excess staff were making full use of the band's capacity to party by planting many of the stories that were drunkenly staggering around the gossip columns.

From December 1995 to June 1996, Catatonia would blaze a trail of heavyweight-sized alcohol indulgence whose highlights(?) would number, one stalker, one publishing deal, two continents, three singles, over 70 gigs and countless crazy 'Tales From the Brains Dark (side)'. It was a tour that would dissolve into a hybrid mix of surreal Monty Python-like slapstick. OTT Spinal Tap indulgence and Fatal Attraction strangeness.

Before Catatonia headed off on their monster-sized booze fest, they released a limited edition Xmas single that was only sent out to members of their mailing list. 'Bleed' had included postcards for fans to fill in and mail back to MRM to be kept up to date about the band's activities. The Christmas 1995 single was a thank you for those fans who had formed an ever-burgeoning fanbase at the onset of Catatonia's career.

Only a thousand copies of the white vinyl 7" single were sent out featuring two new never-before-released tracks – 'Blow The Millennium, Blow' and 'Beautiful Sailor'. 'Blow The Millennium, Blow' was recorded at Grapevine Studios in Cardiff, produced by Catatonia and engineered by studio owners Paul Bowen and Richard Dunn. It's another of those delicate works that Catatonia were so breezily adept at producing. It's an ornately carved, sweetly sung epic, all quiet loveliness hushed along by Cerys's opulent whispered vocals, while 'Beautiful Sailor,' recorded during the sessions at Sawmills Studios, is the exact opposite: a crunching melodic pop romp fuelled by Mark's scything guitar. It's another much sought after Catatonia rarity. The single can be found on Internet auction sites changing hands for anything between £20 and £50.

With their Christmas present to their fans safely delivered, they took possession of a Yuletide gift of their own – a small, but comfortable minibus courtesy of the record company. Catatonia had spent years hunched up in the back of a transit van, now this was more like it. Being signed to a major record label was beginning to pay off. It was a shame the gigs weren't getting any bigger. They were still holed up at those provincial outposts that form the first-rung of the ladder for those aspirant rock 'n' roll stars.

Starting at the Newcastle Riverside on 8 December, they played Sunderland University (9th), Brighton Basement (12th), Weybridge Hum Drum (13th) and headlined a Xmas gig at London Splash Club on 19 December.

1996 got off to a flyer with a gig at Swansea Barons nightclub on 9 January. Barons would become infamous during the following year with the release of the Welsh film *Twin Town* – shot on location in Swansea. The film stars Catatonia's mate, the ubiquitous Rhys Ifans as a petty criminal dope head, who with his brother wreak revenge for their dad's death at the hands of local gangster Bryn Cartwright. Barons is now renowned for being the place where they filmed the infamous karaoke scene in *Twin Town* where Rhys Ifans and his brother (played by Rhys' real-life brother Llyr Ifans) relieve themselves over Bryn Cartwright's daughter!

Talking of the call of nature, Catatonia's own infamy-courting ways were about to come to the fore when the first of many tales of excess (how perfectly has a PR company's name fitted a band's indulgent nature) appeared after they played Bath Moles on 11 January. Here's how the *NME* reported it:

> Not everyone's been living the highlife this week though. No, you can always rely on those Welsh nutters Catatonia to lower the tone, and this week proved no exception. Shortly before taking to the stage at Bath Moles Club recently, singer Cerys paid a visit to the toilets – only to find they were out of order. Still, never one to stand on ceremony, Cerys proceeded to do the necessary squatting on the dressing room sink, before heading off to do the gig. All went well, until the band returned to the dressing room to find Cerys's behaviour had had disastrous results: the sink had fallen from the wall, the dressing room was entirely flooded and the water had short-circuited the electricity supply!

It's probably not a story Cerys has ever told her mum, but as far as music press infamy was concerned it was another triumphant piece of publicity. Excess weren't having to try too hard to garner the band those vital column inches: everything they touched turned to music press gold. It was no wonder journalists loved them. To them Cerys was this mad Welsh wildwoman with the helium squeal who made Björk's squeaky outbursts seem like the keys to the meaning of life. Many writers who encountered the band thought them the perfect collision of rock 'n' roll contradictions. The band could create dramatic yet fragile music that was intense, delicate and unnerving, yet wispy wallflowers they weren't. Roaring good-time merchants, hell bent on reaching the outer limits of simply having it, they were.

The music press didn't have to wait too long after the Moles Club flood, for the next instalment of the young, the surreally wild and the restless.

Gigs at Leicester Princess Charlotte on 12 January and Sunderland University on the 13th had passed without incident before Catatonia rode into Hull to play The Adelphi on the 14th. The 100-capacity Adelphi is more akin to someone's front room than a music venue.

These cramped conditions were highlighted when the band found themselves on the receiving end of what they were delighted to believe was their very first stage invader. Sadly, their joy was cruelly crushed when the punter in question pushed past Cerys to use the fag machine at the back of the stage. Again this moment of bizarre hilarity unsurprisingly found its way back to the music press gossip columns. Catatonia were on a high anyway. It was no surprise that they were in ebullient mood. The band were days away from the release of their debut single on a major record label and everything was new and exciting to them. All of a sudden there's all these opportunities and Catatonia wanted to savour every one of them. Even if it meant burning the candle at both ends and then eating it. This was rock 'n' roll life, and more, importantly it was the rock 'n' roll life they had waited so long for.

So gigs at Leeds Duchess of York on 16 January, Buckley Tivoli on the 17th culminated in a journey down the M4 corridor on the release date of Catatonia's debut major label single.

'Sweet Catatonia' was released on 18 January as a three-track CD, featuring the title song and 'Acapulco Gold' and 'Cut You Inside' as the extra tracks. The 7″ single meanwhile featured 'Tourist' as the flipside. The single's cover art was a painting by Mark and Cerys's housemate, artist Elfyn Lewis, whose work would feature on the covers of the next three Catatonia singles.

The pick of the flipsides was 'Acapulco Gold', stupefying arcane evidence of Catatonia's ability to connect your heart and your mind with their music. It's a song of staggering desolate beauty, a paean to the subject of suicide and/or the poet Sylvia Plath who took her own life. It also fits perfectly with Cerys's lyrical ideology. 'When it comes to lyrics, I like contrasts, presenting themes that have two sides like escapism and reality,' she once related to the *Manchester Evening News*.

The Bristol Louisiana was the lucky venue to receive the welcoming launch party for the single, but the drunken shindig didn't get into full swing until the following night when Catatonia made a triumphant return to Cardiff to play at the city's University Union. Well, that was the plan. What was shaping up to be a jubilant celebration was ultimately to end up casting a shadow over the whole mood of the Catatonia camp.

Unbeknown to their fans and the press alike, Cerys had been on the receiving end of unwanted attention from a besotted fan. Although Cerys didn't want to make too much of it at the time, the *Melody Maker*'s news editor Carol Clerk penned a half-page news report quoting both Cerys and Jayne Houghton.

Speaking to the *Maker*, Cerys said of the stalker: 'The thing is, everyone's got their problems. I don't really want to make a fuss about it.'

Jayne Houghton told the music paper how the French fan's behaviour turned from good-natured to nasty over the period of a few months. 'He met them in France when they played there, and he followed them back on the ferry for their UK tour and turned up at all the shows.

'He was on his own the whole time. Eventually he started to really single out Cerys. The band have always got time for their fans, so she was nice to him, helping him out with a place on the guest list if she could.

'Maybe at this juncture, he started to get the wrong signals. He started to turn up in the foyers of hotels. If she didn't spend much time with him for any reason, he'd over-react and blow-up, or get a bit nasty or emotional. It all became very tense and the band tried to distance themselves from him, but that didn't go down well at all.'

Jayne says that MRM thought he was becoming really obsessed and a bit too scary with it. 'Eventually the police were asked for advice, but they said that unless he did actually bodily harm to someone, they couldn't get involved at all. In America, if you're being stalked, you can get injunctions and restraining orders so easily, but not here.'

Unfortunately, the situation came to a head after the Cardiff University gig. Mark Roberts was obviously concerned for his partner, but had been told not to confront him. Cerys had spent the evening with her friends and family, and was trying to keep the fan at arm's length. 'Which he didn't take too kindly to,' recounts Jayne. 'He was probably pissed, and he went mad and started acting in a really unhinged manner, cavorting around and crying on the fire escape that backs on to some railway tracks. Everyone was worried that he might jump off.

'The security wanted to kick him out, but Cerys wanted to go up on her own to talk to him. She used to be a psychiatric nurse, so she knew how to handle it. She just told him how she felt and if he could see it from her point of view.'

Cerys did manage to calm him down, but he still didn't want to go home. 'I think his family had to come across to get him and take him back home to France,' explained Jayne. 'Cerys did ring them up to find out if he was okay and apparently he is fine now.'

If the band were fraught and anxious after the distressing showdown with a stalker, they would have been wise to have sought solace in the exclamatory reviews for 'Sweet Catatonia'. Catatonia had never yet been on the receiving end of a savage attack by a critic's pen and reviews for their debut continued that winning run.

Time Out's Peter Paphides proclaimed that he was 'seduced into instant replay and left charmed' on hearing the single, while music industry bible *Music Week* reckoned that the time Catatonia had spent in development in recording studios had paid dividends 'with this Stephen Street produced slice of hooky alternapop'. The *Melody Maker* memorably described Cerys's voice as 'psychotic-toddler, Melanie-on-beer-and-sulphate vocals', while the *Observer* described 'Sweet Catatonia' as 'the spikiest bits of Belly with added Bjorkish squeaks and guitars that could wake the most stubborn coma victim'. The now defunct indie glossy *Raw* succinctly labelled it as a debut of 'instant pop catchiness' and reckoned it had 'all the hallmarks of an instant hit'.

Unfortunately the lofty heights of hit record wouldn't be scaled just yet. Catatonia's hopes of smashing into the Top 40 with their first major label single were dashed by the release only peaking at No. 61. The below par chart placing wasn't a disaster but it injected a slice of reality into the euphoria that had surrounded its release. Hopes for the band were high but save the constant championing of Catatonia by Mark Radcliffe, who was still entrenched in the evening schedule at Radio 1, the daytime radio that turns singles into hit records were still conspicuously absent.

'I think it was the case that it took longer then we imagined for people to twig and get it,' explains Jayne Houghton. 'Although she [Cerys] was a potential indie superstar like Louise Wener, we fought against that because we always knew it was more Courtney Love or Debbie Harry or Chrissie Hynde, we knew she was always bigger than just indie, she had more about her and the band were not Sleeperblokes.'

Unlike Sleeper, whose male members were puppets to Louise Wener's puppet-mistress, Catatonia was a dead-set democracy, where everyone contributed. It must have been frustrating for Mark especially, who had formed the band and wrote the bulk of their songs, to see Cerys gaining the plaudits. But as much as Mark knew that Catatonia wouldn't be the same without Cerys, she knew that the band wouldn't be the same without his superlative songwriting. All bands have these creative tensions, but you could envisage this becoming a problem for the band the more successful they became.

'It was very much the sum of their parts – not Cerys's backing band,' Jayne says. 'Sleeper would be the most insulting comparison we would get and we did get it and we always fought against it. We did fight to reposition them before they got stuck with that.'

Blanco Y Negro were choosing the A-sides that were most accessible and commercial, which ultimately only illuminated one side of Catatonia's multifarious talents. Whereas the bands they were being lumped in with – Sleeper, Echobelly and Elastica – offered slightly varying styles of the same punk pop variety, Catatonia were a million lights years away. For one thing, Cerys Matthews possessed a remarkable voice. Unlike the competition she could really sing.

It must have been infuriating for the band, although they staked their hopes on the singles and the album to follow, which they believed would easily change people's preconceptions of them.

This year was to be all about breaking down the walls of chart ache, overcoming lazy comparisons to second-rate bands and building up a sizeable fanbase. The only way they could achieve all these aims was to keep their profile high. That meant constant touring, releasing of records and not a little notoriety snaring on the way.

MRM were attempting to raise the band's profile in Europe by releasing *The Sublime Magic Of*, an understatedly named import only (in the UK) European release on Martin Patton's Nursery Records. It featured nine songs rounded up from the 'Hooked' single, 'Dream On' from the *Volume* compilation, 'Whale' and 'You Can' from the Rough Trade single and the three songs from 'Bleed', plus 'Caradian Ffol' as a secret track. It's another one of those highly collectable Catatonia rarities, selling for around £25-£30.

HIGH TIMES AND HEADLINES

After the eventful Cardiff show there were still gigs to play at Exeter Cavern on 20 January, Norwich Arts Centre (22nd), Chelmsford Attic (24th), Southampton Joiners (25th) and Reading Alleycat (26th), before Catatonia set off for a tour of the south-east as part of a super-charged Welsh double header.

There was only three days respite at home before they were back on the road, this time supporting Newport's premier rip-snortin', drum-crashing, guitar-flailing hedonistic rock 'n' rollers The 60ft Dolls.

Whoever dreamt up this double bill had no caution for the amount of alcoholic carnage that they would wreak, nor for the crowds that would lie quaking in their wake at the venues they visited. The 60ft Dolls – Richard Parfitt (guitar), Carl Bevan (drums) and Mike Cole (bass) – were a band with a finger firmly on the self-destruct button. Journalists 'lucky' enough to be given the task of interviewing them would almost invariably surface days after spending time with them looking like he/she had just starred in a version of the *Blair Witch Project* meets The George Best Story.

The Dolls' manager Huw Williams said that pairing the two of them together was like pitting the unstoppable force with the immovable object. Ironically, neither of the bands particularly suffered, they were both equals in musical and drinking talents, but it was Jayne Houghton's staff who couldn't handle the pace.

Travelling up from a riotous gig at the Brighton Concorde on 29 January – the first date of their double-header – Jayne Houghton's enthusiastic assistant at Excess Press, Martine, threw up over the band on the way back to London.

'She was mortified,' explained Jayne, 'Especially as she was sick all over the band and their brand new minibus. I think it took a while to get rid of the smell!'

Although at that time The 60ft Dolls star was more in the ascendancy than Catatonia's (hence The 60ft Dolls headlining), Dolls' singer and guitarist Richard reckons he could see the band's talents straight away.

'I know it sounds like a cliché to say this, but I believed Cerys clearly had the potential to be a big star,' he says. 'Her voice was stunning. It was so much better than all the other female singers that were around then.'

Obviously Cerys's voice was attracting an enormous amount of attention; however she still needed the songs to illuminate the grand majesty of her voice. You had to feel for Mark. He had stated that he and the rest of the boys were happy to remain in the background, but you can't help feeling he would be miffed by all the attention Cerys's voice was attracting, while his songs were equally worthy of acclaim. However, another huge boost for the band was close at hand.

Catatonia's dates with The 60ft Dolls only lasted for another four gigs – at London's 100 Club (30 January), Weybridge Hum Drum (31 January), Oxford United Supporters Club (1 February) and Tunbridge Wells Forum (2 February), but a mutual admiration society was formed that exists to this day.

The two bands themselves had their own admirer, Sony Music Publishing's Charlie Pinder. Charlie had recently signed The Dolls to a publishing deal and been tracking Catatonia for some two years. Now though he felt the time was right to make a move. 'I sensed things were turning a corner for the band when I heard Bleed on the radio,' he explains. 'I thought musically it was one of the best things they had done.'

However, the turning point for the publishing A&R was the gig at the 100 Club with The 60ft Dolls. 'To put it mildly, I was amazed,' he remembers. 'There was this rock goddess and this brilliant band – I couldn't believe it. Cerys had stopped playing the guitar and they had brought Owen in as a second guitarist. They finally looked like a proper band with a proper singer. There were other publishers sniffing around at the time and I thought to myself, "Fuck, it's all going to kick off, I'd better get in here quick or someone else is going to sign them."

'So, I rang Martin and Richard, who maintain that I said to them on the phone: "I'm wrong, I'm wrong, fuck, they've convinced me!" We all went to Pizza Express in Soho – that's the sort of rock 'n' roll place you'd carry out these negotiations(!) and I asked them what they wanted.' The good news for MRM and Catatonia was that about two weeks before the 100 Club gig, Charlie had been promoted from his first rung of the ladder A'n'R position to Senior A'n'R manager, (he's now the MD of Sony Music/ATV) with a lot more responsibility, and more importantly, a lot more leeway to sign bands.

'If I had tried to sign Catatonia a few weeks earlier, it would have been much harder for me, in my old position, to convince my bosses to sign them up.'

Catatonia signed to Sony Music publishing only a few weeks after the 100 Club gig. Luckily for Charlie it was at the 100 Club he decided to check out the band, if he'd headed up the M40 to see them play with The Dolls he may have changed his mind.

Despite Catatonia's insistence that they were to cut out the booze, the Doll's tour was inevitably – given both bands' reputations – going to be memorable for its hedonistic pursuits. However, it was also unforgettable for spewing out the worst review Catatonia have ever received. While the gig may not have been on a par with their early shambolic performance at TJs, still considered the worst gig they have ever played, Emily Hammond writing for Oxford magazine *The Word*, was so suitably unimpressed with the band's appearance at the Oxford United Supporter's Club (a small venue if ever there was one) that she spat:

> Think of the most boring, clichéd female-fronted band you've ever been (un)fortunate enough to be exposed to, subtract any hints of tunefulness or charm and you start to get an idea of just how bad Catatonia are. They comprise one female singer and (inevitably) an assortment of aesthetically-challenged male musicians. Catatonia's sound is unshaped and messy, the songs blurring into one another like hooligans at a football match. Far from apologising for their shiteness, the band refuse even to acknowledge the audience. A highly unattractive couple are snogging in front of me, and I'm sure it must be somehow symbolic.

Another bad night for the band. They really didn't help themselves sometimes.

Touring was pretty much continuous at this point. The band had played a clutch of European dates in the Netherlands and Germany and had returned to the UK in readiness for an exhaustive 40-date UK tour taking in hitherto uncharted, virgin gig territories like Cheltenham, Bournemouth, Kidderminster and Canterbury.

Before the marathon tour trek began, Catatonia had had a few weeks without any gigs where they rehearsed and carried out press interviews for UK newspapers and magazines. Catatonia did, though, agree to play one gig, as part of the Splash Tour – a series of dates around Wales featuring established and unsigned Welsh bands. Other dates were to be headlined by Gorky's Zygotic Mynci, The Super Furry Animals and The 60ft Dolls.

With the music press having a field day with the emergent Welsh music scene conjuring up inspired headlines like 'Fight The Powys That Be', 'You Make Me Feel Mighty Rhyl', 'You Sexy Merthyrfuckers' and the criminal

'Don't Leek Back In Anger', bands like Catatonia and The 60ft Dolls as well as The Super Furry Animals and Gorky's Zygotic Mynci were blazing a trail for Welsh music.

Alongside Britpop, which was firing a British music renaissance, making heroes of Blur, Pulp and erm, Menswear, Welsh music was in vogue and everybody wanted a piece of the action. Cool Cymru was the unfortunate monicker attached to the scene, but at least this wasn't some media-manufactured hype. Unlike of course the *Melody Maker*'s laughably fabricated Romo scene which lasted for about five minutes in 1996. It revolved around a London-centric rehash of New Romantic ideals by about four people on the *Maker* staff who liked to apply their make-up badly and write horribly verbose prose about Romo's leading lights Orlando and Plastic Fantastic.

Thankfully, unlike Romo, the Welsh music scene was not intent on tunnelling a route straight up its own arse and the Splash Tour represented everything that was good and honest about music. Catatonia headlined their date of the tour at the 600 plus capacity Coliseum Theatre in Aberdare, South Wales on Saturday, 2 March. The support on that day came from Cardiff's spiky mod popsters The Pocket Devils and Cwmaman's tragically named Tragic Love Company.

It was the last gig valley rockers TLC would ever play under their misjudged monicker before singer Kelly Jones would change the band's name to The Stereophonics.

Cerys and Kelly recently reminisced about their first-ever meeting in Aberdare, while both of them posed for a *Melody Maker* cover shoot. The mag's coverlines proclaimed them as 'the new Prince and Princess Of Wales', just proving how far both of them had come since those heady days of 1996. 'They did a brilliant gig,' recalls Cerys, 'and we were ruddy awful! They blew us off stage! You got signed straight after that, didn't you?'

South Wales DJ Steve Johnson was MC-ing the Splash Tour shows and he remembers going backstage at the Coliseum to say hello to Catatonia before they went on stage. He knew that they had a capacity to drink but wasn't prepared for the sight that met him.

'They were completely shitfaced,' he laughs. 'Cerys in particular was staggering about. Although it was a great gig Catatonia walked that fine line between just being drunk enough to play and not being able to see straight!'

After the Aberdare gig, Catatonia had a few weeks to ready themselves for their biggest tour to date. MRM were hammering home the point that they needed to be more professional and cut back on the drink. They ordered more rehearsals. However Cerys was determined to have her cake and eat it. She was nothing but adept at courting publicity, ensuring that she and her band remained fixed firmly in the public eye by carrying out an extraordinary feat of pure-blown hedonism.

Just like The Stone Roses' paint attack on their former record label's offices and Oasis's arrest on a cross-channel ferry, this was a rock 'n' roll tale that would go down in the annals of music press legend. It's a histrionic tale of one woman blazing an alcoholic trail from one country to another that lasted for 48 hours and several hundred miles. It all started when she entered into an alcoholic duel to the death, or at least the nearest toilet bowl with knuckle-hard Geordie grungers China Drum. Well, I'll let the *NME*'s gossip fuelled petrol tank PublicNME take up the story:

> . . . the Newcastle noiseniks were enjoying a quiet night running around shouting, 'Are you a bastard?' at all and sundry, when who should they encounter but our Cerys on a Drink A Northern Band Into Oblivion night. To which end she lured the poor, unsuspecting 'Drummies into a vodka battle that lasted until dawn.
>
> By then the war was over. Cerys, on the other hand, decided she needed an early-morning pick-me-up and, rather than head down the local like any normal psychotic drunkard, opted instead to 'pop' to Marseilles in France with an unnamed showbiz chum. All went swimmingly until the following morning, when Cerys somehow remembered she was due in Brighton that afternoon for an interview. Professionalism, paracetamol and a wad of ready cash to the fore, Cerys strolled into her Brighton hotel foyer three hours later and greeted her panic-stricken band-mates with a hearty, 'Mine's a double!'

The interview in question that Cerys was late for was with the *Melody Maker*'s legendary scribe Everett True. The Brighton-based *Maker* journalist (real name Jerry Thackeray but it's more folk than rock 'n' roll so you can't blame him for his *nomme de plume*) was famed for his interviews with Kurt Cobain and Courtney Love. One interview that passed into folklore centred around the rumour that Courtney had given Everett a blow job (never substantiated!) He was used to firing questions at feisty frontwomen. And a good job too, with a frazzled Cerys Matthews to contend with.

Everett documents the events leading up to Cerys's late arrival in an article he penned for the *Maker* a few days later. 'Two hours before the Catatonia interview is due to take place, I receive a phone call from their manager saying the singer's gone AWOL. The last time she was sighted, she was blind drunk and on her way to France.'

And her excuse? Blame it on The Lightning Seeds! 'I went to see The Lightning Seeds three days ago and woke up this morning in Marseilles,' Cerys confessed to admiring Everett True, who was wholly impressed by the Queen Hedonist's party-loving ways. 'I was drinking champagne in Club Class. I had a big plate of aliens(?) last night and I threw them all up this morning. I woke up crying – I only went to kill a night, and three days later, I woke up in France. That wasn't very glamorous.'

'They were in London and they were doing press as they had a few days off between gigs. We'd arranged some interviews but she wasn't there. She just hadn't come back and she was supposed to be in a hotel in Brighton,' remembers Jayne Houghton, who was anxiously awaiting Cerys's return. 'It turned out she'd got some money off the tour manager and just popped off to the South of France with a mate who said "Do you fancy going?" She just fucked off and then she came straight back after a 48 hour bender on a ferry, then a train from the port and turned up 20 minutes late for the interview I had set up.

'It was the first time she'd ever done it, she was never late for things. The band might sometimes turn up a bit pissed or dishevelled, but this time Cerys just went and we were all really, really panicking – the management and the tour manager – especially the tour manager because he had facilitated her exit from the country!'

As far as Cerys was concerned she didn't know what the fuss was about. 'She just walked in, sat down and went "Hiya!" She was only about 20 minutes late and everyone was going "Where the fuck have you been?" explains Jayne. 'Mark was going mental, the management were going mental. I'd had a coronary several times and she just wandered in and plonked herself down and got on with the interview that had been scheduled. It was so impressive, you couldn't be cross. Just coming back off something like that was admirable. I can't imagine anybody else would have, I don't think I'd have managed it, none of my other bands would have done that. She just went through her press work brilliantly and then crashed completely.'

And her explanation for missing in action? Cerys said. 'Well, my mate said I'm going to the South of France, and I thought that sounds good, I've never been, I'll go.'

'She crammed this big adventure into 48 hours, then she came back and was a pussycat,' says Jayne. 'Everything was exciting for her. Life's a riot. You're out getting pissed, taking drugs every night, out on the road, but a lot of bands can't deal with it and would blow out interviews, they'd fuck you around, they'd be in a bad mood, they'd treat you like shit. A lot of bands do that but Cerys never would and the band never would.

'Conceivably there's no reason why she shouldn't have turned into a drug-addled alcoholic mess, shag around and make a fool of herself. She could have done all of these things but she would still diligently turn up to an interview and be as nice as pie. She never ran rings around me, she always respected what she had and what she was supposed to do. She respected her band mates, she respected me, she respected the job in hand and that's a fuck of an achievement, it really is.'

Jayne Houghton reckons that this comes from the times Catatonia and Cerys struggled to make it, only having their dreams to live off. 'At the end of the day, whatever her personality is, she's a kid from Wales, dreaming of being a pop star. She'd have spent ages like we all did singing in front of the mirror with a hairbrush, wanting to be a star and when she got that, she could have become destructive with it. But she didn't and that's the strength of her personality, that she wanted to taste everything she'd like to taste and savour and stayed true to her own sense of self-respect, and self-worth. It's a brilliant juggling act.'

Juggling? Hmmm. Cerys could have done with a little bit of that when she bagged another excitable fit of press cuttings with a story that you just couldn't make up.

In a colourful interview with the *NME*'s Simon Williams, the writer reveals that after attending a gig at the Clwb Ifor Bach in Cardiff, Mark and Cerys invited most of the crowd back to their house to continue the party where Cerys decided to adhere to the strict dictates of hedonistic rock 'n' roll behaviour by participating in that time-honoured practice of chucking the TV out the window. Except nothing in the world of Catatonia is particularly normal, so their spin on this rock 'n' roll pursuit became Cerys's TV and Cerys's open window through which the TV sailed.

'I dunno, I thought I was being sociologically kind,' Cerys confessed to the *NME*. 'I've never seen the point of throwing a good telly out of the window, but it's a shit telly, and it's my window then, y'know, I just wanted to clear the air in my living room to create some cocktails, and it's an excellent bar so you don't want anything that might take attention from the function of that particular furniture.'

'Any regrets afterwards?' asked Mr *NME*.

'No, it still works.'

NME: 'You threw your television out of your window and it still works?'

'Oh, I'm only on the ground floor!' she shrieks despairingly. 'It's not some blinking ten-storey mansion I live in, is it?'

Cerys's personality was evidently rubbing off on the rest of the band. Next in the dock was Owen Powell.

'Owen got us kicked out of Stringfellows the other day,' Cerys blabbed to the *NME*. 'We were at a party there, trying to befriend Peter Stringfellow, getting into it and that; and Owen sidles up to Stringfellow, then in full view of him jumps over the bar and tries to nick a bottle of tequila, the twit. We all got grabbed by the necks and ejected.'

And it didn't stop there. The quotes and feats of hedonistic excellence just kept on coming. There was the 'I'm not just into debauchery and hedonism. I also like walking in the hills, with a bottle mind, just in case,' quote from Cerys. Then there was the time she found herself in a London hotel throwing bottles at a bloke who tried to come on to her – only to discover on arriving at a TV station for an interview the next day that he and his mates made up most of the staff of the TV station. And finally, who could forget the occasion when Catatonia attempted to steal a mechanical digger from a building site outside a – wait for it – police station, after a particularly heavy night at a North London pub, until the long arm of the law threatened them with a sobering night in the cells?

It was alright for the band to indulge themselves in London because they always had the safety net of South Wales to return to if they wanted to escape the music industry rat race. That was their press officer's view of their shenanigans anyway. Jayne Houghton surely must have had the busiest job in PR-dom just keeping up with her charges high-falutin' extra curricular activities.

'They always went back to Cardiff after doing press work in London and that was a great leveller for them,' she explains. 'Cerys would go home into her little sanctuary with her garden and her mates. Being back in the familiar surrounds of South Wales was good for them. That was probably the thing that helped them stay true to themselves. At least when they were in Cardiff I knew where they were!

'I went down to Cerys and Mark's house once for a meeting. It was a terraced house and there was an alley by the side. Cerys's garden was at the back. I went to the house with Richard and Martin for a meeting to talk about the album. We went to a pub on the corner. It was ridiculous. It was on the street that she was living in and it was full of locals. A drink was about 20p or something stupid. It was like that scene in American Werewolf in London – you'd walk in and everything would go quiet, but it was all so completely normal. Although Catatonia had started to get more press coverage and get bigger, the big thing Cerys was enthusing about was her garden.'

Jayne reckons that Cerys's green-fingered pursuits was one of the saving graces of her sanity. 'She had a secret sanctuary in her garden,' she says. 'I think when everything is going mad you latch on to something to be your anchor. I'm sure friends and family were a help but Cerys's garden became this sort of escape. It was like a magical place. It wasn't especially well-tended or anything because she'd been away so much, but she became almost serene when she was in this little patch behind her house. You knew that it would revitalise her in the career to come.'

Cerys may have gone kicking and screaming to her garden after reading a particularly poison-penned attack from *Melody Maker*'s legendary piss-take exponent Mr Agreeable. To be ripped apart by the music paper's resident manic mirth-making expletive thrower, means you've truly arrived.

Here's the raving rant in full.

> Cerys of Catatonia has described their songs as being 'like snapshots of life in Cardiff'. Cardiff. Right. You know, Cerys it's a fucking crowded marketplace for Britpop out there. Shitloads of bands are fucking screaming for attention, desperate for the main chance, striving to sell themselves in the most positive

and effective manner, urging us in pithy and cogent terms to lend them our ears. And what do you come up with? Our songs are like fucking snapshots of Cardiff. Readers have you ever fucking been to Cardiff? Believe me, like the fucking adverts say, it's definitely not the sort of place you'd want to bring a fucking camera! You might as well have compared your songs to photocopies of drunken office workers' sweaty arses as compared them to fucking snapshots of Cardiff you stupid, stupid fucking bint!'

SPACE INVADERS

Catatonia's mammoth trek around the UK's lesser-used B roads visited some venues that probably hadn't seen a band since rock 'n' roll began. Those outposts included Axiom (Cheltenham), Market Tavern (Kidderminster), Route 66 (Trowbridge) and Lucifer's Mill (Dundee). Luckily the tour, that encompassed 34 dates, was made eminently bearable by the presence of Liverpudlians Space – Catatonia's support band for this mammoth trek around the UK.

If Frank Sinatra, Black Grape, Ray Davies and Cypress Hill were to have an orgy, the bastard love child might be Space. Not pretty perhaps, but what a sound.

They may have looked like ordinary lads from Liverpool, but they weren't Britpop apologists. Space's diabolically catchy pop songs recalled B-movie soundtracks, Fifties show tunes, and Looney Tunes cartoon themes. When he wasn't trying to croon like Sinatra, singer and bassist Tommy Scott was trying his best to sound like the cartoon Mexican Mouse Speedy Gonzalez.

The tour was something of a revelation for Tommy and Cerys who discovered they shared a love of music possessed of a grand style and sweeping melodrama. They both adored crooners whether they be female like Ella Fitzgerald or male like Dean Martin and Frank Sinatra. Singers who had classic style and timeless appeal.

In an interview with the *NME* in 1999 Tommy told of his gratitude to Catatonia for allowing his band to tour with them. 'About three years ago, Catatonia gave us a support tour when we couldn't even get arrested. And that gave us the confidence to believe in ourselves as a pop band and we bonded from then on in.'

Both bands formed an enduring friendship over the 30 dates. More importantly perhaps, a chain of events were set in motion that would climax in a collaboration between the two singers and a music legend whom they both greatly admired.

Cerys had mentioned in an interview with *ID* magazine that her band would love to write songs for Welsh rock 'n' roll icon Tom Jones. 'I'd love to see Tom Jones at number one with a song I'd written,' she told the style bible. No sooner had the article appeared but Tom Jones's manager Tommy Woodward, who also happens to be his son, got in touch with the band and invited them to write a song for his veteran entertainer father. Although this collaboration wouldn't bear fruit until 1999, the band were still thrilled to be offered the chance to work with their fellow countryman. Cerys especially was buzzing about it. She told the *South Wales Echo*: 'He's probably one of the coolest men in rock, isn't he? Even when he was wearing a purple jumpsuit in the '70s he still looked amazing. So you can't really fault him.'

Er, yeah right Cerys.

Despite the usual drunken carousing, there was growing evidence that the band were finally tightening up. They were ultimately pulling the pieces together. The addition of Owen as second guitarist had added a new dimension to their sound and they were becoming consummate live performers. The band's promoter Conal Dodds testified to their flourishing live prowess.

'I saw them at the Clwb Ifor Bach gig in Cardiff,' he remembers. 'I watched the first three or four songs from the side of the stage and thought to myself they had an immense sound. Mark's guitar sounded amazing and they were really tight. It was sold out, about 300 people packed in and of course it was their hometown gig so that made it even more special.'

With over 30 gigs to choose from critics could pick and choose which dates they would review. But it didn't matter which nights they came along the reviews were all the same. Reviewers searched their thesauruses for apt exclamatory praise.

The *Melody Maker*'s Dave Simpson, reviewing the Cats at the Duchess of York in Leeds, recognised that the band weren't just some throwaway Britpop-by-numbers band but much deeper and off-kilter than that, but nevertheless made in a resolutely pop image.

> My first notes read 'Bjork-fronted Britpop', but it isn't that simple. The band's music is at first deceptively conventional 'Evening Session' fare – chunky riffs, powerhouse drums, fast bits, slow bits, blah, blah, blah. But, as it forms, you realise that the verses are where the choruses should be, sometimes there aren't choruses at all, and the whole chaotic mess gels into a glorious and surprisingly pop-oriented row.
>
> To dispense with the boys first; they play this music, do their jobs and if they were in a less adventurous, more careerist and politically dubious Britpop combo, they might be tagged Sleeperblokes. Dull and unglamorous they may appear, but their oblique racket is nevertheless sharp-edged and tempting as a knife laden with honey.
>
> Catatonia evoke the giddy delirium of the beginnings of tipsiness, an image cemented by Cerys as she sways towards the drumkit with half a pint of cider. She's half-cut, possibly alien and most definitely bonkers.

It wasn't just the music press that were scouring for fitting adjectives. Newspapers across the UK heaped on praise, especially when describing Cerys's crystal-cut vocals. The *Scotsman* raving about Catatonia's gig at the Venue in Edinburgh said:

> Both her microphone and her bottle seem like natural extensions of herself: the beer helping to release her innate exuberance and the microphone unchaining her multi-talented voice. At times she's husky, rough-edged yet still seductive; her voice dripping over the blustering, twin-guitar onslaught.

And from that bastion of rock critique, the *Worcester Evening News*, was a slew of prose in praise of the band's show at the Market Tavern deep in the unrock 'n' roll constituency of rural Kidderminster.

'Singer Cerys enchanted the audience with her deep, sooty voice reminiscent of '60s vocal pearl Melanie with the occasional interruption of a Bjork-esque shriek,' trumpeted surely the most under-used member of the newspaper's staff – the Worcester rock critic!

PUSSY GALORE

The Stephen Street produced 'Lost Cat', had been chosen as the next single. Released on two CDs with 'All Girls Are Fly' and 'Indigo Blind' as the extra tracks on CD1 and 'Sweet Catatonia' and 'Whale' recorded live on the Mark Radcliffe show on CD2, Catatonia also released a 7" single for the vinyl junkies with 'To And Fro' as the B-side.

'All Girls Are Fly', 'Indigo Blind' and 'To And Fro' were recorded in the break between Catatonia's tour with The 60ft Dolls and the tour with Space at Grapevine Studios in Cardiff. The 'Lost Cat,' single again featured cover artwork by Elfyn Lewis. The song, a tale of confused love, may have been another harmonious, fizzing pop excursion but the added extra tracks exemplified the band's fertile artistic diversity. 'All Girls Are Fly' is starkly luscious with Mark Roberts weaving his yearning guitar lines around the band's angular sound, 'Indigo Blind', is a poppy plaintive lament alive with Catatonia's sense of mystery and drama, while 'To And Fro' is almost hymnal, Cerys described it as 'the sound of Welsh chapels' and it lives up to that description, featuring a church organ.

Released for maximum effect on 22 April slap bang in the middle of Catatonia's UK travels, the single again ensured that Jayne Houghton's Excess Press files were full to the brim with great press reviews. The pick of the bunch was *Melody Maker*'s inch-perfect words on the single, that neatly identified that this was a band who were increasingly alight with confidence.

> When the drinking stops, Catatonia stand revealed as one of our most ingenious and deeply foxy new groups, with a sound that's waxy and sparkling and singular, oddly light-headed in its gush and glimmer, as though they're trembling audibly at just how good they're getting. Preview cassettes from their album sit among the diamonds and the bottles in my house, suggesting a debut of uncommon confidence and scope, fired along by the raging, uncontrollable creativity of a band just coming into bloom. 'Lost Cat' rolls in on glassy, incandescent waves of guitar that say THIS IS GOING TO BE GOOD, then cranks up, kicks off and starts driving stupid, and even the gruffest grump grins like a Caesarean. Barbed and abstract in equal measure, thin as a razor blade and alive, alive, alive. You really should hear it, because it'll make you happy.

Another outpost of little known musical education, the *Bridlington Gazette & Herald* felt much the same way as their music press comrades, affording Catatonia fulsome praise:

> Who can resist Cerys with her little girl lost voice? Her throaty vocals are joined by catchy harmonies on the irrepressible 'Lost Cat'. Short and undeniably sweet, that's 'All Girls Are Fly', with its slow burning guitars, while 'Indigo Blind' is a soulful breathless beaut of a melody. Two and a half minute wonders. Blink and you could miss them – which would be a catastrophe.

With a big budget afforded to them by the record company the band filmed a video for the single, which, again, almost inevitably ended up in the gossip columns. The London fire brigade were called out to a lamppost in a North London suburb to rescue a poor lady who they were informed was stuck up there. It was only Cerys filming an over-literal story for the 'Lost Cat' video, because, as Cerys said, 'you see cats get stuck up lampposts, don't they?' Obviously.

Mind you, they weren't experiencing any of that cat-type nine lives luck, 'Lost Cat' typified Catatonia's fortunes, or lack of, nibbling at the fringe of the chart by peaking at No. 41, one step short of that hallowed Top 40 placing.

The band didn't seem to mind though. As far as they were concerned it was an upwards curve. Talking to the *Big Issue Cymru*, Cerys was in modestly philosophical mood.

'I don't think we've become big yet. It's just I think we've got good tunes, and now they're playing the stuff on the radio, and that's good. We've been doing it a while, all of us, and it's fucking ace that we're getting somewhere. What the hell, it's not getting to the top of the mountain, it's enjoying it as you're walking around it, that's what the essence is.'

If Catatonia were surprised that they hadn't yet become chartbound superstars they weren't showing it, although they were admitting that life at their local multi-conglomerate mega record company was taking a bit of getting used to.

'It's different because obviously other people are involved and they're working hard for your benefit,' Cerys informed the *Wales on Sunday* newspaper. 'That's hellish weird because you're used to doing it for yourself and cocking up. But because I'm quite stubborn, I miss knowing what's going on and being one of the first people to know about things. Whereas now I don't know and then I lose my temper and that when I shouldn't. But, you've got to work with people, haven't you, and I'm a bit of a loner, usually.'

If anything they were becoming increasingly frustrated at the record company's insistence on moving the date for the debut album's release. Release dates for spring had been pencilled in and then scrapped, with the autumn now looking the most likely date for its long-awaited arrival.

'The trouble with big record companies is that they get so many bands to experiment with on their marketing strategies, as if we're guinea pigs,' Mark Roberts informed Cardiff's *Buzz* magazine. 'It's all bollocks. What we're hoping to do after the tour (with Space) is go straight into the studio and do the second album so they'll have to release that soon after. We'll overload them with material!'

Mark and Cerys along with Owen – who was to come on board and write songs with his two bandmates – were as good as their word. But first there were more gigs to contend with. It seemed that the cycle of touring just didn't stop. The band were beginning to wonder what the inside of their homes looked like. The summer saw them pitching their tent at most of the major festivals in the UK. They stormed the Reading Festival – Cerys challenging to fight the crowd while wearing a huge pair of boxing gloves. They made a successful return visit to the Phoenix Festival and were due to appear at the Essential Festival in Brighton. The band's slot was cancelled due to the fine British summer weather – torrential rain washed out the festival, or as the NME memorably reported it 'Chumbawumba were cancelled to enormous cheers, Catatonia were cancelled to enormous beers!'

What was most thrilling for the band was their appearance at Madstock 3 at Finsbury Park in North London in July. The one-day festival was headlined by those legendary nutty boys Madness who were still fooling their fans into turning up to see them by vowing that this indeed was their last-ever gig before announcing Madstock 4 the following year. Madness had asked Catatonia along personally because they said they liked what they had heard. The gig saw Catatonia slotting nicely into a classy pop line-up that included English tunesmiths Squeeze, funky popsters The James Taylor Quartet and cheesy funsters The Mike Flowers Pops, who were still dining out on their easy-listening smash-hit cover version of Oasis's 'Wonderwall'. The gig was slap bang in the middle of Euro '96 – the

European Football Championships, which were taking place in England that summer. Cerys said that she couldn't understand why when she was onstage an enormous cheer went up from the crowd mid-song, followed by a sudden surge to the right. When she came off she discovered that it was because England were playing and they had scored; the crowd surging towards one poor bloke with a television who was besieged by cheering fans!

Despite the absence of Wales from the summer's footballing finals (no surprise given that the last time they actually qualified for a major tournament was the 1958 World Cup Finals), Catatonia would soon have reason of their own to cheer and generally jump around in a loon-type style befitting that of an English football fan celebrating an Alan Shearer goal.

IF IT TURNS TO BLUE . . .

'You've Got A Lot To Answer For' was the band's third single and the tune that finally propelled them into the Top 40.

Described by Stephen Dalton in the *NME* as a ten-storey love song with a killer twist, sonorous church-bell guitars and a towering Alpine tune, it features the memorable line, 'If it turns to blue what are we gonna do, if it stays on white would it be alright if it all turns sour it's too late.' The song was written by Mark Roberts who came up with the concept while waiting in the queue at the local Spar in Cardiff. A few of his friends had become fathers but had decided not to move in with the mothers of their kids. Consequently they were being hounded by the CSA. The song, a shrewd snapshot of love Nineties style, examines the outcomes and ramifications of having a child.

The song was even more poignant because at that time in the mid-Nineties, Cardiff was fast becoming the single-mother capital of Europe. You couldn't walk the streets of the Welsh capital without seeing a Tory politician accompanied by journalists and camera crews banging on about the supposed abuses of the welfare state.

Again available in two CD formats and with cover artwork by Elfyn Lewis, the single was helped on its passage to the lofty heights of No. 35 by extensive radio play, TV appearances, successful summer festival appearances and Catatonia's debut on that summer radio institution the Radio 1 Roadshow.

CD1 featured the extra tracks 'Do You Believe In Me' and 'Dimbran' – a re-recording of the song that first appeared on the *For Tinkerbell* EP on Crai, while CD2 featured 'You Can' and 'All Girls Are Fly' (Da-De? Remix) – a remix pieced together by Cat bass player Paul Jones and Welsh-language music production guru Gorwel Owen. Meanwhile, the 7" single featured 'Blow The Millennium Blow' as the B-side.

Some songs are just too good for B-sides, so the adage goes, and 'Do You Believe in Me', from CD1 of 'You've Got A Lot To Answer For' is most definitely one of these. It's a majestic, frightening cauldron of bittersweet melody and grandiose anthemics. It's the sound of heartbreak with contorted guitars and Cerys's anguished voice is desperation personified.

The lyrics illuminate the spectacular songwriting partnership of Cerys and Mark with some killer lines that read: 'I'm Andy Cole's tortured soul lost out again in front of goal, I wish I had your cocaine confidence. Some girls are easier on the eye but could you take the silent lives? I wish I had your full-on arrogance. But I'm a white witch, mad bitch, hooked on drugs, the jury's out, the lawyer shrugs. The angel on my shoulder falls asleep. Do you believe in me or are you leaving me?'

Reading between the lines, it's fairly obvious that this immense song is a documentary snapshot of Cerys and Mark's relationship. The song and lyrics tell of troubled minds and troubled times. It just happens that their relationship was reaching the point of no return as the song was having a profound effect on those who listened to it.

In hindsight and with the revelations about Mark and Cerys that would appear a few years later, it's easy to see that this was the point of no return for their relationship. Only the band and their management knew that they were on the verge of splitting up. To the outside world and those around them they kept the heartache secret. Even Jayne Houghton, their press officer had said she was amazed when she discovered they were in a relationship. The fact that she said they didn't exactly act like a couple was the ultimate signpost that the relationship was headed for the rocks and would soon crash and burn in front of the rest of the band.

In keeping with the Catatonia policy of never holding back finished songs for an album Catatonia decided to put this wondrous song, that could surely grace any A-side or album, on the flip of the new single. 'The minute we finish writing songs we have to record them, and if there's no album to be done then they're immediately put out as B-sides,' explains Mark. 'We never save them. We never say, "That's too good to be put out right now." With their debut album long since in the can and awaiting its release from captivity there was only one home for the song.

WAY TO GO!

Riding high on the confidence that the success of 'You've Got A Lot To Answer For' gave them, Catatonia sped off on a couple of sorties across water to promote the forthcoming release of their album, now finally given a release date of 30 September. They played the Temple Bar Music Centre in Dublin as part of the annual 'In The City' music seminar on 10

September. They then headed over to Brussels on 13 September to make their Belgian debut at the 'Botanique Festival', La Rotonde.

After the warm-ups, the long waits, the heartaches, it was finally here. *Way Beyond Blue*, the debut album from Catatonia finally flew into UK record shops on Monday, 30 September 1996.

Given that the 12 songs on the album, plus hidden track 'Gyda Gwen', had been around in one form or another for 2–4 years, it was almost like an Early Years Best Of release.

> *Way Beyond Blue* reads like a greatest hits album already [wrote Stephen Dalton of the *NME*, illuminating the point]. A classy, luxurious pop masterwork that tells the majority of female singers to get their coat on the way out. Big on hooks, high on pop, though no pussycat when it comes to heart-felt introspection, world wise observation. You get the feeling that this is the just the (startling) beginning of something very, very big.

In an interview with *Music Week* magazine Cerys set her hopes out for the album, first hoping that the release of *Way Beyond Blue* would explode preconceptions about Catatonia. 'A lot of people don't know what we're capable of because they've just heard the singles and think 'they're just another indie band like Sleeper,' she says. 'But we're not. What we're doing is spookier and special. We just want it to be an album you can listen to and get a lot of different lines stuck in your head, and there are some really lovely tunes. Hopefully you can get back from a busy night out, put that on and let it be like a warm electric blanket.'

Mark had his own opinion of the album: 'You know how Oasis make good songs for just before you go out to the pub? Well our songs are going to cater for every human emotion.'

Unsurprisingly, given Catatonia were a band that the critics adored, reviews of *Way Beyond Blue* were universally borderline ecstatic.

Johnny Dee in Q magazine chirped that: 'they sound like angels, drink like fish and write songs that sound like whispered threats. In short, they are a great pop band . . . An audacious debut.'

Select magazine's Roy Wilkinson recognised that Catatonia's talents stretched way beyond limited indie music structures.

> Though a superficial listen may put them in fem-fronted indie territory, really these songs can be more usefully compared to the big-playground structures of Blondie, or a grit-enhanced Belinda Carlisle – the latter dimension enhanced still further by the band's noble drinking reputation. Thus, they're able to move adeptly from the power pop of 'Sweet Catatonia' through the kitchen-sink pregnancy-test drama ('If it turns to blue what are we going to do?') of 'You've Got A Lot To Answer For', to muted trip hop leanings and hints of 'Je t'aime'-

◀ All the young dudes: Mark and Paul strike a moody pose in Y Cyrff, 1989.

▶ Getting their heads together: Owen Powell and his Crumblowers bandmates, 1990.

© Rolant Dafis

▼ Brothers in Arms: Owen and Lloyd Powell flying the Welsh flag on St. David's Day at The Powerhaus, 1 March 1990.

▲ Life's a beach: for the early Catatonia line-up as they stroll on the seafront near Crai records at Llandwrog, 1993. The pic was used for the inner sleeve of the *For Tinkerbell* EP. Clancy was none too pleased at being obscured in the picture!

▲ Ooh the Glamour: skint and slumming it. Cerys in transit (van) on the way to London, 1994.

◀ Backstage pass: Cerys, Mark, Paul and Clancy at The Garage, London, February 1994.

▲ On the Last Lap: Cerys and Mark round off their mammoth trek of the UK with Space, at University of London Union, June 1996.

▼ Queen of the Castle: Cerys with guitar rocks out at The Dublin Castle, November 1994.

▲ The nascent Cerys Matthews finds her feet at The Joiners Arms, Southampton, February 1994.

▼ Life Thru A Lens: Cerys scrubs up for one of her first photo shoots, 1994.

▲ Groovy Baby! Mark and Cerys, then known as Sweet Catatonia, in their very first publicity shot – an Andy Warhol-esque 60s homage. The picture was taken by Rolant Dafis in the Autumn of 1992.

▲ Slogan's Run: the infamous photo session at Jayne Houghton's office which spawned a legend.

▶ 'We are the Mob': Cerys surrounded by four 'minders', Aled, Mark, Owen and Paul looking suitably moody and magnificent for a Warners promo shoot..

▼ Paul onstage at ULU,

© Angela Lubrano

▲ Canvassing opinion: Cerys with obligatory beer, having some summer fun in a tent at Reading festival, August 1997.

▲ 'Portrait Of A Girl With A Lovely Voice.' The National Portrait Gallery, Summer 1999.

▲ Cerys Matthews, superbra, superstar, wowing The Reading festival, August 1999.

◀ They come to a Land Down under: streets ahead of the opposition in Melbourne on Catatonia's Australian tour, February 1999.

▲ The epitome of cool: individual, sultry and stylish, the new Queen of Pop, Australia 1999.

> period Serge Gainsbourg on 'Dream On'. And all delivered in a voice that, while it shares some eldritch beauty with Bjork, has more intrigue than Ms Gudmundsdottir has managed in some time.

David Bennun reviewing the album for *Melody Maker* enthused: 'The entire LP is everything it threatens not to be – enchanting, elusive, bold, gorgeous. Sweet Catatonia, for sure. Sour Catatonia, strange Catatonia, cruel Catatonia – but so, so, sweet.

The *NME*'s Simon Williams was on equally ebullient form:

> This is a tremendously assured debut which stands as confidently apart from the indie mainland as the Gower Peninsula, built to a similarly grand design and packing an equally hefty rock content. Most importantly, singer Cerys Matthews is a supremely cool frontwoman who can swing from breathy sensuality to flinty melancholy in the span of a single word . . . Sheer class is written all over this Stephen Street-produced masterpiece. Underneath their polished pop sheen these uniformly majestic tunes are big-hearted, lived-in, lusty, boozy, heartbroken and ready for a fight – or a shag – at all times. That's why 'Way Beyond Blue' is this year's best guitar album.

With these exclamatory reviews ringing in their ears you could have forgiven Catatonia for thinking that the world was theirs for the taking, but as in everything truth is stranger than fiction. What was to come would tear at the very foundations of the group. It was to be an emotional rollercoaster ride, with shattered illusions and relationship heartache at its core. But if you want eventful, then you came to the right place.

10
When it all falls apart

> 'I'd rather stay bold and lonely, I dream that I'm your one and only'
> (Catatonia, 'Mulder and Scully')

With the adulatory reviews for *Way Beyond Blue* reverberating in their ears, outwardly Catatonia wore the appearance of a band with the world at their feet. However, this was just a mask for the internal strife that had beset them. Inwardly, emotional walls were caving in and the epicentre of this state of flux reverberated about Mark and Cerys's stormy relationship.

The cracks had started to show at Sawmills Studios in Cornwall the year before. The location may have been idyllic but the situation both Mark and Cerys found themselves in was anything but. Paul Sampson, the producer who had manned the control desk at Sawmills, had rightly pointed out that when you meld your two greatest passions – your music and your relationship – then sparks are bound to fly.

The quarrels continued into 1996. Their relationship wasn't helped by the excessively gruelling touring which began at Christmas 1995 and eventually foundered under the sun of the summer festivals.

Their fans may have been oblivious to the fact that Mark and Cerys were even in a relationship, but there were interviews the band conducted during 1996 in which tensions visibly rose like red mist from the printed pages. A clash between the singer and guitarist in the 6 April issue of *NME* exemplified their passionately destructive relationship.

> 'You don't need too much passion in music, otherwise you end up sounding like the Alarm,' observes Mark. 'You've got to be very careful. I'd say most of the time we're trying to restrain ourselves, like.'
>
> 'That's bollocks! I don't' says an outraged Cerys. She pauses and stares wildly at the guitarist. 'You don't really do that, do you?'
>
> 'Well, if I didn't I'd be jumping up and down running around and fucking butting you!' retorts Mark.
>
> 'Yeah? Go on then!' yells Cerys. 'He's stoned, he's just talking shit. He's always too stoned to do anything.'

When the *NME* interview appeared Catatonia were just oiling the wheels of the minibus for their mammoth tour with Space. It was obvious that by spending that length of time together tensions were liable to spill over.

A gig at the Tunbridge Wells Forum in Kent was preceded by an interview with local music fanzine *Fiasco*. The interviewer must have sensed some animosity in the air between the couple because, in an interview conducted in a cramped dressing room, he audaciously asked, 'Had any fights yet?'

> Cerys pauses then looks at another member of the band, Mark – the guitarist, who is tucking into a beer nearby. 'We haven't had any mega fights yet, have we? But then we've got about five or six weeks to go, ha ha ha,' Cerys laughs sarcastically.

Both Mark and Cerys are passionate people, so when they meet head on, there is always going to be an avalanche of bruised emotions.

Although Cerys is outwardly demonstrative, the life and soul of the party, whereas Mark is much more outwardly withdrawn, he was more than a match for her legendary drinking prowess. Many people close to the band saw their hedonism as pure escapism, a way of ridding themselves of the troubles they may have had in their relationship. Of course, this was a false economy. You wake up the next day feeling like you could die and then have to cope with the harsh reality of your situation as it floods back into your dulled senses.

In many ways their relationship was ultimately destructive. Cerys was made for the limelight – a party-loving chick who loved to live it up on the road, whereas Mark was a musician's musician: he had no truck with the trappings of fame that encircled a successful band. 'Mark would be far happier staying at home with his mates down the local pub,' says Crai Records' Rhys Mwyn, who has known Mark for years. 'He's happiest when he's just writing songs, I think he can do without all the other flippant sides of rock 'n' roll the band are faced with – the interviews, the excessive touring.'

Mark Roberts is oft portrayed as the mystery man of the group. Invariably seen as moody, aloof and plain miserable, quick to crush a journalist with an acerbic one-liner, he's actually got a razor sharp sense of humour and his dry wit is only seen by those closest to him.

When you parallel Mark and Cerys's personalities they are diametrically opposed people. Cerys would later admit in interviews, when it was revealed that she had had a relationship with the band's guitarist and her co-songwriter, that their relationship 'was always a love/hate thing', but 'then it mostly became hate'.

Cerys's 48-hour bender in Marseilles, drunken nights out and gossip-causing escapades could be interpreted as symptomatic of the state of turmoil she was in as their relationship fell apart. She was living a crazy life, regardless of whether the love of her life was in the band with her or not. But you couldn't help thinking that it was no coincidence that all the stories of OTT excess that she was indulging in reached its zenith during the time she finally split up with Mark.

Mark himself would later admit in an interview that he believed that relationships between band members 'were unnatural', and that both he and Cerys would be better off as bandmates and not lovers.

Imagine how hard it must have been for both of them to have your relationship fall apart and have nowhere to hide, for there to be no escape from the person who has broken your heart. It's tough enough to be in a band pushing themselves hard in an attempt to achieve a modicum of success, whether you are romantically entwined with one of your band mates or not. You've got to be with each other all the time, invariably either stuck in the back of a transit van, propped against an amplifier with only your bandmates' collective body odours for company. Then there's all the time you have to think. When you are touring you are only really busy for those two hours you are on stage. For the two of them it must have been life under the microscope with just too much time to dwell on their confusion.

However it appeared that Cerys was the one bearing the brunt of the hurt. Revelations some years later in the US *Interview* magazine revealed that it was Cerys who had been dumped. She told the magazine: 'He dumped me and had a new girlfriend and then we went on tour a day or two later. So you're stuck in a very small space, singing songs you've written together. I spent time with a hat over my eyes and shades on just to try and get space.'

Incredibly, save their band members and their management, Cerys and Mark did manage to keep their heartache a secret. Many close to the band didn't even know they were involved in a relationship in the first place.

'I would never have guessed they were together,' explains Excess Press's Jayne Houghton. 'They just didn't come across like two people who were in a relationship. I did find it surprising when I was told. But you have to think that they were two very private people and that they managed to keep their emotions in check. They certainly never let their feelings get in the way of their work. They were also very professional with me and you have to pay them a tribute for that.'

Amazingly, the revelation that Mark and Cerys had been an item would only surface two years after they split up. And that would only come to light through the new songs that Catatonia were to write – if they could hold everything together, of course.

PRESSED INTO CHANGES

Mark and Cerys's crumbling relationship may have been having a knock-on effect on the state of the group but there were other rumbles of discontent in the Catatonia camp.

Way Beyond Blue, despite its rave notices in magazines and newspapers in the UK, had failed to substantially dent the album charts. The saga over its protracted release date certainly didn't help matters. It only peaked at No. 40.

Ultimately, *Way Beyond Blue* suffered through a lack of cohesion. Instead of the usual one producer, one engineer set-up of an album's recording, the tracks that make up *Way Beyond Blue* were recorded at studios all over the country with a number of different producers.

Remember also that the tracks, although standing on their own respective merits, represented songs that had been written over a long period of time, between 1992 and 1995. As Stephen Dalton had pointed out in his review of the album for the *NME*, '"Way Beyond Blue" reads like an early greatest hits package.'

If the record company were not overwhelmed with how the album fared, over at the band's publishing company Charlie Pinder was having difficulties of his own. 'Ok, sales were relatively small and it under-achieved, but they had made some key friends in the industry and on radio, so it wasn't all gloom,' Charlie explained.

Nevertheless he admits that he had a difficult time talking Sony into picking up the publishing option they had on the band's future album releases.

'Yeah, I had quite a hard time talking my bosses round. The problem was that they were existing in a sort of first division indie band league. I persuaded Sony that they had the songs, and that Cerys was going to come into her own.' Lucky for him and them he was more than right!

The album's chart position was disappointing given that British music had been undergoing a renaissance with Britpop boosting sales of British artistes for the first time since The Happy Mondays and The Stone Roses lolloped their way out of Manchester with their flares swaying in the breeze.

Even those bands with whom Catatonia were drawing unfair comparisons such as Sleeper and Echobelly were releasing records that would pepper the Top 20 with alarming regularity.

Wales might have been in vogue, but you got the feeling that, despite the unquestionable musical talent that was being unearthed in the Principality, the scene had yet to reach its zenith among mainstream music buyers. Wales was still very much a scene rooted in the indie underground. Much of the uncompromising, leftfield music coming out of Wales just wasn't made for the charts.

Yet, Catatonia's singles, 'Sweet Catatonia', 'Lost Cat' and 'You've Got A Lot To Answer For' were super-charged pop songs in excelsis. These were songs that were made for crossover chart-pop territory. Unfortunately, it was increasingly becoming the case that the music was coming a poor second to the band's headline-grabbing exploits. Despite their burgeoning fame – or infamy – Catatonia were still very much an indie music press band. If they could have transferred their success in the gossip columns to record sales, they would have been one of the biggest bands in the UK.

Every interview that they did to promote *Way Beyond Blue* had read something like:

'Cerys, Catatonia's self-confessed pop princess (who combines the looks and singing voice of a rebel angel, the speaking voice of a particularly innocent five year old chain smoker and the extra-curricular habits of EMF at their most wicked) is trying to justify her latest gossip column friendly exploit, hurling a television out of her own bedroom window. . .'

And 'Cerys Matthews is mad for it. As barking mad for it as Keith Moon was, as the Beastie Boys were; as mad for it as someone fronting one of the best pop bands around should be.'

In short, the way they were being portrayed, as alcoholic party animals, was cheating and undermining the band of their unquestionable music talent. While the band had initially played their part in getting these tired epithets thrown at them, they had made inroads to clean up their act, and they were becoming mightily fed-up with the predictable hedonistic tag.

Change was needed and Warners acted quickly to remove Jayne Houghton and Excess Press from their contract as the band's press agents. Although Excess had formulated the band's press strategy and had positioned them as resolutely mad-for-it – this was the time of Liam Gallagher's swaggering and the boisterous rise of laddism – the strategy had worked too well. What started out as a drive to secure the band some much needed press and publicity, the oxygen of any new band attempting to make their mark, it had ultimately spiralled out of control. Cerys herself was becoming increasingly pissed off with all the stories about her drinking exploits, although most of them were true! She yearned for her band to be taken seriously. In an interview with Southampton-based fanzine *The Edge* she protested: 'I want to be glamorous and they keep printing these stories. I want to be like Kylie Minogue, I don't want to be like Courtney Love.'

Jayne Houghton recognised what had happened and steps to rectify the situation were under way when Warners stepped in.

'They were happy to go along with the hedonistic drinking image at first, but then it got too much, it got too top heavy, it looked as if that's all they did,' explained Jayne. 'Everyone wanted this loudmouth lippy drunk that would go on stage pissed, it became a noose, and we had to reposition them again and show the singing and songwriting talents.'

Sadly Warners pulled the plug before that work could be fulfilled. Understandably Jayne Houghton was upset. It's an event that still rankles with her now.

'In early meetings I would say there wasn't really anyone at Warners at the time who really got it, I don't think,' says Jayne. 'Every label plays games and I'd imagine Warners were telling MRM: 'We pay Excess £X thousand a month, that's £X thousand a year. Now I'm sure you'd get more support from the company if you worked in-house, you might get all the money you wanted for that video and well you'd get that if the band's PR was in-house.'

Jayne says that she reckons Warners just didn't think she and her company had the capability to take the band in the direction the company wanted them to go. 'Warners wanted Catatonia to be their big success story,' she says. 'They wanted them to be like the new Pretenders or something, a big mainstream, cross-over band, and they saw me as a sort of indie PR who was great at getting gossip stories but couldn't necessarily cross them over myself, which is bollocks obviously – we do massive bands.

'We've handled the press for Wet Wet Wet, so we can do bands that aren't just indie bands. And you wouldn't really call New Order an indie band now. But the perception of my company with Warners was that we're an indie company and that they needed their major label weight behind the project.'

Jayne Houghton was distraught at what was happening. She felt immensely close to the group and was incredibly upset when she lost the contract. 'We had a huge fall-out, I met with the band and I was absolutely gutted, there was a big argument,' she remembers. 'I think they realised it would be the logical career-move to go to Warners. At the time, I just wouldn't accept it, but in retrospect it's what I'd have done, it's what anyone would do.'

So off Catatonia went. Ironically press relations between the band and the label didn't exactly get off to an auspicious start on moving in-house. It just typified the gulf between, on the one hand, a relatively small PR company with a small roster of bands who can dedicate time and effort working for their clients and, on the other, a huge record company who have insufficient PR staff to handle their oversized roster of acts.

Iestyn George, was news editor at the *NME* when he received a call from the Warner's press office.

'The person who called me started to rave about this great band from Wales,' explains Iestyn. 'They said I've got this fantastic band called Catalonia, I think they also called them Cefalonia during the course of the conversation. It was bad for one thing because if they had done their homework they would have known my role in their career and known that we at the NME were their biggest champions. They were talking to me as if I had never heard of them.'

Iestyn was bemused. But ironically as Catatonia's fortunes improved, the press office would flex its contacts book and more than justify why the bands PR was brought in-house. Still at the time he was worried that the band were about to become just another record company statistic. 'When *Way Beyond Blue* didn't do anything I thought, well, if the second album isn't successful then that's the last we will hear of Catatonia. I feared the worse when they were taken in-house, because you feel that they are just a small, insignificant cog in a huge wheel that is quick to crush anything that gets in its way. Major record companies don't tend to have a history of patience.'

MANIC STREET TOURING

Catatonia had to deliver, especially when the record company decided to re-release the band's third single 'Bleed'. Released on 18 November 1996, six weeks after the release of *Way Beyond Blue*, it was available in a two-CD format and the cover art was again painted by Elfyn Lewis.

CD1 featured 'Bleed' with an acoustic version of 'Way Beyond Blue' recorded in the summer, backstage at the Phoenix Festival in a live session for the band's old mate Mark Radcliffe and a live version of 'Painful' recorded in August at the Reading Festival for Radio 1.

CD2 featured an alternative version of 'Bleed' and live versions of 'Bleed' and 'Do You Believe In Me' recorded at the Reading Festival.

The cassette version featured 'Bleed' backed by 'Way Beyond Blue', live from Phoenix and 'Bleed' live at Reading, while a limited 7" inch single featured 'Bleed' and the live version of 'Do You Believe In Me' on the flipside.

Despite unstinting support from Mark Radcliffe – who at times seemed to be a one-man, Catatonia-supporting bandwagon – the single stiffed at 46.

The re-release of Bleed bisected yet another furious round of touring. By the end of the year Catatonia would have played over 100 gigs in the UK alone. If Mark and Cerys wanted to escape each other and seek a little solitude after splitting up by taking some time off – a break away from the band – they certainly weren't getting the chance. What all the band wanted to do was close a chapter on *Way Beyond Blue* as quickly as they could and forge a new beginning in every sense of the word.

Mark especially was eager to start demoing new songs and prove to the record company that his band weren't just another workmanlike generic indie outfit. He told *Music Week* magazine:

'Up until Christmas we're going to record as and when we get the chance. We want to book ourselves into a studio in Cardiff and start working because we've got a lot of formulated ideas about what we want to do. Some stuff will be a bit of a departure from what we've done so far – more adventurous with a different approach to arrangement. We'll be experimenting, but it will still be pop.'

Despite Mark's desire to get in the studio it would be difficult finding the time. In October they had started a tour as support with The Manic Street Preachers – a huge thrill for Catatonia who were great fans of The Manics. The Cats sang The Manics' praises in an interview with Stuart Baillie of the *NME*: 'The Manics were never apologetic,' says Mark. 'They were always in your face. Maybe they showed that you could come from Wales and be really confident about what you're doing.'

Owen: 'God bless The Manics for having us. They could choose any support bands in the world and charge them a fortune to buy on the tour. And yet they took Gorky's Zygotic Mynci on the last tour, then us on this one. We're laughing!'

The feeling between the two bands was mutual. Manics bass player Nicky Wire in particular loved Catatonia and tried to get to see them whenever he could. He also memorably dubbed Cerys: 'The Queen of the Council Estates' for her gritty, down-to-earth glamour.

The Manics had recently returned from an enforced exile after the much-documented disappearance of their guitarist Richey Edwards. He had abandoned his car at The Aust Services on the Severn Bridge in February 1995 the day before he had been due to fly out to America with singer James Dean Bradfield for a promotional tour. He failed to turn up for a planned meeting with James and has not been seen since. Despite various alleged sightings in the intermittent years since he has been missing, Richey's disappearance remains one of rock's greatest mysteries.

After Richey had gone, The Manics had to deliberate whether to carry on or not. After much soul-searching they decided to continue as a three-piece and had blazed back to form with their album *Everything Must Go*. It ably demonstrated that they had lost none of their musical fire and lyrical astuteness, despite the departure of the person who had previously written most of the lyrics.

The tour was a success for both Catatonia and The Manics. For The Manics it reconfirmed their position as one of Britain's best live bands, while for Catatonia it allowed them to play to some of their biggest crowds yet. From 5 October to 23 October they played at 2000-3000 capacity venues like Aston Villa Leisure Centre in Birmingham and the City Hall in Newcastle.

While on this UK tour The Manics had confirmed plans to play a special Christmas show at the newly opened Cardiff International Arena. The state-of-the-art venue in the Welsh capital has a capacity of 5,500. It would be by far and away the biggest gig The Manics would have headlined. It was to be their triumphant homecoming and more importantly it would stand as a landmark moment in Welsh rock history because the bill was also to include Catatonia and The Super Furry Animals. It appeared that the Welsh music scene was about to be the scene that finally celebrated itself.

Before their appearance at the festival of Taffpop, Catatonia made an appearance on the fifth birthday issue of *Volume* – the UK CD and magazine that they had appeared on with 'Dream On' way back in May 1994. This time they contributed an acoustic version of 'Mickey' (otherwise known as 'Some Half Baked Idea Called Wonderful') recorded for Mark Radcliffe's evening show on Radio 1.

There was also the first release of the band's music into the lucrative Japanese market. Japanese people are traditionally voracious music buyers and fanatical fans. *Tourist* was a varied collection, featuring the singles 'Sweet Catatonia' and 'Lost Cat' as well as extra tracks from UK single releases 'All Girls Are Fly', 'Indigo Blind', 'Acapulco Gold', 'Tourist' and 'To and Fro', live versions of 'Whale' and 'Sweet Catatonia' recorded on the Mark Radcliffe Show (where else!) and a demo version of 'Cut You Inside' (an early track recorded with Paul Sampson). *Tourist* is yet another of those much sought after Catatonia rarities, valued upwards of £30 by those fans lucky enough to have copies of the highly prized release.

Alongside the *Volume* and *Tourist* releases there was yet more touring as they headed off through November on a headline tour of their own. Catatonia would have been forgiven for forgetting what the interiors of their homes looked like, such was the time they had spent away from home in 1996. The excessive touring was particularly hard on drummer Aled Richards and bassman Paul Jones who both had partners at home with children. But that is one of the occupational hazards of being in a rock 'n' roll band: it can be life in a suitcase.

Aled had two children and Paul one. Aled would drive back to Llanelli where he lived, while Paul would head home to Cardiff at any chance they had in between dates. Paul and Aled are the wiser heads of the band. Paul himself is several years older than the rest of the boys and has served his time as a rock 'n' revolutionary. While they could carouse it up with the rest of the band, it was mainly left to Cerys, Mark and Owen to provide the occasional bout of unruly behaviour. It's no understatement to say that having children changes your world, and for Aled and Paul this was certainly true. Although the band was their job, it wasn't their life.

'I've got children at home, so it's unfair of me to be living it up all the time on the road. My priorities have changed,' he admitted. 'When some of the band head off to parties or accept invites for parties, I'm happy to head off home to Cardiff to see my partner and my kid.'

Sadly, after the gigs at larger venues, it was a case of size really does matter as the band checked back into their far less roomy old haunts like the Leeds Duchess of York, Oxford Zodiac and Manchester Roadhouse.

Catatonia's booking agent Paul Buck must either take credit for the number of gigs and tours he was putting together or be responsible for making a concerted effort to kill the band through excessive touring. No sooner had Paul Jones and Aled Richards reacquainted themselves with their children than they were herded back into the minibus for another round of dates in December, this time supporting York's retro rockers Shed Seven.

No slur on Shed Seven who do that loose-fitting baggy rock thing as well as can be expected from a band with Shed in their monicker and a singer, Rick Witter, with a name made for Cockney rhyming slang, but Catatonia looked like film stars compared to this bunch of Yorkshire builders. It must have pained Catatonia greatly to have to support bands like Shed Seven, when their confidence and belief screamed that their talent was worth a thousand generically indie, dullard, lad rock bands.

Still, their big night out, a chance to dress themselves up and show themselves off supporting The Manics at the CIA (Cardiff International Arena) was now at hand. The gig, on 12 December, was a real homecoming not only for The Manics, but also both Catatonia and the third on-the-bill Super Furry Animals. All three bands had achieved what had been unthinkable years beforehand: the apotheosis of bands from Wales who had gained success pretty much on their own terms, while retaining their own strength of national identity. After years of ridicule and ignorance, Wales and its music scene had helped forge a cultural renaissance and instilled a new found pride and confidence in its people. Now was the time for celebration.

The gig had sold out in a matter of a few weeks and was eagerly anticipated by those who had snapped up tickets. The gig, as you would imagine, was storming. It underlined not only the strength of the country's music scene but its breadth of diversity. So for The Super Furry Animals look under twisted psychedelia, for Catatonia file next to exotic pop, and for The Manics underline anthemic rock.

A leader written by Neil Fowler, then editor of the *Western Mail*, the national morning newspaper of Wales, neatly gauged the temperature of the times. Under the title 'Suddenly it's the land of pop song' he wrote:

> The 1990s have seen two of the most unlikely and unpredicted revivals. The first was in pop music, whose obituary was written in the 1980s when it appeared ready to be swept aside by everything from computer games and the Internet.
>
> The old beast refused to die however, and sprang back to life, inspired by Britpop and a fragmentation of styles. While that may leave today's music scene incomprehensible to over-40s, they were never supposed to understand it anyway.
>
> Just as remarkable is the rebirth of Welsh pop, a phenomenon which reached a 1996 climax last night with a Cardiff show by the three biggest names to have emerged from Wales since many members of their audience were in primary school.

> To have bands as varied and popular as The Manic Street Preachers, Catatonia, Super Furry Animals, Gorky's Zygotic Mynci and more emerge from a confined area in such a short space of time is particularly striking, given the thin gruel Wales has previously served up for the charts.
>
> Wales has had to rely on past glories of the likes of Tom Jones, Shakin' Stevens and The Alarm. Never before has Wales been able to boast such a cluster of success. Suddenly Wales becomes trendy, and the eyes of the music business are on Cardiff, Newport and the rest. The stereotyped vision of a Wales stuck in a 1950s time warp is beginning to disappear.
>
> The short-term effects of Welsh pop on tourism, business and prosperity? Minimal. The long-term effect? By itself, still very small. But it will form part of a larger picture which tells the outside world what we who live here already know: that Wales has changed and continues to change.

Ironically, given their country's shifting cultural landscape, Catatonia were about to undergo a startling regenesis all of their own.

THE VELVET REVOLUTION

After the years of shambling performances, hedonistic headline grabbing and a reputation that took no note of their musical talent, Catatonia started 1997 with a steadfast determination to get their act together. That news was met with gentle hilarity in some quarters. Simon Williams writing in the *NME* quipped: 'Look, Catatonia have been many things – several of them unprintable – over the last three years, but professional has rarely threatened the top of the list.'

An interview in Cardiff University student's newspaper, *Gair Rhydd*, was particularly revelatory, shedding light on the band's new attitude. The newspaper's reporter Mark Williams wrote:

> The pitfalls of pop have threatened to temper the Catatonia career curve, most notably with regard to their well-documented and excessive alcoholic consumption. For Cerys, though, it's all part of the learning curve. 'Last year we were having a lot more fun than maybe we should have been having. We had big rows with promoters for not being able to play, so this is the difference between last year and this year, we're only allowed a limited amount. It's like, you turn up in London at 4pm and just hang about till you play, and wherever you are anyway, it's in pubs all the time, so what do you do?'
>
> 'We were enjoying the prelims rather than the working up to the cup final in the past,' Cerys adds. 'But we're getting there now – we're ready for the European Cup.'
>
> Mark pinpointed the exact period of Catatonia's reawakening: 'Halfway though the last tour we turned from punk to pop.'
>
> 'We always wanted to be a pop band,' insists Cerys. 'But we couldn't do it.

We thought we were Ace Of Base . . .'

'. . . Until we played the live tapes back . . .' growls Mark. '. . . And then we could see all the comparisons with Pinky & Perky and The Slits.'

'And I was going, "No, I'm Whigfield!' [Scandinavian model turned one-hit Euro pop wonder with the abysmal 'Saturday Night'] says Cerys. 'We got it wrong somewhere between me and the microphone. Whereas now it's Shirley Bassey all the way down the line.'

Catatonia have always managed to confound the critics anyway. This situation was exemplified by confused writers attempting to get a handle on the band.

'One writer would say they're a pop-punk band and the next would say: "They're like The Cocteau Twins,"' explains Mark. 'The nearest anyone got was, "They sound like an accident in a knife and fork factory."'

Sadly, for the critics but not for everyone else, Catatonia were going to confound those wordsmiths once again. Mark had already hinted that some of the new songs Catatonia had written while touring throughout 1996 would be a bit of a departure from what they had done so far. He stated that the songs would be more adventurous, experimental with a different style of arrangement, but still pop.

The New Year saw the band back in Cardiff demoing new songs, while Mark found time to don a new hat, that of record producer. He produced a mini-album, *Something To Tell Her*, by emerging Welsh band Topper at Big Noise Recording Studios in Cardiff. Topper are from Penygroes in North Wales, not far from Mark and Paul Jones's birthplace in Llanrwst, but the band had moved to Cardiff to base themselves in the city that was buzzing with a real sense of musical community. That's how they met Mark.

Much of the focus of the music scene in Cardiff was based around Big Noise studios. Big Noise was the new name for Soundspace recording and rehearsal studios, the location where Catatonia had first rehearsed as a band back in 1993. It had been taken over by local musician Greg Haver, a stalwart of the South Wales music scene who had been in various bands over the last 10-15 years. Greg ran Big Noise with his business partner Ceri Collier, himself a local musician who was once the frontman for brilliantly spiky Valleys punk pop combo The Tinmen at the beginning of the Nineties. Just as the Welsh music scene was gaining an admirable reputation so Big Noise was reaping the rewards of the nation's musical success stories. The Manic Street Preachers had worked on many of the songs that had formed the nucleus of the *Everything Must Go* album at Big Noise, while Greg was working with many of the new wave of Welsh bands like Derrero, Topper and Big Leaves, that were emerging as this dynamic movement gathered pace.

Greg Haver had got to know Mark Roberts while he was engineering the sessions that Mark was producing with Topper. 'Mark was impressed with the set-up we had down here,' explains Greg. 'It was very convenient for a lot of bands living in Cardiff and it had a nice atmosphere, so he said he would bring Catatonia in to record some demos.'

These demos formed the nucleus of what would become Catatonia's second album *International Velvet* – the album that would either end their recording career with Warners or elevate them to the lofty heights of major success. While complacency had gripped the indie rock elite, Catatonia had to pull out all the stops or face the dumper. The end result is living proof that when the going gets tough, the tough write a host of heart-stopping tunes and give full rein to one of the most expressive voices on the planet.

Ironically, it was Mark and Cerys's broken relationship that fired the new songs, it gave them a tension and spark that had worked wonders for Abba and Fleetwood Mac before them; two bands with members in relationships who had famously split while still recording together.

The *Melody Maker*'s Everett True had astutely observed in the famous interview conducted after Cerys had returned from her 48 hours AWOL in France, that 'most drinking has a hedonistic edge to it. Catatonia seems tinged with a certain desperation.'

'It's true I really write my best songs when I'm really, really desperate,' Cerys told True. 'And then that song will help me get through that period. I get the biggest high when we write something amazing, so I've got to keep on writing for that feeling. Before I joined Catatonia, if I was in a temper then I'd take it out on something. Now I take it out on my songs.'

That desperation and depth of emotional feeling was to be laid bare on the new songs. Mark and Cerys, as well as Owen who was also penning songs, were all writing and they were particularly prolific in their output. Whether it was a means of exorcising the demons of their broken relationship or just a way of pure fanatical lyrical escapism, the songs that were penned by Robert and Matthews were tales of hope springing from disillusionment, failed relationships, emotional confusion, sensual excess and blasted regret.

Catatonia demoed their new songs in January and February of 1997 and readied themselves to record the album in June. This time they had decided to record closer to home but retaining the same rural setting as Sawmills Studios in Cornwall, by recording at Monnow Valley Studios in Monmouth, on the Wales-England border. The studio is only about 30 miles from Cardiff so it would allow the band time to escape back to their friends and family in South Wales when they wanted.

THIS IS THE WORLD CALLING

Save a few dates in France and Germany arranged by Rhys Mwyn back in 1993 and '94, and dates in Belgium and Holland more recently, Catatonia had rarely ventured outside the UK. Although they had covered the miles in their minibus scuttling up and down the UK's major motorways, it was now time for them to start collecting their air miles: they were off on their first-ever trip to North America.

The group crossed the pond for a trio of showcase gigs in New York, Los Angeles and Austin, Texas in mid-March. Their first bite of the Big Apple came at New York Brownies supporting fellow UK band The Boo Radleys. The Boos, signed to Creation Records in the UK, had just had their first taste of chart success in their homeland with the pop thrill of 'Wake Up Boo', a song that was propelled into the Top 10 on the back of some heavy-duty promotion by Chris Evans, the ginger-topped media mogul, who was then presenting Radio1's breakfast show.

Whether you like to travel or not, playing your first gig in the United States in the skyscraper littered metropolis of New York doesn't get any more impressive. Catatonia, just like everyone else when they first breathe in the enormity of New York life, were suitably overawed. 'It was fabulous,' Cerys raved when asked for her view on New York.

After gorging on the Big Apple, the band headed for the influential South by Southwest music festival, which, alongside the annual CMJ music seminar, is America's premier showcase of up and coming new bands from the UK and America. Catatonia had no thoughts of breaking America. Many bands have tried to get a grip on music's holy grail but, apart from such notable exceptions as The Beatles, The Rolling Stones, U2 and The Spice Girls, few have excelled in cracking the US record market.

Anyway, Catatonia weren't even sure whether *Way Beyond Blue* would even be released in the States. Negotiation was still under way to find the band a home on one of Warners' many subsidiary Stateside record labels. Whether the US market would have the pleasure of sampling the Cat's debut album was still in negotiation. The trip was purely a meet and greet exercise, a getting to know you fact-finding exercise. As well as a chance for Cerys and the boys to sample the glamorous high life. This they did when they breezed into Los Angeles, the City of Angels, and the head office of the American dream.

*

Catatonia were booked to play at the notorious Viper Room, LA's infamous club where Hollywood's young A-list film stars and rock musicians would come to party to excess, and occasionally death. The Viper Room was the scene of the collapse of former Aussie soap star and some-time pop star Jason Donovan, an event which precipitated his descent into rehab. It was also more famously the scene of the death of American actor River Phoenix, after a drugs and alcohol binge. With Catatonia's reputation for burning the candle at both ends and eating it, asking them to play the Viper Room could have been seen as jumping from the proverbial frying pan into the fire. Luckily, for all concerned the blue touchpaper wasn't lit. In fact the Viper Room experience was sadly one big letdown for the band.

'It [the Viper Room] sucks,' spat Cerys. 'You're not allowed to sit on the floor or lean on the wall or you get hassle from the bouncers. It's not cool enough!'

The Viper Room might have disappointed but the rest of their stay in LA was eventful enough. Cerys spent her time star-spotting, impromptu hair dyeing and autograph hunting down pensionable English rock stars.

'It was like we were hallucinating, seeing all these famous people,' bubbled Cerys. 'I was posing in this jacuzzi on top of a hotel in Hollywood and I've got bleached hair, and I went to the bathroom and my hair was bright blue! And Status Quo walked into the same hotel in LA, so it was all a bit mad. I had to get their autographs for my housemates! This was Hollywood, so we did lots of shopping. I got an ant farm and a twinkle ring – you press it and it has lots of coloured lights. None of us had been to America before, so we were just lapping it up. We met loads of people and everyone liked the shows as well. All in all, it was a brilliant trip!'

Not having time to catch their breath and develop their Stateside gig snaps, they threw themselves into yet another UK tour throughout April. They were to play a gig supporting Gene, the fey Smiths-soundalikes led by Cardiff-born Martin Rositter, in Greece at the end of March. However Cerys lost her voice after touring the US and they had to pull out of the Athens gig to give her voice time to recover.

This time though they could introduce the new songs they had penned into their set, giving themselves and their audience a chance to sample these new tunes in a live arena.

They played ten dates in all calling in at The Room (Hull); Hop and Grape (Manchester); Lomax (Liverpool); King Tut's (Glasgow); Riverside (Newcastle); Leadmill (Sheffield); Guildhall (Gloucester); Wedgewood Rooms (Portsmouth); Waterfront (Norwich); and Coal Exchange (Cardiff).

Any time a band tries out new songs on their audience it's always a nerve-wracking affair. You have every faith in your new material but unless you play the songs live, you have no idea how they will be received. Catatonia were confident they had surpassed themselves with the new songs they had penned, and thankfully their appreciative fans thought so too. During the UK tour they debuted four new songs as a teaser for the material to come – 'Game On', 'Johnny Come Lately', 'Mulder and Scully' and 'That's All Folks'.

Listening to the new material it was obvious that Catatonia were once again about to bedazzle and bemuse those critics desperately attempting to tempt the band into a particular pigeonhole. The songs making their live debut were set to drive the music hacks to distraction over suitable analogies and adjectives to pinpoint them.

'Game On', written by Mark and Cerys, is a dayglo pop strumalong, a 24-carat nugget of mellow gold with a lyric full of hope over adversity. It tells of how the song's protagonist will not be beaten however low she/he gets – 'I know that I could never fall from grace, I'm far too clever . . . I will achieve my destiny, my stars ascent a certainty.'

'Johnny Come Lately', penned by the whole band, is an even more intoxicating stab at dewy-eyed acoustic melancholy. Wrapped in gorgeously understated introspection it features Cerys's voice chiming as sweetly and exquisitely as Harriet Wheeler from The Sundays. The lyrics are earthy in both senses of the words, using gardening-type imagery to great effect.

'If I asked too many questions and stayed behind, To find out how to make a garden grow, But he never ever gave away the secret of his godforsaken soil' maybe hints at a sign of Cerys's love of tending to her garden as a means of securing some sanity and escaping from the unnatural world she occupied with her band. She had raved at the time of her favourite relaxing pursuit: 'Gardening is amazingly easy, and it makes you feel amazingly good when you've grown something from the seed. It's the essence of life, with no one packaging it or labelling it or saying it's the next big thing.' So maybe the horticultural aspects of the lyrics ring true.

Although 'Mulder and Scully' is named after the leading characters in cult-hit sci-fi series *The X-Files*, the song isn't actually about them. It's more a case of Ex-Files than X-Files, as the lyrics leave you in no doubt as to what and who the song relates to. It might have the cool cultural referenced title, but the world-weary cynicism of the lyrics, and the ironies inherent in the fucked-up situation they describe, turn what is on first listen a walloping, rollicking pop song, into a barbed epic.

It's the feeling of cracked desperation in Cerys's voice when she sings 'My bed is made for two and there's nothing I can do, So tell me something I don't know', and the howling delivery as she belts out 'If my head is full of you is there nothing I can do, Must we all march in two by two?' You can imagine the authenticity of the song's lyric helped Cerys feel exactly every word that she was singing. The remarkable talking point of 'Mulder and Scully' is that it was written by both Cerys and Mark, which must have been difficult, writing lyrics that struck so close to home.

Cerys would say in later interviews about the writing of the songs on *International Velvet*: 'It was tough, but it also meant the songs took on a different edge. It may have been the catalyst that made the album what it was. The pressure was more exciting. It was more necessary to write these songs and get them out because the friction was there.'

However, the source of friction wasn't only welling up from within Mark and Cerys's broken relationship. Catatonia were quickly learning the harsh practicalities and inherent difficulties of life on a major label.

The band had already had to endure countless delays in the release of *Way Beyond Blue* and release dates of singles being moved at whim. They also despaired at the way they were such a small component of a very large machine that was throwing its money at its megastar cash cows like Madonna and Prince, but seemed to care very little for the bands that were struggling to establish themselves.

As the years have gone on, record companies' impatience with their acts to deliver instantaneous rewards has resulted in rosters being wiped clean and young bands that need to be nurtured being cast aside in favour of quick-hit, bland, manufactured pop rubbish like Atomic Kitten, Westlife and Lolly.

Catatonia, like many of these young bands, were exposed to the strict dictates of their record company. The continual stifling of the band's ideas and blind pursuit of the hit record, had already resulted in all of Catatonia's singles output being of the three-minute pop song variety, masking their abilities to produce a rich diversity of music from potential record buyers. This had given the false impression that Catatonia were just another photofit indie band, whereas they were nothing of the sort.

The fabric of the relationship between Warners and the band was wearing increasingly thin and patience on both sides was even more threadbare. All the soundings Catatonia seemed to be receiving from the record company were negative. Labelmates of the band were being dropped as record companies began to wield their axes and they really did fear that they would be dropped even before they could deliver a second album.

Out of this frustration was borne the superbly acerbic 'That's All Folks'. You won't hear many more sharply written songs laced with such barbed wire lyrics. The song's title not only hints at the demise the band feared but also takes a sardonic swipe at Warner's funded cartoon patron Bugs Bunny and the animated rabbit's key catchphrase.

'I could do without lectures, So heaven protect us, From these bad vibes you're giving . . . I could talk with my label and I am not able, This could do with a remix, Then don't break what's not fixed.'

Even better is the line, 'Did no one warn us, no one want us, They did not warm to us,' the way that Cerys sings 'warn us', 'want us' and 'warm to us' is phrased to sound suspiciously like the word Warners. It was gripping stuff.

INTO THE VALLEY

The positive reception that greeted the four new songs aired from the soon-to-be recorded album gave them great encouragement as they counted the days to the album's recording. Catatonia's profile was heightened even more by the release of *Twin Town*, the hit Welsh movie, directed by Kevin Allen, the brother of Brit actor Keith Allen.

Set in Swansea the film not only featured the mercurial acting talents of Catatonia's old mate Rhys Ifans, but 'You've Got A Lot To Answer' sandwiched prominently in the middle of the film's cool soundtrack.

The success of *Twin Town* was yet another seal of approval for Welsh culture. With a soundtrack that also included The Super Furry Animals and The Manics, it was a landmark moment in the rapid evolution of Welsh culture as Welsh music and film collided in epochal unison.

As the *Twin Town* soundtrack proved, all avenues to raising your profile and publicising your talents are to be welcomed, because who knows where your exploration will end. In Catatonia's case, Canada.

Just like buses, Catatonia had not been to North America, then two trips came along at once. No sooner was their US immigration stamp drying on their passport, than they packed their bags for three dates in Canada.

Although it was a whistle-stop stay, three dates in three days between 9 May and 11 May (at the Warehouse, Toronto, Barrymore's, Ottawa and the Metropolis, Montreal), it was invaluable for experience's sake.

The Cats were playing as support to English band Suede, who were touring under the name The London Suede because of the threat of legal action from an American band of the same name. Suede's fixation with Bowie-era Seventies glam rock and songs that painted images of faded glamour and lowlife bedsit romance was a huge hit in the UK, but was still very much a cult appeal in a country that holds up Bryan Adams and Celine Dion as its musical ambassadors.

Still, for Catatonia as support act there was no pressure: they could just sit back and enjoy the ride.

There was more interaction with their peers when the Cats played at the biggest open-air rock concert to be held in Wales for many years. The Big Noise Festival was held in Cardiff Bay on Sunday, 11 May 1997. A live simulcast on BBC Wales, BBC Radio Wales and BBC Radio 1, it celebrated the centenary of the world's first radio broadcast, sent by Marconi across water from Lavernock in Wales to Flat Holm Island in the Bristol Channel exactly 100 years ago on 11 May 1897. An estimated 10,000 rock fans descended on Cardiff Bay to watch some of the country's top rock acts perform on a specially assembled floating stage in Scott Harbour.

The event starred Paul Weller, Gene, The 60ft Dolls, The Stereophonics as well as Catatonia's good mates Space – whose set Cerys hilariously interrupted as she drunkenly ran on from the wings to join her Scouse mates on stage. The open-air gig saw Catatonia play eight songs in a short set – 'Do You Believe In Me?', 'Lost Cat', 'Johnny Come Lately', 'Mulder and Scully',

'This Boy Can't Swim', 'Sweet Catatonia', 'Bleed' and 'You've Got A Lot To Answer For'.

The outdoor Welsh fest had set the band up nicely for their sojourn to Monnow Valley to record their second album. Monnow Valley Farmhouse Studios nestles in an isolated corner of Monmouthshire, miles from a railway halt, all quiet copses and the River Monnow that weaves its sluggish way nearby. The late Rob Collins, organist with The Charlatans, who always insisted on recording at Monnow Valley, would fish there for barbel. The ultimate irony was that the keyboard maestro met his death when he died in a car crash driving through the lanes near the studio. Not far down the road from Monnow Valley is the famous Rockfield Studios, the location for The Stone Roses' famously protracted attempts to record a follow-up to their epochal, eponymously titled debut album.

Monmouthshire may not immediately resonate in the mind as the rock 'n' roll capital of the UK, but the recording studios that are situated there have been responsible for some of the most famous albums in UK music history. A list of bands and musicians that reads like a Who's Who of UK rock 'n' roll have chosen Monmouthshire as their rural setting of choice: Queen, The Flamin' Groovies, Rockpile, Iggy Pop, Black Sabbath, Robert Plant, Motorhead, Echo & the Bunnymen, The Undertones, The Icicle Works, The Pogues, The 60ft Dolls, Super Furry Animals, Manic Street Preachers, Gene, Cast, Paul Weller, Ash, Black Grape, The Charlatans, The Boo Radleys, The Stone Roses, Dodgy, The Bluetones and Oasis have all availed themselves of the rural ambience to produce their own particular masterworks.

In an interview with Cardiff's *Buzz* magazine Cerys and Owen described how much they were looking forward to finally recording their second album at Monnow Valley.

'I'm sure it would be a different album if we'd decided to do it in a city,' explained Owen. 'Everything at Monnow Valley is laid back and countrified and its got a completely different feeling to it. And also because we're all used to living in a city, if somebody takes you out of that and puts you in the country you feel like a different person straight away.'

'I was so glad to get in the studio because we had a batch of new songs and we'd been touring too much last year,' added Cerys. 'We were geared up for doing new material.'

In contrast to the recording of *Way Beyond Blue*, which had been marked with the fingerprints of a number of different producers and engineers, Catatonia were adamant that things would be different this time around. They were determined that *International Velvet* would not suffer from the same fragmented recording that had afflicted their debut.

The man entrusted with ensuring this happened was Tommy D. Tommy was already known to the band. He had engineered a few of the tracks on *Way Beyond Blue* and he had reworked the 'You've Got A Lot To Answer For' single. A DJ in clubs during the late Eighties and early Nineties, Tommy had travelled the world playing sets. However, it was an unlikely meeting with two muscle-bound wannabee pop stars that got his production career under way.

'I used to do DJ at the Limelight [on Shaftesbury Avenue, London] on Wednesday nights, and one day, two guys I used to book for the downstairs part gave me this tape to listen to,' Tommy explains. 'One of these tracks was called, "I'm Too Sexy". It sounded like a great track and I thought I could do something with it. I played it to them and they liked it and so we went to a studio and did it, and then thought nothing more of it.'

Of course, 'I'm Too Sexy' was a massive hit and made stars, albeit briefly, of those two guys otherwise known as Right Said Fred.

'That opened up a lot of doors for me,' says Tommy. 'After this people started calling me a record producer, although I never really thought of myself like that much. I did some work with The Shamen, Björk, some remixes of Michael Jackson tracks, some quite good stuff really. Then I worked with a band called Laguna Meth, an American band who were a bunch of nutters. But, they were managed by Geoff Travis [owner of Blanco Y Negro]. Geoff came down to the studio one day and hung around to see what I was doing. He gave me a tape to listen to, which was by Catatonia. I'd sort of vaguely heard of the band but never really heard much of their stuff. It was a demo of "You've Got A Lot To Answer For".'

Tommy liked it, so he talked to Geoff about it, and he was informed that they'd done the album but the band were looking to release this record as a single and would Tommy like to have a go with it?

'So I reworked the song by adding some backing tracks and vocals, fixing the drumming sound – all sorts of little things, and then we released it as a single,' says Tommy. 'I actually thought it was too slow – which is a common thing I have with Catatonia. Many of their tracks, the demos at least, are just far too slow. I told them to crank it up a bit, and it worked much better. When they play it live it's normally much faster and sounds much better.'

Tommy had obviously made a good impression on the band, who evidently liked the way he worked. On the strength of his work on the single and his ideas he was offered the producer's chair for the second album. It would be during that recording session that romance would blossom between the producer and the band's enigmatic frontwoman.

'When it came to doing their next album – since I'd become a fan immediately it seemed natural. I was impressed by them all. I thought Cerys was the tops, a really exciting person to be around and a great figure head. In fact, I'm a great fan of "bands" – when you get four or five people as individuals coming together and the pushing and pulling between the characters involved end up making this sound, which if you took one of them away you'd never get. Like when John Bonham died from Led Zeppelin, or Keith Moon from The Who – if you take one of them away, its the sound that goes. And that's what I loved about Catatonia, the sound that they made is just great. The two contrasting styles of guitar just sound fantastic.'

Tommy's first job was to ensure that the new album rang true with a consistency that was lacking on *Way Beyond Blue*.

'There's basically a couple of jobs a producer has to do. The most important job is to get the bloody thing finished, because very often if you leave it up to the artists they'll just faff around with it for ages,' he explains. 'The second job is different. I don't like doing just "tracks". Although I do do that, I don't like doing it. I prefer to sit down with the band when they're about to make an album. Get to know the band, and hang out with them and try and understand what's going on in their heads and try and understand what type of record they want to make. Then I use my knowledge to try and figure out the best way to approach the problem.'

Tommy reckoned it helped that he came from an age of listening to albums by Pink Floyd, Led Zeppelin, Bob Dylan and The Beatles.

'They were whole albums which you couldn't turn off once you'd put it on,' he says. 'I think that's important and at the end of the day, if you were to say that an album is a snapshot of a band or individual's ideas at this time, then there should be some kind of theme to it. One of the reasons that *Way Beyond Blue* doesn't have this feel is because it was done by lots of different people over time and maybe seems disjointed. *International Velvet* was recorded in about two months, and was produced entirely by me, and it was just done in that time. So it is what it is. Bang.'

The songs that were recorded – 'Mulder and Scully', 'Game On', 'I Am The Mob', 'Road Rage', 'Johnny Come Lately', 'Goldfish and Paracetamol', 'International Velvet', 'Why I Can't Stand One Night Stands', 'Part of the Furniture', 'Don't Need The Sunshine', 'Strange Glue', 'My Selfish Gene' and 'That's All Folks' – were explosive. Not in a turning the speakers up to 11 and shaking the studio to its very foundations with a thunderous rock noise way. This was a quiet storm full of songs that were both awash with heartfelt sentiment and emotional poignancy, but also swirling with lyrics that stung as sharp as lemon juice in open wounds. Most of the emotionally troubled tracks on *International Velvet* were co-written by Cerys and Mark, songs that laid bare tortured emotions. Those 'tricky' songs, 'Mulder and Scully', 'Game On', 'Road Rage', 'Part of the Furniture' and 'Why I Can't Stand One Night Stands', are a naked examination of emotions laid bare. It's gripping as well as harrowing material, songs as melancholy drama and stark theatre.

Two years later, when news of Mark and Cerys's relationship was made public, Cerys talked about the 'difficulties' to the *Daily Telegraph*.

'It must have been hard to keep working so closely with someone after a painful break-up?'

'Well, yes, and I'm proud of it. It ['International Velvet'] worked because it was getting more and more difficult to stay together,' says Cerys. 'So we had a lot at stake; more and more to put in to make it a better record.'

Still, what a nightmare. 'Yes, but it's like running off a hangover. It's the only thing you can do. We just poured it into the music.'

Perhaps that's why 'International Velvet' is such a successful album; it feels real. When Cerys shouts out, 'Now you're doing my head in', on 'Why I Can't Stand One-Night Stands', it feels like her heart was in it. 'It was,' she says.

The *Daily Telegraph*, not usually revered for its concise rock 'n' roll interviewing, had captured the essence of the depth and complexity of *International Velvet*.

Of course, the whole album isn't just one long session on the therapist's couch, there's also the self-empowerment anthem 'I Am The Mob' and the album's title track cum new Welsh national anthem 'International Velvet' to decode.

Despite its Mafia-tinged nuances 'I Am The Mob' doesn't reveal the members of Catatonia as secret gangsters. It features Cerys's voice fizzing with searing malevolence as the song kicks off with a sample of a young girl spitting out the words, 'Alright then you think you're some bad girl, but you just wait until someone gets hold of you and beats the living daylights out of you.' The sample is from a discussion on bullying lifted from *Jenny Jones* – an American talk show.

Mark explains that the song is open to interpretation but to my mind there's no ambiguity about it. I get the feeling they'd like to do something criminal to their bullying record company.

'We're constantly faced with people in places higher than ourselves,' Mark explained to the *NME*. 'They're telling us why don't you do it this way or that way. Making excuses that it's all for our sake, in our best interests. What they mean is, "We can make more money out of you if you do it like this."'

Evidently that's where the line, 'Don't try and tell me it's not one for the money, two for the money, three for the money, Am I your Easter bunny', comes from. If that's not a veiled reference to Warners and Bugs Bunny, then I don't know what is. Again this just exemplified how disillusioned Catatonia were with Warners, who were interfering, attempting to get them to change their sound to suit what they thought would sell. There's a line in 'I Am The Mob' – 'Stop mucking around with a brand new sound', that speaks volumes. It was a snarling two-fingered riposte to their paymasters, saying you do it our way or you don't do it at all.

International Velvet meantime features verses sung in Welsh and the chorus sung in English. Opening with an oddly offbeat cod-reggae swing, another inventive musical departure for the band, the song swaggers around the Welsh lyrics and bursts into swathes of pulsating guitars as the chorus erupts with the words, 'Everyday when I wake up I thank the Lord I'm Welsh.'

Although on first appearance the song states a heavyweight case for a new national anthem, everything isn't exactly as it first appears. It's definitely not tub-thumping jingoistic nationalism.

'Could it become a new national anthem?' pondered Mark to *Select* magazine. 'Probably not. The melody's too difficult to have them singing it at closing time in the streets. And, besides that, not everyone in Wales is going to like it. The verses [sung in Welsh] just list a whole load of clichés about what it is to be Welsh, taking the piss out of Welsh culture. Also, it's written in a strict Welsh poetic metre, just to annoy people who are puritanical about the Welsh language. And English people might not like the chorus. Hopefully we'll get everybody to hate us!'

'The thing with *International Velvet* is that it celebrates differences,' says Cerys. 'Aye, we're Welsh, but we could just as easily put it in Finnish. You shouldn't be fearful of being proud of something. Everybody has their favourite chip shop or place they feel attached to.'

Taking a swig of orange juice, she elaborates on her theme, 'One thing's for sure, Wales have the best flag in the world. Who else has got a bloody great big red dragon? Talk about a mythological nation . . .'

International Velvet, the song and the album push the envelope right out there. There's anger, pain, suffering, confusion and a world-weary dose of cynicism swirling around in a maelstrom of human emotions, while the music is equally on the edge. There's the rollicking pop gems that fire 'Mulder and Scully', 'I Am The Mob' and 'Road Rage'; the gorgeously honeyed lilts that light up 'Game On', 'Johnny Come Lately' and 'Don't Need Sunshine'; the brooding rock of 'Part Of The Furniture'; the dub scarred 'Goldfish and Paracetamol'; the darkly trip-hopped 'Why I Can't Stand One Night Stands' and the grandiose musical theatre of the two immense ballads 'Strange Glue' and 'My Selfish Gene', that bring the album to a nerve-wracked, frazzled climax.

It's a testament to the band and Tommy D that, against all the odds, 'The sound which comes out of the speakers is magical, it's just something else,' as Tommy puts it. 'This magic might only last 10 seconds, but it's there. I remember when we first got "Johnny Come Lately" going, and I was just sitting there listening to it. It sounded absolutely beautiful – it's such an amazing track.'

What is clear is that Tommy and the band clicked, with both parties contributing ideas. It wasn't only the band and Tommy that clicked: he and Cerys were working closely together. And like in films when the leading man falls in love with the leading lady, romance was soon to blossom, between the two of them. Tommy was very much a confidante and a very good friend to Cerys initially. He understood the music business intimately and was a good shoulder to cry on. However, it wouldn't be until the recording of the follow-up to *International Velvet* that they would become an item.

'They are very receptive to other ideas,' explained Tommy. 'When we did *International Velvet* it was different from what they had done before. They'd done an album so I knew what they were capable of doing, and I'd done several albums so they knew what I was capable of doing. I tried to encourage everything they wanted to do and not worry about it, if they want to get a brass band in, then I'll get a brass band in. If they want a huge orchestra, I'll get it sorted. It was different – what we do is just let them stand there and make a sound. They are a band after all.

'If you let them make the sounds, and then suggest maybe to silence that bit, or turn that bass up a bit, or try a different key. Whatever. They'll try it out, and in the end we all pretty much agree when we've got a take. Generally we do about two or three, but maybe up to ten takes for a song. With the tracks on *International Velvet*, a lot of them had been played live and also been demoed up. So they'd already done quite a lot of work on the tracks.'

This creative democracy drove the album's creation, while Monnow Valley Studio's peaceful, pastoral location only added to the clear-headed, sparkling recording process that was drawn out over eight weeks of long, hazy summer days.

Although the Catatonia mindset outside Monnow Valley was to be firmly tuned into mass record company dissatisfaction and the invariable tensions arising from the Cerys and Mark split, inside the confines of the studio they were single-minded and determined. The recording of *International Velvet* was an undoubted catharsis for the band.

It was a testament to their abilities that while the odds were stacked against them they produced an album that was simply stunning. It was as brave as it was revelatory. Catatonia may have thought they were drinking in the last-chance-saloon, but they could never have even dreamt at that stage that in reality the champagne was on ice.

11
Mob Rule

Throwing themselves into work obviously helped Catatonia to escape the clawing paw of their record company who were hardly receptive to the band's hopes and ideals. The eight weeks in the studio may have provided some solace from their paymaster's demands, but worse was to come.

The first single to be released from *International Velvet* was planned to be the zeitgeist encapsulating 'Mulder and Scully'. It was originally pencilled in for a summer release and although *The X Files* was fast approaching iconic status on both sides of the Atlantic, it was pulled from the release schedule. Incredibly, given that you couldn't walk into a newsagents in the UK without seeing Agent Scully, aka US actress Gillian Anderson, draped provocatively over a men's magazine cover, Warners didn't think it a strong enough choice for a first single. That decision was a case for Mulder and Scully in itself. However much Catatonia cajoled and protested, Warners pointed out the band's position in the grand scheme of their burgeoning empire and that evidently was that.

Next single to be mooted was the coruscating pop thump of 'I Am The Mob'. The empowerment anthem was scheduled for a September release date to coincide with another UK tour and the planned release of *International Velvet* a few weeks later. Of course, just like your typical supermarket trolley nothing in the world of Catatonia ever followed a straight course. The next few months before the appearance of 'I Am The Mob' in all good record shops were to be a real rollercoaster ride.

The 'fun' started when the band were booked to make their first appearance at the Glastonbury Festival at Pilton Farm in Somerset. Held in June, Glastonbury is invariably open to the unkind dictates of the 'glorious' British weather. The day Catatonia were geared up to make their debut outing at the legendary festival was no different. Like some Biblical occurrence, the heavens opened and a torrential downpour turned the festival site into a haven for hippos. To the festival's human inhabitants it was a misery-inducing, sodden mudbath. The Cats were booked to play the *NME* stage – until it started to sink into the mud.

'We'd arrived and managed to get our gear out of the van and take it to the stage when we were told that we, the Sneaker Pimps [moody trip hoppers] and Kenicke [shouty all-girl punk popsters] had been cancelled,' explains Catatonia's disappointed guitarist Owen Powell, who had always wanted to play the festival.

'So, we had to get back in the van, plastered in mud and go back to the studio [Monnow Valley]. It was sort of depressing because I've always really wanted to do Glastonbury because I used to go there every year – that was my holiday, basically. And I'd always thought that it'd be great to play there, but the weather was stinking – it was awful. It wasn't just mud, it was liquid mud everywhere. So in the end, they couldn't get the stage ready and all the electrics were knackered and everything, and so we just piled in the van and came back to the studio. Mark doesn't like festivals anyway, although I think they're good because you've got a chance of playing to a big crowd, most of whom won't have heard of you and it's your chance to convert them.'

After extensive sessions in the Monnow Valley studios laundrette they packed their barely clean kit and headed off for more festival bookings at the Reading Festival and a date at the newly launched Swansea Festival the day after.

The Reading gig over August Bank Holiday weekend was a much more whiter than white performance. Catatonia delivered a knockout performance to a big crowd rammed into the *Melody Maker* tent. Despite their growing critical acclaim, Catatonia's lack of high chart-snaring positions meant they were still very much rooted in the second string 'new band' tents, away from the prestigious environs of the main stage.

If Reading was a high, a return for Cerys to one of her old stomping grounds, Swansea was very much a low, a complete letdown. After playing the Reading Festival on the Friday they returned home to Swansea on the Bank Holiday Monday to play the inaugural Swansea Festival with fellow performers Mike Peters of The Alarm and Yorkshire's mentallists Terrorvision. They were disappointed to be shoved on the side stage:

'That was a load of shit really especially 'cos it was home-townish and it was the first time my family had come to see us,' said Cerys. 'It just sounded like crap, the sound wasn't coming off the right stage. It's just amateur innit? Never again. It was the Swansea Rotary Club – a mishap.'

AND THE OUTLOOK WILL MAINLY BE CONTROVERSIAL!

Thursday, 18 September 1997 was a memorable night in Wales, one of the most historic occasions in the country's history. Grandly billed by the media as 'Wales Decides', the country was about to find out whether its inhabitants had voted either 'Yes' or 'No' for devolution, although in the watered-down form of a Welsh Assembly, unlike the fully fledged Parliament that Scotland was also about to vote on.

Wales had always been run by a centralised government at London's Houses of Parliament. Under devolution a newly established Welsh Assembly would take control of all the current responsibilities of the government appointed Secretary of State for Wales.

On the night of the vote, Welsh-language television, S4C, hosted a discussion on the vote from Giovanni's Restaurant in central Cardiff. One of Cardiff's most famous eateries, it's situated next door to the equally famed Spillers record shop in The Hayes.

In an attempt to obtain a cross section of views and inject some sense of cool credibility, Catatonia were invited to state their views on the vote. Instead of getting stuck into politics, the band tucked into the free beer and wine that was on offer. As the evening wore on, the band were becoming more and more pissed and equally as animated. The audience included a clutch of Welsh sportsmen, politicians and celebrities – including annoying TV weathergirl Sian Lloyd – who were becoming wide-eyed at the antics of this rising Welsh band.

The debate didn't air until 1am, by which time the band were inebriated to the point of collapse. Some bright-spark S4C presenter decided to ignore the demon-eyed look the band were wearing and ask Cerys what question she would ask about devolution. Cerys promptly piped up in Welsh: 'Who's Sian Lloyd fucking tonight?' The question hung in the air for what seemed like an eternity, as the assembled throng didn't quite comprehend what Cerys had just said on live TV!

Cerys herself, nonchalantly stepped down back to her seat to rapturous applause from her table, sat down, grabbed a beer and carried on talking as if nothing had happened. In terms of impact Cerys's sole contribution – to query the social life of another guest – not only won her a £10 bet with a mate who dared Cerys to ask the mischievous poser, but a ban from S4C.

The peeved weather girl turned-pro Welsh assembly campaigner drafted a 'defamation of character'-type writ only to miraculously reconsider when it was pointed out to her that the youth vote was integral to winning the referendum. The TV weathergirl, one of the founder members of the horrendous clique of Welsh luvvies that is the SWSS (the Single Welsh and Sexy Society) then laughed off the incident and admitted she was a fan of Catatonia. However, the band did later receive a letter from Welsh TV bosses advising them they would not be welcome on live TV again.

'What it was, there were all these media darlings air kissing and telling each other how much they loved each other at the political party which was on devolution night,' Cerys told *Melody Maker* of the incident. 'And I just questioned their nightly habits.'

It may have appeared that the band were behaving like some snotty punkish upstarts, but it was a brilliant reaction and a defiant two-fingers to the tedious backslapping antics of the nepotistic Welsh establishment that populated the S4C debate.

The release of 'I Am The Mob' gave vent to their feelings. The lyrics plainly demonstrate their unquestioning belief in their own abilities, even if people close to them were doubting that they could deliver.

Ironically, Warners didn't suss that the ambiguous lyrics could be construed as a thinly veiled attack on them. Although if the record company had bothered to take a gander at the Cats inflammatory press cuttings they would have easily gauged the rising ire in the Catatonia camp. The fact that the record company didn't clearly showed that they obviously couldn't have been that bothered. It was just symptomatic of the whole situation.

Signing to a major label wasn't turning out to be quite the spectacular breakthrough it might have been. Over the last year Catatonia had had to get back to the basics of writing and recording, preparing for another assault on the nation, while shielding themselves from the demands of Warners who quickly wanted to recoup the money they had already laid out on the band's critically acclaimed, but commercially unsuccessful, debut album.

'It's been slow and frustrating, but that's just been one part of it,' Cerys explained to the *Scotland on Sunday* newspaper. 'We'll keep churning the songs out as long as we can, as long as we're still getting something out of it, and you can't really think of it in any other way.'

Read between the lines and you see a band disillusioned at the predicament they found themselves in. The fall-out of Mark and Cerys's relationship was still affecting the group, who were quickly learning to cope with the tensions that arose. An interview with *Melody Maker* again saw those niggling edges collapsing in front of the press.

When asked by the writer whether Cerys had ever considered contracting a hit man:

> Mark Roberts, Catatonia's lead guitarist and co-writer turns to Cerys and says: 'You know somebody, don't you?' The look he receives in reply is matched in intensity only by Cerys's sealed-lipped silence. 'I wouldn't use them,' she whispers. 'I have enough nightmares as it is without having violence and death on my conscience, thank you.'

The tension that was coursing through the band on several fronts – internally and externally – was later acknowledged by Cerys in an interview with the *Independent on Sunday*. When asked by the writer when she last felt miserable, Cerys replied:

'There were moments within the band which made it very awkward to continue, but we got through them. I love the guy's [Mark's] songwriting abilities and that's why I'll always want to work with him, even though we argue like dingoes. You know each other very well. You know the good points and the bad points. There's a competitive streak there. It just shows how much he respects what I do in the band and how I respect him. The other band members have to just put up with the tension. It goes back a way, but the edges get worn down after a while.'

That wasn't exactly fair on the band, but they had become adept at dealing with the tension over time and let it wash over them. To Paul, Aled and Owen it was all part of edgy life in Catatonia.

FOLK OFF

At the time that promo copies of the 'I Am The Mob' single were being sent out to journalists and DJs, advance copies of *International Velvet* were also being circulated in an attempt to build a buzz ahead of the album's scheduled release at the start of October.

However, the buzz that was gathering pace concerned 'That's All Folks', the final track on the promo versions of *International Velvet*. This six-minute towering colossus of a song, an all-out assault on their record label, features Cerys wailing like a possessed banshee as her voice spirals out of control. 'They did not warm us, did not want us, they did not warm to us . . . I could talk to my label but I am unable', the words are piercing and biting, delivered with a frightening intensity.

The way she screams 'That's all folks' in such a distressed manner makes your spine spasm as you wonder just where her mindset was when this was recorded. It's one of the most amazing vocal performances you will ever hear, the sound of anguish, frustration and bitterness flooding out and colliding with a stampeding, defiant guitar sound as the song races to a frenzied climax.

Catatonia thought their days were numbered. As Cerys had admitted the band were near to splitting through personal and professional tensions: fear of being dropped had resulted in frustrations in the band which had in turn led to rows, so they were going to vent their collective spleen in the only way they knew how. 'That's All Folks' not only parodies Warners' favourite cartoon rabbit, they believed it would be a fitting epitaph. The curtain-closer, the final track on the final album, the final nail in the coffin of their career.

Incredibly, Warners couldn't have paid too much attention when the album was delivered to them, as promo copies had been sanctioned and sent out. It was only when a Warners executive decided by chance to listen to the album that any action was taken. But the situation just neatly underlined how Catatonia were regarded by the label. The unnamed exec brought the track and its lyrical content to the attention of label bosses who were otherwise oblivious to the song's barbed content. Warners ordered that 'That's All Folks' be taken off the album and its release postponed.

Before they could cop any flak the band raced to Scotland where they filmed the video for 'I Am The Mob' with Kevin Allen, the director of *Twin Town*, who was making his first foray into video directing.

Filmed in the rural surrounds of the highlands, the video can only be described as a widescreen vision featuring the band racing around in the countryside in a slightly oddball, psychedelic manner. There's mushrooms, cheesy grins, bagpipes, toy boats, goldfish in drums and a none-too serious air about Kevin Allen's first promo vid.

'The whole idea was that we didn't want it to look like a pop video,' explained Owen. 'We wanted it to be slightly different. So it was his suggestion that we go up to Scotland to do it, to have big spanning shots and make it quite cinema like. But then the risk doing that was that it would all look a bit serious, and look like a U2 video where people are stood on top of hills. So we thought we'd put a bit of piss taking in it to show that we were not entirely serious. Which was the idea behind Mark having a little toy boat to play with, and me going fishing.'

And an unidentified person with bagpipes that actually turns out to be Cerys and a submerged drummer.

'This guy turned up with his bagpipes, thinking that he was going to play them for us, but it was the actual bagpipes that we wanted,' says Owen. 'I wanted him to be in the video, because he was funny, but we just gave the bagpipes to Cerys. He taught her how to hold them and then she marched up and down with them. Aled's drum kit is in the water, with goldfish in it. We got the idea from Keith Moon. The drum kit Aled's got now, Keith Moon used to have one exactly the same, and he used to put goldfish in it. That's what Aled wanted – a sort of homage to Keith Moon.

'The whole idea with our video was that too many bands do videos where they try to look cool and spend a million pounds on it and we just wanted to show people that even though we're doing a song about putting horses' heads in people's beds; we have got a sense of humour. We're not completely unapproachable. It was good fun to do, which is unusual for videos, because they're normally a bit boring. Take after take after take. It took two days to do, but the working atmosphere was somewhat laid back.'

Of course, given the song's content, most people thought Catatonia were semi-psychotic pop nutters. Cerys and Mark explained the song to a journalist from the *Melody Maker*. 'The song's open to interpretation,' says Mark. 'But there's only one interpretation which Joe Bloggs on the street's gonna come up with. Basically, it's a song for people who've just had their head kicked in. They can go and play this song and fantasise about giving whoever gave them a good beating a good beating back.'

'It's not really about the Mafia, so much as using that idea to express frustration and anger that we were feeling over the last year,' adds Cerys.

In the interview the *Maker* journalist describes 'I Am The Mob' as:

> a mean slug in the face, the kind of song which can part hair at high volumes; it strip-searches you with a yell-along melody, ties you up with lacerating guitars and leaves you for dead as it speeds off for a night of total debauchery at the coda. It's also funnier than Catatonia's previous work, starting with Cerys's euphoric holler, 'I put horses' heads in people's beds, 'cos I am the mob.'

'People just haven't picked up on the humour before,' says Mark. 'This is more upfront but it's not blatantly trying to be funny. We were trying to get over a feeling of supreme confidence. It's a very confident song.'

Owen Powell had his own particular, unique take on 'I Am The Mob'. 'When we finished it, I described it as what My Bloody Valentine [legendary Creation Records band famed for their squalls of guitars and shoegazing ideology] would have been like if they'd drunk loads and loads of coffee every day instead of smoking loads of dope. It's sort of a firepower sort of song. It's a good attitude song.'

It was certainly a rip-snorting riposte, but as with all Catatonia records it wasn't exactly representative of the bigger picture. As usual, the extra tracks on the single illuminated their multi-stylistic approach. Those three tracks, 'My Selfish Gene', 'Jump or Be Sane' and 'I Am The Mob' (Luca Brasi Mix) all represented different strands of the Catatonia geneology.

'Jump Or Be Sane' is a Madness-like rollicking ska-pop romp, although while the music is breezy pop the lyrical content is anything but.

'I'd describe it as a song where the verses are quite dark and the choruses are quite pop,' explained Owen, 'but if you listen to the words they're still quite heavy.

'The kind of clues in there would be say if you were passing a tall building and there was someone stood up on the ledge of this building and a small crowd gathered below, with everybody going, "Oh no, no don't do it, don't do it." And you're thinking in your head, "Well, jump or be sane." It's either come down off the ledge or fucking jump and get on with it. When you're on the window ledge you can either think to yourself "Well, am I going to be completely mad and jump, or am I going to be sane?" And there's a line in it, "Be not vexed by remorse. I'm not lost but one who has gone before", which is actually taken off a gravestone in the church yard that was next to the studio [Monnow Valley]. If you walk from the studio into Monmouth which is about a 30 minute walk, you pass this little church, and we went for a wander around the churchyard one day and one of the gravestones has got that line on it. Basically we interpreted that as "Don't be sad for somebody who's died – they haven't been lost, they've just gone on ahead" – "Be not vexed by remorse. I'm not lost but one who has gone before".'

Then there was 'My Selfish Gene', an extra track that was too good to be an extra track, and which ironically ended up being both an extra track on 'I Am The Mob and replacing 'That's All Folks' on the forthcoming album due to the track being pulled.

'It ['My Selfish Gene'] is a sort of a piano torch song,' explains Owen. 'It's all about how man is basically selfish.' The song's title comes from the famous book by Richard Dawkins, *The Selfish Gene*. 'It's either uproariously funny or very very sad, it depends on which way you listen to it,' adds Owen. 'It could be taken as being a terribly sad song, but it's actually quite funny when you listen to it. The tracks on the single are actually all quite varied.'

That was definitely true of the final extra track on the single, the Luca Brasi remix of 'I Am The Mob'. Recorded at Rockfield and mixed by the Cat's bassist Paul Jones, it showcases the bass player's technological wizardry that he would put to good use on future Cat releases.

For those who are wondering, Luca Brasi was one of the characters in the famous Francis Ford Coppola *Godfather* films, tying in with the song's mobster analogies and the line from the song, 'Luca Brasi, he sleeps with the fishes.'

The song was scheduled for release on 30 September, but was postponed to a week later. It finally surfaced on 6 October.

Despite almost minimal publicity, except for its being 'Worm of the Week' on the Mark Radcliffe show on Radio 1 – it received scant air-play everywhere else. That was baffling given that it was a very radio-friendly slice of pop euphoria. The official line put out was that certain stations deemed it to be non-radio friendly, unlike songs such as 'Smack My Bitch Up' by The Prodigy that were released at around the same time, of course. More of an excuse, less of a cogent explanation I would say. Disappointingly, 'I Am The Mob', charted at No. 40, and fell out of the charts the following week.

Although those around Catatonia cited that a line from 'I Am The Mob': 'Stop blowin' the don, put his keks back on' – could have adversely affected their chances – the obvious reason was that it just wasn't lent the full weight of the press and marketing might of Warners, who were viewing their Welsh signings as extremely troublesome.

The single bombing didn't bode at all well. And any confidence the band were vainly attempting to instil in themselves was quickly dissipating in the face of strained relations with Warners and another poor chart placing.

If Catatonia only had the services of a crystal ball and a good fortune teller, the future would have appeared a lot brighter than the dark clouds they were presently shrouded in.

RUNNING TO STANDSTILL

A little light relief from their present state of depressive inertia was quickly offered with a gig at Liverpool's Sefton Park with their old mates Space.

The live event was Space's biggest-ever headlining show in front of 5,000 rabid Scousers in a specally erected circus marquee.

Ironically, the last time the two bands played together was the year before when the two bands undertook a marathon trek around the UK. Then it was Space supporting Catatonia. Now the roles had been reversed. Space had notched up a series of chart hits with 'Neighbourhood', 'Me And You Versus The World' and 'The Female Of The Species' propelling them into the limelight of Top 20 chart regularity. The Space star was definitely in the ascendancy, although Tommy had hatched a plan that would soon allow both him and Cerys to share the limelight.

Both singers were fervent admirers of Tom Jones and both Catatonia and Space had had overtures made to them to work with the Welsh colossus. Born out of this interest was a song that Tommy had written, 'The Ballad Of Tom Jones'. It was penned as a dramatic Sonny and Cher style ballad about how two desperate lovers stave off impending doom by listening to Tom Jones.

Tommy had written it some months previously, but was terrified to ask Cerys if she would record it with him for fear of what she would say. 'It took me a while to pluck up the courage to ask her,' admitted Tommy. 'I was so nervous I thought it was going to be a duet between me and Yorkie (Space's session bassist who comes an extremely poor second to Cerys in the glamour stakes!)

Luckily Cerys eagerly agreed and she quickly headed into the studio to record the duet with Tommy and his bandmates. At that time the song was only planned for inclusion on Space's forthcoming album, but unbeknown to the two of them, within six months it was about to take on a life all of its own.

For Cerys, a couple of days of dreaming of herself as a glamorous Sixties chanteuse dueting with a famous crooner was unfortunately offset by another round of gigs at venues that the band were now beginning to become uncomfortably over-familiar with.

They were down to their last few units of self-belief and running critically low on drive and determination. But they had come this far and there really was no turning back, so off they went again, accompanied by the usual exclamatory critical bouquets while the thorns of underachievement stung as deeply as ever.

The 15-date tour would, though, contain some undoubted highlights, most noticeably the band's return to North Wales for another of their secret gigs, a first-ever show in Belfast and the band's biggest headlining show at the London Astoria.

The tour to support 'I Am the Mob', and to promote an album that was now postponed to a date yet to be scheduled, kicked off on 7 October at Betws-Y-Coed Swallow Falls, then called in at the Olympia (Dublin); Empire (Belfast); Roadmenders (Northampton); Hop and Grape (Manchester); Aberyswyth University; Wedgewood Rooms (Portsmouth); Warwick University; Bangor University; Alleycat (Reading); Fleece and Firkin (Bristol); Venue (Edinburgh); Riverside (Newcastle); and Bradford University, culminating in a gig at London Astoria on 4 November.

The tour was marked by some particularly riotous shows. The Swallow Falls gig was meant to be a secret but word got out through a series of ads on trees and an article in the local paper. The venue, a pub in picturesque

Betws-Y-Coed, was rammed as was the band's date at the Bristol Fleece and Firkin, while Manchester was memorable for Cerys's very first attempt at stage diving.

'Bristol was excellent,' explained Owen. 'It was meant to hold 270 people in it, and we got 430 in there, so the fire regulations went out the window! Manchester was really good because Cerys went stage diving for the first time ever, which was interesting, until the security and tour manager dragged her out. It was quite amusing, and she looked a bit bemused after it!'

Caitlan Moran, *The Times*' renowned rock writer, penned a memorable article about the secret Swallow Falls gig that provided a brilliant snapshot of the eccentricity of country life and how it coped with the arrival of a bunch of pop stars.

> Halfway up the mountain, by the waterfall, underneath a sky salted with stars – and, more pedantically, just outside Betws-y-Coed – is the Swallow Falls pub. This is the Hacienda of North Wales: Fred at the hotel has already warned us of its fights-kicking-off potential.
>
> Tonight, Catatonia play their secret warm-up gig here: publicity has been limited to a small ad in the local paper, and a board nailed to a tree which proCerys Matthews, Catatonia's lead singer, is warming up for the gig by shooting pool and drinking gin and tonic. 'We played our secret gig here last year,' she says, in that gorgeous Welsh lilt that sounds as intricate and warming as a crocheted blanket. 'It was mad! All these girls dressed up in boas and heels, and they have to climb back over the mountain to get home. In the dark! Drunk!'

Catatonia rounded off their UK tour much as they had started with some of the most erudite wordsmiths heaping noteworthy praise in their general direction. John Mulvey, deputy editor of the *NME* noted how Cerys had acquired a consummate stage presence that was simply bedazzling to behold.

> Intoxication costs, you want to get catatonic fast, you buy your booze off the shelf, mix your drinks and, before you can say Merthyr Tydfil, you're flying. Just past 9pm on the London Astoria stage, and Cerys Matthews is a fly girl cruising the warm currents of a dependable pop high.
>
> With practised ease, she lifts a wine bottle to her lips, swigs it back and dumps it down next to the can of lager. Her inhibitions are gone, her belly button is communing with the crush of fans . . . her arms are aloft, twisting in the sensual jangle as age displays the formidable confidence of someone blessed with the symmetrical good looks, the voice of a playground sweetheart and a pair of great trainers. Cerys is on good form tonight. Her voice is shagged like a four year old Janis Joplin on 'Stars In Their Eyes' but she still holds every available attention-grabbing second.

As the record company machinations ground on, the UK tour had helped Catatonia take their mind off their manifold problems and boost their self-esteem by playing to packed and enthusiastic crowds. The new material was well received everywhere they went, and there was a universal anticipation in the music press about the forthcoming album.

Of course, there was the little matter of when Warners would decide to release the album. The record company had decided to replace the inflammatory 'That's All Folks' with 'My Selfish Gene', although it had already appeared as an extra track on the 'I Am The Mob' single. Both songs were climactic torchlit ballads, so it made sense to replace like with like, and end the album with a similarly moving finale, even if 'My Selfish Gene' had already made an appearance in the public domain.

Although relations were fraught, Warners were now making concrete decisions on the album's release and what singles would be released from it. In a turnaround from their original decision not to release 'Mulder and Scully', it had obviously been pointed out to Warners that in cold cynical marketing terms, releasing a song that had nothing to do with *The X-Files* (except for its use as a metaphor for decoding emotional confusion) made sound commercial sense.

The single was pencilled in for release in January. A wise decision given that it's traditionally a downtime for the release of singles, coming just after the much-hyped chase for Christmas No. 1. If Catatonia were going to be in with a chance of securing anything like a high chart-placed single, this was the time to do it. This is invariably the period that most record companies attempt to blood their new acts and push them on to chart success.

The album *International Velvet* was also tentatively pencilled in for release within two weeks of 'Mulder and Scully' in the first week of February, with the release of the band's other zeitgeist-snaring titled single 'Road Rage' set for release a few weeks later.

As 1997 came to a close the band decamped to Cardiff. Since the split, Mark and Cerys had moved out of their legendary house in Gold Street, Mark moving in with members of rising young Welsh band Big Leaves (formerly Welsh-language prodigies Beganifs), while Cerys had moved to a house on the same street as one of the band's favourite pubs, the Yellow Kangaroo, with one of her best mates sculptor Angharad Jones, famed for once building a 45ft vagina out of scrap metal!

The autumn of 1997 was a great time to be in Cardiff. The city continued to reverberate with the buzz of the music scene's rapid ascension. Meanwhile, the release of *Dial M for Merthyr*, a diverse and exhilarating compilation of 21 Welsh bands, helped further the cause célèbre.

The compilation was a collaboration between Hue Williams's Cardiff-based Townhill label and *NME* journalist Simon Williams's renowned London-based Fierce Panda label. Williams is a journalist with the same gonzo turn of phrase as his equally speed-freaked *NME* colleague Steven Wells, who memorably penned Catatonia's first *NME* single of the week, 'For Tinkerbell' .

Simon's sleeve notes make for typically manic reading: 'Forget scenes, give us the 'zines, dreams and (cough) sonic SCREAMS for here be dragons,' he raved, 'a stack of tracks with no tricks attached; a 100 per cent Welsh album inspired by last year's Splash mini-tour; a 1000 decibel roar through the best, brashest talent around on the right side of the Severn; a 100,000 mile-an-hour joyride through the punk, the spunky and the downright DUNKY!' Phew.

Catatonia contributed an early song, the lilting 'To & Fro' replete with its church organ and its gentle resonance, to the album. The Cats appeared alongside the first wave of Welsh stars like The Stereophonics, The 60ft Dolls, Ether, Dub War, Novocaine and The Manics, as well as newer additions to the Welsh constellation such as Mark Roberts's housemates Big Leaves, contributing 'Mill Lane' (their psychedelic pop tribute to Cardiff's former city-centre eyesore, now reinvented as a swank Parisian Quarter). There was also the darkly brooding 'Rollercoaster' from former Cat's keyboard player Clancy Pegg with her band Crac, as well as equally intriguing offerings from the classy Derrero and Melys.

The band rounded off what had been a difficult and troublesome year by decamping to Big Noise studios in Cardiff to record the B-sides for 'Mulder and Scully' and 'Road Rage'.

Catatonia had built up a good working relationship with Big Noise's Greg Haver and Ceri Collier. The Cats also liked the Big Noise studio. Indeed 'Johnny Come Lately' from *International Velvet*, recorded as a demo on a 16 track at Big Noise, was the version that was to be included on *International Velvet*. 'They said they tried to replicate the song as well as the take they did here, but just considered the Big Noise version better,' said Greg proudly.

Catatonia recorded four tracks for inclusion on the singles – 'No Stone Unturned', 'Mantra For The Lost', 'I'm Cured' and 'Blow The Millennium'.

'No Stone Unturned' is another of those sweetly melancholic gems Catatonia have the unerring knack of writing. 'I did not leave the sinking ship, The sinking ship left me,' Cerys croons wistfully in her crisp Welsh lilt, surrounded by a luscious arrangement and an equally delicate burst of gorgeous la la la's.

'Mantra For The Lost' is similarly downbeat, but beautiful nevertheless. There's a desolate wonder about the lyrics, a song about the confusion and pain of adolescence. 'Oh, for the life of me, I don't know where it is I'm going. I'm growing. Somebody swapped the signs from nursery rhymes.'

Anyone who had doubted the band's talent would just have to listen to these extra tracks for ample evidence of Catatonia's innovative musicianship, use of offbeat stylistic inflections and fearless experimental approach. 'Mantra' uses what can only be described as dub brass. It's lovingly created and Cerys's mellifluous refrain of 'This is all there is,' is opulently fragile, tenderness personified.

Catatonia's sharp-eyed observations of relationships, much of it coming from their own experiences of course, are richly etched all over 'I'm Cured'. Mark's lyrics, as usual, are of the highest quality, underpinned by not a little humour – a quality most wouldn't immediately attach to the Cats' songwriting. Cerys sings, almost knowingly: 'How abstinence can wipe the slate clean, I'm through with that, It ain't my time, I'm rewarded poorly, I'm cured – hurrah! I no longer feel the urge, If lust is sin then what price our extinction? Yes, it's all starting to make sense.'

'Blow The Millennium Part 2' picks up from 'Blow The Millennium, Blow', the track that appeared alongside 'Beautiful Sailor' on the Cats' Xmas 1995 fan club single. It's spookily atmospheric, twinkling softly like a widescreen vision of utopia. With its filmic qualities it's ideal soundtrack music, again underlining the band's consummate musicianship.

Greg Haver could testify to the band's skills: he saw them at close quarters and has nothing but praise for the band. 'They're very studio sussed, they knew exactly what they wanted, and although the band members are all quite different, they all have qualities that they bring to the party,' explains Greg.

'Paul is the thinker, he's a brilliant musician. He's very underrated because he's the bass player and on stage he's content to stay out of the limelight, but he's very technology minded and he's the computer wizard of the band. Owen is a great guitarist and like Paul, he loves the gadgets, he's well up on the latest innovations. Aled is another of the unsung heroes. He's a brilliant drummer, a drummer's drummer who just loves playing. Mark is probably the most misunderstood of the whole group. Some people might think he's sullen or a miserable bastard, but he's really talented and a brilliant songwriter.

'He only opens his mouth when he has something important to say. He might not say anything for a while and then he'll say why don't you try this or that and it will be fucking brilliant. That's because he only speaks when he's got something really important to say and you think fuck what a great idea. Mark just likes writing songs, that's what he enjoys the most, but he could do without being away from home all the time. He likes to be home and going to the pub, whereas Cerys is more naturally predisposed to the parties and the limelight.'

Of course, the limelight and the parties had been restricted to strictly minor league soirees, many drunken nights at dank and dimly lit indie venues. That was glamour of sorts, albeit in a world they didn't want to inhabit, because this was a band who were 'Pop' with a capital P. They existed to make hit records, not carve a cult niche with limited edition 7″ singles, handmade sleeves and residencies at the Camden Falcon. That wasn't their raison d'être. They aspired to make a home in the Top 20, the dream of sell-out crowds and long-awaited commercial acclaim for their art. As the flame of 1997 burnt itself out, Mark and Cerys had been joined in Catatonia union for five long years. They were in severe danger of having to enrol in Underachievers Anonymous. For the Cats it was now or never. The dream or the despair. After a year like the one that had just passed, 1998 had to be an improvement. Surely, it couldn't get any worse?

CONQUERING ALIEN TERRITORY

Catatonia had around six weeks' respite before they wound themselves up for the promotional onslaught surrounding the release of a new single and album. If the band were filled with trepidation, it was understandable. Their last single had hit the wall of the Top 40, relations with their paymasters were stretched to breaking point and their first proper album after *Way Beyond Blue*'s early greatest hits' collection was set to be unleashed upon the mercy of the UK's fickle record-buying public.

'Mulder and Scully' was the first release. A video for the song was filmed at the end of December. The venue was the Severn Bridge, the colossal structure that spans the divide between England and Wales and Newport's Legendary TJs, adding yet another slice of mystique to the infamous venue's already mythical reputation. Again at the helm was director Kevin Allen and completing the *Twin Town* connection for the video was the ubiquitous Rhys Ifans, Catatonia's favourite actor and all-round 24-hour party person who starred in the video alongside a couple of Mulder and Scully lookalikes. Also in attendance was a journalist from the *Melody Maker*, there to document every little bit of action, and I mean every little bit:

> Things are getting strange I'm starting to worry/This could be a case for Mulder & Scully. Or it would be if they could tear themselves away from each other. Right in front of our eyes, Mulder and Scully are in full clinch. Snogging the faces off each other. Hands everywhere. All around them, a full-on gigging crowd takes no notice, instead focusing their attention on the band onstage, who in turn seem oblivious to the fact that right next to them, Rhys Ifans – one half of the double trouble 'Twin Town' duo – is similarly at it with a luscious blonde. Tongues? Even lizards would be turning greener with envy.
>
> This is TJs nightclub in Newport (the unlikely venue which saw Nirvana's first ever UK show) and the truth is we're at the video shoot for Catatonia's chart-bound new single, 'Mulder & Scully'. Director Kevin Allen [brother of Keith and director of *Twin Town* and the Tonia's 'I Am The Mob' video] has enlisted the help of the snogging Mulder and Scully lookee-likees as well as

calling in a favour from Rhys and his most lovely girlfriend, Jessica. A whole bunch of fans have turned up to play the audience and fellow countrymen 60ft Dolls – who are playing at TJs tonight – are marvelling at the chaos as they wait to sound-check.

It was about time that Lady Luck finally found her way round to visit.

THREESY DOES IT!

'Mulder and Scully' was released on 19 January 1998 on CD, cassette and 7" blue vinyl single with a free poster. Alongside the title song was a strong line-up of extra tracks – 'No Stone Unturned', 'Mantra For The Lost', and 'Mulder And Scully' (The Ex-Files), a startling remix by Paul Jones. This alternative take on the title track not only underlined Paul's ever-growing remix skills but featured a gorgeous ambient orchestration. It was produced at Paul's home studio and at Rockfield Studios in Monmouth, just down the road from Monnow Valley.

Whereas, 'I Am The Mob' was the first single to feature a pic of the band on the cover after using their friend Elfyn Lewis's distinct artwork for their first four Warners' singles; it was back to anonymity for the new single, replaced by stunning artwork from London-based design agency Stylorouge.

The cover featured a striking image of a spaceship beaming down on Cardiff's City Hall. The cover artwork was created by Stylorouge's Carl Rush.

'Well, when I first started coming up with ideas for that [the single] it was all to do with alien imagery,' explained Carl. 'And then I hit upon the idea of a spaceship flying over London Bridge, and it was basically this big composite of London with a huge spaceship flying over the top. I showed the band, and they liked it, but said could I put Cardiff in there instead. So, that was when I went to the Welsh Tourist Board and bought a picture of Cardiff. We then turned that picture to night, and bought a plastic spaceship from Forbidden Planet [cult sci-fi shop], and made it up and then photographed it. So it's just a model with a whole load of lights stuck on it. We then had to touch up Cardiff as well by drawing all the lights in and making it night time.'

So with new artwork, came a new outlook and, incredibly for them, a whole new raft of record buyers. From perennial chancers and daydreaming believers, Catatonia's fortunes were about to spin on its head, do a double back flip with extra tuck and land on its feet, magnificently.

'Mulder And Scully' made no attempt to knock politely at the door of the Top 40, no pushing past into the Top 20, it barnstormed its way into the Top 5 with a look on its face that was pure glee and disbelief.

For a band that had waited so long, so very very long for a modicum of success, 'Mulder And Scully's' blinding pop brilliance had deftly flicked a one touch pass to No. 3 – a mere 32 places above their previous highest chart placing at No. 35, 'You've Got A Lot To Answer For.'

The band were rightly stunned. It had been a long time coming.

'I was sure it would happen in 1993, and then I thought 1995 would be the one,' Cerys told Japanese magazine *Big O*, about the band's unstinting belief. 'I don't like even numbers, see, so when it didn't happen in 1997, I mean, eight, 1998 for God's sake. Eight is my least favourite number. We have always had tremendous faith in our songwriting abilities. We would put one single out, and when that didn't get popular, put another one out. I think it's just a matter of time.'

And of accusations, that 'Mulder And Scully's' ascension to the Top 5 has been helped by some cynical marketing tactics. Cashing in on *The X-Files* perhaps?

'I would probably say that they're quite right! [laughs] No, really, we're not cashing in on the X-Files, because I know "Mulder And Scully" is a good song. But it has helped a lot that everyone knows who Mulder and Scully are. Yes, you can be quite cynical and say, yah, the song is popular because of its title, but it wasn't written with that in mind. It was written because that was how the song was written. We haven't heard a thing from the X-Files people. We'd like a call from the producers of the show to include the song on the soundtrack of X-Files, the movie. That would be great. That would be better – we could exploit the song a little more!'

NME's very own terrorist wordsmith had his own unique thoughts on 'Mulder And Scully's' rapid-fire rise.

> It's not that Catatonia write crap lyrics it's just that they love the big Morrissey/Meat Loaf-style two-liner pop pun – and two-liner pop puns are, by definition, daft. This is not A Bad Thing. The brilliant 'Mulder And Scully' (which also, in an act of Abba-esque genius, manages to rhyme 'worry' with 'Scully') seethes with them: 'I'd rather be jumping ship/I find myself jumping straight in . . .' For instance. For not only is M&S a braincrushing juggenaut of a tune – it is also a work of unquestionable lyrical genius. The irresistibly sticky chorus – with its utterly desperate cry for help aimed at Ginger and UFO Boy from The X-Files – is a solid-gold nugget of cross-referenced pop-culture cool worthy of Shaun Ryder at his least overdosed. But look beyond that and the song is an almost operatic roar of confusion and pain from a woman who is both dizzy with the euphoria of sexual love AND utterly pissed off that she's once again let herself become an emotional Siamese twin. She wants to have her beefcake AND eat it. She equates love with dependency and dependency with brain death and er, getting fat.

Perhaps it was that 'Mulder And Scully' was of the time, perfectly encapsulating the craze for all things X-Files-like, or that given wider exposure Catatonia could justifiably share their talents with a whole new audience, a mainstream pop audience who had never encountered them before. Maybe it was none of those things – just the simple, inescapable fact that 'Mulder And Scully's' rollicking pop sense embedded itself into a nation's consciousness and wouldn't let it go, and irrefutable evidence that Catatonia had arrived. Finally.

When 'Mulder And Scully' crash landed into the Top 3, Catatonia had embarked on yet another UK tour. This time though there was at least a variation on the same old venues that the band had made their second homes over the last four years.

The Cats might have felt they were headed off on holiday, with the tour kicking off at Tenby de Vallens Pavillion on 7 January. The West Wales holiday resort isn't usually associated with thrilling pop sounds – the only rock you'll find there is the kind you shove in your mouth – nevertheless the Pavilion was striking a chord for the ever-increasing youth population that live in Tenby all year round. The Super Furries and Gorky's had played there so it was only fitting that the Cats kept up the Welsh end and showed their faces too, although they were already doing their bit for Wales by taking Cardiff-based Derrero out with them as support, having performed the same feat by yanking Topper along for the ride before Xmas.

The band's promoter Conal Dodds had figured Catatonia had played most of the mid-sized venues in the UK's major cities at least a dozen times in their attempt to pull themselves above the parapet of indie obscurity. Conal reckoned it was time for something different. So added to gigs in Leeds, Liverpool and London were shows at the Buckley Tivoly in the wilds of Powys, the Hanley Stage in Stoke, and the Princess Theatre in Port Talbot; the town situated midway between Cardiff and Swansea that's famed for its huge steelworks and naturally enough, considering the whacking great steelworks on its doorstep, its pollution.

The change to venues that are more off-the-beaten-track was almost prophetical, given what was to occur. It was the last time those lucky enough to catch the band in such small venues would have the chance to again.

Catatonia might have started the tour as indie also-rans in the eyes of some but they ended it as new supernovas of British pop. 'The transformation was quite incredible,' says Conal Dodds. 'The tour had been going well, but when "Mulder And Scully" hit the charts everything changed. The crowds seemed more up for it, more fervent and by the time we got to Port Talbot on 1 February, which I guess was their homecoming gig (Aled is from just down the road in Llanelli and Cerys has lived in both Cardifff and Swansea), the crowds were clambering for tickets. The show was sold out, but there was also a huge crowd outside who wanted to get in.

It was chaos and we had to call the police so we could get the band into the venue and restore order.'

It wasn't quite a step-by-step reconstruction of the Beatles' *Hard Day's Night* film, that saw The Fab Four high-tailin' it around Liverpool being chased by an adoring mob, but it was certainly a culture shock and a sobering introduction to the big time.

'We've always had the utmost faith in what we were doing, but nobody else understood, and now it seems a bit strange 'cos it was always our little thing,' said Cerys explaining to the *NME* her attitude to her first brief glimpses of fame.

'When you're writing songs, you always think they're brilliant, and when they don't do as well as you expected you think you must be listening with different ears,' added Owen, reassured that he was now sporting the right pair of lugholes.

Sensing that their charges were finally set to repay them, Warners quickly set about gearing themselves up for the launch of *International Velvet*. Ironically, and quite fittingly, the album was released the day after the Port Talbot fireworks. Warners' marketing muscle was finally flexed and the record company's press officer Ginny Luckhurst suddenly found herself besieged by magazines and newspapers all wanting a piece of the band.

Ginny joined Warners in April 97, not long after the record company and the band parted company with Jayne Houghton's Excess Press.

'Catatonia were quiet at that time as they were finishing *International Velvet*,' remembers Ginny. 'I asked if I could work on the project as I was familiar with *Way Beyond Blue* and loved the band. There was no major strategy discussed, I just knew that as *International Velvet* was such a great record this new material represented their best chance for mainstream success. And Cerys was the archetypal star-in-waiting: fantastically quoteworthy, undeniably talented, and in possession of her own off-beam sense of style and unique worldview.'

But even Ginny couldn't have quite gauged just how busy she was about to get.

'It did go pretty crazy in the press office when "Mulder And Scully" broke (as it does with any act). There was such a great feeling toward them in a lot of areas of the press and I believe a lot of supportive journalists were just dead chuffed for them. I already had an idea about what I wanted to do press wise. I was definitely ready for the explosion of interest. I don't think the band were quite as prepared, but who would be? It was totally uncharted territory for them.'

After the fraught machinations with the record company it was a relief for everyone to see the album finally appear in the shops, albeit minus the Warners-baiting 'That's All Folks' but plus 'My Selfish Gene'. It was made available in CD, cassette and a vinyl edition of the album limited to 1000 copies with free 12" featuring Radio 1 session versions of 'International Velvet', 'No Stone Unturned', 'Mulder And Scully', and 'Strange Glue'.

Debuting at a very encouraging No. 11, it would soon rise much higher and exceed everyone's expectations. Neil Kulkarni wrote in the *Melody Maker*:

> It ain't just that Catatonia have some incredible songs and words here. It's not merely that they play with a feel and reach and tenderness that makes the likes of Travis and Embrace sound as pitifully tepid as you'd suspected. It's this: in an age when the young want to be old and the smart want to be stupid, 'International Velvet' is a clued-up stretch 'n' flex towards some kind of livid new cool you can't help but get wet about. Make eye-contact and let it shoot you down. Fucking skill.

Select magazine's own in-house Catatonia aficionado, Roy Wilkinson, pinpointed the beating heart of the group when he wrote:

> And the music gives voice to such all-embracing sentiments. Populist in the best way, 'International Velvet' has the potential to enter the hearts of everyone from Suede aficionados to Virgin Radio listeners . . . If a regional comparison is in order, Catatonia are miles from the lost-valley lunacy of Gorky's Zygotic Mynci, even the frazzled idiosyncrasies of Super Furry Animals. But though their song structures are cut from time-honoured archetypes and frequently sing of love heading toward the rocks, that's not to say they're Meredith Brooks. This band are more of a Welsh Beautiful South – suppliers of subtly radical everyman music . . . Their other main strength remains Cerys's remarkable voice. From the rasping Janis-gone-pop of 'I Am The Mob' to the sweet tones of 'Johnny Come Lately', her stylistic range is ever more impressive. It complements her beautifully humanist lyrics – heartbroken but never histrionic, her words have a rare understated warmth.

With the plaudits boosting their once tattered confidence, the rush had really set in. Cerys and the rest of the band were spending every waking hour either on the telephone to, or in the company of, journalists who all wanted the definitive line on the Catatonia ideology. It was noticeable how high the band's currency had risen that rock magazine aristocracy like *Q* now wanted to share an alcoholic beverage or seven in the company of the girl the band called Queenie – well she was fast approaching Welsh royalty, so it was only fitting!

'We used to make excuses not to do press.' Owen told the *Melody Maker*. 'It's taken us this long to realise that we have a certain amount of responsibility. I was reading this interview with Thom Yorke and everybody just asks him about the bleak side of what they do. I think he'd prefer to have a bit of a laugh. Well, you'd hope so, anyway. It's impossible not to enjoy being in a band; when I read interviews with people whingeing about how awful it's been . . . I mean for fuck's sake, it's hardly hard work is it? Yeah, there's a lot of hanging around, but I was hanging around on the dole for years so hanging around and getting to play music at the end of it is like . . . I'm basically being paid for doing something I'd be doing for free, but don't tell the record company that though, because they'll probably stop my wages! We thought instead of making jokes about paying members of the crew to do phone interviews for us, we'd better do it ourselves.'

Although Owen, Paul and Mark, and occasionally Aled, who – by rarely uttering a word during interviews – nicely lived up to the drummer's billing as the fountain of quiet mystery, would lay themselves at the mercy of the press, it was Cerys that everyone wanted a piece of. The Catatonia frontwoman endeared herself to the music press by just being herself. She was gracious and funny, confident without being arrogant and completely natural and assuming without a trace of it being an act. Her endearing eccentricity was another important component in her favour, as was her distinct, high-pitched speaking voice, which intrigued most people who interviewed her. She was possessed of a voice that *The Edge* fanzine described as 'a tight trousered Minnie Mouse on helium'. It amusingly compared her to some other day Tarzan. 'She can communicate with bats and schools of dolphins have been seen changing direction on hearing her speak. It's very cool,' raved the fanzine.

Within six weeks Cerys Matthews would have quickly risen through the ranks of rock 'n' roll royalty to the UK's new pop queen. And it's not hard to see why, when you have press cuttings that are so wildly positive.

'There she is, warts and all, screaming through bad PMT, the anger of betrayal and the joy of sex. She's Janis Joplin without the self-hate and Alanis Morrisette without the sleeves-longer-than-her-arms cuteness, Debbie Harry without the discipline' (*Daily Telegraph*).

'Cerys Matthews defines the word eccentricity. She has everything – beauty, talent and a great personality. So if you haven't heard Catatonia before, take your chance now (*Scotland On Sunday*).

'A lady singer whose voice sounds exactly like Shirley Bassey puking five pints of Jack Daniel's (with snakebite chasers) into the Grand Canyon through a megaphone during an earthquake' (*NME*'s Stephen Wells – who else!).

What was noticeable from these first stabs at success, was how every conceivable sort of magazine wanted the definitive Cerys Matthews viewpoint. Women's magazines were interested in her because she was an enigmatic ballsy chick; the broadsheets wanted her because she was intriguing and Catatonia were an unpindownable quantity, cool enough to be adored by both indie and pop camps; while teen music mags wanted to quiz Cerys because her band represented great crossover – commercial pop chic. Catatonia had always professed their alignment to the pop hierarchy, and now they had finally arrived.

The Cerys Matthews effect meant that she frequently had to adapt her interview technique for whomever was setting the questions. Invariably the posers she was set were never about the music.

New Woman magazine: 'OK, the final question: if you had to fill up the car and flee the country, what would you take?'

Cerys: 'My guitar, bags of cash that I've robbed from the bank – because it wouldn't matter – a passport, and someone who's really good at bull-shitting so we can get through customs. A blagger. Maybe someone from a record company who's used to blagging their way into clubs, because I'm always at the back of the queue waving. I can't stand it, I go red; I'm not used to it. I'm a hick really; it's the way I've been brought up. I'd rather pay. Actually, I wouldn't rather pay. I just do!'

Top Of The Pops magazine: 'What kind of things were you always being told off about when you were little?'

'I was always being told off for something. My parents used to think I was prone to fits 'cos I'd throw so many tantrums when I didn't get my own way. I'd go blue in the face and they'd think I was dead. On a number of occasions they'd take me to the hospital and there was nothing wrong with me, it was just pure temper. I was a real rebel. Every rule was meant to be questioned and boy did I question them!' (*Laughs with glee!*)

Cerys coped admirably with whatever came her way. She was a natural. But this wasn't surprising. She had waited years for this opportunity and wasn't going to waste it. Although she was taking the lion's share of the limelight, Mark, Paul, Owen and Aled were content to sit in the shadows, secure in the knowledge that though outwardly Cerys was becoming the group's enigmatic figurehead, inwardly it was a definite democracy.

'In the heady Sleeper days, when everybody thought bands should be her and them, we resisted attempts to make us like that,' Paul explained to the *Melody Maker*. 'We're five individuals who contribute different things to the band. We've all got our own strengths and weaknesses. There's no big boss and cowering band members, we're all realistic enough to realise that the singer is going to be the one who is at the front and that's the way it should be.'

'I don't think about female-fronted bands,' admits Cerys, 'I just think about good songs and good singers. . . but Fleetwood Mac, Sonny and Cher, Lennon and McCartney, the way you hear about them having this mad rivalry that would never be spoken about, that fascinates me. People look at Catatonia and think it's me all the time, think it's me doing the lyrics and none of the music but its never been that simple, ever. It pisses me off when they go on about my voice. There's more going on with us. Sometimes people write about us and ignore the boys completely, when in fact we're a full band where everyone contributes. Only the people who know us know the score.'

The score being, roughly, that although Paul, Owen (who himself contributes songs) and drummer, Aled Richards, all have a sizeable input, the spark, the majority of the actual songwriting is split 50/50 between Mark and Cerys. As Mark doesn't care for the superfluous trappings of fame, it was naturally always going to be Cerys that stepped into the spotlight.

But although Cerys was out front, behind the scenes was a markedly different story. She had admitted in an interview that Catatonia were prone to rubbing each other up the wrong way: 'We fight like all the time,' she said. 'That wears you down, but because you have a measure of success, everybody believes it's their input that makes it successful, so you get egos creeping in and you won't stand down. Sometimes things do get fraught but I think all bands are the same. Perhaps we all hate each other.' Many a true word was said in jest. And if that was true, it was slightly worrying.

STAR STRUCK

It was incredible that after one single and the release of their new album, Catatonia were being fast-tracked to success, and experiencing some altogether alternative environments. Although they had appeared many times on Welsh television, they quickly had to acclimatise themselves to appearances on kids' pop programmes like *The O Zone* and *Live And Kicking*, as well as their debut performance on that British music institution *Top Of The Pops*. *TOTP* aside, what was a huge thrill for Cerys was appearing on *This Morning with Richard and Judy*.

Cerys had become a devout fan of the programme that's beloved of housewives and students alike, during the band's dole years. It was ironic that she used to watch it while her band were struggling to make ends meet, and now here she was on the programme itself. It was hard for Catatonia to see how things could get any better, but this was just the beginning of their ascent to the pop summit. The firsts just kept coming.

The *Melody Maker* felt so confident in the band's abilities that they put Cerys on the cover and awarded them their Single Of The Week. The band also rendezvoused with The Stereophonics in Amsterdam on 13/14 February, where both bands were playing the prestigious London Calling Festival at the city's Paradiso venue. It was the first time Catatonia had played with the fast-rising Stereophonics, who had recently signed to Richard Branson's fledgling V2 label, since their appearance with the then Tragic Love Company at the Aberdare Coliseum, as part of the Splash Tour, in 1996. It was a riotous affair with the Welsh bands and their Welsh road crews indulging in typically Welsh pursuits of excessive drinking and falling down.

As one of the gigs fell on St Valentine's Day, Cerys was experiencing some welcome attention from her fellow Welshmen. The Stereophonics' Richard and Stuart, who were evidently smitten with the Cats' frontwoman, dared singer Kelly to send Cerys a Valentine's card, which he duly did. She was suitably flattered to be the centre of this good-looking Welshman's ardour, except for the little problem of Kelly's long-time girlfriend! Cerys and The 'Phonics did become great friends – but just that!

Cerys had a suitably close relationship with Tommy from Space, but again this was purely platonic, although when they worked together sparks definitely flew. The single the duo had recorded at the tail end of 1997, 'The Ballad Of Tom Jones', was released on 23 February. It couldn't have been put out at a better time, especially for Catatonia. A second single from *International Velvet*, 'Road Rage', was scheduled for release in April, but the duet with Tommy would keep Cerys in the public eye and hopefully have a knock-on sales effect on *International Velvet*.

The song, a big old-style ballad written by Tommy in which they both sing, Sonny-and-Cher style, of their love for Jones the Voice, recalls the days of the wonderful duets of Nancy Sinatra and Lee Hazelwood. It was drama pop with a big bruised heart, a sweeping ballad loaded with a sizeable tongue in its cheek. 'I don't throw my knickers at you,' squeaks Cerys cheekily. 'And I don't come from Wales,' crooned Tommy ruefully.

Helped by a fantastically gothic video – or perhaps Gothamic, as it was designed by someone who worked on the Batman movies – it featured a car teetering at the edge of a cliff in the pouring rain at night, with Tommy hanging on the outside and Cerys in the car. The single smashed into the Top 10 at No. 4.

The duo made a memorable appearance together as panellists on cult music quiz show *Never Mind The Buzzcocks* and Cerys survived the Record Police on the equally hip *Adam and Joe Show*. However, Cerys got closer to her own personal nirvana when she spoke to Tom Jones via a live satellite on TV, after she and Tommy had performed 'The Ballad of Tom Jones' at Space's London Astoria. She described the conversation at the time as 'one of the highlights of my life' and went on a £1000 champagne bender afterwards to prove the point!

It wasn't just the UK that was taking to Cerys and the boys. Europe was beginning to wake up and wish they could thank the Lord that they were Welsh. Both 'Mulder And Scully' and 'The Ballad Of Tom Jones' had been minor hits in the major European countries. Catatonia were about to head out on a European tour to promote the album and forthcoming single 'Road Rage'.

First though, their sights were set across the Atlantic, as the problem surrounding an American home for the band was finally resolved.

Catatonia signed to Vapor Records in the US, a subsidiary of Warners, owned by legendary American rock survivor Neil Young. A statement from the label read:

> Vapor Records is proud to announce our latest signing, Catatonia. The UK chart toppers will release their first Stateside album 'International Velvet' in May. Catatonia have been creating quite a stir recently with their latest single 'Mulder And Scully' which has been in the UK charts for weeks. Hopping to the other side of the pond, Vapor will release 'Mulder And Scully' in the next few months. Yanks beware. . .

In an interview with the Virtual Cardiff website, Paul and Cerys explained the background to the American deal.

Paul: We were looking for a branch of Warners really, to take us to the giddy heights in America.

Cerys: Yeah, 'cause we're tied to Warners, anyway. They're an independent label but their distribution comes through Warners. It's Neil Young's label, isn't it?

Paul: Yeah, it's all overseen by Neil Young. He seemed really keen, didn't he?

Cerys: Yeah, he did.

Paul: And Warners seemed to be having sort of cold feet 'cause we haven't released anything over there yet – so we're really keen to get started. The idea with Vapor is that they'll release singles and 'International Velvet' over there. Everyone has sort of been 'umming and 'arring about which division Warners wants to take us on and all this – but it's far easier just working with them (Vapor) because he (Neil Young) seems a lot more personally involved, and he's got loads of experience and he seems really into us.

Back in the UK, Catatonia had been picked as one of the bands to head out on the road for a UK mini-tour with Scottish bands Travis and Idelwild as part of a Radio 1 sponsored Steve Lamacq Evening Session tour. The dates, at the start of March, called in on venues in England, Scotland and a memorable show at the Newport Centre in South Wales. It was a frenzied gig which saw Catatonia headlining to a tumultuous reception from the packed crowd. Ironically, given Cerys's admiration for the man who has made a living out of women throwing their knickers, Cerys was treated to a little Tom Jones treatment of her own. Mid-set Cerys caught a pair of Welsh flag boxer shorts that were hurtling towards her. She inspected the patriotic flying undergarments and discovered they were etched with the legend 'Love from the boys from Maesteg'!

Life for the band was now non-stop but they were loving it. I mean who wouldn't. This was the life they wanted and they were going to wring every last drop out of it.

Next up was a 10-date, six-country jaunt around Europe between 18

March and 15 April, stopping off at Barcelona and Madrid in Spain, Brussels in Belgium, Copenhagen in Denmark, Oslo in Norway, Stockholm and Malmo in Sweden and Bonn, Hamburg and Berlin in Germany.

Then they would only have three days to catch their breath before kicking off a 10-date UK tour in support of the new single 'Road Rage', released on 20 April.

The tour was dubbed the 'Ride the Tiger' tour, as a precise approximation of what life was like with the band on the road – one 100mph hedonistic roadshow. 'Ride The Tiger' is taken from a book called *Up and Down with The Rolling Stones*. The Stones, infamous as the original good-time indulgers went on tours that became legendary excess fests of sex, drugs and rock 'n' roll. The book claims that 'You have to ride the tiger with the band, and if you fall off – you're out!' In Catatonia's case the falling off related more to the alcohol than any possible drug-addled casualties, but at least it was the thought that counted!

The tour called in at Llandudno North Wales Theatre on 18 April, stopping off at Leeds Metropolitan University, Newcastle University, Leicester University, Southampton University, Sheffield University, Bristol University, Ipswich Corn Exchange and finished up at London Shepherds Bush Empire on 1 May.

A gig in Dublin was scheduled for 3 May, while a gig at Liverpool L2 had to be re-arranged from 21 April to 4 May, as the band had been booked to appear on *Later with Jools Holland* the same day. An appearance on the premier UK music TV show was another sure-fire sign of the band's ever-growing stature. A reputation that was about to be enhanced with the new single 'Road Rage'. Its timely release, midway through the UK tour and the day before the Jools Holland appearance, ensured the single was backed by some heavyweight promotion. This was promotion that included Cerys and Owen appearing on *The Big Breakfast*, Cerys popping up as a guest on Channel 4's Jo Whiley TV show, the band performing on kids programme *Fully Booked* and Cerys doing a phone-in with Mark Goodier on Radio 1.

'Road Rage' was released on 20 April and available on CD, 7″ and cassette. It was backed by the two songs recorded at Greg Haver's Big Noise studios before Christmas – 'I'm Cured' and 'Blow the Millennium', as well as a remix of the title track – 'Road Rage' (Ghia Mix). Again another fine effort by Paul Jones at the mixing desk.

The video and cover art for the single carried on the futuristic space theme of 'Mulder And Scully'. The cover featured a yellow spacecraft whizzing around a futuristic Cardiff skyline, while the video kept that theme running, seeing the band performing in futuristic surroundings in front of a large window that looked onto a Cardiff some time in the year 2080.

The video was immediately picked up by music video television channels MTV and The Box, who both featured the single in heavy rotation. The single also saw the unanimous support of both Radio 1 and commercial radio stations.

No surprise then that Catatonia snapped up their second Top 5 single, as 'Road Rage' sped its way to No. 3 in the UK charts. Cerys could hardly believe what was happening to her. She'd scored three Top 5 singles in the space of three months. It was an extraordinary feat, but one that was about to be topped.

International Velvet had entered the UK charts at No. 11 but had fallen several places the following week. However, following the subsequent releases of 'The Ballad Of Tom Jones' and 'Road Rage', as well as innumerable amounts of TV, radio and press promotion, the album had started to climb steadly back up the charts.

Come 5 May, astonishing reports were filtering through that *International Velvet* had recorded an amazing midweek chart position of No. 1. The album's ascent was capped on Sunday, 11 May as it sat proudly on top of the pile, knocking Massive Attack's *Mezzanine* down to No. 2 and in the process handing the band their first No. 1 record. Not bad for an album that had arrived in the album chart at 11, fallen into the 20s and then made a meteoric rise back to the top.

Of course there was unbridled joy in the Catatonia camp. It was a cue for another of Cerys's famous benders, this time a £2000 champagne rampage with her bandmates and close friends that lasted a week and ended with some of the largest hangovers ever subjected to prolonged paracetamol use. Cerys also fittingly roped Catatonia's best pop chums Space, into the celebratory equation by appearing with the chirpy Scousers on stage at the University of East London's Ball on 19 May.

SUMMER FUN

As well as the huge successes of Catatonia's singles and album, there were other ways of gauging the band's increasingly profound effect on the UK music scene. One of those clues resided in cyberspace.

1998 saw a real revolution in the use of the Internet to promote bands. Fan sites were cropping up at an incredible rate and Catatonia had one of the best. The unofficial site – http://easyweb.easynet.co.uk/~durandal/catatonia/ – was masterminded by Adam Shutes, an impressive Catatonia fan in more ways than one. The brains behind the website is also a boffin by day. He is currently finishing a PhD in cancer research at the National Institute of Medical Research, in Mill Hill, North London.

'The site started while I was doing a Biochemistry degree at Oxford University, I think it was the summer of 1994,' Adam explains. 'It started out as a pretty small affair, since my email account allowed no more than 4 megs to be stored on my University web space. Now, this site occupies over 100 megs of disk space, all of it about Catatonia.

'I had a couple of the Cats records, and I wanted to see if I could write a website about them. Plus I had a Mac LC computer, which I wanted to use to do things other than practicals and essays. There was no single catalyst for doing it though. I just loved their music.'

Although its inception was around 1994, the site didn't really make much impression until 1996, and then really started to be the natural stopping off point for Catatonia fans all around the world in 1998.

'There was a massive huge upsurge in hits by people visiting the site when "Mulder And Scully" was released,' says Adam. 'You could really sense that something big was happening and that the band were well on their way to becoming stars. When the band aren't busy, neither am I. When they are it's hectic. I hope to make the website feel like somewhere where people can come and chat and discuss. There's nothing more interesting than other people after all. And we've had a few meetings between fans who have met by using the site.'

The last five months had been a non-stop storm of extensive touring and gigs. It had been a hugely successful time, but the band – and especially Cerys – needed a rest. Due to Cerys working far too hard over the last few months, the Liverpool gig that had already been moved once was postponed.

The gig was rescheduled for the summer as a pre-festival warm-up. Before they headed off for a few weeks' rest and recuperation before the churn started to turn once again, the band recorded a video for the US release of 'Mulder And Scully', in Windsor in Berkshire, of all places. It depicted Cerys running through a city of filing cabinets attempting to find the rest of the band.

While the band went their separate ways, either back home or on holiday, the Catatonia schedule was being rapidly filled with gigs at conceivably every major summer festival, both home and abroad.

The band were booked to play at Cheltenham racecourse with Space and 60ft Dolls on Saturday, 6 June, followed by support slots with Madness and Pulp on consecutive Saturdays at Finsbury Park in North London at the start of June. Then it was off finally to attempt to make their debut performance at Glastonbury, popping up to Scotland to play T In The Park in July, and then V98 at Chelmsford and Leeds in August.

In between UK festival dates the band were to play festivals in Europe including Rockpalast, at Loreley in Germany in June and Expo 98 in Lisbon, Portugal in July.

For Cerys there was some escape before the band's frenetic festival activity as she headed to the sunny climes of clubbers' paradise Ibiza in the Balearic Islands with her girl friends. Even there Cerys couldn't resist the allure of getting up and singing. She clambered on to a small mobile stage in a packed bar to perform one of her own songs. 'I was very drunk,' she confesses. 'Somebody put "Mulder And Scully" on the karaoke machine and I got up and gave it loads. I shocked everybody. They were like, "It's not her, is it?" And then the stage collapsed and I fell right on my bum, legs in the air!'

When back home Cerys admitted she was aiming to indulge in her hobbies – marrows and gnomes! 'I'm fed up with reading about the silly things I've done. I don't think I'll get any respect for my music if I'm just seen as a brainless idiot ruled by drink. My problem is that I just can't sit down,' she says. 'I need something to occupy my time so I've taken up gardening. I know it sounds daft, and no-one believes me, but I really want to grow a championship marrow. I've been fascinated by them since I went to a garden festival. I've already organised the garden at my house in Cardiff.' Unfortunately, clearing the space for her marrows meant Cerys struggled to accommodate her other backyard occupants – a collection of gnomes.

'I know it's not very rock 'n' roll but I've got about six hundred,' she laughs. 'They're starting to take over the house. We've had to invent a game to try and get rid of a few of them. It's called Millennium Gnome and basically we put them on the garage roof and try and knock them off with champagne corks!'

HERE, THERE AND EVERYWHERE

As well as the summer festivals both home and abroad, the Cats were scheduled on the Horde Tour, a package deal of bands with various line-ups that were touring around the US under the Horde banner. The tour featured bands like The Dave Matthews Band, Blues Traveller and The Barenaked Ladies – quite an older bluesy line-up compared to Catatonia's insouciant pop sense, but still it was exposure, whoever they were playing on the same bill as. Although The Horde tour kicked off in July, it wouldn't end until the beginning of September so Catatonia were set to hijack the tour around late August.

Still, they first had the summer festivals to contend with. After their break they were once again raring to go. Although Catatonia had played Reading and the now defunct Phoenix Festival, the summer would see them cropping up at all the major music ports of call.

There were many highlights – starting off with their two Saturday tenancy at Finsbury Park with Madness and Pulp. 'All my mates were down for those gigs, the sun was out, and we had a really good time,' Cerys told the *NME*. 'We played with Madness about four years ago, and they asked us to play with them this summer because they liked us then. It was so much fun. Watching them is like watching Abba, single after single.'

Then there was Glastonbury, at last. 'Glastonbury was a big highlight because the album had really taken off and it was just amazing to see all these people who knew the words better than me,' Cerys recounted to the *NME*. 'We did have to contend with the mud a bit, but we got lucky because it stopped raining for the hour we were on stage. Which was great because we had tried to play Glastonbury before, but we couldn't because of the weather, so we were owed a bit of luck.'

Probably the highlight of the summer though was two storming gigs at Chelmsford and Leeds as part of the V98 festival. The V festivals sponsored by Virgin, are new festivals in the summer calendar and are probably the most professionally run.

The two-site festival had a strong line-up in 1998 with the Godfather of Soul, James Brown headlining one of the stages. However, even the soulman's dazzling stage show could do nothing to dampen the supernova performance of Catatonia.

Cerys, who was fast becoming something of a style icon, with an ever-changing, chameleon-like attitude to her wardrobe, was wowing the crowd in a cowboy hat, white cropped top and two-tone Tommy Hilfiger trousers. She was also on sparkling form, knocking back a bottle of wine as she engaged the crowd in a stream of humorous banter. It was estimated that two-thirds of that day's festival-goers had flocked to the *NME* stage to see Catatonia play. That was an estimated audience of 25,000 plus. No mean feat. It just underlined the band's ever-rising currency. Track after track was played from the album, and it seemed that everyone owned a copy of *International Velvet*, such was the noise the crowd generated. As a blazing sun set on the festival site the crowd sang along lustily to every song the band played. It was a special gig and a wonderful climax to a beautiful day.

Unbeknown to Catatonia, the management – MRM, in tandem with Conal Dodds, the band's promoter – had been planning a spectacular event for the following summer. Conal was backstage at V98 and was so excited about the plans that he decided to sound them out to the band.

'They had just come off stage after playing a great gig in front of a huge crowd,' explains Conal. 'By this time we knew that this was it, they were on the up. They could definitely achieve a decent level of business, but at that time we hadn't talked to the band about what we had planned.'

What was planned was headlining a 30,000 capacity open-air show at Margam Park, a natural beauty spot, just outside Port Talbot in West Glamorgan. 'I just steamed in and told them,' recalls Conal. 'I saw Cerys and we went and had a bit of a chat, I took her to our [the promoter's] bar backstage and told her about Margam. She was really into the idea, having gone there as a kid and visited the place. I think Paul and Aled go to Margam with their kids, so everyone knew of it. We bought them all some champagne because they had played a great gig that day, and I gave the bottle to Cerys who poured some out for everyone and she proposed a toast, 'Here's to Margam Park next year!'

The Margam show was scheduled for Saturday, 29 May 1999. Conal also wanted the band to do some warm-up shows before Margam. 'The Albert Hall was mooted, but the band didn't want to do it,' says Conal. 'I struck on the idea of playing a couple of gigs the weekend before at Llangollen International Arena in Denbighshire, North Wales – the site of the Welsh national Eisteddfods. The arena holds 6000, and I thought that would make the perfect warm-up to Margam.' Everyone else thought so too.

Conal, who was the driving force behind the organising of the shows, even came up with a great name for the gigs, The Home Internationals, based on the old four nations' football tournament that was a stable fixture of Wales' international football calendar. So it was scheduled in that Catatonia would play two shows at Llangollen on 22 and 23 May 1999. If all went well and ticket sales were good it would have meant that Catatonia would have played to 40,000 fans in the space of a week. An extraordinary feat, given that it was little over a year ago that they were struggling to score chart singles any higher than No. 40. This really was an epochal moment in their career and Margam would be the undoubted highpoint.

In the UK they had the midas touch: *International Velvet* was fair steaming towards an incredible double platinum mark, 600,000 copies, but in the US it was like 1992 all over again. They were starting from scratch.

The Cats jetted off to the States at the end of August with no preconceptions of what to expect. *International Velvet* had been released in May and 'Mulder And Scully' not long after that. Both achieved steady if unspectacular success, with the single picking up decent airplay on the US's college radio network, the natural home for all those alternative-minded bands, which Catatonia weren't of course. So they were at a disadvantage to begin with.

Through Vapor Records and the links with Neil Young, Catatonia managed to charm themselves onto the Horde Tour, but not in their wackiest Welsh dreams would Cerys and the boys have dreamt of playing to the crowd that they encountered – a raggle taggle mix of hippies, drop-outs and stoners. 'People kept saying how great it was that we would be playing with Blues Traveller,' Cerys recalled in an interview with the *Washington Post* newspaper. 'And we were like, "To be honest, we don't know anything about them. What do they sound like?"' In essence it was hippie rock. Catatonia's sparkling pop thrills were as suited to the tour as an Englishman wearing a daffodil.

'We all had a lovely time, but I couldn't understand the little differences, such as why they'd never heard of the Wombles,' says Cerys mockingly. 'I can't respect any country that doesn't know who Uncle Bulgaria is!'

The best thing about the US experience was that it allowed the band time to write and demo new songs on the road. Although singles were still to be released from *International Velvet*, the band were looking ahead to recording the next album quickly. The songs from their second album had now been written some time ago, and the group are particularly prolific, so they had a new batch of songs just itching to be recorded.

In an interview with *Music Week* magazine Cerys explained that the basic ideas for the new songs were worked out while they toured throughout 1998 and occasionally played in embryonic form live on tour. They were then demoed in the 'back of a bus with the microphone swinging' while touring in the US.

'I think you carry on doing songwriting all the time. It's not a case of writing one on the road and then one in a hotel ... we just wanted new songs to play,' explained Cerys. 'We were keen to get back in the studio. You've got to keep fresh, keep alive. It's like recharging your batteries. We usually just like to get on with it. And we work best without people hearing stuff when we're going along.'

'If you can keep going you'll be all right – it's the promotion and touring that grinds you down.'

STRANGE DAYS INDEED

While Catatonia were writing and demoing new songs, they found themselves in a situation where they were still releasing singles from an album they had written over 18 months ago.

While the band were touring in America, Warners released 'Strange Glue' to keep the interest bubbling over in the UK. The song, written by Owen Powell, highlighted Owen's talents as a songwriter, penning some of the best lyrics from the whole album.

'It was strange glue that held us together when we both came apart at the seams ... When faced with my demons I clothe them and feed them.' 'Strange Glue' was another of their big-hearted ballads, loaded with the emotional turmoil of fragile relationships. Mark beautifully described the song as 'a Bryan Adams ballad fucked up the ass with a log'. An intimate picture that most people would like not to conjure up in their minds. But what Mark sarcastically meant was the tune was commercial enough to rival the annoying 'Everything I Do' song, the Canadian's record 26-weeks No. 1 single from the soundtrack to the Robin Hood film. It had more intelligence and meaning that the mindless slush of Adams's song could ever have. Even if the song did border on soft metal balladry.

What was unique about 'Strange Glue' was that the vocal on that track is totally from scratch. Normally when bands' record tracks, they are recorded with the producer concentrating on the bass and drums. Then they would go back and over-dub the other instruments. He/she might use the guitars, but more than likely they'd go back and rerecord the guitars to get a better sound, and tailor the sound to the track. Vocals are largely used to just guide the rest of the band – then the producer would go back in and fix them properly. But with 'Strange Glue', when the band recorded the track Cerys gave such a great guide vocal that repeat takes were tried, but the band couldn't get the sentiment and intonation as good as the original vocal.

'It just told the story of the song perfectly, and so both Cerys and I decided to go with the guide vocal as the main vocal in the track,' explained Tommy D.

'And it's quite ironic, because the lyric in there "She said your place or mine" is sung because Owen had written the song from a man's perspective, and Cerys just sang it because it was the guide vocal. But we didn't think anything of it – I was going to go and ask her just to sing one sentence of the entire song. And now it seems quite funny because it bends the meaning of the whole song.'

The other most noticeable thing about the single was the inclusion of 'That's All Folks', the controversial track that was pulled as the album closer on *International Velvet* in favour of the less-inflamatory 'My Selfish Gene'.

The band had battled hard to get the song included on the single, rightly thinking that it was just too good to be consigned to the dumper of record company history. The inclusion of the anti-Warners tirade was a welcome addition to the single, being one of the most climactic and downright scary songs you are ever likely to hear.

Due to a new regulation on chart singles allowing only three songs on a CD single, the extra tracks to 'Strange Glue' had to be changed. A live version of 'Mulder And Scully' was to be included, but it was removed when the new rule was announced. A live version of 'Road Rage' recorded at the Shepherd's Bush Empire in London got the nod instead.

While 'Road Rage' and 'Mulder And Scully' were in-yer-face stomping pop gems, 'Strange Glue' being a slow-burning ballad was more subtle, not as immediate as the previous two singles. Despite again accruing the support of radio, it only managed to get to No. 11. Nevertheless, if you had offered Catatonia the chance of three singles attaining chart positions of 3, 5 and 11 at the start of the year, they would have bitten your hand off. And remember that 'Strange Glue' was the fourth single from the album, so all things considered, 11 was a fine effort.

1998 was presenting one amazing opportunity after another. This time last year, the surname Matthews conjured up nothing more than nibbling turkey drumsticks; Mulder and Scully were just two American actors; road rage was something that happened on the M25 and the only strange glue you'd heard of was Pritt Stick. It was amazing just how their fortunes had changed.

Catatonia were nominated at two of the most prestigious music awards ceremonies in the UK. *International Velvet* was up for best album at the Mercury Music Prize Awards, while Catatonia had been nominated for best single at the *Q* Magazine awards.

Amazingly for a band who only 12 months previously had been propping up the bars at the UK's seedy indie watering holes, they were invited to play in front of the high fashion brigade at the Versace show in Milan.

Cerys, being the abstract clothes horse and part-time style icon that she was rapidly becoming, enjoyed the trappings of glamour that the show afforded, although Mark, Paul, Owen and Aled would rather have been down the pub.

'We were invited along to play a soundtrack to the fashion show,' Cerys explained. 'And me being a pretty typical lady, I like a lot of fashion and that, so I said, 'yeah!' and it was brilliant. I've never been to a fashion show before. What an experience, all the models and the clothes, we only played about five songs, but it was all very classy.'

As much as Catatonia were gaining plaudits for the music, Cerys was also a fast-rising feature of the nation's style bibles. Her appearance was as interchangeable as a voice that could be growling one minute, girlish the next.

She was glamorous in a way that her idols like Shirley Bassey, Edith Piaf and Billie Holliday were. She also loved the Hollywood films of the Forties and screen sirens like Greta Garbo and Grace Kelly. Cerys eschewed trends for her own fashion ideology. A way of dressing that relied on one dictum – do what the fuck you like.

'I change like the wind,' she said. 'I just like dressing up. I had my tracksuit phase, then the Spice Girls started wearing my shoes – my platform shoes – so I had to change because I don't want to be doing the same as everybody else. I've got my hippy period at the minute. I had my Queen period with my tiara. I wear what-the-hell I want.'

On video shoots, Cerys would drive stylists mad by doing her own thing. Whatever they would recommend she would do the opposite. She laughed at the po-faced fashion press and the pretentious sniping attitudes that went with it.

'I remember being at a fashion shoot with her and the stylist was cracking up,' says Excess Press's Jayne Houghton. 'She was going "That's not how it's supposed to be worn" – and these were really expensive things. Cerys just flung them on, wore them whichever way she wanted and it quickly became Cerys's style. She's really got her own style, that's very Courtney Love. She just wears what she likes, when she likes. Her view is fuck fashion and fuck style.'

Cerys exuded the dangerous charm and domestic glamour of a pop star and soap star all rolled into one – not only celebrated but also looked out for as one of 'our own'. She was a star with attainable glamour and down-to-earth chic, with an appeal that stretched from the council estate to the manor born.

She was the first 'real' female pop star there had been for years. Robbie Williams, the former singer with boy band Take That, also possessed that tongue-in-cheek, self-deprecating charm and ability to transcend pop star barriers to appear to be everyone's mate. In 1998 he and Cerys were the true King and Queen of pop music.

Just to underline Cerys and Catatonia's broad church appeal, what other band could have appeared on the National Lottery Show, Radio 1, and Radio 4's Woman's Hour in the space of a few days? Here was a band that was rapidly becoming all things to everyone.

A BLESSED RELIEF

After a summer that saw the band as a permanent fixture on every conceivable festival bill both home and abroad, Catatonia were about to dip their heads temporarily below the parapet for a few months, but would be no less busy for it.

Their enforced absence due to the recording of their third album, again at Monnow Valley Studios in Monmouth, would see them reappear in December as guests of their fellow countrymen and close mates The Manic Street Preachers.

Before the recording and touring, there was the little matter of the superfluous fluff of the music industry to contend with.

The Mercury Music Prize is billed as one of the most prestigious fixtures in the music calendar. Held at London's swank Grosvenor House Hotel, the top prize is awarded to the musician/s who an independent panel of judges drawn from radio, TV and press consider to represent the best in British music.

Catatonia's *International Velvet* was shortlisted alongside a diverse array of music makers that included the doomily anthemic Wigan rockers The Verve; the brooding trip hop of Massive Attack; Robbie Williams' cheeky pop melodies; Asian Dub Foundation's bristling agit-dance style; the dayglo asian dance pop of Cornershop; eclectic electro merchants The Propelerheads; Gomez's grizzled swamp boogie; Britpop stalwarts Pulp; classical composer John Surman; folk singer Eliza Carthy and soulful gospel-lites Four-Hero.

'These albums of the year reveal a new landscape – multi-musical, multi-cultural, ever fascinating and exciting' declared Simon Frith, chairman of the judge's panel. 'British music is alive and well.'

Catatonia were third favourites for the prize, but even if they didn't win, they vowed they were going to enjoy yet another epochal moment in an epoch marked year. Although the head of the judging panel had spouted on about British music's new landscape the award of the Mercury prize shocked many by being given to Gomez, who themselves couldn't quite believe they had won. It's hard to take awards like this seriously – especially when they are supposed to reward innovation and design a new blueprint for British music, yet the prize is meted out to the most backward-thinking, retro-styled bunch of young musicians who aspire to be Louisiana swamp bluesmen you are ever likely to come across.

Despite the slight setback ('we didn't expect to win anyway,' Cerys said later), The Cats had their own table and access to as much free alcohol as they wanted, so there was enough liquid refreshment to soak up any hurt feelings. And anyway, another chance to lay their hands on some silverware was lurking around the corner at the *Q* Awards in late October.

First, there was some welcome reparation from the breathless bouts of touring and promotion, as the Cats headed to the becalmed surrounds of Monnow Valley, to record their third album.

Following up a double platinum selling album so soon after the immense triumph of *International Velvet* might have been strange to some people who reckoned they should have basked in the reflective glow of that album's success. However, this was a band of three songwriters that were always writing.

'If you just delegate a certain time to writing I think it puts pressure on you, so we just try and keep it in mind and write all the time,' explained Cerys. 'I don't think it's really inspired by the success we've had, our brains take about a year to catch up.'

'The Jam used to write an album a year,' chips in Mark. 'And look at how good their albums were. So we're well on course to release *Equally Cursed And Blessed* a year after the last album.'

Anyway, this was a band who had waited four years for their first album to be released, and they still felt there was lost time to be made up. They had seen at first hand how fickle and changeable the music business was. They'd had their own moments of immense self-doubt and fears that the record company axe was soon to drop on their heads. Although they were now Warner's 'golden children' helping the company to one of their best ever years in the UK market, they didn't take anything for granted. They wanted to make every minute that they were in, what they believed was a privileged position, count.

Cerys was particularly moved by a quote from Tony Curtis, the film actor. While he was being interviewed on the *Clive Anderson All Talk* programme, he said: 'You live for now, because now is the time – not one minute ago, and not one minute in the future.'

That summed up Catatonia's prolific approach to recording – make the most of what you have got, do the best you can, while you can.

They say time is a great healer and Cerys and Mark were both learning to live with each other on the road. It was two years since they split and old wounds were being healed. It also helped that the band were afforded bigger and better facilities, a larger touring coach and better hotels. If the two of them wanted to put some distance between each other they could.

The rest of the band had acclimatised themselves to any friction that arose. The band's situation and their fraught history made them the band they were.

Perhaps if there hadn't have been a relationship breakdown between the singer and the guitarist there wouldn't have been an *International Velvet*. Maybe if the pair hadn't gone through hell and back, they wouldn't have come up with such a perfect album.

You sensed the two of them realised this fact by naming the album that had the onerous task of following up a smash-hit album *Equally Cursed And Blessed*. In equal parts this was a band who had spent the last five years prior to 1998 rueing their cursed luck, while then spending what followed thanking their blessed stars.

As they headed to Monnow Valley, again with Tommy D at the producing helm, the central theme that would run through the album would be hope over adversity. In essence the 12 tracks that would adorn their new album would be redemption songs with a sunny reproach. While *International Velvet* was angst and turmoil painted in bright pop colours, *Equally Cursed And Blessed* would present a more thoughtful, pared down approach in equal parts wistful and elegant, downbeat and reflective.

While Warners were banking on the band reproducing the sheer pop highs of 'Mulder And Scully' and 'Road Rage', Catatonia as usual were their single-minded selves, set on doing their own thing.

What was consistent with *International Velvet* was the breadth of variation in style. As a grand sign of their consummate musicianship, the songs that would make up *Equally Cursed And Blessed* would be wildly different as was the array of equipment the band used in the recording. Monnow Valley studios was strewn with old gear and new technology, microphones and effects, analogue delays and space echoes aligned with experimentation with keyboards, drum machines and even hurdy-gurdy and saw players feature.

The recording was a much more relaxed affair for Catatonia. The pressure was less intense on recording *Equally Cursed And Blessed* in comparison to *International Velvet*, where the band faced the possibility of being dropped. As a result the songs on *ECAB*, are far warmer, sunnier and humorous than past efforts.

There's an all-purveying confidence about the album that is reflected in its fearless approach to recording. Catatonia were unafraid to embrace old and new technology while stretching themselves musically. That confidence and belief could have only come from their not appreciating the glory of feeling alive until they had faced the opposite and found the strength to overcome it. Catatonia had taken numerous knocks, hit interminable lows both professionally and personally, but had come back fighting hard. They had succeeded despite all the odds, and that triumphal confidence was shining through.

'I suppose a lot of people were expecting International Velvet II, but I prefer bands that come out with something a little different each time,' explained Paul Jones. 'When we were in the studio, we had all these songs that stood on their own but we wanted to so something different to them. We always like dabbling with stuff like that.'

'We got a hurdy-gurdy player and a harpist in and had someone playing the saw on one track. We had been doodling around with putting strings on the songs and because we could afford it, we though we'd get a big string section in.'

As a consequence of this Catatonia were more receptive to trying things out and exploring different avenues. 'They definitely wanted to have a go at new things,' says Tommy D. 'We used different musicians, a harpist and a saw player, for example. I think that creativity runs throughout the album.

Tommy was right. *Equally, Cursed And Blessed* was an album that didn't pander to trends or follow a radio-courting route. It wasn't obviously packed full of hit singles nor did it loosely sound like anything else around.

The album opens with 'Dead From The Waist Down' – a perfect example of the lavish production Tommy D wrapped the album in. Lit in a dreamy netherworld of sumptuous strings and golden Bacharach melodies, the song radiates with mellow sunshine and positive 'make hay not war' vibes.

'Londinium' is a biting riposte at London's fickle excesses coated in ironic melancholy. Mark's caustically biting but clever lyrics lay bare his distrust of the place and strikes a blow for the provinces. 'London doesn't breathe, it just sucks the life out of me . . . I come alive outside the M25 . . . oh Euston, Paddington, train station please, make the red light turn green endlessly,' snipes Cerys and you are in no uncertain terms at the band's contempt for the English capital.

'Postscript' is probably the weakest link on the album, a track that rallies against the false moralities of the church ('if you live a lie, you'll die a liar') but whose slow-tempo melody doesn't shift much out of first gear.

'She's A Millionaire', however, is a song that twinkles like a rare gem. Offbeat feminist-like lyrics that namecheck Versace, tampons, gynaecology and pushchair rage weave their way around shimmering verses and a bubbling chorus. The song also features the first unfurling of Cerys's recorder playing skills as she parps her way through a neat recorder solo!

If you had been lulled into a false sense of calm after the album's opening four slices of mellowness, 'Storm The Palace' will jolt you out of your dreamy state. A proverbial punk pop hurricane is kicked up as a strident anti-monarchy rant – 'Storm The Palace, turn it into flats, make them all ex-pats' – belts along on the back of Mark and Owen's fiery guitars and Aled's tub thumping drumming. The song climaxes with some decidedly electrifying 1977 punk-encrusted feedback. To get the band in the mood for some anti-monarchy bile spitting, Tommy D encouraged the Cats to pin up pictures of the Queen Mum to help them vent their anti-royalist spleen. The album was recorded around the time it was leaked to the press that the Queen Mother had an overdraft of millions of pounds.

Pop thrills in abundance are delivered by 'Karaoke Queen' – a song written in homage to Cerys's adventures in the bars of Ibiza during her summer holidays, and specifically her arse-over-tit escapade when belting out 'Road Rage' while out of her head in an Ibiza bar. It encapsulates the no-brainer joys of the perfect pop song. 'It's just a three minute song, It doesn't last very long, But it'll take you to a place you'd rather be.' 'Karaoke Queen' is as infectious as it is sweet pop confection; interspersed with smatterings of sugar-kissed 'ooh sha la la's', and a chorus that imbeds itself in your brain like only the catchiest tunes ever can do.

It's typical Catatonia, with their wilfully eclectic approach, that they follow 'Karaoke Queen's' unadulterated pop romp with an eerily icy ballad.

'Bulimic Beats' was a ballad that took everyone by surprise as it documented Cerys's flirtation with an eating disorder. She hadn't given any indication in any previous interview that she had suffered either from bulimia or any other eating disorders and when the music press seized on the suggestion, she brushed them away by saying, 'Most girls have suffered from them, I just laughed at it and got on with my life.'

The song itself features the singer's beautifully fragile vocals gently tiptoeing over spine-tingling harp and sweeping strings accompaniment. It's as gorgeous and bewitching a ballad as you are ever likely to hear. However it's not a harrowing tearjerker. Not when Cerys makes light of her once bulimic state with the brilliant pay-off line, arguably pop music's first attempt at making light of vomit, 'here in my kitchen . . . a front line with labels, where I witness custard's last stand.' The harp on the song was played by Elinor Bennett, the wife of one of Wales' leading nationalist politicians, Plaid Cymru's Dafydd Wigley.

'Valerian' is as wistful and elegant as 'Bulimic Beats', Mark's coyly strummed crystalline guitar line wraps itself around Cerys's coyly luxuriant vocal and it's like The Sundays or The Cocteau Twins never existed. 'Valerian' is a natural alternative to sleeping pills. Ironically the song is strongly rumoured to be about Mark and Cerys's relationship. If it is, it seems almost fitting that, like 'Valerian', it finally puts to sleep the past.

'Whatever the case I always felt out of place, as a matter of fact I always felt like that around you.'

Again it's all change as Cerys adopts yet another vocal style, underlining just how diverse her range is by transforming herself into an Edith Piaf-Marlene Dietrich-style Forties cabaret singer on the bawdy burlesque of 'Shoot The Messenger'. The song allows Cerys a little role-playing by stepping into the shoes of a prostitute, while the music is given a spooky veneer by the accompaniment of that rarest of musical instruments, the bowed saw. The saw was played by carpenter Paul Whyman who was invited to Monnow Valley studios by his friend, the album's engineer Joe Gibb. Amazingly the Cwmbran based chippy hadn't played a saw and over five days taught himself how to do it, before joining the band in the studio.

'I'm quite musical anyway because I play the guitar and I've been in a few bands,' explained Paul. 'So I just bought myself a violin bow, and tried playing but after a few hours, all I was getting was a screeching noise. So I logged on to the Internet and there were a lot of sites devoted to playing the saw. I learnt some technique and took it from there.'

Paul ended up playing his saw down the phone to Cerys. 'She said it was the sound the band wanted, so I went down to the studio and did it. I was there for a few hours, did four takes and that was it. It was great hanging out with the band and an honour to play on *Equally Cursed And Blessed*.'

That was Catatonia for you, unpredictable to the end. Just like their album. The closing two tracks on *Equally Cursed And Blessed* are diametrically opposed but no less good for that. The Owen Powell penned 'Nothing Hurts' is a hushed lullaby, a breathy ballad with sparkling atmospherics as Cerys coos: 'words plain with lullaby refrain, so sweet sleep, enjoy the time you keep'.

The album's closer *Dazed, Beautiful And Bruised* meanwhile picks up the theme of personal empowerment that coursed through 'I Am The Mob' from *International Velvet* and continues on this clarion call to the downtrodden. The chorus cascades with the words 'I dream one day I'll find the one that lives within my mind and they'll feel the same way too we've all been used, Dazed Beautiful and Bruised', while the song wells up to a climactic ending. Cerys delivers yet another astonishing vocal performance, as her voice stretches itself to its outer limits at the songs end.

'Equally Cursed And Blessed' was put to bed safe in the knowledge that when reawakened for release in March its eleven songs of varying shades and colours would again have the critics straining to decode the band's diverse manifesto.

If you wanted your bands to baffle and bemuse, then sign up now – Catatonia are the band you've been looking for.

IT'S ALL OVER THE FRONT PAGE

After missing out on the Mercury Music Prize, the band soon got their first taste of silverware by picking up the Welsh Communicator of the Year Award by the Institute of Public Relations in Wales.

The Communicator of the Year Award is given to the person or persons who, in the eyes of the members of the IPR, have done the most to promote Wales and the interests of Wales. 'This is the first time the award has been given to anyone other than an individual, and Catatonia follow in the footsteps of actor Sir Anthony Hopkins, athlete Colin Jackson, broadcaster John Humphrys, and choir boy Aled Jones,' trumpeted the press release.

The band were presented with their PR gong in the middle of recording at Monnow Valley. The Cats were given the award for their enormous success, and on the way they have used their limelight to popularise Welsh culture and language. Cerys was typically gracious on receiving the award. 'This is actually the first award we have ever been given, she said, 'we've been nominated in a few music awards, but this is the first we've actually won, and its great that it is something so closely related to Wales – diolch yn fawr!'

With nominations in place for the *Q* magazine awards and the Ivor Novello songwriting awards, the Catatonia mantelpiece could soon be groaning under the collective weight of its silverware additions.

As the band put the finishing touches to the album, they found themselves in the bizarre position of having to promote a single from their second album, just after finishing their third. Warners were set to release 'Game On' as the fifth single from *International Velvet*, which didn't make much sense, but Warners wanted to squeeze every last drop of profit out of their charges, so they weren't going to listen to the artistic reasons for not putting the single out.

'Game On' was released on 26 October and rather predictably it stiffed at 33. That was five singles from the album and given much of the general public already owned *International Velvet* there was no way they were going to go out and purchase another single from it. Only die-hard fans would buy 'Game On' for the B-sides – 'Mulder And Scully live in Newport' and an acoustic version of 'Strange Glue' .

Despite its low chart placing it was a relief for the band to close a chapter on *International Velvet* and move on. The churn of promotion and forward planning was spinning into full effect and Catatonia were being lined up for appearances around the globe.

In the UK the band would confirm their broadband appeal by performing at the Smash Hits Poll Winners Party in front of thousands of screaming kids and appearing on *Jools Holland's Hootananny*, a special treat for serious music lovers recorded in November and aired on New Years Eve.

The band had also been invited to appear on some major US shows in

November – *David Letterman*, *Penn and Teller*, and *Viva Cabaret*, while they were also confirmed for a tour of Australia and Japan in February 1999 – their first visits to the Asian and Australasian sub-continents.

More importantly, in the immediate future maybe, was the announcement to the press and public of the Home Internationals at Llangollen and Margam Park in May. There was nervousness within the Catatonia camp whether a band whose phenomenal rise had been accelerating for all of 10 months could sell over close to 60,000 tickets for three gigs scheduled for the following year.

Although 'Game On' had not done as well as the record company would have liked, the release of the new album and subsequent singles would be the perfect aid to boost tickets sales nearer the three big May shows. And, of course, the cult of Cerys Matthews showed no signs of abating. She was gaining increasingly populist appeal across all sections of the media. She was as likely to appear in a women's magazine pontificating on her perfectly offbeat fashion sense as to appear in a full-on sassy photo shoot in any number of the UK's legion of growing men's magazine titles.

Tickets for Margam Park went on sale in October 1998 and they sold over 2500 on their very first day, 12% of total ticket sales – a brilliantly encouraging figure to begin with.

The personal triumphs, of what was without doubt rapidly turning into an astonishing year for the band, continued as they ran away with the Best Single Award for 'Road Rage' at the *Q* Awards. Legendary British singer-songwriter Elvis Costello was due to present them with the award but was stuck in traffic and TV presenter Mariella Frostrup ended doing the honours. 'This is nice, thank you very much. It's a bit too early to say anything really, isn't it?' Cerys's acceptance speech was memorable for mentioning Ron Davies, the recently disgraced Welsh secretary of state, who was caught soliciting on Clapham Common. Why couldn't we have been last? I've only had two glasses of champagne. This one's for Ron Davies, what the hell was he doing?'

Elvis Costello did roll up later and asked if he could get the group out into the lobby so he could read his specially prepared list of famous Welsh people. The *Q* Awards allowed the band to rub shoulders with the their fellow rock colleagues and Cerys ended up on the cover of the following month's *Q* magazine posing with fellow award winners Michael Stipe of REM and James Dean Bradfield of The Manics.

And it was, rather fittingly, that Catatonia rounded off an incredibly momentous year by again joining forces with The Manic Street Preachers for another jaunt around the UK's arenas including two ecstatic Christmas gigs at the Cardiff International Arena.

The Cats also helped see in the last year of the century with an appearance on Jools Holland's New Year's Eve Hootenanny. The band performed 'Road Rage' and 'Nothing Hurts', while Cerys realised her dream of teaming up with grandfather of Welsh pop Tom Jones to sing a duet of the old standard 'Baby It's Cold Outside'. The two Welsh icons had met previously, but their appearance on Jools Holland would trigger a chain of events that would see Tom Jones restored to hipdom and elevated to the cool echelons of the music business once more.

If that wasn't enough, the band could hardly catch their breath as the plaudits kept on coming. They swept the board in both the *NME* and *Melody Maker* end-of-year polls walking off with the top placings in the Best Album, Best Single and Woman of the Year categories. As the cliché goes – 'it really doesn't get much better than this'.

Cerys's face adorned the front cover of the Christmas double issue of the *Melody Maker* and you couldn't help thinking that this was a band that had deserved every single success the year had brought them.

Writing lines like 'I will achieve my destiny, my stars ascent a certainty,' (from 'Game On') have never been so prophetic.

12
Iechyd g'day mate

How apt. You travel for 24 hours, raking up both chronic jet lag and a healthy fillip for your air miles entitlement in equal measure, yet find yourself on stage in front of an audience that is more 'hometown' than any hometown show could ever be.

Journeying to the other side of the world does strange things to your sense of patriotism – it accentuates it into the realm of pantomime-like cliché. That's how Catatonia found themselves playing the 'you-just-can't-make-this-up' Prince of Wales venue in Melbourne, Australia in front of a rabid crowd of Welsh rugby shirt wearing ex-pats, exiled travellers and any Australians who cared to lay siege to their Welsh ancestry for one night only. Welsh flags were waved and the 'Everyday when I wake up, I thank the Lord I'm Welsh' chorus of 'International Velvet' drunkenly bellowed as if it was the new Welsh national anthem. Which it was – for pissed-up Welsh people too drunk be able to pronounce the words to the original anthem.

Still, this was welcome relief for Catatonia. Uncharted territories are always faced with trepidation by any pioneering band. The Cats had also been due to make their debut bow in Japan, but this had been put on hold to late spring 1999. However, the Australian gigs, in Brisbane, Sydney, Canberra, two nights in Melbourne, and a one-night-only stopover for a gig in Auckland, New Zealand, were like a night out in Wales without the rain and cold, replaced instead by Australia's characteristic late summer heat and humidity.

The Melbourne show brought a surprise meeting with one of the journalists who was to discover the shooting star called Cerys Matthews as she had drunkenly whizzed into his orbit after her notorious French bender. Everett True was writing for the *Melody* Maker when he had sat listening to Mark tell him how he had a wager with Owen of £30 that Cerys wouldn't show, only having to blow the bet when she staggered into Brighton for their planned interview two hours later. That, however, was the Catatonia from a lost era; drinking too much and partying too hard to be taken seriously. But Everett was a believer, even if too many others weren't at the time. Via a stint as editor of the now defunct monthly music magazine *Vox*, he'd headed down under to turn Australia on to his own particular brand of rock 'n' roll journalism.

So he found himself at the Prince of Wales penning a review for the local paper, 24 hours after injecting the Catatonia legend with even more mystique with an ecstatic preview of the gig in a Melbourne paper.

'There are stars, drab little beasts, all grey sullenness and fake angst, and then there are stars,' he had written. 'I always loved the idea that Cerys has so neatly managed to reinvent herself as a modern-day swaggering, female counterpart to Tom Jones, a Shirley Bassey for the Nike generation,' he said. 'Stardom is all about straddling the fine line between insanity and insanity. Stardom is Catatonia's birthright.'

After the show Everett said that few were inclined to disagree with his comments. 'Most were inclined to throw flowers at Cerys – and Mark's, Owen's, Paul's and Aled's feet. I've never seen so many ex-pats claiming to be Welsh in my life: the chorus from "International Velvet" was roared out like everyone in Melbourne were paid-up members of the Welsh Assembly.'

Cerys, amazed at Everett's presence at the gig (she didn't know he'd upped and left for warmer climes) invited him across the road to a karaoke bar, where the redoubtable Karaoke Queen wowed the drunken punters with sparkling renditions of songs that neatly summed up the singer's mental mind jukebox.

So alongside The Beatles' 'Blackbird' and Lulu's 'To Sir With Love', there was an airing of Kylie Minogue's kitsch pop classic 'I Should Be So Lucky', topped off with a teary-eyed show-stopping version of the perennial Irish pub closing-time classic 'Danny Boy'. *International Velvet* had just gone gold in Australia and all the gigs had sold out, so everything was set-up nicely for the band. News of the buoyant Welsh scene had filtered through to Oz via the country's cool national youth radio station Triple J and the thousands of Aussie travellers who had spent the previous summer living in the UK. So Australia was shaping up well. For a country whose pop chart resembled the inside of a diseased radio DJs mind (ear-bleedin' hardcore metal noise clashing with blandly manufactured teen pop confection), Catatonia's sizeable inroad was quite an achievement.

While the Cats had been down under, the finishing touches were being applied to *Equally, Cursed And Blessed* in London. Meantime, the buzz surrounding the new album was reaching fever pitch.

It had been decided that 'Dead From The Waist Down', the album's mellow, sunny day opener, was to be the debut single. First, before the rounds of heavyweight UK promotion for the new single could get under way, there were still some loose ends from 1998 to contend with. There was the little matter of being shortlisted for the Brits, the music industry's official beano, where the band were up for best band, best album and best single. Some weeks later attending the back-slapping, black-tie soirée, they discovered they had made a clean sweep – namely they didn't win a single award in any of the categories for which they were nominated.

Owen reckoned he knew they weren't going to win anything because they were being allowed to go back and forth to the toilets. 'And all the bands who win are not allowed to go to the toilets, just in case they are in the loo when their name is read out,' he revealed. After Cerys had ripped up the three speeches she had prepared in case of a shock result they did what they do best, attempted to drink the Brits' free champagne quota dry. Now if only awards were being doled out for that.

NO NEED TO BE DOWN

Six weeks before the release of 'Dead From the Waist Down' the hype surrounding the single was causing the UK's radio stations to fall over themselves to playlist it.

Radio 1 and Virgin Radio took it, while the band scored a first as Capital Radio placed the single straight on it's A-list, amazingly the first time the stoutly commercial London-based radio station had playlisted a Catatonia single. Proof, if any were needed, that Catatonia were well on their way to achieving that much craved after crossover appeal.

It was only fitting that now the band were cresting along on a pop wave, two guys who had given the band their much needed support during those dark early days had been charting new territory of their own. Mark and Lard, previously redoubtable cult bastions of late night Radio 1, had been handed the unlikely role of anchoring the Radio 1 breakfast show.

Chris Evans had walked out on the station after finding his ego no longer fitted through the door of BBC Broadcasting House and Radio 1 found themselves desperately in need of a suitable crowd-pleasing replacement.

It's a long way between late-night Radio 1's student fraternity and those Radio 1 breakfast listeners, but the station in their infinite wisdom believed that Mark and Lard could translate their cult late-night appeal to early morning listeners. It wasn't the brightest idea ever mooted.

Mark and Lard had no choice but to go along with it, although they knew they were as predisposed to early mornings as Catatonia were to alcohol-free rides. To be fair to Mark and Lard they gamely attempted to throw themselves into it and peppered the show with their usual off-the-wall ideas. One of their brightest brainstorms was to accrue some much needed publicity by staging a mock engagement between Lard and Cerys.

It was a story that ran for about a month and had a nation guessing whether this was really true or not. With both Lard and Cerys not denying the story, the intrigue built. The DJs even phoned Cerys and got her to play along with the ruse.

As a pre-publicity stunt for both single and album it was right on the money. 'So many people believed that Cerys would actually get engaged to a tosspot like Lard, it was quite frightening,' explained Mark Radcliffe.

'Although we did also have lots of messages saying "How can someone as pig ugly as Lard get someone like Cerys?" Fair play to her though, she played the part perfectly. We had thought of getting Louise Wener from Sleeper to do it, but we reckoned Cerys had more universal, across the board appeal.'

The 'Dead From The Waist Down' pre-publicity might have neatly transformed itself from a whisper to a scream, but the song itself was strictly low-key.

If the Cats legions of newly acquired fans were expecting another big and bold, Mulder And Scully-like, *zeitgeist*-shagging pop romp, they were in for quite a surprise.

'It was important we led off with a single which would surprise most Catatonia fans,' Tommy D remembers, 'We had to give them something they didn't expect.'

So it was on 29 March, mixed with a double dose of trepidation and relief, Catatonia let 'Dead From The Waist Down' loose on the record-buying public. The indie press, who had so staunchly supported the band when they bore the mantle of gossip-column-squatting, beer- monster quote machines, were cautiously praiseworthy while the more mainstream press were fulsome in praise of the band's subtle but bold shift of their own musical axis.

While Suede were predictably gathering a Single Of The Week in the *NME* for another jaded rehash of their 'Stars In Their Eyes' Bowie routine, stylistically Catatonia were light years ahead of Brett Anderson and his glam rock circus. In terms of adaptability, imagination and experimentation there was no contest. The release of *Equally Cursed and Blessed* and its stylistic smorgasboard, would bear that out. However, 'Dead From The Waist Down' and its two extra tracks were evidence enough of this change through the gears. While the title track swooned into full string-laden effect, the first extra track 'Branding A Mountain' is Cerys finally giving full rein to her love of traditional Welsh folk standards. With a campfire swagger lit by acoustic guitars, penny whistles and recorder, full raggle-taggle weight is lent to Cerys's lusty, swaggering vocals. 'Bad Bad Boy' meantime is melodic quirk pop that works just by dint of its hooky chorus, urgent vocals and euphoric, crashing guitars. It just proved that Oasis weren't the only band that wrote quality B-sides.

The video to 'Dead From the Waist Down' not only helped push the single, but signposted a notable development in the Catatonia career curve. They had obviously gained some much needed popularity within their record company, after the successes of 1998. Given the amount of money they were allowed to spend on their new video anyway – substantially more than they had been allowed before.

The video was a technicolor fantasy. A west London studio had been transformed into what to all intents and purposes was Kansas City just before the Wicked Witch Of The West came visiting in the *Wizard of Oz*.

Directed by Patricia Murphy, it featured Cerys as Dorothy-meets-Nell Gwyn in full-corseted sexy milk maid garb, singing about the joys of making the most of what you have while you have it, while romping with a half-naked hunk and laughing at her bandmates' costumes.

There was Mark as country bumpkin via tea-cloth shirtwear and sporting a gingery hair-style calamity; Owen dressed as a blacksmith, who is pegged out on a washing line; while Aled was masquerading as an orange-skinned scarecrow with a sack on his head and Paul dressed up as a bloke chopping wood.

Unfortunately, on the week of its release, a number of novelty records also entered the fray. And 13-year-old kids being susceptible to the charms of unadulterated rubbish, snapped up the novelty pap and forced Catatonia down from a midweek chart placing of No. 1, to its eventual arrival in the chart at No. 7.

However, the album was to be released two weeks later, so expectation was still high. With all the excellent publicity 'Dead From the Waist Down' had garnered, would *Equally Cursed and Blessed* enter the Charts at No. 1?

All signs were nicely posted towards the album hitting the top spot.

As 'Dead From The Waist Down' was marking the band's third Top 10 single, Catatonia had set off on yet another UK tour. As a sign of their pulling power, it seemed the nation could not get enough of the live Cat experience.

The two Llangollen shows in May had sold out and more tickets had to be made available, while over 20,000 tickets had already been pocketed for Margam Park. Meantime, their 12-date jaunt around the UK saw them playing their biggest venues yet, accompanied by sold-out signs adorning venue doors on each night of the tour.

Live was where the band had really started to come into their own. Gone were the shambling live spectacles of yesteryear, replaced by stagecraft that was both professional, disciplined and exciting. Add Cerys's enigmatic stage presence and natural bonhomie to the band's watertight set list – drawing on the best tunes from their three albums – and you had gigs that were ribald celebratory affairs. On many of the songs you would be hard pressed to hear Cerys's voice, her lung-busting vocals drowned out by the sheer volume of their fans singing along to every word.

The band's audience stood as evidence that Catatonia were nimbly making the transition from successful riders of the cool indie vanguard (for which they never wanted to be cut out) to crossover pop stars and household names (which is what they always wanted).

Dates on the tour would be populated by 14-year-olds, experiencing their first gigs, while wanting in on the band's easily consumable pop thrills, and thirtysomethings holding each other tight during the Cat's fragile and tender moments.

To gauge the age you only had to ask the T-shirt seller. 'A real cross-section buy the shirts,' explained Shaun who worked on the merchandise stall on the Cats' UK tour. 'I was expecting it to be young kids, but there was everybody from little kids of nine or ten with their mums right through to a granny who got a poster. That's quite a surprise, but it just goes to show how popular the band are getting.'

Cerys's popularity was such that she was a wanted woman. So although the band had the music to concentrate on, Cerys had double the workload. Every facet of the UK media wanted a few words of eccentric Welsh wisdom from the woman who had been dubbed 'the country's only genuine female pop star for years.'

The media loved her sheer affable earthiness and the incredible chameleon-like way she could be all things to all people. The public saw her as 'one of them', the pop star with the common appeal. And that's because Cerys is 'normal life' through and through.

There was also the curious matter of Cerys's sex appeal. UK men's magazine *FHM* reinforced the singer's sex symbol status by plastering her over their May 1999 cover. *FHM* had experienced something of a similar supernova-like trajectory to Catatonia. As the men's magazine boomed buoyed by record sales, *FHM* magazine had led the pack with huge circulation figures edging over the 750,000 mark.

Draping yourself half-naked over the cover of the UK's leading men's magazine was seen as a canny career move by semi-clad movie stars and rising TV actresses aching for their big break. Instead of publicity agents chasing the magazine's editor for cover shoots of their aspiring starlets, the *FHM* shoot with Cerys came down completely different avenues. *FHM* had received numerous letters on the subject of Cerys's sex appeal addressed to its Burning Questions section, where experts attempted to answers readers' most taxing questions.

The gist of the problem went as follows: 'I know I shouldn't, but I really, really fancy that girl out of Catatonia. Can you please tell me why?'

The magazine answered:

> Cerys is no supermodel, but she has a wildly flirtatious streak that shines through wherever she appears. She's a girl you fancy for being worldly-wise. A bit on the naughty side. The sort who'd drink you under the table in the pub, then be assertive enough to drag you back home to teach you a thing or two – while all the time maintaining the pretence of complete innocence.

Cerys had met FHM's then editor Mike Soutar and their meeting coupled with the letters the mag received resulted in a PVC catsuit-clad Cerys staring moodily from the cover clutching a dagger and looking for all the world like a Welsh Emma Peel – Steed's sexy, sassy sidekick in *The Avengers*.

Cerys did admit, though, that she had doubts before agreeing to the cover shoot. 'Yeah I was cautious, because I don't like to see bland-looking females in white knickers on magazine covers all the time,' she explained. 'But I also think the female form is gorgeous – I've no qualms about showing or using mine. I met the editor of the magazine and we got on well, so we decided to have a go.'

Despite the fact that she likes to think of herself as a lady, saying that she prefers men who can woo her with 'gold and diamonds', both her 'no bullshit' attitude and natural coyness are her trump cards. Those unique attributes were reflected in the pictures shot for *FHM*, some of the weirdest and sexiest the magazine had ever published.

In one picture she's clutching a sword above her head, flashing her legs while coming on like a cross between Joan of Arc and the heroine of a Ken Russell film. In another picture she's squeezed into a rubber body suit, touting two rather large guns and acting up a storm as a super heroine space vamp. She looks like she'd eat Lara Croft for breakfast.

'I think they're lovely pictures,' says Cerys. 'Most people say it doesn't look a bit like me. They go, 'They're gorgeous – it doesn't look anything like you!' and I'm like, 'Oh, OK.' But if you don't try and surprise yourself and test things, you might as well just sit at home and knit a jumper.'

The pictures were nothing short of a revelation, doing little to quell the Cerys Matthews fever that was spreading across the land and doing everything to reinforce her mystique as the sassiest pop star in the UK today.

As well as revelatory photographs Cerys was also baring her soul to the music press, letting slip revelations that had only been known within the band's close circle. Tensions had become evident in the band and Cerys was ready to hold forth on her feelings. While in Australia Cerys had inadvertently 'outed' her relationship with Mark. In an interview with an Aussie online magazine, the interviewer had posed the question: 'And is there a true partnership between you and him when you are writing?'

Not realising he had meant a proper songwriting relationship, Cerys had replied: 'There was before we broke up. It was tough, but it also meant the songs took on a different edge and I think it was just before the success came. It may have been a catalyst to the success. The pressure was more exciting. It was more necessary to write these songs and get them out because the friction was there. I love the guy's songwriting abilities and that's why I'll always want to work with him, even though we argue like dingoes.'

Surprised, the interviewer then asked: 'When you say "we broke up", does that mean there was more to the relationship than just songwriting?'

Cerys, to her credit, admitted: 'Yeah. It was at one point. It happened a long time ago and it's not something we get into. In fact, the most juicy questions have been in Australia. Across Europe, in the UK or America, no one ever asked.'

Well, no one ever asked because no one never knew. Although it didn't take long before the British music press got a whiff of the story. Only a few weeks after she and the band had arrived back in the UK from their antipodean adventure, Cerys was interviewed by the *NME*'s Sylvia Patterson. As candid interviews with Cerys Matthews went, this was one of the most deeply personal she had ever undertaken. Considering that she went to great lengths to stress that her personal life was nothing to do with the music that she made and that the press questions about her personal life were strictly off limits, this *NME* interview was a revelation.

When Sylvia Patterson asked Cerys, 'Some people of our idiotic generation believe that they're too scared to allow themselves to fall in love, what'd you say to them?' The singer replied: 'Well it's like that song, what is it . . . "nothing left to lose" – if you don't take the risk, you're not gaining anything, you're just losing. It's quite good actually. The best thing that ever happened to me was having my heart broken. Mmmm yeah it was.'

'When was this,' asked Sylvia Patterson. 'Oh it was . . . mid-20s.'

'So this was Mark?' inquired the journalist.

'Possibly.'

'Cerys looks genuinely hurt,' wrote Patterson. 'Her relationship with Mark from Catatonia spanned four of the five dole-living "wilderness years" and informs much of their kitchen sink lyrical rumness. Cerys is famously and fiercely protective of her emotional life and *NME* feels like a great big bully. Sorry.'

'I don't, I mean, I don't wanna, I just don't think it's particularly relevant,' Cerys manages, 'but it's a good thing that's happened, so I don't think anyone should fear . . . love. Oh don't ask me about it. But once you know it's happened, and once you know you can pull yourself back, and you get on with each other you can just go on, and you can do better things.

''Cos suddenly you can see really, like clear again. That's like another song (Cheers up and begins singing), "Ah can see clearly now the rain has gone . . ." It is! It's brilliant. And you think, "What the hell was I worried about?" You can do anything you want anything! Except if you get run over by a rolling steamer or whatever, you might find that a bit hard!'

Cerys was ensconced in a relationship with Catatonia's producer Tommy D, the pair having grown close to each other during the recording of '*Equally Cursed And Blessed*'. It was evidently going well and Cerys was full of the joys of a new relationship.

The *NME* interview was run in the issue that had a cover image of Cerys shot on the set of the 'Dead From The Waist Down' video. In impact terms it was just as eye-catching as the *FHM* cover; a cartoon-like cascade of colours with Cerys sitting on a flower strewn swing, her heaving bosom almost as prominent as the snarl etched across her face.

Both the issues of *FHM* and the *NME* with Cerys emblazoned across the front appeared within a week or two of each other, just before *Equally Cursed And Blessed* was to be released. It was a publicity masterstroke, with both publications having a huge impact, heightening the already fever-pitch anticipation of the band's third album.

The album's promotion was helped by the band headlining a show for Radio 1 at the Forum in London, a week before *Equally, Cursed And Blessed* was to be released. The gig was broadcast live on Steve Lamacq's Radio One show.

The London date came only two weeks after the band had headlined two nights at the Brixton Academy. The fact that they could sell out another London show so soon gives you an indication of their pulling power.

Equally Cursed And Blessed was released on Monday, 12 April 1999 on CD, cassette and a vinyl version limited to 5000 copies that included a free 7″ featuring a version of 'Nothing Hurts', recorded on *Later With Jools Holland*. Everyone surrounding the Cats were hoping that they would notch up their second No. 1 album. Ironically, for a band who unashamedly wore their pop influences likes badges, they would face competition for the top spot from those Swedish doyennes of pure unabashed Seventies pop, Abba. The Super Troupers were experiencing yet another wholesale revival on the back of a musical, *Mama Mia*, featuring Abba songs, that had recently opened in London's West End to much acclaim.

As the midweek chart was announced the Cats were streaking ahead by 15,000 sales and it looked certain they would crash into Sunday's chart at No. 1. Despite a late rally by the Swedish scourges of the world's karaoke machines, the Cats held on to claim their second No. 1 album.

Unlike the crazy rounds of celebrations that accompanied *International Velvet*'s arrival at the top spot, Mark and Cerys were in Europe undertaking the normal rounds of TV and radio promotion, so any wholesale hedonism had to wait until they returned to Wales.

Underlining the peak Catatonia were experiencing in popularity, as the dust settled on the album charts they had three albums in the Top 40: *Equally Cursed and Blessed* at No. 1; *Way Beyond Blue* at No. 32; and *International Velvet* at No. 36. Some achievement.

Another popularity barometer was measured by Adam Shutes's definitive Catatonia website voted into 15th place in a UK-based award for favourite music websites on the Internet. A staggering result given that there was the little matter of 900 entrants to deal with.

PARTY IN THE PARK

With Mark and Cerys newly returned from their European promotional jaunt, the Catatonia air miles would soon be piling up again, with Euro festival dates in Germany, Denmark and Holland planned, as well as a return to Australia in late July and a first trip to Japan in early August.

Although Margam Park and the biggest gig of their lives was only a matter of weeks away, the band were being kept busy in the UK with numerous radio and TV appearances, as well as a number of one-off London gigs.

There was a special show arranged on the afternoon of Saturday, 8 May at the London Astoria. The gig was filmed for a Japanese Fuji TV television station, allowing Japanese fans a first 'live' glimpse of the band they would soon see in concert in a couple of months. Tickets were given away through the London-based alternative radio station XFM and Adam Shutes' website. Adam had the administrative headache of sifting through the thousands of e-mails he received from fans eager to snap up the 140 pairs of tickets he had to give away.

Ten days after their Astoria show, the band were back in London. MTV had chosen Catatonia to headline one night of their newly conceived Five Night Stand Festival, five nights of shows at the Shepherd's Bush Empire.

The gig saw the Cats reuniting with Pureessence, a band they had last played with four years previously when the bands had shared a triple bill on a UK tour with feisty Mancs Marion. In stark contrast to Catatonia's recent meteoric career curve, Pureessence's early promise had amounted to nothing and they had disappeared, before making a comeback with the magnificently moody *Only Forever* album. Completing the exciting and eclectic bill were Supergrass, Reef, and Belgian art-rockers Deus.

Unbelievably this was Catatonia's fifth London show in as many months. London fans really were being spoilt. While they were in London, Cerys and Owen played an unplugged show on Jonnie Walker's BBC Radio 2 show, another sure-fire indicator of Catatonia's widespread appeal. Remember this was a band that was being interviewed by both *Smash Hits* and *Q*, appearing on both children's and late-night television as well as being playlisted on Radios 1 and 2.

The day after the Johnnie Walker session, the band reconvened to BBC Television Centre to record another appearance on *Later with Jools Holland*. The former Squeeze pianist and presenter of Eighties cult music show *The Tube*, was fast becoming the televisual version of the band's main radio supporter Mark Radcliffe, having now invited the band onto his programme four times.

Later is one of the most ingenious yet simple shows in the history of music broadcasting. Take one large studio, invite four bands or five bands to set up in a circle around the studio. Bands perform live and their songs are usually recorded in one take. *Later* has been such an effective and enduring show that it's now into its eighth year and has played host to over 400 of the world's finest bands.

Catatonia were offered the prestige of performing three songs, an honour only afforded to the show's headlining band. On each of their last three appearances the band had played two songs, but now that they had seemingly become the UK's omnipresent pop band of choice, the flame of popularity burnt brighter than ever. The Cats chose three shades of their chameleon-like third album, starting with 'She's a Millionaire', 'Dead from the Waist Down' and playing out with 'Londinium'.

But although the band may have been skimming the upper echelons of pop success, you could rely on the record company to bring them back down to earth with a bump.

The next few weeks saw great confusion over the identity of the second single. Initially it was to be 'Karaoke Queen' – indeed, it reached promo stage where all the artwork had been done and a run of promos had been pressed and sent out to journalists. But, despite Catatonia's protestations to the contrary and under advice from the industry as well as pressure from the record company, 'Karaoke Queen' was dropped in place of 'Londinium'. A surprising and brave move, considering the albeit tongue-in-cheek poke at London which ran through the song.

The second single from *Equally Cursed And Blessed* was scheduled for release in July. But the trifling matter of that release paled into insignificance with what was at hand. The most important week of Catatonia's career? That would be a fair estimation.

BARD BEHAVIOUR

Llangollen is a tiny little picturesque town in Denbighshire in North Wales. The Llangollen International Pavilion usually plays host to the Bardic traditions of the Eisteddfod, but for one week, it was to pay lip service to the past but strike out for a glorious new Welsh present.

The 6000 capacity Pavilion had sold out within weeks of tickets going on sale. As a boon to the local economy, it was a tremendous fiscal fillip.

The band's promoter was to be the man at the eye of the storm for the three biggest gigs in the band's career. He described the scene in Llangollen, when the weekend got into full swing.

'It was like a tribal invasion,' he remembers. 'We'd sold tickets to all the local kids but kids came from all over the North West, all over Wales, England. That weekend it was a great, buzzing little town. All the hotels and B&B's and campsites were sold out. All the pubs and offies did fucking amazing business.'

Conal, himself, could only manage to get a B&B on the outer limits of the town and his paymasters were putting the gig on.

Despite the storm of activity that was blowing around the band, the Cats remained the fount of calm at its epicentre.

If the band were nervous they weren't showing it. 'The night before the first gig, Catatonia came down to the venue and sound-checked,' explains Conal. 'Then the rest of the band went back to the hotel and Cerys waited for three hours for the harpist Eleanor Bennett, who couldn't get there until 9pm. Cerys just sat in catering with a bottle of wine, read the paper, did the sound-check with Eleanor, it was great and everyone was relaxed. They adjusted to it. It had only been 18 months previously when nothing was happening and now they were faced with this. But they'd always wanted it, so they were just glad to be at this stage of their career. They just seemed to be able to step up a gear without a problem.'

Supporting Catatonia at Llangollen were fellow Welsh bands Gorky's Zygotic Mynci and Big Leaves, naturals for support slots given the locale – both Gorky's and Big Leaves hail from North Wales.

In terms of location, Scousers Shack were almost a local band, although they were offered the chance to play thanks to Cerys's love of the band's enigmatic and eminently talented singer Michael Head.

1999 saw Shack return after a lengthy hiatus with *HMS Fable*, an album brim full of heartfelt reveries to loves lost and found and of life lived on the edge. Shack's history mirrored the tragi-comic content of their psychedelically imbued pop fables; how you can't appreciate the glory of being alive until you have faced the opposite and found the strength to overcome it. If any band were held up as a shining example of survival it was Shack.

'We did the *NME* Premier Awards at the start of 1999 – that was Shack's first big comeback, supporting Mercury Rev at the London Astoria,' says Conal. 'Cerys came down to that gig with Tommy D, their producer; they were both suitably impressed with Mick Head, Cerys loved the songs, so we got them on to both gigs (Llangollen and Margam Park).'

The Saturday found the Cats' Manchester United supporters (Cerys, Mark and Paul) celebrating the Red Devils' FA Cup Final win. 'They sent us out to get bottles of champagne for the support bands,' remembers Conal. 'They all got a bottle of champagne for Man United winning, it was all a bit of a drunken haze. Amazingly, I remember the audience were more inebriated than the band themselves.'

After the gig the band retired to their hotel and more partying. 'The band were staying in the middle of Llangollen which I thought was silly but they couldn't get anywhere else,' he explained. 'The band were there with their families, Cerys's parents, the other parents, everyone, Shack, their management, all the Metropolis crew went down.

'We went to our hotel before we headed up to theirs, but we couldn't get a cab back for love nor money, so we managed to get the landlady of our hotel, to drive us into town to drop us off there.' And then the beers started flowing?

'Yeah, we just started drinking solidly with everyone else. As the night wore on the other guests went to bed and it was down to about 20 of us, then 10. Mark was there with his mates and wanted to go out for a game of football. Then Cerys and Mark's girlfriend and I think it was Cerys's cousin decided to go and sit outside the hotel by a river that ran nearby. This was about 5am and the three of them are sat there singing Welsh folk songs at the top of their voices. Then I'm thinking I've got to try and get her to go to bed, she'd got a gig to play tomorrow in front of 6000 people. I'm telling her to go and rest herself and her voice.

'But while they're singing their heads off, all the windows at the front of the hotel started to open up and you can see all these different members of the bands poking their heads out and shouting at the girls, "Shut that noise up!" That was quite amusing.

Finally, at around 6am, Conal managed to persuade the Queen Hedonist to get some sleep.

'I was telling her off, but she wasn't having any of it, she was saying, "I'm going to be fine stop worrying,"' laughs Conal. 'The last thing I said to her was, get a good night's sleep, make sure you can sing tonight.'

The next time Conal sees the band and Cerys is when their coach rolls up at the back of the venue at 4pm later on that day. 'I was standing there worrying what state she was going to be in,' he grins. 'I'm stood by the coach door and Cerys bounds down the steps merrily singing "La la la la la" to herself, then she turns and looks at me, before chirping, "I told you my voice was fine, there's fuck all wrong with it" and amazingly it was a much better gig the second night. That band never failed to astound me!'

PARKLIFE!

Margam Park has the dubious distinction of being the only area of outstanding natural beauty situated next to one of the biggest steelworks in Europe. That was the incongruous setting for the biggest gig Catatonia had ever headlined. Set in 850 acres of glorious parklands, Margam Country Park houses a magnificent Orangery and an impressive gothic Mansion House. It held special significance for both Cerys and the boys, as they had all visited the park either as youngsters or more recently with their children. As a venue for an open-air show, it offered the perfect setting. The park had a natural amphitheatre that fitted perfectly the requirements needed for staging such a big show. There was easy access to the main site, a natural incline that would offer perfect views to the crowd and of course, the beautiful surroundings that just enhanced its superior setting.

While Catatonia could head back to Cardiff to recuperate after Llangollen, Conal and the Metropolis roadshow headed from North to South bound for Margam.

The site had started to be erected on the Monday, the following day immediately after Llangollen,' explained Conal. 'It would take five days to build everything, to get all the food and merchandise vendors in, sort the security out, bring in toilets and water, organise a car park and even ensure that there was a crèche for the band and their kids.'

Of course, months and months of planning and negotiation had already been put into making the show a reality. 'As the promoter it's your role to oversee absolutely everything to do with the show,' explains Conal. 'For instance, we spent the last four or five months going to endless council meetings, meetings with the police, fire officers, licensing officers, the venue, security companies. Basically we're doing an open air show in a green field site – it's not a stadium site – so there's nothing to work with. So you've got to put a fence in, you've got to build a stage, we have to bring in caterers, there's so much to consider. And the most important thing is advertising it, and selling tickets!'

Ticket sales had been bouyant. They were fast approaching the 30,000 sales. Everything was being put in place, operations guided by Conal were running smoothly; there was only one factor that threatened to spoil the band's biggest day – the weather.

Long-range forecasts had predicted that rain would sweep through Wales at the end of the week, but it was touch and go whether the heavens would open on Saturday or Sunday.

'I'd been at Margam all week,' explains Conal. 'When we had started work on building the site on Monday, the weather was a bit murky but it was getting better. On Friday night the band came down, did the sound-check, looked around the site and were all really excited about it. It was a really gorgeous evening, a real "red sky at night" sort of thing, a beautiful sunset.'

The BBC were recording the Margam Park show for an edited live *Later* special and spent the Friday setting up their cameras. 'I went into the BBC truck watching the stuff on the screens and it looked fantastic,' says Conal. 'We were all geared up for a fantastic day.'

The following morning, the day of the gig, Conal awoke to the news that he had dreaded. 'We'd received weather reports saying possibly there'd be some rain, so I left for the site quite early in the morning, at 9am, then we got this report at about 10am of a severe weather warning.

'We didn't know whether it'd hit us or not. We were opening the gates to the site at 2pm, and at about 1pm there was an almighty downpour which didn't stop for about two hours. It rained very heavily for two hours which turned a third of the site into a bit of a mud-bath. There was a three foot wide river running in front of the hospitality tent which we had for all of the guests – we had to put down boards over this river to get people in there. It was really depressing, basically, for me, having spent the last eight months from having the show confirmed to getting it on sale, to getting the support bill together, to seeing the sales progress and us creeping along and maintaining our sales pattern.'

Meanwhile, Cerys had woken up on Saturday morning, looked out of the window at her home in Cardiff and started crying. 'I was crying because you know, you can't imagine how much work people have put into organizing everything,' she said. 'The day before had been so beautiful, and you could see the oil refinery, and the abbey, and it was so green, and it was just beautiful, so beautiful, the setting, and then the rain clouds, and the thunderstorms . . . oh, I don't know . . . it was mad, but I think we tried our best.'

However, this event had been the focal point of both the band and their fans' excitement for too long to let a little bit of rain spoil everything.

Fortunately, the skies did soon clear, saving the event from being a total wash-out, although thousands of boots ensured that conditions underfoot would remain quagmire-like for the whole day.

THE STORY SO FAR

'It was just disappointing for all the punters,' said Conal ruefully. 'There were kids queuing up just getting soaked. It killed the walk-up for us as well because anyone that had been planning to come and pay on the gate might have been put off because of the weather. I'd travelled in from the West in the morning and I rang my girlfriend, who lives in Bristol, who said she had seen a huge storm there at 10 o'clock, so anyone coming from that direction would have been put off, knowing what the weather was like.

'Thankfully, it stopped raining after about three o'clock, and as soon as Richard Parfitt, who was the opening act, came on stage and started strumming, it stopped raining. All hail Mr Parfitt!'

Richard was just coming to terms with the disbanding of his group The 60ft Dolls, the thrill-a-minute punk-pop band that had blazed an alcohol-fuelled trail for the Newport scene some five years previously. The Dolls had been dropped after their record company Indolent had been swallowed up by yet another record company merger. This left the Dolls in limbo and a second album *Joya Magica*, temporarily on the shelf, before the band released it through their own label.

Richard, a veteran of the Newport scene after being in a succession of quality bands that scratched the underside of success without fully breaking through, had decided to concentrate on writing his own songs and using his encyclopaedic knowledge of the UK music industry to try his hand at management.

Only weeks before the Margam gig he had spotted a band playing at Le Pub who blew him away. That band was Terris, an amalgam of sonic noise and Stone Roses grooves. The band has been awarded the onerous task of living up to the much-vaunted tag of the future of British rock 'n' roll. Still, that wasn't a bad start to any former musician's managerial career. Richard faced a similarly large task; opening the day's proceedings and playing to a crowd that were pretty much soaked to the skin. Still, the sunny vibes from the sky and the stage helped dispel any dark clouds that may have dulled people's optimism for the day's events.' It was, er, an experience, laughs Richard. 'I've played hundreds of gigs, but you can't help feeling vulnerable in front of a crowd of that size staring up at you. Especially when it's just you and your guitar.'

He didn't have to worry, he was on home turf and most of the crowd knew who he was and afforded him a reception that reflected his highly respected standing on the South Wales music scene.

Shack and Big Leaves had both made the journey from Llangollen to join the bill at Margam and were joined by Abba tribute band Bjorn Again, reinforcing Cerys's love of pop credentials. However the most noticeable support act was former Stone Roses' singer Ian Brown.

Brown, had recently been freed from prison after being convicted of assaulting an air stewardess on a British Airways flight back from Spain. It was thought he wouldn't be doing any gigs, choosing instead to lie low while he commenced work on a second solo album.

'We'd approached Ian Brown while he was still in prison, in January,' Conal recalled. 'The band wanted him, being huge fans of The Stone Roses. We spoke to his agent, who'd written to Ian Brown in prison and said Catatonia would love you to play at this gig. Apparently he didn't get the letter in prison and then Cerys bumped into him in London. They got on really well, and he agreed to play. I think Ian Brown's always had a bit of an affinity with South Wales – the Stone Roses did the *Second Coming* at Rockfield Studios in Monmouth and I think he's got a house in Wales.'

If Ian Brown was looking forward to meeting his public for the first time in a while, he was to get the chance sooner rather than later. The singer found himself marooned at the entrance to the site, after a mix-up at the gate.

'Ian Brown got there and there was a problem with security so he had to get off at the main gate,' Conal remembers. 'Fair play to him. He didn't throw any tantrums. He got out of his car, and had to walk through the punters all the way through to the backstage. There were a lot of autograph hunters, but he was fine, he was great about it, a really nice bloke. He was quite chilled out, in fact he felt quite touched that Catatonia had given him this opportunity to play, it was a positive thing for him to come back to.'

The sun was just beginning to squeeze the wetness out of the crowd's dripping clothes when Big Leaves took to the stage. The Cardiff-based four piece were quickly becoming accustomed to the large crowds, after having supported Catatonia on tour during March. They had recently made an appearance at the Voices of a Nation concert in Cardiff's Docklands to celebrate the opening of the Welsh National Assembly, so had had their taste of a big stage and a large crowd.

The Leaves' blues-imbued sunny delights swept the rain clouds away and slowly deflected the crowd's minds from their sodden clobber and to their highly entertaining and hugely endearing psychedelic quirk pop.

While Big Leaves weren't undaunted by the size of the crowd, revelling in playing such a huge gig in their homeland, Shack seemed intimidated by the sheer vista that spread before them.

Unfortunately, mud fights and recreating a trenchlike Glastonbury vibe seemed to be the main source of entertainment for the crowd, while Shack gamely attempted to grab their attention. Shack's affecting tales from the dark side of the human psyche are beautifully crafted and gorgeously played, but the crowd needed something a bit more dynamic to feed off. Cue the perfect glitz-laden entrance then of the world's favourite Abba tribute band Bjorn Again. On first reflection the doppleganger Swedish pop icons might have seemed an odd choice as a support band, but it's easy to understand why Catatonia wanted their two boy, two girl showbiz presence.

'We wanted a good glitzy, fun-time band to get the audience going,' explained Conal. 'Catatonia see themselves as a pop band, which they are. There's no greater pop band than Abba. You can't have Abba so Bjorn Again's the next best thing, isn't it?'

Injecting the proceedings with some vigorous Seventies anthems seemed to enliven the crowd and get those who weren't caked in mud hell, dancing stupidly and grinning inanely like you should be when you are in the presence of Abba songs.

For all his revered status as iconic leader of the one of the UK's greatest ever rock 'n' roll bands, Ian Brown post-Stone Roses is an entirely different proposition to the once mighty King Monkey that swaggered menacingly afront the Roses' luscious baggy sound.

Sadly, Brown's voice that was once a honey-dipped, mellow croon has degenerated into the sort of howl usually reserved for Hammer House of Horror films. Following Bjorn Again, the crowd were hoping for the former Manc Messiah to weave a bit of magic, but his voice was as flat as the atmosphere he and his band generated. Considering that Brown was performing in the land of song, this was a problem. The Welsh crowd were just not having it.

Brown eschewed The Roses' heavenly Sixties psychedelia for a sound resolutely in keeping with the times, but singularly forgot that you have to be able to sing to lace your ideas together with any sort of conviction. The low point had to be his droning slaughter of Michael Jackson's 'Billie Jean', the Eighties disco pop classic mutated into a risible plodding mess. Brown was guilty as charged; sentenced to solitary confinement with singing lessons. The irritation and impatience for the main act that had spread through the crowd only heightened Catatonia's entrance. However, before the Cats could make their hugely anticipated arrival on stage, the management deployed the first of a few surprises they had planned for the day.

A stop-go camera had filmed the whole site being erected. Building the suspense by rapidly compressing the week of preparation for the concert into a dramatic two-minute film, the filmic climax met the band's grand entrance to the stage.

Was it only 18 months ago that the band had feared they were to be dropped from their record label and that their career was headed for the dumper? It had taken seven years of blood, sweat and tears, as well as a few thousand beers to get to this epochal point in their lives. Catatonia's ascension to pop fame had been a road followed full of diversions and delays, not least many of their own making. How faraway now were those shambling, drunken nights at the Falcon and the Monarch, where their performance was only notable for its shambolic appearance and their musical abilities took a backseat to their hedonistic press cuttings. However, it couldn't be denied that this was a band that had earned their rewards, through sheer persistence and determination in the face of personal and professional adversity.

Of course, the focus for their flamboyant entrance revolved around the whirlwind in sequins that was Cerys Matthews. Poured into a dress that was pure Forties filmic glamour and chic, no one could doubt that they were in the presence of a singer and fastrisingglamourpusspopicon that was one part Greta Garbo, one part Valley girl.

Despite the scenery, the occasion and her appearance as starry pure pop vamp, Cerys couldn't help being humble. One of the first things she said when she stood on the edge of the stage surveying the amazing sight around her was to express her gratitude to a crowd that had 'endured the bloody awful thunder clouds'. The irony of the weather wasn't lost on her. She quipped sarcastically: 'Biggest day of our lives and it rains. It never rains in Port Talbot does it!'

Despite the fact a huge section of the 30,000 strong crowd camped centre stage were encrusted in mud, aching with tiredness and bruised and battered, Catatonia needn't have worried about their audience – the crowd couldn't have been happier.

Margam Park was where Catatonia's dreams had come true. Gigs didn't come much bigger or better than this. Realising the sheer enormity of the occasion, Cerys endeared herself to the hordes by telling of how when she was a little girl she dreamt of coming back to haunt this place and how nice it was to do it while she was still alive.

This gig, the biggest outdoor show in Wales at that time, not only signposted Catatonia's long-awaited ascension to pop stardom, but underlined how a nation's music scene had pulled itself up from the depths of ridicule to the lofty heights of worldwide respect. Tell any Welsh musician at the turn of the Eighties into the Nineties that this story would unfold and they would have laughed in your face. Now, as the last year of the decade burnt itself out towards a new millennium, 1999 typified the huge success of Welsh bands.

The Stereophonics, The Manics, Gorkys and The Super Furry Animals were all squeezing plaudits out of even the most hard-nosed of cynics. Fitting then that The Manics' Nicky Wire, The Super Furry Animals and The Stereophonics should form an impressive backstage line-up at Margam Park as guests of The Cats.

The set list chosen for Margam reads like a Greatest Hits package. The best moments from *Way Beyond Blue*, *International Velvet*, and *Equally Cursed And Blessed* were served up to a rapt crowd. While the band played, they were happy to take a back seat and allow their inspirational front-woman her rightful place in the limelight. Cerys had rapidly needed to adapt to life in the full glare of publicity after 'Mulder And Scully' and 'Road Rage' had made her, Mark, Paul, Owen and Aled the longest overnight success story in British pop history.

It was a position that Cerys had learnt to revel in. The success and acclaim that she has richly deserved had so obviously boosted her own confidence, she fitted like a glove the role of both singer and celebrity. To see her perched on the edge of the cavernous Margam Park stage holding reign like the Queen of British Pop that she had most definitely become was a wondrous sight to behold. If Cerys and the lads were daunted by the size of the crowd they didn't show it. They knew the songs they were playing so well, they were like second nature, so they could play their set while fully inhaling the atmosphere of a great day. Cerys herself, was personality personified playing up to the crowd with her cheeky chit chat and matey bonhomie that had so endeared her to Catatonia's huge fanbase and ensured her iconic status.

That she swigged from a wine bottle, drunkenly danced like you or I would after a few too many only heightened the human aspects of her personality and the everyman and woman appeal of the band. The diverse Margam Park crowd lapped it up. From the young Cerys clones in their best Saturday night get-up – slinky dresses and glamorous high heels sinking in the mud – to the families with their young kids, this was quickly becoming a crossover pop celebration par excellence. It didn't matter if it was the unfamiliar-to-many white knuckle ride of the early singles 'Bleed' and 'You've Got A Lot To Answer For' or the lush giddy heights scaled by 'Gyda Gwen', the bewitching psychedelic track from the *For Tinkebell* EP – featuring the first unveiling of Cerys's twinkling, bewitching vocals – the crowd were as receptive as the world's biggest satellite.

The *NME*'s maniac scribesmith Stephen Wells, whose mad prose had elevated 'For Tinkerbell' to *NME* single of the week, reviewed the Margam Park gig for the music paper in his own inimitable fashion. 'Cerys stomps, hoots, hollers, murmurs, bellows, billycoos, smiles, flutters her eyelids and we come – again and again and again. This is class. Sheer, unadulterated, copper-bottomed, brontosaurus-bollocked pop class.' It was hard to disagree with him.

As hour-and-a-half rollercoaster rides of luscious pop dips and rollicking rock 'n' roll highs went, Margam Park was a sea of hands and a cauldron of singing. There's 'I Am The Mob's' raucous stomping guitars forcing everyone to jump around like loons while Cerys bobs and weaves in her cowgirl-on-smarties-and-Smirnoff way. Then Cerys's open-throated roar pins the ears of the first few rows back as she exhibits pure pop drama on the band's most constantly loved B-side, 'Do You Believe In Me'.

Of course, everyone is aching to scream along to the earthquake choruses of 'Mulder And Scully' and 'International Velvet', but no one quite expects them to be volleyed to the crowd in quite the way they are. Cue MRM's second surprise. While the band had left the stage with the crowd's deafening acclaim ringing in their ears, much activity was taking place behind a huge curtain at the back of the stage. Then . . . 'I'd rather be liberated, I find myself captivated . . . Stop doing what you . . . Keep doing it too . . . I'd rather stay bold and lonely, I dream I'm your one and only . . . Stop doing what you . . . Keep doing it too . . . Things are getting strange, I'm starting to worry . . . This could be a case for Mulder and Scully.'

Well, it was 'Mulder And Scully', but it wasn't Cerys Matthews's twin-lunged assault that was firing the song. As the curtain that swept across the back of the stage dropped, it revealed the 80-strong members of the Pontardullais Male Voice Choir belting out the band's huge hit. For moments of sheer spine-tingling exhilaration this was hard to beat. The idea had come from Catatonia's managers Richard Lowe and Martin Patton, who had reckoned that this link to the great choral traditions of Wales past, bridging the music traditions of past and present, would provide a fitting climax to the show. Two coaches ferried the 80 singers, average age 50 plus.

'They were great,' says Conal Dodds. 'They didn't sound-check. They just got on with it. They were excited to do it, I think a few of them wanted the opportunity to flirt with Cerys! But true to their professionalism they sounded great.' Conal had made the wise decision of making his way to the side of the stage for a rousing, tear-filled rendition of 'International Velvet'. The phrase 'blown away' may be bandied about loosely nowadays but the vocal whirlwind of Cerys Matthews backed by a male voice choir belting out the song's storming chorus of 'Everyday when I wake up I thank the Lord I'm Welsh,' was more than fitting of the phrase.

'It was hairs on the back of your neck effect,' laughs Conal. 'I'm glad I was at the side of the stage, it was awesome.' The song brought this most memorable of days to a grand climax and by once again thanking the Lord she was Welsh, Cerys – emotionally wracked with tears in her eyes – got the dream concert she feared the weather might ruin and Catatonia ended the day on an explosive high. Especially as a cascade of fireworks lit up the Margam sky, lighting a path for the exhausted crowd to find their way back home.

FOLLOW THAT

The Llangollen and Margam shows had presented the band with the gigs of their lives. How would they pick themselves up after the emotional excess of those epochal shows? So, how do support slots with two of the biggest bands in the world sound? Not a bad way to follow the biggest gigs of your lives with some equally seismic shows with two rock legends. First up was a one-off support in Gronigen, Holland on 2 June with everyone's favourite rock behemoths, the decidedly rock-dinosaur-like Rolling Stones.

The strolling bones were obviously looking to inject their two millionth tour with a little credible spark by adding one of the coolest and credible bands in Britain to their rock 'n' roll circus. It was the chance for Catatonia to chalk up yet another landmark moment in their history and meet Mick 'n' Keef 'n' Ronnie 'n' Charlie.

'Keith was stretchered on to stage,' jokes Cerys. 'Allegedly. They were actually brilliant, they treated us really really well, considering that they're the biggest band in the world. They really looked after us, invited us for a drink, it was a really really good day out we all had.' Meanwhile, at the other end of the rock spectrum, residing in the toxin-free world of tofu and health food shops were America's favourite alternative music stadium act REM.

Catatonia had been offered two dates with the band in Germany; Hanover on 29 June and Berlin on 30 June. Playing with REM was a thrill for the Cats in more ways than one. Mark and Cerys used to play REM's 'I Am Superman' from their early *Life's Rich Pageant* album when they were busking in Cardiff city centre. The occasion of playing with REM had obviously got to Cerys, who in a moment of drunken madness and overcome by the excitement of playing with this band that she admired so much, stormed the stage on their first night with REM and gave the band's bass player Mike Mills a big kiss on his cheek.

Apparently Cerys's mini-invasion didn't go down too well with the band's studious singer Michael Stipe, a man who prefers to hang around with serious-faced musicians like Radiohead's Thom Yorke, rather than mad Welsh nutter lasses like Cerys Matthews! As the British summer sprang into life bringing with it the inevitable rain clouds, Catatonia's career was anything but uneventful. There were festival dates in Finland –

the Ruisrock Festival and Denmark – the Midtfyns Festival, while back in the UK, capped their crossover pop credentials by playing the Party in the Park.

This annual event held in Hyde Park is organised by Capital Radio in aid of the Princes Trust charity. It features the best (worst?) in mainstream pop acts like Boyzone, Westlife and Steps. A cynic might call it a production line of insipid, manufactured bland pop acts; however, Cerys was thrilled to be playing the event. She was especially chuffed at appearing on the same bill as Steps, a group she greatly admired. Featuring two Welsh members, Steps, have become one of the most ridiculed pop acts in UK music history, for their appalling cover versions and OTT stage shows, yet that hasn't stopped them becoming one of the most successful UK acts of all time either.

Whatever their respective merits or otherwise, Cerys loved them. 'Yeah, Steps just make me laugh,' she explains, defending her pop favourites. 'I watched from the side of stage. I like them an awful lot more than Boyzone, 'cos Steps have got a sense of humour. They know they're cheesy, they know they're silly, but then again folk dancing at the turn of the century was serious, but people joined in for a bit of fun. But Boyzone, God, they just seem to think that they're ace, like. Some people do think they're ace. But they take themselves so seriously, when they're miming all the time, and I don't understand that.'

LONDON FROWN

'I have to promote a single that I don't even like.'

Cerys had made no disguise of the fact that she was not happy with the release of 'Londinium' as the follow-up to 'Dead From The Waist Down', appearing on Radio 1 and telling DJ Jo Whiley as much. 'We wanted to release a different track,' she explained, 'because a lot of people think it's a negative song and I'm like, "Well I don't want it to be a single, I just don't want it to be."' Cerys also complained that the video had cost 'a lot more' to make than their entire album. 'It's just crazy,' she stormed.

Catatonia would have preferred the next release to be 'Karaoke Queen', the single originally mooted as the second single, which had already been sent out to DJs and journalists in promo form. If not 'Karaoke Queen' then the band favoured 'Storm The Palace' as the next single. However, Warners executives and the band's management had made their ruling, and Catatonia once again had cause to rue their paymasters' decision. 'Londinium' was a risky choice as a new single, given its potentially inflammatory attack on all things London-like. Airplay for the single was, however, not great and the hype which had surrounded 'Dead From the Waist Down' wasn't there for 'Londinium'. Despite the song's uplifting chorus 'Londinium' was essentially not as commercially 'pop' or as 'up' as more energetic songs like 'She's A Millionaire' or 'Storm The Palace'.

Still, 'Londinium' it was. The second single from *Equally Cursed and Blessed* was released on 12 July, with two extra tracks, 'Apathy Revolution' and 'Intercontinental Sigh'. While the A-side failed to set the radio playlists alight, the extra tracks again at least showed that Catatonia's quality control was high as ever. 'Apathy Revolution' fizzes with the sounds of synths, sequencers and effects as Mark, Owen and Paul give full reign to their experimental tendencies, while the chorus is, curiously enough given the electro verses, pure blue-eyed pop.

Another Cat gem illuminating another side to the band's multi-dimensional musical character. 'Intercontinental Sign', meantime, starts worryingly like Bonnie 'Big Hair' Tyler's 'Holding Out For A Hero', but fortunately any worries of a Jim Steinman-esque operatic rock ballad, are banished by a gorgeous, downbeat lament with Cerys cooing dreamily over woodwind and strings. Despite appearances on the UK pop programmes *The Pepsi Chart Show, CD:UK* and *Top Of The Pops*, the single charted disappointingly at No. 20.

While the single may have failed to propel the band back into the Top 10, Cerys's unstoppable rise to iconic pop status showed no sign of abating. First up, was the singer's appearance in an exhibition at the National Portrait Gallery, entitled *Icons of Pop*. Subtitled 'From Cliff to Cerys', the exhibition was a history of popular music photography over the last four decades. The many pictures on show included a youthful Tom Jones, Billy Fury rocking with his Tornados, the ever-changing face of David Bowie, and Cerys in a pastiche of Jack Kerouac. The picture, taken by cult Cardiff photographers Klanger and Boink, featured Cerys looking suitably radiant and iconic.

The Cerys picture was the only commissioned piece of the whole exhibition. And as luck would have it, Terence Pepper, the National Portrait Gallery's photographic curator, was an avid fan of Klanger and Boink's fine art photography.

The gallery wanted to complete the Icons Of Pop Exhibition with a picture of someone they considered to be the 'hottest property' in pop music. To them Cerys was the natural choice and so were Klanger and Boink the obvious team to shoot the Welsh pop queen. The two parties knew each other anyway, so there were no problems arranging the schoot.

One half of Klanger and Boink, Paul Jeff, was good friends with Cerys' housemate, sculptor Angharad Jones. Paul had met Cerys many times and the two had often talked of Klanger and Boink photographing Cerys and the band.

'Cerys photographs to the 'nth degree,' says Paul. 'She's very photogenic, very bubbly and that radiates from the picture. We had a great time shooting the pictures. We all quaffed Cava and joked around. Cerys doesn't mind having a laugh at her own expense.'

The Icons Of Pop picture was named by Klanger and Boink as 'The Girl With The Lovely Voice'. A title that really is simplicity itself.

In terms of her growing fame, the fact that she appeared in an exhibition alongside such rock legends as The Beatles, Marc Bolan and The Who told its own story. Most magazines were desperate for a Cerys Matthews interview to boost their credibility. However, the workload on the Catatonia singer was becoming ever burdensome and there were attempts by Ginny Luckhurst in the Warners press office to limit the amount of interviews Cerys was doing. Purely because, as the figurehead of the group, she shouldered the bulk of the band's promotional workload.

Still, there were some nice confidence boosters to assuage any media stress, as Cerys capitalised on her triumphant *FHM* front-cover appearance only three months previously by scoring a remarkable 36th place in the men's magazine's annual poll of the world's sexiest women. The *FHM* poll has become something of an institution with UK males who every year vote in their thousands for their favourite *femme fatale*.

To underline the magnificence of Cerys's first appearance in the poll, she finished higher than a glittering array of sexy film stars, TV personalities, supermodels and pop personnel. 'In a world populated by Anthea Turner, Victoria Adams, and The Corrs, Cerys makes a refreshing change,' explained the *Western Mail*'s women's editor Catherine Jones.

'She appears to be totally her own person and is so happy with herself she doesn't mind dressing up in anything; during the devolution campaign she wore a Yes T-shirt – because, let's face it, the clothes alone do not maketh the woman.' As for Cerys's sexuality, Catherine reckons that is down to her not unattainable glamour. 'Physically, she takes a no-nonsense approach. She has a decent-sized body, a nice big face, and looks stylish, whether it be street or edgy glamour, without appearing to try too hard, if at all. Cerys isn't a frail rag doll with tiny chicken bones and a curly mane on the cover of a chocolate box but she gives the impression of having a soft centre.

'What better icon for Wales than a woman who possesses all the best stereotypes of Wales – passion, gutsy vocals and presence that cannot be equalled by any other nation. Cerys makes the Spice Girls seem as wooden and unimpassioned as a line-up of Russian dolls.' Still, it was some weight to carry on her shoulders – the expectations and hopes of a nation.

They say fame doesn't come without a price and that was certainly true of the secret life of Cerys Matthews. As her star soared ever higher in the ascendancy, so the UK's tabloid newspapers became increasingly interested in her as a celebrity. What followed was some intrusive probing into her personal life which had some unfortunate spin-offs. One tabloid had already exposed Cerys's relationship with Tommy D, while another had incredibly named the street in Cardiff where Cerys was living at the time.

Unfortunately, that act of tabloid stupidity had the knock-on effect of attracting hordes of fans to Cerys's home. A splash story in South Wales evening newspaper, the *South Wales Echo*, under the headline 'A Nightmare On Elm Street' (the street on which she lived) told of a horror story for her neighbours.

'Fans of superstar Cerys Matthews are making her neighbours' lives a nightmare – by flocking to her home,' trumpeted the newspaper. The story told of how fans 'from all over Britain' gather there hoping to catch a glimpse of their blonde idol. Although the paper printed quotes from Cerys's neighbours saying how it was becoming a nuisance with so many fans heading for her address, what it ultimately underlined was how careful Cerys had to become. She had already suffered with one stalker early on in her band's career; now she was becoming a household name, she would have to become even more vigilant.

Just to underline these safety fears, the Elm Street story broke only a few months after TV presenter Jill Dando had been shot dead on her home doorstep in Fulham, south-west London. If Cerys was worried about the ongoing strain of fame she, at first, wasn't showing it. Cerys featured in a specially themed 'Fame' issue of music magazine *Select*, where she was probed on her attitudes to life in the limelight. When asked how she deals with all the attention, Cerys explained how she was coming to terms with the rush of people wanting to deconstruct her character in the pages of newspapers and magazines.

'Mmmm, you know when you're in school, and you have your report written? With this, all of a sudden you get reports on what you're like as a person. It's very interesting to see what people think of you. When people write about the band, they usually write about my personality. I'm not bothered; it's almost a privilege. But imagine waking up and reading a report about how you come across as a person, it's very funny. But it's not like I'm Camilla Parker-Bowles.'

Of course, fame also affects those around you. Cerys explained how her fame has affected friends and family.

'It's pretty weird,' she muses. 'Like with your grandparents; they learn more about you through reading stuff than visiting. That's weird. And it's strange when your mum and dad, or your ex-boyfriends, or your sisters get hassle. They're thrown in the deep end with you.' Cerys had become one of the more instantly recognisable British pop stars, with her own definitive style, a situation that has also brought its own downsides.

'I went shopping in Cardiff and a lot of kids followed me around,' she explained, sounding pained. 'I don't understand it. Come and say hello by all means, but this was for three-quarters of an hour, while I was doing the most mundane things – buying a tupperware dish.' Still, despite this infant stalking episode, she was apparently still maintaining a philosophical air about the cult of celebrity, while having a pop at the tabloids' obsessions with the personal lives of the nation's pop stars.

'I've shopped for 27 years without any hassle, so I'm not going to complain about a little bit of hassle in the last year,' she told *Select*. 'I haven't had any bombs or anything like that. Some funny letters, but it's nothing very much. I just think we should all take up embroidery, get a hobby, you know? Stop worrying about all this tabloid bollocks.'

However, despite Cerys's protestations that celebrity was just a niggly aside to her own very full and happy life, cracks were beginning to show. Long stretches away from home, cocooned in a tour bus with your band mates constantly at close proximity can make anyone run screaming to the hills.

But Catatonia were about to head off on a multi-nation world-skimming gig itinerary that would stop off in Europe, Australia and Japan, before collapsing in a heap back in the UK. It would mean months away from home, for band members who had families and for Mark, someone who didn't like touring at all. On the Cats' first visit to Australia in February *Q* magazine had tagged along for the ride. Writer Nick Duerden observed at first hand the personal peculiarities of the five distinctly different people that make up Catatonia.

The *Q* journalist managed to coax an interview out of Mark – something which is no mean feat, given he is as adverse to interviews as Wales are to winning rugby matches. He quickly discovered that the songwriter and guitarist is a man who loves his home comforts. 'We're all very different people, you'll never find all five of us sitting around having a laugh at the same time. Cerys has her mood swings, I've got mine. I tend to get bored very easily, and when I'm bored I like to moan. But it's never trivial moaning, nothing like, Where's the lemon for my tequila? It's more like, I'm miserable I want to go home. I don't travel well. Just the other day I invited everyone on the tour bus outside because they were keeping me awake. I just about ripped the door off in anger. Well, I didn't quite rip it off, just yanked it a bit. Home comforts is what I miss most of all.'

Sadly, being on the road for months on end can cause you to pine all the more for the comfort and familiarity of home. What makes the Catatonia situation even more precarious is two ex-lovers who don't particularly like each other thrown together in a band of five distinctly different personalities expected to maintain an upbeat camaraderie and friendly bonhomie for the duration of gruelling gig schedules. Even the most forthright optimist would find it hard saying that difficulties aren't going to arise.

While Cerys had admitted that it could be difficult being in a band with your ex-lover, Mark admitted to *Q* that he didn't see what the problem was. When the music magazine suggested that it must be difficult being in a band with a former girlfriend, painful even, Mark retorted, 'Not at all. To be honest I think it's embarrassing when band members copulate with each other. It's ungainly. We're much better off since we've split, actually.'

It wasn't just Mark that was in confessional mode. *Q* interviewed Cerys when the band had returned from Oz. Although fame and success had been a long time coming, they had a profound effect on the Catatonia frontwoman. To say that becoming a British music icon can take a lot of getting used to is something an understatement. It's often been said that fame and celebrity are a prison from which you cannot escape, that your life is not your own, but is run by managers and PRs drawing up endless itineraries that dictate your day. After 18 months on the celebrity merry-go-round, Cerys evidently wanted to get off.

'I never really wanted fame,' she confessed. 'I just wanted to be a great singer. This life . . . it's not natural, is it? People have this image of me as loud and brash and feisty. But that's only half the time. There's a different side to me that people don't see. I need a break from all this constant attention. I just want to go home. I want to go walking along the cliffs, find some mussels, cook them, put them in a big bowl of rice with some fresh parsley and take time eating it. Then I want to go and see the sheep, it's been ages since I've done that. I want to be alone. Just for a few days.'

Cerys would probably open herself up to accusations of hypocrisy in the coming months as she became even more illuminated in the public gaze, but at this point she was obviously yearning for some time away from it all. Touring was grinding her down, although one trip that she had confessed she had always wanted to make was just around the corner.

ORIENT EXCESS

Come 1 August and there would be at least some excitement in the Catatonia camp caused by the band's first trip to Japan. Cerys had confessed she had always wanted to visit the land of the rising sun. The opportunity for Catatonia to make their debut Asia appearance came at the Fuji Rock Festival – Asia's biggest outdoor rock festival.

The Japanese date had been preceded by the band's return to Australia for dates in Melbourne and Sydney. Outside of the UK and Europe, Oz had taken the band to its sunny heart; *International Velvet* had already eclipsed the 100,000 sales mark there, while *Equally Cursed And Blessed* had just been let loose in record shops.

The dates Down Under signalled an increasing notification of the rising stature of the princess of Welsh pop, as TV, radio, newspapers and magazines – alerted to the singer's penchant for a perfect soundbite – all clambered for an acutely observed Cerys quote.

Of course Australia didn't need an overworked interpreter trying to decode the Catatonia frontwoman's unorthodox and off-kilter take on the world. The translator used for the band's first Japanese adventure would need the patience of a saint and the broadest of multilingual skills properly to convey the Cerys Matthews manifesto to the massed ranks of the Far East Catatonia fan club!

Still, the trifling matter of a language barrier hadn't deterred a whole squadron of British bands from being, 'big in Japan'. The fact that Japan tends to like to be force-fed dayglo pop with a side order of kitsch fun ruled the band more in than out of the race to earn their yen.

'Not one of us has been to Japan before, but I've always wanted to go,' Cerys explained to a Japanese website. 'I've been waiting for about five years, since we signed with the record company. Everyone has been saying how good it is and they've been promising me every year. I can't quite believe it. I won't believe it until we actually arrive in Japan. It's absolutely going to be one of my highlights. I really can't wait.'

Although they've released a Japanese version of *International Velvet* and the early album *Tourist*, a compilation of early singles and B-sides, the band has only done limited PR and never played live there. Because of this Cerys remained realistic but optimistic about their chances of cracking the lucrative Japanese music market. 'I think it's early days for us in Japan,' she explained. 'Our profile is quite low at the moment, which needs remedying. Three weeks ago we did a live TV linkup, which was amazing, and we've done a few interviews with Japanese magazines. But until you actually go there and show what you do live, you never really know what it will be like.'

'I'm excellent with chopsticks,' she proclaims. 'I use them all the time. I carry chopsticks round with me wherever I go and people always make fun of it because I eat steak with chopsticks. I get given them now by people and I've got a huge collection.'

If hope sprung eternal in the Far East, it had run dry in the Midwest. Catatonia's career in America thus far had been handled as smoothly as a dingy in a Force 10 gale. Navigating a British band to success in America occurs as frequently as Halley's Comet. Dress up the band a wrong way, hype them as something they're not and slot them in the wrong pigeonhole then you'll fail miserably. To all intents and purposes the Cats' US label Vapor had made the mistake of steering the band on a course toward an older alternative American music nirvana populated by their label boss Neil Young and alternative with a small 'a' acts like The Dave Matthews Band and Hootie And The Blowfish.

The warning signs were there when Catatonia headed out on the Horde tour – the alternative hippie fest – where the band's colourful pop nuances stuck out like the proverbial sore thumb.

While, *International Velvet* had seen a small-scale release, it had made little inroad towards cultivating any sort of niche or presence in the US market.

Catatonia's alliance with Vapor had shown to be nothing but ill-starred, and was soon brought to an end when the band were dropped from the label's roster. Although this might have reflected badly on the Cats, the fact that they had little heavyweight support, lack of a cohesive strategy and most importantly a record label that just didn't 'get' the band, dictated this ignominious departure was for the best.

Despite the souring of their American dream, the band's career steadily trod an upward curve in the rest of the world. As they headed off for their much anticipated debut appearance in Japan at the Fuji Rock Festival and more dates in Australia, the band had announced other festival dates in Portugal and Germany, as well as another high-profile appearance in the UK.

Previously, the Cats had only ever appeared on the Reading Festival's peripheral stages. Now they had snared a prestigious slot on the main stage, second only to headliners Blur. This was the year that the Reading Festival would become a two-location event, with a new second site in Leeds. Catatonia would play the Saturday night at Reading and Sunday night at Leeds over the August Bank Holiday weekend.

FEST AND PANTS

The Fuji Rock Festival was a fine first taste of the Orient as Catatonia played on a bill that also included reformed hellraisers The Happy Mondays, ensuring if nothing else the two bands' combined riders would resemble a riotous night out with Oliver Reed and George Best.

Luckily, there was no drunken repeat of earlier live escapades. Catatonia played a tight and assured set that left the crowd impressed with their first glimpse of the Welsh band they had heard so much about.

Similarly, the Australian dates – in Sydney and Melbourne – passed off without too much incident, apart from the fact that they resembled a Welsh flag convention and meeting point for Welsh ex-pats. What was noticeable was that the crowds were bigger and this time there were more native Australians who had heard the band's songs played on Australia's Triple J radio station and read articles about Cerys in the media. All in all, steady if not unspectacular success was being made.

A gap of three weeks between returning from Australia and Japan and the band's European festival dates saw them either resting and recuperating or working on side projects. Cerys dashed off into the studio to record her duet with Tom Jones – 'Baby It's Cold Outside' – to be featured on Tom Jones's forthcoming duets album *Reload*. The ageing belter had begun to experience something of a renaissance after joining Robbie Williams on stage at that year's Brit awards. With his cool credibility seemingly undiminished from the years hammering away on the Vegas cabaret circuit and his questionable medallion man past, Jones and Gut Records, who had released Cerys and Space's 'The Ballad of Tom Jones', started to record a collection of songs featuring the grandfather of Welsh pop duetting with some of pop music's hippest acts. Alongside Cerys there was a Welsh contingent that also included The Manics' James Dean Bradfield and Cwmaman's finest The Stereophonics, as well as duets with, among others, Space and Sweden's ice-cool popsters The Cardigans.

Paul, meantime, was contributing a track to *Commemoration and Amnesia*, a joint venture between poet and writer Patrick Jones (the older brother of the Manics' Nicky Wire), Big Noise Recordings and a host of talented Welsh artists. The album compiled 22 of Patrick's poems and put them to a musical backing.

The track listing read like a Who's Who of the Welsh music scene. There were the usual suspects: members of The Manics, The Super Furries and Gorkys all contributed tracks, while a sprinkling of the new wave of Welsh bands such as Manchild, Derrero and Pink Assassin also featured.

Catatonia's contribution, 'Hiraeth', (Yearning) is a stark soundtrack put to Patrick Jones's harrowing overview of Wales. Assembled by Paul Jones who played keyboards and programmed the track, 'Hiraeth' also features samples from the Cats' 'Mantra For The Lost'.

The weekend before their dates at Reading and Leeds, Catatonia found themselves playing at the Rockpalast Bizarre Festival in Germany on Saturday and the Vilar de Mouros Festival in Portugal. The band have a loyal following in Portugal thanks to a dedicated support that's centred around the 'Angel On My Shoulder' website run by the Cats' Portuguese superfan Olga Barrios. Olga and her friends swarmed the festival site and ensured the Cats met with an ecclesiastical welcome.

By the time that Catatonia had arrived back in the UK for their Reading Festival appearance they were, to coin the catchphrase of their mate Mark Radcliffe, 'cooking on gas'. They had hit a rich vein of form. Cerys's voice, a fragile instrument at the best of times, was holding up well and the band were at the height of their musical powers.

If Cerys was privately suffering the growing pains of life in the public eye, she wasn't showing it. Outwardly she wore the appearance of someone taking to fame like the diva she had spent her younger days dreaming of becoming. Stages don't get much bigger than the one that presented itself at Reading and Cerys wasn't going to miss the chance to make a big impression.

After Margam, stadium dates with REM and The Rolling Stones as well as the European festival dates, the Cats were getting a taste for huge outdoor crowds. And what better way to reach the greatest number of potential new

Catatonia fans while hitting the tabloid headlines than by upstaging headliners Blur with a flash of your bra and knickers in front of 30,000 festival goers?

Whether it was Cerys acclimatising herself to her new-found sex-symbol status or the time spent with the man in receipt of more knickers than Marks & Spencer, Tom Jones, she stunned the crowd with her sexy apperance – pink bra and knickers barely covered by a fishnet dress – and sensual confidence.

As soon as she stepped out on to the stage, the crowd surged forward as suddenly as the male contingent of the crowd's testosterone levels soared amid the wolf whistles and dropped jaws.

Teasing, preening and pouting, she wove her sultry way across the stage belting out the band's hits like Marlene Dietrich meets Mae West. The crowd duly responded by screaming their way through the band's singles and jumping around in a suitable frenzy to the more up tempo songs and dutifully swooning in the more relaxed moments.

The effect of Cerys's performance couldn't have been more profound. The tabloids were full of pics of Cerys's underwear, while reviewers raved over the band's show, widely acknowledging it as one of the best ever Reading performances. Strange to think that all those years ago they were renowned for their shambolic live performances; now they were famed for their untouchable live prowess. But then they weren't a household brand. Back in the days of hazy back-room gigs at the Camden Falcon they skulked moodily on the periphery of success, crowds never quite knowing whether they were to witness magic or mayhem. Now they basked in the full glare of the limelight while their consummate musicianship shone just as brightly.

You had to feel sorry for Blur, having to follow the Catatonia whirlwind on to the Reading stage. You almost wondered if Damon had contemplated shaving his legs and popping on a frock after witnessing the Cat's seismic show as he watched aside the stage. Blur had no chance. Pop had dealt indie a knockout blow and there was no doubt who were the champions of Reading '99.

A tabloid newspaper report that Cerys 'had demanded a paddling pool full of champagne for her dressing room' at Reading, just underlined that this was a band most noticeably with a singer whose fame had made her into a prime target for showbiz gossip. Cerys Matthews had arrived at the point at which fantasy and reality become entwined in a minefield of ego and hype, with the boundaries between fractured truth and fantasy blurring at the edges.

Despite her candid assertion about rock 'n' roll life – 'it's not natural is it' – Cerys, for all her desire to escape the limelight occasionally, still revelled in the glamorous perks that the music business afforded her.

While the rest of the band would retire to South Wales and into the safe arms of domesticity with their families, Cerys was still burning the flame of hedonism as brightly as ever. And despite her singing the lines 'London, it just bleeds the life out of me' in 'Londinium', Cerys was becoming an increasingly regular fixture on the London party scene. She was regularly snapped staggering out of the Met Bar, the *de rigueur* West End hang-out for TV presenters, models and pop stars.

It's said that fame and the accompanying acclaim can do strange things to a person's head and people close to the band were worrying that Cerys was spending a little too much time in a showbiz vacuum with Meg Matthews and Kate Moss for her own good. The *Melody Maker* started to make a joke out of it, printing regular pictures of Cerys in various drunken poses at the Met Bar. Great play was made out of Cerys's spending the night partying with Tom Jones at the launch of his album *Reload,* which featured their version of 'Baby It's Cold Outside'. The Welsh superstars past and present were snapped sharing a lengthy snog. Cerys might have found the stories and pictures amusing, but the rumours coming out of Cardiff were that the rest of the band found their singer's behaviour embarrassing.

While the picture was innocent enough, a chance to exploit an opportunity which wouldn't harm either of their reputations, it was rumoured that the band didn't need what they believed was stage-managed publicity. They couldn't stop Cerys doing what she wanted, but the band were in it for the music. They reckoned Cerys was becoming too caught up in a showbiz lifestyle for her own good.

Cerys had once vehemently slated London and its false excesses and here she was seemingly embracing them. The band prided themselves on maintaining a resolutely grounded approach to the music business, yet Cerys was mixing it in the land of inflated egos. To friends back in Cardiff it seemed very odd to revel in the excesses that you had once rallied against.

Everyone knew that the band weren't exactly the greatest of friends, but for a group that had endured a stormy passage to this point, the last thing they needed was another rift within their ranks.

STADIUM ROCK!

Whatever the respective merits or otherwise of Cerys's party-loving lifestyle, the girl was certainly in demand. Cerys had agreed to record a song for a new animated TV version of *Watership Down,* based on the novel about the trials and tribulations of a group of rabbits forced to find a new home. The song she sang – 'Thank You Stars' – was written by Mike Batt, who wrote the music for The Wombles in the 1970s. Cerys was a massive fan of those furry residents of Wimbledon Common, being one of the greatest exponents of their pioneering rubbish-collecting conservationist tactics herself when she worked as a refuse collector on Swansea's beaches.

The Cats' singer did her pop cred with the kids no harm at all by being pictured with Boyzone member Stephen Gately – who had re-recorded 'Bright Eyes', the famous Art Garfunkel hit from the original animated film version of *Watership Down* .

Cerys had also recorded two songs for films – the Chris Montez song 'The More I See You' for Brit film *Fanny and Elvis* and 'We'll Gather Lilacs' by famous former Cardiff resident Ivor Novello for an upcoming film by Welsh director Sara Sugarman.

If Cerys was raising her profile then the band was gearing up to do the same. Although they hadn't long returned from the Far East after playing the Fuji Rock Festival, gigs in Osaka, Nagoya and two nights in Tokyo had been planned for the start of November.

More importantly for those Cat fans closer to home, the band had announced their biggest indoor shows to dates – a pre-Xmas jaunt that would see them calling in at arena-sized venues the Glasgow SECC, Doncaster Dome, London Arena, Blackpool Empress Ballroom and climaxing with two nights at Cardiff International Arena on 12 and 13 December.

Announced immediately after their Reading Festival, so as not to dilute ticket sales from Reading, the gigs were trailed by a torrent of publicity. The posters publicising the gig were duly dispatched, the promoter took out ads in all the music press and magazines and 'Karaoke Queen' was finally to receive its release in November.

Originally planned to be the follow-up single to 'Dead From The Waist Down', 'Karaoke Queen' was pulled much to the annoyance of the band in favour of 'Londinium'. However, the record company had committed something of a U-turn and the single was set for release in the first week of November.

After announcing dates for the biggest indoor shows they had ever played, a year that had been brimfull of landmarks acquired two more 'momentous occasions' in the Cats' eventful career curve. On consecutive Saturdays, Catatonia were due to play live in front of in excess of 150,000 people, while millions and millions would watch the band on TV. First up, on 2 October, was a date at Cardiff's newly opened Millennium Stadium. A pint pump away from one of the band's favourite watering holes, the City Arms, the state-of-the-art stadium was due to host its first major showpiece with the opening ceremony of the Rugby World Cup.

Catatonia had been invited to perform at the opening ceremony, providing the 'youth' interest alongside fellow Welsh stars Shirley Bassey, opera star Bryn Terfel, Michael Ball and stalwart Welsh comedian Max Boyce.

The band performed 'International Velvet' to a rapturous crowd who roared the 'Everyday when I wake up I thank the Lord I'm Welsh' chorus in suitably fervent fashion. Cerys had already teased the crowd when she had taken to a specially erected stage in the middle of the pitch, by customising a Welsh rugby shirt in glamorous Cerys fashion with glitter and gem stones. The band's appearance not only underlined their reputation as one of Wales's favourite bands but provided them with a huge sales fillip.

As a result of their performance, televised around the world, sales of *International Velvet* soared, propelling the album back into the UK charts at No. 12.

The album, which had by this point sold more than one million copies worldwide, had dropped completely out of the charts before the band performed the title song at the ceremony, watched by an estimated three billion people. The power of television was evident for anyone to see. This was incredible publicity for a band that only two years previous had been playing to crowds of little over 500.

It was to be an unforgettable week for Catatonia. Cerys punctured the band's slots at the Millennium Stadium and Wembley stadium by appearing on *An Audience With Tom Jones*. The show, filmed in front of an invited audience of celebrities, featured Cerys duetting with the granddad of Welsh pop on 'Baby It's Cold Outside'. The song from Jones's *Reload* album was being heavily tipped to be released as a Christmas single, although nothing had yet been confirmed at that point.

Over 10 million people tuned in to the TV special, so add that to their appearance at the Millennium Stadium, and Cerys and Co were gathering amazing blanket media coverage.

But it didn't stop there. Seven days after Cardiff, on 9 October, the band found themselves sharing the stage at London's Wembley Stadium with a multitude of pop superstars performing at Net Aid.

This multi-venue charity concert – aiming to duplicate the success of Live Aid, but adapting itself to the twenty-first century with simultaneously broadcast and webcast gigs in the US and Geneva in Switzerland – was arranged chiefly to benefit the crisis in Kosova. Catatonia would share the stage at Wembley with rising Welsh superstars The Stereophonics as well as Robbie Williams, The Corrs and a much-lauded appearance by George Michael – his first live performance since his infamous arrest in a Hollywood public convenience.

Shows didn't come any bigger than this and the band didn't disappoint, rattling out their hits and performing a heart-stopping version of fans' favourite, 'Do You Believe In Me', a huge song made for an even bigger arena.

That day Catatonia played to an audience of millions. More than 100,000 people attended the concerts. Hundreds of thousands of homes and villages north and south of the equator tuned in on television and radio, and

2.4 million people logged on to receive a live webcast. As weeks go, Catatonia had just experienced one of the most phenomenal.

The lads in the band remained their customary low-profile selves, while it was left to Cerys to deal with the world's media. At Net Aid she was in typically outspoken form. That was part of the reason the press, and for that matter the general public, loved her. They knew that, unlike some bland pop stars who wouldn't open their mouths without asking their press officer, they would get a great quote from the singer. And Cerys didn't disappoint, informing the assembled press hordes when asked if she thought that Net Aid would make a difference:

'Of course it won't. It'll make fuck all difference . . . but we've got to try.'

Not exactly toeing the official line, unlike all the other star performers who had spent the day boring journalists senseless with a string of bland, clichéd quotes. However, Cerys, as she always did, told it like she thought it was – with a brutal but refreshing honesty.

TOUR DE FORCED

After their stadium appearances and multi-media coverage, everything in the Catatonia garden looked rosy. But if there was one band that easily lived up to their most recent album's title – *Equally Cursed And Blessed*, it was Catatonia.

The news filtered through that Cerys' relationship of over six months with Tommy D was over. The rumour circulating was that they had just drifted apart as they were both incredibly busy and hardly saw each other, then even more of a surprise was the news that was released from Catatonia HQ.

Tickets for their December arena shows had been on sale for over a month when a statement was issued by the band informing their fans that they had scrapped their UK tour because of exhaustion. The statement read:

> Dear All.
>
> After much soul searching and thought we have unfortunately decided to cancel our forthcoming UK tour. We don't want to use the usual excuses – production problems, visa problems, etc., etc.
>
> The simple truth is that after 22 months of whirlwind success we need a break and as a band haven't been able to put together a new show we'd be proud of. By charging ahead with the tour we feel we wouldn't be doing justice to ourselves or to our magnificent fans, who have supported us through thick and thin.

We know many people will be disappointed – for this we apologise, but feel in our hearts that this is the best course of action for all of us.

We will be back better and stronger next year.

Thank you for everyone's support.

Diolch am y cefnogaeth a phopeth arall efo cariad mawr.

Aled, Cerys, Mark, Owen and Paul

As announcements go it was a bit of a bombshell. It was true that the band had worked constantly for almost two years, but these were only six dates.

Nevertheless Catatonia's press officer Ginny Luckhurst defended the band, saying 'The band haven't really had a break between making albums. They have worn themselves out with all the concerts and publicity, but they will be back next year.'

Now all of this would have made perfect sense, yet what followed confused a lot of the band's fans. Soon after the announcement of the cancelled UK dates, the band confirmed a ten-date European tour that would take them to Denmark, Germany, France, Belgium and Sweden, only days after arriving back from a tour of Japan. It was announced that the Cerys and Tom Jones duet, 'Baby It's Cold Outside', would be released as a single in time for the race for the Christmas No. 1. Cerys was scheduled to perform a host of promotional engagements and live appearances for the single's release.

It all seemed very odd. There were rumours circulating that the gigs hadn't been selling well and that was the real reason for the cancellation – rumours that were vehemently denied by the band's management and promoter Conal Dodds.

Conal admitted that the gigs wouldn't have sold out, but said: 'The sales were fine. At the end of the day, we'd have done good business. We wouldn't have done exceptional business, but it would have done good business.' The promoters couldn't have been happy about the situation as they would lose the money spent on the advertising and promotion of the gigs, although Conal remained philosophical about it all.

'Well I wasn't happy about it because we lost that money. We (the promoters – Metropolis) were obviously pissed off. We lost a substantial amount of money on the dates being pulled, but if you see that the other option is the band do the dates and get so fed up about it that they do a crap gig which leads to the split up of the band. It's in all our interests that the bands don't tour when they're unhappy. It's rare for this to happen.'

The announcement of the cancelled shows came only two weeks before the release of 'Karaoke Queen' on 1 November. It wasn't exactly a great climate to release the single in. What made the single's release doubly baffling was that the band wouldn't be around to promote it, having already committed to their dates in Japan which commenced on 4 November.

The band managed to squeeze in two performances of the single – on *TFI Friday* and kids' Saturday morning programme *Live And Kicking* – before they jetted out to the Far East.

The single seemed to be beset by problems. The record company held its hand up and admitted its release had been delayed due to the time it took to get the right remix of the single, which was noticeably different from the album version.

Released in three formats, CD, vinyl and cassette, CD1 featured 'Karaoke Queen' (Remix), 'Don't Wanna Talk About It', a sweetly coy new song given a rural, pastoral feel thanks to some nimble banjo accompaniment from Owen, and a new remixed version of an old song, 'All Girls Are Fly'. Meantime, CD2 – a special 3" Japanese-style CD, featured 'Karaoke Queen' (Remix-Edit) as well as a version of 'Karaoke Queen' and 'Dead From The Waist Down' without lyrics for those karaoke-loving Catatonia fans. The cassette and 7" single featured 'Karaoke Queen' (Remix) and 'Don't Wanna Talk About It'.

In a similar fashion to 'Londinium', air play and promotion for the single was pretty minimal. The best publicity the band received was Cerys pictured with The Stereophonics' Kelly Jones on the front cover of a relaunched version of *Melody Maker*. The music paper had changed to magazine format for the first time in its history. To celebrate, it beamed an image of Cerys and Kelly with the line, 'The new Prince and Princess of Wales' on to the side of Buckingham Palace. It caused a stir, making a few morning papers the next day.

However, despite this welcome publicity, but given that the band were hardly in the UK to promote their new single, the warning signs were there. 'Karaoke Queen' entered the charts at No. 36, which for a band the size of Catatonia was a huge disappointment. Ironically, 'You've Got A Lot To Answer For', released a few years earlier, and which many would argue was a better song, actually entered the charts one place higher, at 35.

Probably the best thing about 'Karaoke Queen' was the video. It was a kitsch classic complete with transvestite dancers and a calf called Cattlelonia! Although many watching the video might not have realised it, the cow did bring with it a serious political message. The band wanted to highlight the plight of livestock being sold for ridiculous prices due to the BSE scare – an issue that was seriously affecting the livelihoods of farmers in Wales. Cerys, whose family are part-time farmers in Pembrokeshire, said: 'It's absurd that you can buy a calf for £2 – and that's a great price. Some farmers are having to sell their calves for just 10p.'

Cattletonia will be seen in the video with a £2 price tag around its neck. 'People probably think I'm bonkers starring a calf in a pop video,' she added. 'The politicians don't seem to be making any effort to help so I thought I would.'

The failure of the single can be attributed to various factors: the lack of any substantial promotion, fans fed up at the cancelled arena dates, the negative publicity that the cancelled dates brought and maybe, just maybe, there had been too much Catatonia for people to stomach. It sounds strange but bands can get too much coverage, when publicity gets to saturation point it's time to beat a hasty retreat. You only had to look at the number of times Catatonia had played London, at least six, to show how much in the face of the general public they had been.

Whatever the reasons were for the cancelled dates, the band were right to believe that they needed a break. While Cerys would still be busy promoting 'Baby It's Cold Outside', at last the rest of the band could finish the European tour in mid-November and then spend what was left of the year recharging their batteries and spending time with partners and children whom they had hardly seen for 22 months.

The time was right for the band to take a break from the exhausting machinations of the music business. In the light of this, the disappointing chart placing of 'Karaoke Queen' and Cerys's impending single release with Tom Jones, plans to release 'Nothing Hurts' from *Equally Cursed And Blessed* as the fourth single were shelved.

HEADLINE HITTING ANTICS

After cancelled dates and failed singles, December started with some good news for Cerys Matthews: she was named as the 'Coolest Star In Rock Music' in a poll compiled by readers of *Melody Maker*.

Wales continued its reputation as a cool country with two of the other top five contenders in the poll also being Welsh. The Manics' Nicky Wire was voted the second coolest star in rock and The Stereophonics' Kelly Jones clocked in at No. 5.

This Top 10 read: 1. Cerys Matthews, Catatonia; 2. Nicky Wire, Manic Street Preachers; 3. Brian Molko, Placebo; 4. Paul Draper, Mansun; 5. Kelly Jones, Stereophonics; 6. Huey, Fun Lovin' Criminals; 7. Jarvis Cocker, Pulp; 8. Brett Anderson, Suede; 9. Dominic Chad, Mansun; 10. Cliff Jones, Gay Dad.

It was quite a coup, given the opposition and that she was the only woman in the Top 10, and a timely boost for Cerys who had faced much criticism over the band's last few rocky weeks and her continued appearances on the London social scene. It was also good publicity to take into the week of the release of 'Baby It's Cold Outside.' Although originally tipped as a Christmas No. 1, planned Xmas single releases from teen popsters like Westlife and S Club 7 made a Top 20 placing a more realistic aim.

The single was helped by a brilliant video, featuring Cerys and Tom flirting outrageously with each other as Cerys hammed it up in two guises – as a white clad virginal innocent and then as a sultry black bodice-ripping vamp after Tom has had his evil way with her.

Despite her claims that she was exhausted, Cerys certainly did a fine job of promoting the single, popping up with the rockin' granddad on virtually every youth-oriented pop programme you could imagine. The duo even gatecrashed that grandiose gathering of the great and the good of the teen pop world, the Smash Hits Poll Winners Party. They left the shockingly young crowd (average age 11) bewildered by this big ballad that was being sung at them by 'that Cerys Matthews and an old bloke with a curly wig'. When the camera panned to the crowd, they did look suitably bemused by the virtuoso performance they were witnessing.

Still, it didn't harm the single's chance of success. In the end and in the face of fierce competition from some big names the single charted at a commendable No. 14.

The two Welsh stars evidently shared some unique chemistry, though spurious stories of their having some sort of relationship were strictly in the realms of tabloid fantasy. As Tom Jones said in a newspaper interview: 'I'm old enough to be her dad, for God's sake!'

Those ridiculous claims were underlined as pure fantasy when it was unearthed by one tabloid that Cerys shocked everyone by getting engaged to musician, Anthony Genn. Maybe the pressure was getting to Cerys but most people near to the band thought this was totally out of character. Yes, she was impulsive, but to be getting engaged to someone you've only just met . . . Well, eyebrows were being raised off foreheads.

A guitarist with Joe Strummer's band The Mescaleros, Genn's better known in the music industry for streaking on stage at Glastonbury when he was a member of Elastica. One of the more lively characters in British pop music, he would at least act as an equal foil to Cerys and her love of a night out.

Given that they had only been seeing each other for a short space of time, it was a huge surprise to everyone – fans and band personnel alike. Cerys had turned 30 and while showing no visible signs of cutting down on her love of a lively social life, she had admitted to wanting to settle down one day with the right man and have children. It was just that no one thought that this would be 'it'.

One horoscope specialist once wrote of Cerys Matthews: 'On the face of it, Cerys is a very confident, organised soul, but in the inner sanctum lies an insecurity about love and being loved.' The rumour was that Tommy D had finished their relationship abruptly and Cerys had been deeply hurt. Maybe, her shotgun engagement to Genn was fallout from the Tommy D affair. Whatever, no one was betting on the engagement lasting.

Given her star status the tabloids were increasingly willing to enshrine Cerys in their showbiz columns. Up until now she had never felt the sharp side of tabloid practice. That was until she did an interview with *Melody Maker* and was asked for her views on drugs. Little did she know then that she was about to prompt a tabloid feeding frenzy.

When asked by the music magazine what she would do if she discovered that her closest friend was a heroin dealer, she replied with tongue planted firmly in cheek: 'I'd get some of them cheaply.'

Her quote, although said flippantly, was enough to prompt the Welsh edition of the *Daily Mirror* to splash Cerys all over the front page with a banner headline that screamed in suitably indignant tabloid fashion: OUTRAGE AT CERYS HEROIN BOAST.

Astonishingly, the saga escalated horribly from there. The story got airtime on TV news bulletins and even more incredibly a question was asked about it on the BBC's *Question Time* programme. Then Cerys had to incur the wrath of anti-drugs campaigners who queued up to crucify her. Linda Pearce, from RAID (Rhondda Against Illegal Drugs), was typical of those who wanted to slate Cerys. 'Doesn't she realise how many kids who think she's cool will read that article,' she raged. 'She's sending completely the wrong message to them.'

A shell-shocked Ginny Luckhurst at the band's press office had to field a flood of calls. She did her best to defend Cerys's seemingly innocuous quotes by saying: 'Cerys says a lot of things very tongue in cheek. People take them the wrong way and it's just one of her usual tearaway comments.'

The barrage of criticism was enough for Cerys to be forced into issuing a statement through the record company. She said: 'I am shocked that the *Welsh Mirror* has taken a flippant remark by me out of context and reported it as me condoning the use of heroin. Nothing is further from the truth. I support the work done by drugs rehabilitation charities and nothing I say is intended to undermine them.'

Although those of us with an ounce of sense could tell she was just joking, it was a salient lesson learnt by Cerys Matthews, that in future such a high profile public figure had to be careful what they say, otherwise they would face the full wrath of a tabloid press that are able and more than willing to blow stories out of all proportion in the name of sales figures and a sensationalist story.

The end of the year and the holiday season couldn't come quickly enough for Cerys and co. 1999 had been both cursed and blessed, littered with both highs and lows. It had been a rollercoaster ride and now they wanted to get off. They could retreat into anonymity to spend time getting their lives back into some sort of perspective in the company of their friends and families, and at last put some semblance of sanity back into their lives.

In a fitting end to the twentieth century, most of the band congregated at the Millennium Stadium to witness the biggest-ever Welsh pop happening. The Manic Street Preachers had announced some months previously that they wanted to see the millennium out at the new shrine to Welsh sport.

Although it was rumoured that the Cats would be lining up on an impressive supporting bill that included fellow countrymen The Super Furry Animals, Feeder and Nicky Wire's brother Patrick Jones performing tracks from his *Commemoration and Amnesia* album, they sensibly opted for a seat in the stands.

As occasions go, it was an amazing event. If nothing else it signified just how far Welsh music had come in the last decade. Back then it was unthinkable that any Welsh band could become hugely successfully, let alone sell 54,000 tickets for a state-of-the-art stadium show. But it summed up perfectly a decade that had witnessed an astonishing Welsh pop revolution. An uprising that had forged a new dawn for both Welsh music and Welsh culture.

Even curmudgeonly old soothsayer Nostradamus would have been hard pressed to predict that.

The Final Chapter?

The Year 2000 signified a new start for everybody. Many people make New Year's resolutions but the fact that we were entering a new century meant even more to most people, who saw the dawn of 2000 as *the* opportune time for a new beginning. For those who wanted to make a fresh start, make new plans or even reinvent themselves, this was the time to do it.

The band had started to write new songs for the next album, but as opposed to the last two albums which followed each other in a short space of time, it would be good for all concerned if the band took advantage of their much-needed break to take their time over the new material.

While the UK had, for the time being, had its fill of Catatonia, the US had been positively undernourished. Having been dropped by Vapor Records six months previously, steps had been taken behind the scenes of Warners USA to find the band a new home. Although Catatonia might have been depressed at how things hadn't worked out at Vapor, they must have been ecstatic when they heard that Atlantic Records had agreed to sign them.

Atlantic has a grand tradition in America. It's one of the oldest labels and has been responsible for serving up some of the greatest music in rock 'n' roll history. The label has been responsible for the careers of some legendary performers – Ray Charles, Otis Redding, Aretha Franklin and Led Zeppelin – to name but a few. If any label had a chance of breaking the Cats stateside then Atlantic did.

Catatonia joined an impressive roster that included The Corrs, Everything But The Girl, Jewel, Stevie Nicks, The Pet Shop Boys, Sugar Ray, The Stone Temple Pilots and Tori Amos.

Having decided to throw their full weight behind Catatonia in an attempt to break the band in the most difficult country in the world to break bands, Atlantic at least had the financial clout that would enable them to give Catatonia every chance of achieving what other British bands had failed miserably to do in recent times.

The first part of the plan was to fly the band to the States for two showcase gigs in January. The first in New York at the Bowery Ballroom and the second on the opposite coast in Los Angeles at the El Ray Theatre. This would be followed by a heavyweight round of interviews with America's leading magazines throughout February and March, with the Stateside release of *Equally Cursed And Blessed* on 28 March.

Although *International Velvet* had received a small-scale US release, it was planned that *Equally Cursed And Blessed* would meets its American public with fanfares and trumpets blaring. To ensure the album would meet with maximum exposure, Atlantic employed a canny tactic. They added both 'Mulder And Scully' and 'Road Rage' to the album's track-listing. This shrewd ploy enabled the record company to utilise the band's biggest hit singles as the tunes that would trail the album's release on American radio stations.

It was a smart move and gave the band a great launch-pad into the American market. Equally pleasing were the two showcase gigs. Both were sold out and both received rapturous reviews from papers in New York and LA.

Atlantic's press office had been working overtime to get the band maximum coverage in America's coolest magazines. They had done well. Atlantic had rightly pinpointed Cerys as the cool focus of the group. The record company had traded heavily on Cerys's charismatic, ballsy chick credentials and built her up as a Courtney Love or Debbie Harry for the twenty-first century.

The magazines went for it hook, line and sinker. The pick of the press were articles in *Billboard, Rolling Stone, Interview* and *Details* magazines. *Billboard*, the American music industry bible would be able to spread the word about the band to those inside the industry. *Rolling Stone*, America's authoritative music tome would afford them some credibility. *Interview*, the cool, cutting-edge publication pioneered by Sixties pop artist Andy Warhol would put Cerys and Catatonia on a stylish footing, while leading American men's magazine *Details* offered something of a coup for the Catatonia press campaign. They were so impressed with Miss Matthews that they offered to splash her all over their front cover. This was a major triumph for Atlantic and a huge fillip for the band's career Stateside. Making the cover of *Details* carries immense kudos, so signs at this early stage were encouraging to say the least.

After their Stateside gigs in January the band were flown back in February for photo sessions for the album. Unlike their albums in the UK, the plan was to feature the group heavily on the cover and the inner sleeve of the Stateside version of *Equally Cursed And Blessed*.

It was obvious that the crux of Atlantic's campaign was to trade on Cerys's striking looks and personality. That was the plan and it seemed to be working. The results of the American photo sessions were simply stunning. The record company's photographer had transformed Cerys into a supercharged sex siren. They were amazing pictures. The image chosen for the cover featured the band in the back of a stretch limo with Cerys coyly smiling into the camera while the rest of the band, all dressed in black, sit moodily behind her. Other pics that would constitute the inner-sleeve images were equally as excellent. They were stylish without being too pretentious. The nearest comparison would have been vintage Blondie – Cerys possessing that same Debbie Harry icy cool.

The Details cover too, featured a strikingly sexy image. This time Cerys dressed in blue vest that bore the legend 'I Love You' matched with white pants with zip undone and plenty of flesh on show, ably demonstrating why she had been voted as one of *FHM* magazines' Top 100 sexiest women in the world. Details rounded the whole image off nicely by adding the tagline, 'The next Courtney Love only better', to the cover.

From what it had seen so far, America was suitably impressed. Ray Rogers, music editor of *Interview*, explained the Catatonia effect. 'Everybody is going crazy for them. Cerys is a very beautiful woman and a fabulous singer. She has loads of charisma and that's working wonders for them.'

The band themselves seemed to be warming to the idea of giving America their best shot. Cerys told the *New York Times* that, despite earlier disappointments, the idea of doing well in the US has grown on her.

'If you'd said a year ago, "Do you want to break America?" I would have said it was the last place in the world I was interested in. When you start off, everything is a bed of roses, the world is promised, then you suddenly realize America's massive. But it's much better now, Atlantic is so much behind us, and at least they're going to give it a go.'

But would Catatonia show the same level of commitment required to propel themselves to glory stateside? As many times in the past the band had showed they were more than adept at snatching defeat from the jaws of victory.

Cerys had commented in the past that truly big stars had learnt to instil in themselves a strict discipline and a healthy work ethic that would keep them on top of their game. Given that Catatonia seemed able to press the self-destruct button at any time and admitted to constant rowing within their ranks, they would need a huge amount of self-control to tackle a task as big as cracking the States.

What they needed to do was strike while the metaphorical iron was hot. Trying to make it in America carries the sort of odds only a fool would bet on. However, Atlantic had forged some once-in-a lifetime opportunities for the band to take advantage of. They just needed the band to show the same amount of commitment back.

Catatonia were due to fly back to the States the week following the album's release to undertake some amazing promotional dates. They were to appear on one of America's biggest TV shows, *The Tonight Show with Jay Leno*. They were also to film a number of concerts, including a 120 minutes special for MTV. These were all brilliant opportunities to hammer home their advantage in the States. However, you should always rely on Catatonia's penchant for unpredictability.

First, the news broke that Cerys had called off her relationship with

Anthony Genn. Although the couple were still together, Cerys and former-fiancé took the unorthodox step of calling off their engagement on St Valentine's Day. While doing press interviews for American magazines Cerys had let slip the news, saying, what most fans of the band had been thinking, that the engagement had been a mistake and that they were both too hasty in their actions. This news was then followed by a second bombshell.

Equally Cursed And Blessed had been released in the US when it was announced that the promotional dates had been postponed due to drummer Aled's being rushed to hospital with suspected appendicitis. Although this story was widely reported in the press, rumours started circulating that the band were about to split. Fans pointed out that some of the promotional dates only required Cerys's presence. Wouldn't it be easy just to draft in a replacement drummer for TV appearances – surely these dates were too important to postpone?

What was clear was that not everything was how it seemed. The band's management rubbished the stories that were being put out and insisted that the American dates would be rescheduled. MRM also stressed that writing and recording of a new album would take place this year, with the possibility of a new single before the end of 2000, with their fourth album to follow in 2001.

The one nagging question remains though. Can a band made up of such strong willed musicians, which is fronted by a superstar-in-waiting who shapes Catatonia's personality but who chooses a life divorced from the rest of the band, have the discipline, drive, commitment and energy to drive the band on to even greater heights?

Early indications are that they can. The band have been on a rollercoaster ride for two and a half years and it's time they got off and took a long break away from the unreal world that is the music business.

Let them recharge their batteries, seek some sanity in the arms of their families, which might allow them to rediscover the reasons why they formed a band in the first place. Time apart from the inevitable tensions of living in each others' pockets can only do them a power of good. Hopefully that well-deserved hiatus can bring them back bigger and stronger than ever.

Critics reckoned that *Equally Cursed And Blessed* suffered because it was recorded so soon after *International Velvet*. Now here's the chance to prove to the dissenters that whatever problems have beset the band, a clean break will heal old wounds and give them the creative space that will enable their songwriting talents to shine once again.

You do fear for their future when you hear Cerys telling any available journalist that: 'We fight like all the time with the band, that wears you down. It's because we've had a measure of success and everybody believes it's their input that makes it successful, so you get egos creeping in and you won't stand down.' However, as she adds, 'Sometimes things do get fraught but I think all bands are the same.' Exactly, that's the vagaries of creative life in a pop band. If you didn't agree with each other you would probably be a member of Boyzone.

Catatonia's brilliant songwriting more than suggests that there is, at the very least, another immense album left in the band. Especially as the nucleus of the band, Matthews and Roberts, have been together for fast approaching a decade and against all the odds have confounded their detractors.

The fact that their prolific output has already resulted in a clutch of new songs for a forthcoming album is just cause to be confident of their future plans.

No doubt there are those who believe that Cerys Matthews is destined to be the 'new Shirley Bassey', a big-voiced Welsh diva and solo superstar in waiting. In the future, yes, maybe. Yet you have to remember that Catatonia is a highly saleable brand name in the UK, Europe and Australia that is poised on the edge of adding America to the countries it has conquered.

The States may have fallen in love with Cerys's charisma, but they've also fallen under the spell of the evocative songs that were penned by Mark Roberts and Owen Powell. Catatonia are the sum of their parts, not just the entrancing aura of their singer.

To walk away from these potential creative, artistic and financial rewards would be career suicide.

The only question that hangs in the air like a helium-filled question mark is: can a band whose songs explore the fuzzy-edged fragilities of the human psyche keep their own emotions sufficiently under wraps to ensure the group's continued survival? Catatonia's legions of fans, myself included, hope and believe they can.

It seems that this could be a case for Mulder and Scully . . .